Teaching ESL Composition
Purpose, Process, and Practice

Teaching ESL Composition
Purpose, Process, and Practice

Dana Ferris
California State University, Sacramento

John S. Hedgcock
Monterey Institute of International Studies

LEA LAWRENCE ERLBAUM ASSOCIATES, PUBLISHERS
1998 Mahwah, New Jersey   London

Lawrence Erlbaum Associates, Inc., Publishers
10 Industrial Avenue
Mahwah, NJ 07430

Cover design by Kathryn Houghtaling Lacey

Library of Congress Cataloging-in-Publication Data

Ferris, Dana.
Teaching ESL composition : purpose, process, and
practice / Dana Ferris, John S. Hedgcock.
p. cm
Includes bibliographical references and index.
ISBN 0-8058-2450-2
1. English language—Study and teaching—Foreign
speakers. 2. English language—Composition and exercises. I. Hedgcock, John. II. Title.
PE1128.A2F47 1998   98-9490
                                          CIP

Books published by Lawrence Erlbaum Associates are
printed on acid-free paper, and their bindings are chosen
for strength and durability.

Printed in the United States of America
10 9 8 7 6 5 4 3 2 1

*For our ESL student writers
—past, present, and future*

CONTENTS

3 SYLLABUS DESIGN AND LESSON PLANNING IN THE ESL WRITING CLASS
                                                                      51

4 TEXT SELECTION, MATERIALS DEVELOPMENT, AND TASK CONSTRUCTION IN THE ESL WRITING CLASS
                                                                      85

Application Activity Thematic Reference Guide

AA#	Title	p. #	Reflection	Observation	Needs analysis	Curriculum/syllabus design & evaluation	Instructional planning	Classroom task analysis or design	Materials evaluation & selection	Teacher response	Peer response	Writing assessment	Computer-assisted instruction	Action/field research & secondary research
1.1	Retrospection assignment	18	•											•
1.2	Classroom observation task	18		•										
1.3	Introspective process analysis	19	•	•										
2.1	Encouraging extensive, self-initiated reading	45						•						
2.2	Maximizing reading–writing relationships in the classroom: Writing from texts using reading journals	45						•						
2.3	Writing-to-read task development	46					•	•						
2.4	Writing from texts: A sample assignment sequence	47				•		•						
2.5	Text analysis	48						•	•					•
3.1	ESL writer profile	77			•									
3.2	Syllabus assessment	78				•	•							
3.3	Assessing lesson plans	78				•	•							
3.4	Working with lesson plans	78				•	•							
4.1	Practice textbook evaluation	119						•	•					
4.2	Writing task analysis and assessment	119						•	•					
4.3	Writing task adaptation	119			•			•	•					
4.4	Writing assignment critique	120						•	•					
4.5	Constructing a writing assignment	121					•		•					
5.1	Surveying teachers and students about responding practices	148								•				•
5.2	Analyzing teacher feedback—1	149								•				
5.3	Responding to student errors	149								•				
5.4	Responding to student papers	150								•				

AA#	Title	p. #	Reflection	Observation	Needs analysis	Curriculum/syllabus design & evaluation	Instructional planning	Classroom task analysis or design	Materials evaluation & selection	Teacher response	Peer response	Writing assessment	Computer-assisted instruction	Action/field research & secondary research
5.5	Analyzing teacher feedback—2	150								•				
5.6	Self-analysis of response patterns	151	•							•				•
5.7	Examining research on teacher response	151								•				•
6.1	Investigating the effects of peer response on revision	190		•							•			•
6.2	Surveying student attitudes toward peer response	191		•							•			
6.3	Designing peer response forms	192					•	•			•			•
6.4	Giving and receiving peer feedback	193						•			•			•
7.1	Assessing students' and teachers' opinions about grammar feedback and instruction	220			•					•				•
7.2	Analyzing a research review	221												•
7.3	Analyzing errors and giving feedback	221						•		•				•
7.4	Assessing the formal grammatical knowledge of a target population	222			•			•						•
7.5	Comparing reference sources on a particular grammar point	222					•	•	•					
7.6	Developing grammar/editing lessons	223					•	•	•					
8.1	Holistic essay scoring practice	261										•		
8.2	Analytic essay scoring practice	261										•		
8.3	Designing and testing a rubric or scale	262										•		
8.4	Designing a writing portfolio plan	263				•			•			•		
9.1	Comparing research studies on computers & revision	284								•			•	•
9.2	Reflecting on your own computer-assisted writing process	284	•							•			•	
9.3	Surveying student writers about their experiences with computers	285			•		•						•	
9.4	"Cyber-tutoring" an ESL student writer	286								•			•	•
9.5	Using a spelling/grammar checker to analyze student writing	287											•	•

PREFACE

The purpose of this book is to present pedagogical approaches to the teaching of ESL composition in the context of current theoretical perspectives on second language (L2) writing and writers. It should therefore appeal to at least four different audiences:

1. Teacher-educators and graduate students in TESOL preparation programs;
2. In-service ESL instructors currently engaged in teaching composition to L2 students;
3. Mainstream composition teachers wanting to know more about meeting ESL writers' needs;
4. Researchers involved in describing L2 writing and/or investigating ESL composition pedagogy.

The text addresses the needs of the first three groups by providing overviews of research related to ESL writing, as well as numerous opportunities to reflect on, develop, and practice the teaching skills needed for effective ESL composition instruction. Researchers in the field will also appreciate the current and extensive reviews of the literature on various topics in ESL composition. The discussion and review questions at the beginning and end of each chapter are designed to stimulate readers' thinking about the material presented, and the Application Activities at the end of each chapter are designed to serve as "hands-on" tasks for pre- and in-service teachers as well as teacher educators. The Application Activities provide a range of ideas for evaluating and synthesizing research and for undertaking action research. Because of the book's dual emphasis on theory and practice in ESL composition, it is appropriate as a primary or supplementary text in classes focusing on L2 writing theory as well as practicum courses that emphasize or include writing instruction.

Because of the relative newness of L2 writing as a field of expertise, very few resources have been produced to help pre- and in-service teachers *become* experts. Therefore, one of our primary goals is to furnish readers with a synthesis of theory and practice in a rapidly growing discipline. We have consistently and intentionally focused on providing apprentice teachers with practice activities they can use to develop the complex skills entailed in teaching ESL composition. Although all topics of discussion are firmly grounded in reviews of relevant research, what we feel distinguishes this book from others is its wide array of hands-on, practical materials and tasks. By presenting theory and research in a way that pre-service teachers can understand, readings and exercises will enable readers to see the relevance of the material to their own classroom settings and their own student writers.

The book as a whole moves from general issues to specific pedagogical topics. Chapter 1 begins with an argument for the importance of theory as it shapes pedagogical practice. It also provides an overview of the history of L1 and L2 composition theory and teaching as well as in–depth discussion of the issues and variables unique to L2 writers and ESL composition instruction. Chapter 2 highlights the important issue of the reading–writing connection, focusing specifically on what is known about how reading affects writing and how teachers can exploit these critical links between literacy skills.

Chapters 3 and 4 deal with fundamental issues related to approaching any ESL writing class: syllabus design, textbook and materials selection, and lesson planning. The remaining chapters then focus on specific topics pertaining to L2 composition instruction: teacher response to student writing (chapter 5), peer response (chapter 6), developing grammar and editing skills for writing (chapter 7), models of writing assessment (chapter 8), and the role of computers in L2 writing instruction (chapter 9).

Although the organization of individual chapters varies somewhat according to the topic under discussion, all contain the following components:

- Questions for reflection. These pre-reading questions invite readers to consider their own prior experiences as students and writers and to anticipate how these insights might inform their own ESL composition teaching;
- Reflection and review. These follow-up questions ask readers to examine and evaluate the theoretical information and practical suggestions provided in the chapter;
- Figures and appendices. These textual illustrations provide numerous examples of authentic activities, lesson plans, ESL student writing, etc., which teachers can use or adapt for their own classrooms;

- Application Activities. Icons (e.g., $\boxed{\Rightarrow AA\ 1.1}$) at various points within the chapters direct readers to specific Application Activities that correspond to the principles or concepts discussed in the previous passage. Application Activities follow each "Reflection and Review" section and propose a wide range of hands-on practice. Tasks include evaluating and synthesizing published research, writing commentary on sample student papers, developing lesson plans, redesigning classroom activities, planning field research projects, and executing and evaluating classroom tasks.

To assist readers in locating the different types of material included in this book, a matrix of Application Activities follows the Table of Contents. We have consciously attempted to make this text as reader-friendly, helpful, and informative as possible. However, we know that readers may still have questions. Readers are thus encouraged to contact us through the Lawrence Elrbaum Associates, Inc., World Wide Web home page so that we can address questions, comments, and suggestions [www.erlbaum.com].

As writers, researchers, teachers, and teacher-educators, we find the field of L2 composition to offer many challenges as well as many rewards. We hope that this book will not only provide its readers with accurate information, meaningful insights, and practical ideas, but that it will also convey some of our enthusiasm for this rapidly evolving and engaging field of intellectual inquiry and professional practice.

ACKNOWLEDGMENTS

We would first like to express our heartfelt thanks, admiration, and appreciation to our editor at Lawrence Erlbaum Associates, Naomi Silverman. Her support, encouragement, and enthusiasm made the development of this book a true pleasure. Debbie Ruel, our production editor, also deserves our gratitude for her professionalism and patience as this project neared completion.

Paul Markham at the University of Kansas and Ellen Smith at Contra Costa College provided us with incisive reviews that were highly beneficial. We thank them for their suggestions, which helped us keep our audience in mind and make sensible adjustments.

Also instrumental in the development of this book were Professor Diane Belcher and her students at The Ohio State University, who provided us with extensive and constructive comments on draft portions of the manuscript. We similarly acknowledge our own graduate students at California State University, Sacramento, and the Monterey Institute of International Studies for their patience in reading draft versions and for their insightful feedback at various stages of the writing process.

xviii PREFACE

Special thanks go to Catherine Apostolidis and Luba Schmid, MATESOL candidates at CSUS, who provided extensive comments.

We are also grateful for the technical and clerical contributions made by Michael Larsen and Luba Schmid (CSUS), as well as Kelly Crosby and Kathleen Burke (MIIS), who worked as our graduate assistants at various phases of the manuscript development process. In a similar vein, we would like to thank our respective institutions for release time and for funding our graduate assistants' awards. Personal thanks go to Randy, Laura, and Melissa Ferris for their patience and understanding during the writing process. Also deserving of recognition for their perpetual moral support are Martha Bean, Elizabeth Bradbury, and Jean Jewell.

Dana Ferris
John Hedgcock

CHAPTER	Introduction:
1	Theoretical and Practical Issues in ESL Writing

Questions for Reflection

- What do you remember about the primary language writing instruction you received during your elementary, secondary, college, or even graduate education? What were the principal features of the method(s) used by your instructors?
- What aspects of that writing instruction contributed most to your expertise as a writer in your primary language? In your opinion, what aspects contributed least to that expertise? Why?
- In your experience as a writer, have you been made aware of any explicit or implicit theories of writing that might have motivated instruction? In other words, were there any instances in your education in which teachers of writing exposed their philosophy concerning the teaching of writing? If so, what were the stated principles and how did they influence your learning?
- If you have received formal instruction in a second or foreign language, were you given any training as a writer of that language? If so, compare that experience to your experience as an apprentice writer in your primary language. Describe specific similarities and differences.

THE RELEVANCE OF THEORY AND RESEARCH
FOR TEACHERS OF ESL WRITING

Books and articles used in teacher education courses frequently begin with a theoretical background that explains and/or justifies the premises of the instructional approaches and methods to be presented. This convention sometimes frustrates pre- and in-service teachers who may wish to forego a careful study of abstract

1

theories and principles in favor of acquiring practical methods and techniques for effective classroom teaching. This book will provide its readers with a principled set of instructional tools for teaching writing to secondary and postsecondary English as a Second Language (ESL) learners. To achieve this goal, we begin by laying a theoretical foundation so that readers can make reasoned and informed decisions about the pedagogical processes and procedures presented throughout the chapters of this book. By developing an understanding of the historical and formal origins of the discipline of second language (L2) writing, readers can approach current instructional paradigms from an informed, critical standpoint.

We believe that the development of effective instructional skills for the L2 writing classroom relies partly on an explicit awareness of the fundamental precepts that guide current beliefs and practices. Because current knowledge about composing processes and how to teach them is disparate and constantly evolving, teachers now "have to consider a variety of approaches, their underlying assumptions, and the practices that each philosophy generates" (Raimes, 1991, p. 412). A familiarity with formally articulated theories and principles enables teachers to discover and build on their own theories (Bartholomae, 1986; Grabe & Kaplan, 1996, 1997; Johns, 1990; Knoblauch & Brannon, 1984; McKay, 1994; Tsui, 1996). This knowledge also helps teachers become aware of the strengths and weaknesses of their own teaching, an aspect of teacher education that encourages teachers "to become critical and reflective practitioners, researchers of their own professional life, and agents of change" (van Lier, 1994, p. 7).

Formal theories, coupled with the findings of empirical research, can thus play a vital role in our thinking about teaching and the conduct of our classes. In a compelling argument for the utility of theory in composition instruction, Zebroski (1986) characterized the ways in which theory serves his day-to-day teaching:

> Theory has helped me to excavate and to uncover my own assumptions about writing. It has aided me in crafting a more coherent and unified course structure. It has encouraged me to try out some new methods of teaching writing. It has helped me to relinquish control and to emphasize classroom community. (p. 58)

Rather than being viewed as abstract and distant from the challenges faced by teachers and students, theory can have enormous practical utility when viewed as knowledge to be used for responsible classroom planning and decision making. As Lewin (1951), a pioneer in social psychology, wrote, "there is nothing so practical as good theory" (p. 7).

THEORY AND RESEARCH IN ESL WRITING

It would be convenient, indeed, if we could survey a tidy corpus of conclusive L2 writing theory and research as an easy introduction to processes of learning and teaching L2 composing. Unfortunately, our task in this chapter is a bit more difficult than that; as Silva (1993) accurately observed, "there exists, at present, no coherent, comprehensive theory of L2 writing" (p. 668). This observation has been largely supported by other leading researchers and theorists (e.g., Grabe & Kaplan, 1996; Johns, 1990; Krapels, 1990; Krashen, 1984; Leki, 1991c, 1992; Raimes, 1991). The field of L2 writing is nonetheless far from atheoretical. Although substantive L2 composition research did not appear until the 1980s, its theoretical frameworks can be traced directly to first language (L1) rhetoric and composition research (Grabe & Kaplan, 1996; Johns, 1990; Krapels, 1990). The following sections examine major approaches to L1 rhetoric and composition, focusing on those paradigms and philosophies that have played particularly influential roles in shaping theories of L2 writing. As these approaches are examined, one should keep in mind that no single theory or paradigm is necessarily autonomous or exclusive. In fact, one should expect to find a number of common features and overlapping points of view even among so-called "competing theories" (Knoblauch & Brannon, 1984).

Origins of the Field: L1 Composition Theory and Research

From the early 20th century into the 1960s, the principles driving composition instruction in U.S. schools, colleges, and universities were largely rooted in an educational philosophy that featured the reading and analysis of literature. In this tradition, native-speaking students were required to read novels, short stories, plays, essays, and poetry, and to analyze these works in written compositions or "themes." Because the pedagogical emphasis was on understanding and interpreting canonical literary texts, little instructional time was devoted to the act of writing (Kroll, 1991; Squire & Applebee, 1968). Of course, then (as now) students were expected to develop mastery of a number of school-based written genres (e.g., description, narration, argumentation, and exposition, including exemplification, process analysis, and comparison/contrast, to name just a few). To achieve this goal, many textbooks of that era followed a fairly prototypical model of instruction. In the first phase, the teacher would introduce and define a rhetorical form or pattern (e.g., comparison) in terms of a set of rigidly established rules or formulæ. Next, students would read a work of literature, which they would discuss and interpret in class. The teacher would then assign a writing task based on the literary text, referring back to the rhetorical principles introduced earlier; this would often be accompanied by a linear outline for the students to follow in preparing their compositions. Finally, the teacher would evaluate (and perhaps comment on) students' assignments before re-initiating a similar cycle based on a new literary text. This model, known by some as "the traditional paradigm" in U.S. English language education (Hairston, 1982) and by others as the "product approach" (Kroll, 1991), was not well grounded in a clearly articulated theory of learning or teaching. Moreover, it reflected a perspective in which students' written products were viewed as static representations of their knowledge and learning. Therefore, in the traditional paradigm, little if any attention was paid to the procedures or strategies involved in putting pen to paper and composing a coherent, readable piece of writing (Knoblauch & Brannon, 1984).

A strongly influential trend in L1 composition research and pedagogy that emerged in the 1960s and 1970s and was popularized in the 1980s in U.S. educational institutions is known broadly as the *process approach.* This model emphasizes the writer as the creator of original written discourse, focusing particular attention on his or her procedures for producing and revising text (Applebee, 1978, 1984; Berlin, 1988; Grabe & Kaplan, 1996; Hillocks, 1995; Johns, 1990; Knoblauch & Brannon, 1984; McKay, 1984; Tarvers, 1993). According to Faigley (1986), process proponents can be divided into two distinct categories: the *expressivists* and the *cognitivists.* For expressivists (e.g., Coles, 1974a, 1974b, 1978, 1980; Elbow, 1973, 1981a, 1981b; Macrorie, 1984; Murray, 1985), composing is viewed as "a creative act in which the process—the discovery of the true self—is as important as the product" (Berlin, 1988, p. 484). Founded on the premise that writing instruction should be nondirective and largely personal, expressivist pedagogy involves tasks that promote self-discovery and empowerment of the individual's inner writer. For example, Elbow (1981b) enthusiastically advocated journal writing and personal essays as tasks in which students can "write freely and uncritically" to "get down as many words as possible" (p. 7). Thus, expressivism values fluency and "voice" (Elbow, 1981b) as principal tools for achieving proficiency in writing.

Because it has affected the construction of theory in L2 writing pedagogy more directly, cognitivism (sometimes described as a "writing as problem-solving" model) shares with expressivism an explicit appreciation of writers' composing processes as personal and recursive. However, cognitivists place considerably greater value on higher order thinking and problem-solving skills such as planning, defining rhetorical problems, positioning problems in a larger context, operationalizing definitions, proposing solutions, and generating firmly grounded conclusions (Flower, 1985, 1989; Hayes & Flower, 1983). Hallmarks of the cognitivist approach to process writing pedagogy include invention and prewriting tasks (cf. Lauer, 1970), drafting multiple versions of writing assignments, abundant text-level (as opposed to sentence-level) revision, collaborative writing, feedback sessions (cf. Murray, 1992), and the postponement of editing until the end of a composing cycle. Thus, cognitivist rhetoricians focus principally on developing writers' mental processes, particularly strategies used to create and revise text on their own (Berlin, 1988; Flower, 1985, 1989; Hirsch, 1977).

A feature that distinguishes some cognitivist views of process-oriented L1 composition theory and pedagogy is an explicit recognition that writing is an inherently social, or transactional, process that involves mediation between the writer and his or her audience (Berlin, 1987). As a transactional endeavor, writing is understood as a process that must be undertaken with the reader's background knowledge, needs, and interests in mind. By understanding his or her reader and anticipating the latter's expectations, the writer can shape his or her texts so that they meet those expectations as effectively as possible (Flower, 1979; Hinds, 1987; Kroll, 1978). In such a social constructionist view, the audience or discourse community largely determines knowledge, language, and the nature of discourse, both spoken and written (Bruffee, 1986; Coe, 1987). According to Swales (1990), a discourse community is composed of a minimum number of expert members and a frequently larger number of apprentice members who operate on the basis of implicit and explicit public goals. It is informative to examine discourse communities because their members develop and use systems of speech and writing that are sometimes quite specific to a particular community's needs and goals. Within these systems, we often find participatory mechanisms used by community members to transmit information and feedback (e.g., meetings, publications, etc.), as well as text types or *genres* that promote collective goals (e.g., letters, journal articles, etc.) with particular formal (rhetorical, grammatical, lexical) features (Johns, 1990; Swales, 1990).

Students' access to academic discourse communities depends fundamentally on the mastery of certain types of communication skills (Horowitz, 1986c). These skills might include the writing of expository or persuasive essays for college composition courses (Bizzell, 1982, 1987, 1992) or preparation of research reports for the physical sciences (Bazerman, 1985, 1988; Myers, 1990). Given these social and institutional demands, composition instruction must provide novice writers with opportunities for practicing and appropriating the content knowledge, language, and rhetorical patterns represented in the academic discourse community (or communities) that students wish to join (cf. Grabe & Kaplan, 1996; Johns, 1995a, 1995b; Reid, 1989; Spack, 1988). A number of pedagogical models have been proposed to assist L1 writers in gaining control over written genres and in becoming apprenticed to the discourse communities that these genres characterize (cf. Berkenkotter & Huckin, 1993; Briggs & Bauman, 1992). Because L2 writing pedagogy has largely paralleled L1 composition instruction in terms of both theory and practice (Krapels, 1990; Leki, 1991c, 1992), we explore in the next section methodological developments and approaches as they pertain specifically to the teaching of composition in ESL classrooms.

The Emergence of L2 Writing as a Subdiscipline: Issues and Methods

Based on presumed and observed similarities between L1 and L2 composing processes, practitioners of ESL writing instruction in the early 1980s largely imitated L1 classroom practices in their own classrooms (Leki, 1992). Not only did research in L1 composition and rhetoric provide sound theoretical underpinnings for L2 composing pedagogy, but emergent L2 writing research also began to show that ESL writers already proficient in writing in their L1s tended to demonstrate strategies and skills quite similar to those displayed by native English-speaking (NES) writers. For example, investigations by Cumming (1989) and Zamel (1976, 1982, 1983) indicated that ESL writers with well-developed L1 writing abilities were able to transfer L1 skills and strategies to their L2 composing processes. ESL students in these studies exhibited skills that included planning, fulfilling the purposes of specific writing tasks, organizing ideas, and revising texts to reflect their intentions as writers. Cumming also reported that his intermediate- and advanced-level writers' ability to practice these strategies as they composed in English functioned independently of their measured L2 proficiency. This study and others like it have led some L2 writing researchers and practitioners to conclude that ESL students' needs are essentially comparable to those of basic L1 writers with regard to writing instruction.

Although non-native linguistic ability does not seem to prevent ESL students from becoming effective writers of English, many such learners require assistance in developing written fluency and practice with a variety of composing strategies. Based on research outcomes, some authorities have determined that what ESL writers need is not more language instruction, but more extensive and directed practice with global writing functions (Jones & Tetroe, 1987; Zamel, 1983). Research involving ESL students who are also inexperienced L1 writers tends to show that, like their NES peers, they: (a) lack a sense of direction as they undertake composing tasks, (b) experience difficulty organizing information, and (c) often get stuck at intermediate steps in their composing and revision processes (Bereiter & Scardamalia, 1987; Cumming, 1989; Raimes, 1985). Consequently, less experienced L1 and L2 writers often focus prematurely—and with less than satisfactory results—on microlevel features such as grammatical, lexical, and mechanical accuracy, as opposed to macrolevel concerns such as audience, rhetorical structure, purpose, clarity of ideas, and so on (Cumming, 1989; Jones, 1985). Because inexperienced L1 and L2 writers appear to share these characteristics, many models of L2 composing pedagogy (particularly those that emphasize process writing) assume that L2 writers benefit from the same instructional techniques as those used in L1 settings (Krapels, 1990; Leki, 1991c, 1992).

Shifts in Pedagogical Focus

Raimes (1991) provided a useful historical account of how ESL writing theory and practice have evolved since the 1960s and of how the field has achieved status as a discipline in its own right. Reflecting parallel (although by no means simultaneous) developments in L1 composition and rhetoric, approaches to L2 composition can be categorized according to the following four foci, each of which can be linked to a particular school of thought:

1. *Focus on form and "current-traditional rhetoric," 1966–*

Raimes traced the form-focused orientation in L2 writing to the audiolingual tradition in second language teaching (Fries, 1945), in which writing served merely to reinforce oral patterns of the language being learned and test learners' accurate application of grammatical rules (Rivers, 1968). In L2 writing instruction, early emphasis was on the production of well-formed sentences; a writing task that typifies this paradigm is the controlled composition, a narrowly focused paragraph- or essay-length assignment designed principally to give students practice with particular syntactic patterns (e.g., the past tense in English) and/or lexical forms (Kroll, 1991; Silva, 1990). In an extension of this model, "current-traditional rhetoric" (Berlin & Inkster, 1980; Kaplan, 1967; Silva, 1990; Young, 1978), students were also led to generate connected discourse by combining and arranging sentences into paragraphs based on prescribed formulae. Representative composing tasks might involve the imitation of specific rhetorical patterns (e.g., exposition, illustration, comparison, classification, argumentation, etc.) based on authentic and/or student-generated models.

2. *Focus on the writer: expressionism and cognitivism, 1976–*

Congruent with process approaches in L1 composition (described earlier), the focus on the writer in L2 composition has drawn researchers' and teachers' attention to what writers "actually do as they write" (Raimes, 1991, p. 409). Thus, researchers in this paradigm have attempted to characterize the heuristics and procedures used by writers as they plan, draft, revise, and edit their texts (see Krapels, 1990, for a summary of some of this research). Classroom procedures resulting from this writer-based orientation include practice with invention strategies (see chap. 4), the creation and sharing of multiple drafts, peer collaboration, abundant revision, and attention to content before grammatical form. Syllabi reflecting this approach may likewise allow writers to select their own topics and take more time to complete writing tasks than would be possible in a form-focused paradigm.

3. *Focus on content and the disciplines, 1986–*

Reservations concerning writer-centered instructional approaches have been expressed by researchers and practitioners who argue that the "almost total obsession" (Horowitz, 1986c, p. 788) with how writers construct personal meaning overlooks the need of many ESL writers to compose texts for academic readers with particular expertise (Horowitz, 1986a). In response to this perceived need, experts have proposed shifting the methodological emphasis in the direction of the knowledge and written genres characteristic of ESL students' specific academic disciplines. Rather than replacing writing processes with the pedagogical material characteristic of traditional English courses (viz., language, culture, and literature), content proponents assert that ESL writing courses should feature the specific subject matter that ESL students must learn in their major and required courses (Brinton, Snow, & Wesche, 1989; Horowitz, 1990; Shih, 1986; Snow & Brinton, 1988). In this model, students in adjunct, multiskill, and/or English for Academic Purposes

(EAP) courses are given assistance with "the language of the thinking processes and the structure or shape of content" (Mohan, 1986, p. 18). However, this focus on content does not preclude the use of writer-based, process-oriented principles and procedures such as prewriting, revision, peer collaboration, and the like (cf. Horowitz, 1986b). The main emphasis "is on the instructor's determination of what academic content is most appropriate, in order to build whole courses or modules of reading and writing tasks around that content" (Raimes, 1991, p. 411).

   4. *Focus on the reader: social constructionism, 1986–*
Like the content-based model, the reader-focused model of ESL writing instruction has emerged partly in opposition to the prescriptions of the writer-centered approach, described by Horowitz (1986a) as a form of "humanistic therapy" (p. 789). A reader-focused composition pedagogy is instead founded on the social constructionist premise that ESL writers need to be apprenticed into one or more academic discourse communities and that writing instruction should therefore prepare students to anticipate and satisfy the demands of academic readers (i.e., their professors) as they generate their written products (Horowitz, 1986a; Johns, 1990; cf. Bruffee, 1986; Coe, 1987; Flower, 1979; Hinds, 1987; Kroll, 1978). Clearly, the reader-focused approach is highly compatible with the content-based approach, both philosophically and methodologically. Interestingly, some have interpreted its implementation as entailing a return to a somewhat directive stance with respect to materials selection and classroom pedagogy (cf. Hairston, 1982). For example, Reid (1987) issued the following recommendations for deploying a reader-centered pedagogy dominated by an emphasis on discipline-specific rhetorical forms: "Teachers must gather assignments from across the curriculum, assess the purposes and audience expectations in the assignments, and present them to the class" (p. 34). In this view, writing instruction most appropriately centers on identifying, practicing, and reproducing the implicit and explicit features of written texts aimed at particular audiences.

   As Raimes (1991) pointed out in her survey, these empirical and methodological orientations reflect neither discrete historical periods nor mutually exclusive theoretical paradigms (cf. North, 1987). That is, although each focus represents a distinct instructional purpose and area of core interest, there is considerable chronological, conceptual, and practical overlap among them. The conflicts and compatibilities that exist among these orientations can certainly cause confusion among ESL writing teachers in search of answers to key pedagogical questions. According to Silva (1990) this "merry-go-round of approaches ... generates more heat than light and does not encourage consensus on important issues, preservation of legitimate insights, synthesis of a body of knowledge, or principled evaluation of approaches" (p. 18).

   To make sense of this perplexing situation, Silva first proposed that we systematically approach L2 writing as "purposeful and contextualized communicative interaction, which involves both the construction and transmission of knowledge" (p. 18). Working within this framework, we can then consider the following components of composing processes as we assess research and theory and make decisions about our own teaching practices:

- *The ESL writer*
  The writer as a person—that is, his or her personal knowledge, attitudes, learning styles, cultural orientation, language proficiency, and motivation, in addition to his or her composing strategies (see chap. 3);

- *The NES reader as the ESL writer's primary audience*
  The L1 reader's needs and expectations as a respondent and/or evaluator of the ESL student's written products (see chaps. 5, 6, and 7);

- *The writer's text*
  The writer's product as represented by its purposes, characteristics, and constituent elements—genre, rhetorical form, discursive mode, features of coherence and cohesion, syntactic properties, lexicon, mechanics, print-code features, and so on (see chaps. 2–7);

- *The contexts for writing*
  Cultural, political, social, economic, situational, and physical dimensions of the text (see this chapter, as well as chap. 6);

- *The interaction of all of these components in authentic educational settings.*
  (based on Silva, 1990)

By adopting a critical view of L2 composing theory and research and how this work has been informed by developments in L1 composition and rhetoric, we can begin to formulate our own operational theories of how ESL writers learn to write and how we can shape our instruction to meet their needs most effectively. A solid understanding of theoretical and pedagogical paradigms can sensitize us to our students' strengths and weaknesses. It also can equip us to implement a balanced, informed, and effective pedagogy that takes into account the multiple dimensions of L2 writers' developing composing skills (Grabe & Kaplan, 1997; Tsui, 1996).

$\Rightarrow AA\ 1.1$

$\Rightarrow AA\ 1.2$

$\Rightarrow AA\ 1.3$

Schema Theory and Its Implications for Teaching L2 Writers

One of the primary differences between NES and NNS writers lies in the prior experience they bring to the writing classroom. Differences in background knowledge manifest themselves in a variety of ways—in NNS students' responses to texts and topics, in their reactions to the activities of U.S. writing classrooms, and in their familiarity with the rhetorical patterns (at the discursive and sentence levels) of U.S. academic English (see Fig. 1.1).

A. Knowledge brought to the writing class:
  - about reading/writing topics and texts
  - about rhetorical patterns of U.S. academic writing
  - about the expectations of U.S. academic readers
B. Reactions to the writing class:
  - about assignments requiring personal writing
  - about peer response and teacher–student conferences
  - about using the work of others in their own writing
  - about teachers' responding techniques

FIG. 1.1. Cultural and rhetorical differences between L1 and L2 writers.

Weaver (1994) defined a *schema* as "an organized chunk of knowledge or experience, often accompanied by feelings" (p. 18). In L2 reading/writing research, schema has been discussed in terms of both content and formal knowledge about texts (Carrell, 1984, 1987; Carrell & Eisterhold, 1983), and particularly the facilitating or debilitating effects of the presence or absence of the appropriate schemata for the L2 reader or writer.

The notion of schema as it relates to pedagogy rests on several precepts: (a) that literacy events involve an interaction between a reader and a text (Eskey, 1986; Eskey & Grabe, 1988; Rumelhart, 1980), (b) that readers' responses to and understanding of a text will vary according to individual readers' schemata and other circumstances at the time of the interaction (Weaver, 1994), and (c) that schemata include not only the content of a text, but its organization as well (Carrell, 1984, 1987). For example, imagine that you are reading a recipe in a magazine or cookbook. What would you expect the *content* and *organization* of that text to be like? You would probably anticipate finding a list of necessary ingredients and then the steps you would need to follow in order to prepare the recipe. A recipe that deviates from this expected order might be frustrating or confusing. These expectations constitute your schema or schemata (content-specific and formal) for the presentation of recipes in written form. Of course, if you have never cooked a meal, your schemata related to recipes will be different from those of experienced cooks. Moreover, your experience with reading that text will vary depending on the circumstances: Are you merely glancing at the recipe to consider it for some point in the future? Are you in the kitchen at this moment preparing dinner? The specific situation will affect the level of concentration and attention to detail that you bring to the reading task.

L1 and L2 research has concluded that "when content and form are familiar, reading and writing are relatively easy. But when one or the other (or both) are unfamiliar, efficiency, effectiveness, and success are problematic" (Reid, 1993a, p. 63). A major implication of schema theory for writing instruction is that teachers must take pains to ensure that students find the texts and topics of a class accessible from a cognitive standpoint. This can be accomplished either through selecting reading materials and writing assignments that allow students to capitalize on their prior experience and/or through in-class activities that develop students' schemata where they may be lacking (specific suggestions for schema activation and development are presented in chaps. 2, 3, and 4).

Contrastive Rhetoric and Its Implications for Teaching L2 Writing

As already noted, one specific way in which the schemata of L2 students differ from those of L1 writers is in their expectations about the rhetorical patterns or logical organization of a text. The study of contrastive rhetoric (CR) examines the differing expectations and their effects on L2 literacy development. According to Connor (1996), "contrastive rhetoric maintains that language and writing are cultural phenomena. As a result, each language has rhetorical conventions unique to it. Furthermore, the linguistic and rhetorical conventions of the first language interfere with the writing in the second language" (p. 5).

The Genesis of CR.   The study of CR was initiated in a pioneering article by Kaplan (1966). The historical context of the term was that, at the time, the application of contrastive analysis (CA) to teaching second language grammar and phonology was very much in vogue. In the CA approach, the structures of students' L1s were compared with those of the L2 they were trying to acquire. Hence, areas of potential difficulty could be identified, and students could be directly taught about those aspects of the language.

In his article, Kaplan suggested that students' L1s also have contrasting rhetorical and logical patterns. Based on his analysis of more than 600 texts written by international students at a U.S. university, Kaplan made the following generalizations: Arabic speakers make extensive use of coordination (considered excessive by readers whose first language is English), "Oriental" writers tend to circle around

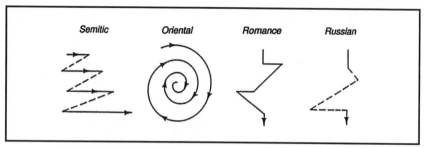

FIG. 1.2. Kaplan's (1966) "doodles" diagram on cross-cultural differences
in paragraph organization.

a topic rather than approaching it directly, and French and Spanish writers digress and introduce extraneous material more than English writers do. Kaplan summarized these observations in a now-famous diagram reproduced in Fig. 1.2.

The Impact of CR.   The implication of Kaplan's 1966 research and the resulting CR hypothesis appeared, to most readers and teachers at the time, to be that L2 writers needed explicit instruction and modeling in the rhetorical patterns of English. Of course, this view dovetailed nicely with the current-traditional view of composition that prevailed at the time. However, as time went on, a number of criticisms of CR surfaced. Kaplan's study was characterized as being too crude and general (e.g., his classification of all Asian writers under the broad category "Oriental"), too prescriptive (leading to a rigid and ethnocentric view of what correct English rhetorical patterns are), and too simplistic (for attempting to induce L1 rhetorical patterns from L2 compositions).

Nonetheless, over the past 30 years, a number of studies have produced evidence of differing rhetorical patterns across diverse languages, indicating the impact of L1-specific discursive and sentence-level patterns on ESL writing (for reviews, see Connor, 1996; Connor & Kaplan, 1987; Kaplan, 1983, 1987, 1988; Leki, 1991c, 1992; Purves, 1988; Reid, 1993a). Hinds' (1983a, 1983b, 1987) work on Japanese and English argumentation provides a clear and compelling example. Hinds found that English-speaking readers expect a writer to make a clear and straightforward statement of his or her point of view (usually near the beginning of a persuasive text), whereas Japanese-speaking writers deliberately obscure their own opinions as they carefully present the various sides of an issue, only taking a stand at the end of the piece, if at all. Thus, English persuasive writing, in which the author states his or her view up front and then supports it by means of linear argumentation, can seem dull, pointless, and self-involved to Japanese readers, whereas Japanese argumentation can appear circuitous and evasive to U.S. readers.

Most scholars today, including Kaplan, would not claim that CR has strong predictive power. Nonetheless, even the most conservative authorities acknowledge its explanatory value. In other words, we cannot assume, based on the findings of existing CR research, that all writers from a particular L1 will have the same difficulties in a given L2. Nonetheless, the knowledge that logical patterns of organization differ cross-culturally and cross-linguistically can help both teachers and students understand some of the issues and difficulties faced by L2 writers. Leki (1991a) and Reid (1993a) suggested several ways in which an understanding of CR can be valuable in the writing classroom. These suggestions are summarized in Fig. 1.3.

Implications

1. Helps teachers to avoid stereotypes by understanding culturally informed preferences in writing styles.
2. Helps students realize they are influenced by cultural patterns and rhetorical traditions, rather than suffering from individual inadequacies (adapted from Leki, 1991b).

Applications

1. Teachers can collect reading–writing assignments across the curriculum in order to "become more informed about appropriate U.S. academic discourse patterns."
2. Teachers can analyze different assignments "to inform their ESL writing students about discourse differences and audience expectations."
3. Teachers can then plan lessons around this information "to provide practice with the imposition of appropriate patterns upon experience and to offer opportunities for practice and experience with the new schema" (adapted from Reid, 1993b, p. 63).

FIG. 1.3. Implications and applications of contrastive rhetoric.

Therefore, it is important for L2 writing teachers to be aware of the differing schemata (including rhetorical variations considered by CR researchers) that their students bring to the writing class—backgrounds that differ not only from those of NES learners, but from the schemata of other L2 students. These differences affect students' abilities to (a) comprehend, analyze, and respond to the texts they read; (b) function effectively in the L2 reading and writing classroom; and (c) construct texts of their own that fulfill the expectations of NES readers. Consequently, teachers of L2 writing must consider the implications of schematic differences in the (a) readings they choose, (b) tasks they assign, (c) instruction they provide, (d) assessment instruments they use, and (e) feedback they give to their students.

THE UNIQUENESS OF ESL WRITERS:
CLASSROOM IMPLICATIONS

The preceding sections of this chapter dealt with aspects of L2 composing theory, research, and pedagogy that draw on parallels with L1 composition and rhetoric. They also touched on theoretical assumptions, empirical findings, and instructional approaches that make implicit and/or explicit distinctions between L1 and L2 composing processes and strategies, particularly with respect to research in contrastive rhetoric. As Silva (1993) plainly observed, "L2 writing is strategically, rhetorically, and linguistically different in important ways from L1 writing" (p. 669). Therefore, it is crucial for teachers of ESL writing to understand fundamental characteristics that distinguish L2 writers and to appreciate the diversity of learners that they may encounter in their ESL writing courses. This variety of backgrounds, goals, and expectations on the part of novice ESL writers accentuates the complexity of an already challenging educational endeavor.

Raimes (1991) succinctly noted that, "there is no such thing as a generalized ESL student" (p. 420). If there were, our task as composition teachers might simply entail making decisions about the optimal instructional approach or approaches to adopt based on the existing literature. However, ESL teachers in many (if not most) educational settings are keenly aware of the challenges posed by working with student populations that are heterogeneous in terms of linguistic, ethnic, and cultural background, not to mention language proficiency, literacy, and cognitive development. Also of concern to classroom teachers are their learners' attitudes toward learning, formal instruction, and the target subject matter, in addition to students' motivation to acquire linguistic, cognitive, and academic skills. Other factors known to influence learning include age, academic goals, aptitude, anxiety, cognitive and metacognitive strategy use, language awareness, and social distance (see Ellis, 1994, for a complete literature review).

We mention these variables here to acknowledge the enormous complexity of the educational challenges facing ESL composition teachers (Silva, 1997; Zamel, 1997). At the same time, however, we would like to point out that there are ways of identifying, categorizing, and working with these multiple variables. The individual differences (ID) research in second language acquisition has contributed enormous insight into the multiple learner-specific and environmental factors that bear on L2 learners' success (or failure) in their attempts to acquire L2 knowledge and skills (see Larsen-Freeman & Long, 1991; Skehan, 1989, 1991, for excellent surveys of this research). Globally speaking, ID research "has concentrated on investigating the effects of different ID variables on learner proficiency, achievement, or rate of progress, measured in terms of performance on some kind of language test" (Ellis, 1994, p. 473). Although this body of empirical and theoretical work is seldom cited in the L2 composition literature, it is worthy of our careful attention because it offers a systematic framework for identifying roughly hewn, but easily identifiable, ID factors known to influence language proficiency and academic performance, as well as students' predispositions toward writing processes and tasks (cf. Reid, 1995).

Of particular relevance to ESL composition teachers are dimensions of learners' knowledge and training that have shaped their current linguistic and literacy skills in both L1 and L2. Figure 1.4 summarizes a few of the major differences that may set ESL writers apart from NES writers.

As observed in some detail in the previous sections on CR and schema theory, a primary feature that sets ESL writers apart from their NES peers is that ESL students come to the classroom with the ability to speak (and often write) one or more languages other than English (Leki, 1992). This bilingual, bicultural (and, in many cases, biliterate) knowledge gives ESL students a unique status as learners that entails a set of linguistic, metalinguistic, cognitive, and metacognitive skills that may be very different from those of their monolingual, NES counterparts (Carrell & Monroe, 1995). Based on the findings of research in CR and genre studies, we have suggested that this bilingual/bicultural knowledge can both facilitate and impede progress in the development of L2 writing proficiency (cf. Connor, 1996).

SUMMARY

The individual cognitive, linguistic, ethnic, and socioeconomic background factors highlighted in the previous section (which is by no means an exhaustive list) underscore the importance of taking into account students' unique personal and educational profiles, as well as the characteristics of particular educational institutions. Clearly, individual differences and institutional factors can have direct and rather specific implications for classroom practice in the ESL environment. Despite the apparent parallels between the composing processes of L1 and L2 writers highlighted in the first part of this chapter, ESL writers represent a unique learner population. Therefore, developing an effective approach (or set of approaches) to the teaching of ESL composition necessitates an appreciation of these unique features and strategies for accommodating them. Based on the work of a number of researchers cited throughout this chapter, the following summary statements are presented as a general foundation for considering the topic-specific content of succeeding chapters:

- ESL writers, by virtue of their emergent language proficiency and literacy skills in English, should not be expected to perform as well as NES writers on writing tasks and tests that are designed for NES writers (Silva, 1993). The form and content of ESL writing is inherently (and thus naturally) different from NES writing in qualitative terms (Leki, 1991c, 1992).

	NES Writers …	ESL Writers …
Knowledge of Language and Writing Systems	• begin with intact, "native" knowledge of spoken and written English; are principally acquiring English *composing* skills;	• begin with an intact L1 and a *developing* knowledge of spoken and written English as a second language; are simultaneously acquiring *language* and *composing* skills;
	• are familiar with the Roman alphabet and English orthographic conventions;	• may or may not be familiar with the Roman alphabet and may thus still be learning English orthographic conventions;
	• produce sentence-level errors that are not influenced by knowledge of another language;	• may produce sentence-level errors influenced by their primary language(s);
	• are not influenced by rhetorical knowledge emanating from another language or writing system, although they may be unfamiliar with formal rhetorical conventions (i.e., organizational patterns, markers of cohesion and coherence, etc.);	• may have L1-specific rhetorical knowledge (i.e., organizational patterns, markers of cohesion and coherence, etc.) that could facilitate or inhibit the learning of English rhetorical conventions;
Schematic and Rhetorical Knowledge	• have topical/schematic knowledge specific to U.S. culture and education;	• may not have the same topical/schematic knowledge as NES writers due to home country educational experience;
	• have access to (and perhaps some knowledge of) U.S. reader expectations;	• may be unfamiliar with U.S. reader expectations;
	• have, by virtue of U.S. educational experience, exposure to (and experience with) rhetorical conventions of U.S. academic writing;	• may have little or no experience with rhetorical conventions of U.S. academic writing: may have been trained in rhetorical conventions of L1 educational tradition, which may be quite different from those promoted in the U.S.;
Responses to the Writing Class	• may have experience with personal writing;	• may have little or no experience with personal writing (particularly in the context of school);
	• may have experience with peer response (and may expect it);	• may have little or no experience with peer response;
	• may have experience using outside sources, paraphrasing, quoting;	• may have little or no experience using outside sources, paraphrasing, quoting;
	• may have extensive experience with U.S. teachers' response and feedback styles (e.g., questioning, indirectness);	• may have little or no experience with U.S. teachers' response and feedback styles (e.g., questioning, indirectness); may expect little or no feedback for revision;
	• may expect to revise assignments significantly	• may not expect to revise assignments significantly (if at all)

FIG. 1.4. Overview of differences between novice NES and ESL writers.

- ESL writers come to the composition classroom with needs specific to their status as NNS students. That is, given their implicit and explicit linguistic knowledge, prior educational training, L1 and L2 literacy skills, and cognitive/metacognitive skill and strategy use, ESL writers have unique instructional needs that may not be appropriately or effectively addressed in NES-oriented or mainstream composition courses (Silva, 1993).
- These special needs can be most accurately identified and productively accommodated by composition teachers who are equipped with theoretical and practical knowledge of L2 writing processes and the unique expertise of L2 writers (Leki, 1992; Silva, 1993).
- Apprentice ESL writers may require "more of everything" in terms of procedures, heuristics, content, practice, and feedback than their NES counterparts (Raimes, 1985, p. 250). That is, L2 composition teachers offer their learners the greatest benefit by devoting "more time and attention across the board to strategic, rhetorical, and linguistic concerns" (Silva, 1993, p. 670).
- L2 writing pedagogy may be most effective when it directs writers' attention toward macro- and micro-level textual concerns, including audience expectations, patterns for producing unfamiliar rhetorical forms, and tools for improving lexico-grammatical variety and accuracy (Grabe & Kaplan, 1996; Leki, 1991a; Silva, 1993).

Reflection and Review

1. Discuss the similarities and differences among the following theoretical orientations toward L1 and L2 composition and rhetoric: the traditional paradigm, the process approach (expressivist and cognitivist perspectives, as well as the social constructionist view), and the current-traditional model. What do these models have in common philosophically and practically?
2. What factors do you think have contributed to the "merry-go-round of approaches" that Silva (1990, p. 18) claimed characterizes L2 composition pedagogy? What solutions might you propose to address this problem?
3. To what extent do you feel the following emphases in L2 writing instruction are compatible or incompatible: (a) focus on form, (b) focus on the writer, (c) focus on content, and (d) focus on the reader? Which of these foci might be seen as complementary? Explain and justify your point of view by referring to your own experience as a novice writer and/or teacher of writing.
4. Summarize and evaluate the cognitive, perceptual, and creative consequences and advantages of being bilingual and/or biliterate in a society

that is predominantly monolingual. In a predominantly monolingual educational system? In what ways can bilingual/biliterate knowledge promote learning?

Application Activity 1.1: Retrospection Assignment

Directions.   Reflect again on your experience as a composition student in an L1 or L2 setting either in written form or in an informal discussion with a classmate. Explain how you would characterize the instructional approach(es) used in one or more of these courses in terms of one or more of the major theoretical orientations presented in this chapter (i.e., the traditional paradigm, expressivist and cognitivist views of the process approach, the social constructionist view, the current-traditional model, etc.).

Application Activity 1.2: Classroom Observation Task

Directions.   Individually or with a classmate, arrange to visit one or more NES or ESL composition classes. Before going into the field to conduct your observations, select and/or develop a set of focused and easy-to-use classroom observation tools for capturing classroom behaviors and processes of specific interest to you (e.g., see Wajnryb, 1992). Use these tools to focus your attention as you take field notes. Following your observation, prepare a written observation report in which you describe and make inferences about the following:

1. Basic information concerning the level of the course, the writing curriculum, the assignment types in progress, the institution type, the students (ESL proficiency, gender ratio, L1 backgrounds), and so on;
2. The contents, sequence, procedures, and tasks that took place during the lesson;
3. The instructor's explicit and/or implicit goals and objectives for the lesson and its component parts (i.e., tasks, activities, assignments);
4. The extent to which the instructor's goals and objectives seem to have been met;
5. The instructor's and/or the institution's dominating theoretical-philosophical orientation toward composition and rhetoric; and
6. Evidence of the students' learning as manifest in their behaviors and written products.

Use the prior steps as basic guidelines for reporting and reflecting on your classroom observations. You may also wish to consider the following as additional options for maximizing your observational experience:

1. In one or more observations, focus specifically on a single writer and his or her behaviors throughout the lesson. If possible, interview the student before and/or after the lesson to learn about his or her impressions concerning the composition class, his or her composing and revision processes, and so on;

2. Meet with the instructor before and/or after your observation to learn about his or her explicit expectations for and perceptions of the lesson that you examined. Compare his or her impressions to your own; and

3. Compare a NES composition class to an ESL composition class in terms of goals, objectives, procedures, tasks, and student behaviors. Discuss the similarities and differences between the theoretical orientations of each class.

Include an appendix with your field notes and any other materials related to the course (e.g., the syllabus, assignment sheets, etc.) as part of your complete observation report.

Application Activity 1.3: Introspective Process Analysis

Directions.

1. Select a substantial academic writing task that you have been assigned in one of your regular courses (e.g., a research study, a position paper, a bibliographic essay, etc.). Take care to select an assignment that requires extended prose and that involves revision (i.e., not a 24-hour take-home exam or a short homework assignment).

2. Maintain a chronological log in which you record notes on your processes and procedures throughout the development of this assignment. At the beginning of this process, for example, you may wish to begin by taking notes on the task or assignment sheet. Date your log entries so that you can use them to compose a retrospective meta-analysis of your writing and revision processes. You should include this log as an appendix to your completed analysis.

3. Refer to the following questions and prompts repeatedly and systematically throughout the process of completing this assignment:

   a. What is your assigned topic and what are your purposes for writing?
   b. Whom did you envision as your audience as you started? Why?
   c. How did you get started? Describe the procedures in specific terms.
   d. Characterize the processes involved in producing a preliminary draft. Note the time, place, and length of time this took. Describe brainstorming, planning, reading, and other processes that were involved. Record instances in which you made progress, took backward steps, abandoned your original plans, and so on. Always try to reflect on *why* you made these decisions.

e. Describe what you were pleased and displeased with on completion of your preliminary draft.

f. Note your thoughts about your audience as you completed your preliminary draft and considered revising it. Did your perceptions of the audience change at all? Why or why not?

g. Characterize the process involved in composing your second version. To what extent did it resemble (or not resemble) the first draft? Why? What changes did you make and why?

h. If you received oral or written feedback from another reader (a friend, a classmate, the instructor), discuss how that feedback influenced your revision process.

i. If you went through more than one revision process, return to items d–h and record your impressions.

j. Perform an honest assessment of your effectiveness in addressing the assignment. To what extent do you feel you accomplished the instructor's goals? How might you have adjusted your process? Describe your sense of satisfaction with the final product.

k. Summarize the principal features of your composing process in completing this assignment, noting its strengths and weaknesses.

l. How do your current impressions of your composing processes agree with your original beliefs about these processes? What have you learned from analyzing your process?

m. Try to characterize the foci of your writing processes. That is, are your writing processes predominantly form-focused, writer-based, content-focused, or reader-based?

4. Based on your journal reflections and findings, compose a report on your own writing and revision processes that synthesize the central features listed in items 3a–l.

(Adapted from a course assignment developed by Cherry Campbell and Lynn Goldstein.)

CHAPTER 2	Reading–Writing Relationships in ESL Composition

Questions for Reflection

- In what ways has your academic and other reading influenced your L1 and/or L2 writing proficiency?
- To what extent do your writing skills and styles match the kinds of reading you have done for academic and recreational purposes?
- Why might reading be an especially important factor in how ESL students become writers of English?

TEXT AS THE SOURCE OF LITERATE KNOWLEDGE

The role of reading as a function of general language proficiency has received considerable attention among researchers and teachers over the last two decades or more. As "an intrapersonal problem-solving task that takes place within the brain's knowledge structures" (Bernhardt, 1991, p. 6), reading is understood not only as a cognitive activity, but as a social process that is vital to the success of academic L2 writers (Eskey, 1993; McKay, 1993). Furthermore, the act of reading involves a transformation of the reader's state of knowledge. To characterize this transformation, Just and Carpenter (1987) maintained that we must minimally take into account the following components:

- what information in the text starts the process
- how long the process takes
- what information was used during the process
- the likely sources of mistakes
- what the reader has learned when the process is finished. (p. 4)

This final component, "what the reader has learned when the process is finished," is widely believed to be the basis of how learners become *writers*. This information contains the message that is encoded in print as well as clues about how the message's grammatical, semantic, lexical, pragmatic, and rhetorical forms combine to make the message meaningful. Therefore, teachers interested in the learning and teaching of writing skills require a fundamental understanding of reading–writing relationships, their socioeducational dimensions, and their implications for instruction.

Not surprisingly, empirical studies in the field of literacy almost overwhelmingly show that reading for academic and recreational purposes positively influences L1 and L2 development among both children and adults (Krashen, 1985b, 1993). Despite the large body of evidence that supports the positive influences of reading on language and literacy skill development, we still lack a comprehensive understanding of exactly *how* the act of reading impacts literacy skills, particularly composing skills. Many researchers have attempted to explain how writing proficiency develops as a result of readers' interactions with print (Grabe, 1991). Recent findings have important classroom implications for ESL teachers, particularly those who teach writing.

To maximize the potential of reading in L2 academic literacy development, it is vital for classroom teachers to know how reading promotes an understanding of the purposes, functions, and structures of academic and non-academic texts (Kroll, 1993). Due to the vast nature of the field and the overwhelming quantity of research on reading–writing relationships, however, a truly comprehensive survey is not possible. This chapter addresses major issues in reading and writing research that are particularly relevant to ESL writing instruction. It also contains brief descriptions of empirical studies suggesting specific pedagogical directions and implications.[1] The material that follows is necessarily somewhat descriptive in nature and attempts to outline a theoretical approach to reading–writing connections that includes concrete principles for incorporating reading skill development into writing pedagogy. The recommendations and sample tasks in this chapter are intended to serve as general guidelines for exploiting and strengthening reading–writing relationships.

READING PATTERNS IN L1 AND L2 LITERACY DEVELOPMENT

A fundamental principle of L2 education is that students acquire more knowledge and learn more efficiently when abundant and meaningful input is made available to them (Krashen, 1985a, 1985b). The common wisdom of communicative language instruction extends to the ESL composition setting, where many teachers

---

[1]For a detailed treatment of the role of reading in the ESL composition classroom, readers are referred to Carson and Leki (1993). The following volumes also present theoretical, empirical, and pedagogical perspectives on L2 reading development: Bernhardt (1991); Carrell, Devine, and Eskey (1988); Devine, Carrell, and Eskey (1987); Goldman and Trueba (1987); Gunderson (1991); and Peregoy and Boyle (1997).

operate on the general assumption that nearly any type of reading is beneficial to apprentice writers. For example, numerous studies have indicated that extensive reading correlates highly with improved writing performance in L1 (Belanger, 1987; Stotsky, 1983) and L2 (Krashen, 1984, 1993). Consequently, many ESL writing courses are founded on the premise that "writing competence results somehow from exposure to reading, and that good readers make good writers" (Carson, 1993, p. 85). Enthusiastic reading proponents have further argued for the primacy of reading over explicit writing and grammar instruction in L2 classrooms (Goodman, Goodman, & Hood, 1989; Krashen, 1984, 1985b, 1993, 1994; McQuillan, 1994; Peregoy & Boyle, 1997). Although the research literature offers some support for the view that reading is the single greatest factor in promoting compositional skills, it merits cautious evaluation and interpretation. ESL composition teachers can benefit from understanding the advantages and limitations of empirical studies of reading–writing relationships, particularly as they pertain to the teaching of academic literacy (Cummins, 1981; Kroll, 1993). The following sections examine a sampling of these studies and their implications.

Reading Habits: Book Ownership, Voluntary Reading, and Writing Proficiency

Apart from investigations that account for the amount of reading reported by students in relation to their language proficiency, a number of reports have focused on the connections between book ownership and various measures of L1 and L2 linguistic performance. Most of these studies assume that book ownership reflects an individual's level of literacy and claim that book ownership reliably predicts learners' performance on academic reading tasks (Briggs & Elkind, 1977; Milner, 1951; Roberts, Bachen, Hornby, & Hernandez-Ramos, 1984; Ryan, 1977; Sheldon & Carillo, 1952; Stevenson, 1985; Williams, 1981). Because book ownership alone is unlikely to be a wholly valid measure of literate behavior (let alone performance), reading–writing researchers have endeavored to look more closely at the reading behaviors of children and adults. A growing body of evidence suggests that extensive reading—most notably, reading of a voluntary nature—may dramatically enhance the development of linguistic skills, especially those related to comprehending and producing written text. Flower and Hayes (1980) observed that good writers demonstrate significant amounts of tacit knowledge of conventional and formal features of written text. Using this unconscious knowledge "may be one way in which extensive reading affects a person's ability to write: A well-read person simply has a much larger and richer set of images of what a text can look like" (p. 28).

Krashen (1984, 1985b, 1993, 1994) summarized much of the L1 and L2 research related to this topic, which leads to his unequivocal assertion that "reading exposure is the primary means of developing language skills" (1985b, p. 109), including grammatical knowledge, vocabulary, and writing proficiency. Controversial and subject to frequent criticism, Krashen's more extreme claims are nonetheless important for ESL composition teachers because they highlight a fundamental argument: The emergence of academic literacy must, to some extent, depend on learners' exposure to and processing of print matter. As Smith (1988) observed, knowledge about written language and its use "must be found in what other people have written, in existing texts ... We learn to write without suspecting that we are learning or what we learn. Everything points to the necessity of learning to write from what we read, as we read" (p. 20; cf. Johns & Davies, 1981; Smith, 1982, 1984, 1985, 1986).

Studies of voluntary reading among L1 and L2 learners in various age groups offer empirical confirmation that the ability to produce written text emanates at least partly from long-term, self-initiated reading and that this ability can develop without learners' conscious awareness. Generally, individuals who report reading extensively are better readers and writers than those who do not read extensively or at all (Krashen, 1993; Stotsky, 1983). In Birnbaum's (1982) study of fourth- and seventh-grade NES students, for example, the more proficient writers had typically engaged in voluntary reading as well as self-sponsored writing. Birnbaum suggested that voluntary reading experiences teach young learners the multiple uses of writing in school, the workplace, the world of communication, and literate societies in general. Such literacy experiences transform apprentice writers' composing behaviors "from detached mechanical compliance with an external demand to an involved commitment to transforming a personally meaningful experience into written language" (Birnbaum, 1982, p. 256). Similar patterns, most of them very striking, have been reported in studies of children learning ESL (cf. Elley & Mangubhai, 1983). Elley's (1991) synthesis and review of nine "book flood" studies conducted around the world confirms the "spread of effect from reading competence to other language skills—writing, speaking, and control over syntax" (p. 404). Thus, voluntary exposure to print may thus heighten learners' awareness of the multiple functions of written language and of how various text types are constructed, even at a relatively young age. Research results seem to reflect the general principle that self-initiated reading is good and that more self-initiated reading is even better (Krashen, 1993, 1994).

Strong correlations between reading habits and measured writing ability have been discovered among older learners as well. Fader (1976) reported the outcomes of numerous L1 studies in which adolescent participants in pleasure reading programs consistently demonstrated more fluent and complex writing skills than did students who were not program participants and who reported little or no voluntary reading. Not surprisingly, the readers also outperformed nonreaders on measures of reading comprehension accuracy. Applebee (1978) likewise discovered that high school students who read an average of 14 books during the summer vacation were also successful writers whose composition scores were superior to those of students who reported reading significantly fewer books. These studies and others like it (e.g., Donalson, 1967) systematically indicate a positive relationship between good reading habits (e.g., reading extensively, reading for pleasure outside of school, etc.) and a demonstrable ability to compose fluent, meaningful, and grammatically accurate text (cf. Krashen, 1984).

Parallel findings have been reported among college- and university-level L1 and L2 writers. Ryan's (1977) study of L1 college freshmen showed that students enrolled in remedial writing courses reported owning and reading significantly fewer books than did their counterparts who were enrolled in regular (nonremedial) composition courses. Woodward and Phillips (1967) found that college freshmen judged to be good writers (identified by their placement composition scores) reported frequently reading newspapers and other nonassigned texts outside of their classes. Meanwhile, students with lower composition scores reported reading significantly less often, if at all. Findings such as these point to a salutary role for self-initiated reading as a means of accelerating the growth of academic literacy in general and writing skills in particular. Although not all of the L1 studies have produced statistically significant correlations between reading habits variables and writing proficiency (e.g., Illo, 1976), research outcomes consistently support the claim that learners who report reading on their own tend to be better readers and writers, both in L1 and in L2 (Krashen, 1984, 1993; Stotsky, 1983).

Because of ESL learners' unique and complex situation (see chap. 1), the positive effects of self-initiated and assigned reading on their English writing proficiency are more difficult to discern than they might be for L1 writers. The task of literate ESL writers involves challenges that L1 writers never confront. For example, the ESL writers with whom this section is concerned bring to the ESL composition class a set of L1 literacy skills that may be well developed (Carson, Carrell, Silberstein, Kroll, & Kuehn, 1990). Nonetheless, their English literacy skills require support "from a language system which, in the early stages at least, is insufficiently developed to allow those learners the full range of literacy practices to which they are accustomed" (Eisterhold, 1990, p. 94). Therefore, ESL composition teachers must take into account their students' not-yet-native knowledge of the structure and use of written English, not to mention the possibility of transfer and nontransfer of L1 literacy skills into L2 performance (Eisterhold, 1990; Friedlander, 1990; Hedgcock & Atkinson, 1993). Some L1 abilities and strategies (e.g., decoding, inferencing, morphosyntactic prediction, etc.) may certainly transfer to emergent L2 literacy (Canale, Frenette, & Belanger, 1988; Edelsky, 1982; Elley, 1984; Goldman, Reyes, & Varnhagen, 1984; Johns, 1988b; Mace-Matluck, Dominguez, Holtzman, & Hoover, 1983; Roller, 1988; Sarig, 1987; Wagner, Spratt, & Ezzaki, 1989). However, it is important to recognize that such transfer is not necessarily automatic. In fact, transfer may require explicit instruction (Alderson, 1984; Carrell, 1987; Clarke, 1978; Cziko, 1978; Eisterhold, 1990; McLaughlin, 1987).

These potential difficulties notwithstanding, observational and experimental studies still underscore the advantages enjoyed by ESL learners who read extensively in English over those learners who read very little in English. Most ESL reading–writing studies emphasize learners' vital need to become familiar with multiple text types as they learn to compose in English. Salyer (1987) compared the English writing performance of two groups of college ESL students: The first group reported extensive pleasure reading in English, whereas the second reported almost none (although students said that they read for pleasure in their L1s). Whereas the two groups had begun their ESL composition course at the same level of writing proficiency, the group that reported frequent pleasure reading showed significantly greater improvement by the end of the course. In an analogous study, Janopoulos (1986) examined the reading habits and writing performance of graduate ESL students. Based on significant relationships between amount of self-initiated reading and standard composition scores, he concluded that "the amount of pleasure reading a foreign student does in English may be used as a reliable predictor of his/her English writing proficiency" (p. 767). Also significant for the ESL composition teacher is the widespread finding that L2 students find self-selected reading pleasurable and thus potentially facilitative of literacy acquisition (Flahive & Bailey, 1993; Hafiz & Tudor, 1989; Krashen, 1988; McQuillan, 1994; van Naerssen, 1985).

Large-scale and long-term voluntary reading programs sponsored by schools and local libraries are typically geared toward primary and secondary students (Krashen, 1993, 1994). ESL writing teachers in secondary and higher education may find it impractical to participate in or initiate such programs because of preestablished curricular objectives or low student interest. Small-scale efforts to encourage voluntary or self-selected reading are nonetheless practical in ESL programs where teachers select their own instructional materials and participate in curricular decision-making. Perhaps the most effective way to encourage ESL learners to read English texts on their own is to dramatize the value of voluntary reading by describing, discussing—and, if possible, modeling—reading for personal enjoyment and enrichment (Dupuy, Tse, & Cook, 1996). This could mean devoting class time to exposing the short- and long-term benefits of reading for writing and for education in general. The teacher might also help students discover resources where texts of personal interest might be located. For example, ESL students might not realize that the campus library probably subscribes to an array of daily newspapers and popular magazines and is a good place to keep abreast of current events. The teacher may also discuss with students ways of making time for pleasure reading and for fitting it into a busy academic schedule. By addressing these issues in the writing class, the teacher accentuates the value of reading for enrichment.

In courses where reading is an integral component of the composition class, teachers may offer their students a range of texts from which they can make individual selections, rather than requiring a single textbook or set of readings. This plan can work effectively in content-based courses as well, where students might be further encouraged to seek out their own reading materials based on topics to be covered in the course. Even in courses where teachers' hands are essentially tied in terms of materials selection, writing assignments (e.g., summaries, reviews, essays, research reports) may be designed to allow students to choose their own sources. Because reading is a required element of ESL instruction, these options do not constitute *voluntary* reading in the truest sense, although the texts may be self-selected. However, they may serve as a viable compromise for the teacher working under tight constraints and for ESL students whose time is at a premium.

$\Rightarrow AA\ 2.1$

Assigned Reading and Writing Proficiency

Like its voluntary counterpart, assigned reading has also proved to be a positive influence on developing composing skills. For example, De Vries (1970) suggested that, under some circumstances, assigned reading may serve as an effective and useful substitute for conventional writing practice. De Vries compared two groups of fifth-grade L1 students: The first practiced traditional essay writing in class, whereas the second did no writing but instead did extensive reading in and out of class. The second group produced superior writing samples at the end of the experimental period. Heys (1962) related parallel findings in an experiment involving high school L1 writers who were divided into a reading group and a writing group. The reading group wrote one third the number of essays produced by the writing group, using class time normally dedicated to writing for reading. At the end of the term, the composition scores of the reading group were significantly higher than those of the writing group.

Christiansen's (1965) investigation of L1 college freshman writers was designed along similar lines. In the study, a writing group wrote three times the number of assignments as a reading group and did no reading in class. Although the reading group did not produce higher quality essays than the writing group, both groups showed the same degree of improvement by semester's end. Experimental outcomes such as these suggest that, under certain circumstances, the time that students spend reading may be as valuable as writing instruction and practice in enhancing writing performance. Some have even argued that reading may actually make a more significant contribution to writing proficiency than the practice of writing, particularly when reading is self-initiated or self-selected (Krashen, 1984, 1993, 1994; McQuillan, 1994; Smith, 1984, 1988). Such claims should be viewed with caution, however, especially when they pertain to L2 writers, because there is no reason to assume that extensive reading of any sort *automatically* leads to competent reading or composing skills (Shanahan, 1984). As Hughey, Wormuth, Hartfiel, and Jacobs (1983) were quick to emphasize: "Being a good reader does not make one a good writer. Reading serves to give the writer ideas, data, model sentence patterns, and structures, but a student will be able to become a good writer only by writing" (p. 49).

It has also been shown that college ESL writers may need to develop an explicit awareness of rhetorical and grammatical conventions before they can reproduce academic texts such as summaries, essays, reports and research papers (Carrell, 1987; Carson et al., 1990; Connor & Farmer, 1990; Eisterhold, 1990; Johns, 1986, 1988b, 1993, 1995a, 1995b). In fact, the ability to read and make sense of academic content actually entails a large number of microskills that may not be apparent to those of us who take many such skills for granted. Gunderson (1991) presented the following microskills as necessary for L1 and L2 readers who must cope with the complexity of academic materials:

1. Recognize the significance of the content.
2. Recognize important details.
3. Recognize unrelated details.
4. Find the main idea of a paragraph.
5. Find the main idea of large sections of discourse.
6. Differentiate fact and opinion.
7. Locate topic sentences.
8. Locate answers to specific questions.
9. Make inferences about content.
10. Critically evaluate content.
11. Realize an author's purpose.
12. Determine the accuracy of information.
13. Use a table of contents.
14. Use an index.
15. Use a library card catalogue.
16. Use appendices.
17. Read and interpret tables.
18. Read and interpret graphs.
19. Read and interpret charts.
20. Read and interpret maps.
21. Read and interpret cartoons.
22. Read and interpret diagrams.
23. Read and interpret pictures.
24. Read and interpret formulæ.
25. Read and understand written problems.
26. Read and understand expository material.
27. Read and understand argument.
28. Read and understand descriptive material.
29. Read and understand categories.

30. Read and understand adjust reading rate relative to purpose of reading.
31. Adjust reading rate relative to difficulty of material.
32. Scan for specific information.
33. Skim for important ideas.
34. Learn new material from text. (pp. 145–146)

Although ESL composition teachers must appreciate their responsibility to promote productive reading habits and skills among their students (Carson & Leki, 1993), they should be careful not to subordinate writing practice to reading: "The more experience students have writing about specific topics in particular genres and contexts, the more confidence they gain and the more fluent their writing becomes" (Scarcella & Oxford, 1993, p. 122).

$\boxed{\Rightarrow AA\ 2.2}$

$\boxed{\Rightarrow AA\ 2.3}$

$\boxed{\Rightarrow AA\ 2.4}$

READING ABILITY, WRITING PROFICIENCY, AND INTERLINGUAL TRANSFER

Another major dimension of reading–writing research involves the examination of quantitative and qualitative relationships between measured *reading ability* and/or *achievement* and measured *writing performance*: "Good writers are often good readers" (Reid, 1993a, p. 43). The reciprocal relationship between the two processes has, in fact, become a primary focal point of L1 and L2 literacy research. Empirical findings have led researchers to recognize that reading and composing both involve the construction of meaning, development and application of complex cognitive and linguistic skills, activation of existing knowledge and past experience, and ability to solve problems to control thinking (Berhnardt, 1991; Boutwell, 1983; Cumming, 1990b; Flower et al., 1990; Grabe, 1991; Kucer, 1985, 1989; Reid, 1993a). This knowledge and experience forms structures, or schemata, which behave like open databases (Carrell & Eisterhold, 1983; see chap. 1 for a discussion of schema theory). Reid (1993a) held that, as readers read, they enter ideas (in the form of words and sentences) into these databases, which they can subsequently search and modify as they encounter new textual information. In building, activating, and reworking schemata, L1 and L2 readers engage in a dynamic and interactive process in which they formulate meaning for a given text. They construct meaning by storing "newly acquired knowledge, accessing recorded and stored knowledge, and attending to the writer's clues as to the meaning intended for the text" (Cohen, 1990, p. 75).[2] If successful, this process results in the transformation of existing knowledge into new understandings and ideas. Schema theory highlights important links between reading and writing by identifying the processes in which readers discover ideas and views that become available as subject matter for their writing. As readers consciously and unconsciously build more numerous and complex schemata, they develop an implicit and/or explicit awareness of various formats of writing and of the expectations of NES readers (Reid, 1993a).

Early L1 studies have largely borne out the interdependent connection between reading and composing. For example, Evanechko, Ollila, and Armstrong (1974) and Zeman (1969), reported finding significant correlations between measured reading ability and composition scores in their studies of elementary school learners. Birnbaum (1982) conducted an in-depth study of the behaviors of 10- and 13-year-old learners during reading and writing episodes. Like Loban (1976), Birnbaum claimed that efficient reading habits and strategies were related to a clearer understanding of the act of reading on the part of the learners, as well as to a higher level of writing proficiency. In general, skilled readers and writers in these studies viewed themselves as good readers and writers. Perhaps more important, they demonstrated a measurable capacity to understand text based on their knowledge of rhetorical and grammatical structure (cf. Reid, 1993a). For instance, Birnbaum's participants displayed a solid knowledge of how narrative and expository texts were constructed in English. This pattern lends weight to the prediction that proficient and experienced readers may develop an underlying or implicit awareness of discourse structure, rhetorical conventions, and grammatical regularities (Krashen, 1984; Reid, 1993a; Smith, 1988). Birnbaum further reported that more proficient readers appeared to know how to make inferences and reason as they read texts and wrote compositions: The skilled readers in the study "seemed able to monitor the success or failure of their attempts to construct meaning in or from written language" (Birnbaum, 1982, p. 257). This kind of sensitivity, wrote Birnbaum,

> ... may be a prerequisite for experiences in one process [reading] to enhance development of the other [writing] ... it seems reasonable to assume that, barring a negative response to a context, these subjects are drawing upon a richer set of cognitive and linguistic sources as they engage in both oral and written language. (p. 257)

Statistically significant relationships between reading ability (e.g., comprehension accuracy, speed) and writing proficiency (as measured by standard essay exams) have similarly been discovered among high school and college L1 writers

---

[2]For research on schema theory and interactive reading, please see Carrell (1981, 1983a, 1983b, 1990); Carrell and Eisterhold (1983); Eskey and Grabe (1988); Grabe (1988, 1991); Haas and Flower (1988); Hamp-Lyons (1985); James (1987); Johnson (1986); McCormick, Waller, and Flower (1987); Peregoy and Boyle (1997); Petersen (1986); Rosenblatt (1988); and Swaffar (1988).

(Belanger, 1987; Bridwell, 1980; Flower et al., 1990; Grobe & Grobe, 1977; Mathews, Larsen, & Butler, 1945; Stotsky, 1983). These studies have examined various aspects of the reading–writing relationship and have found a striking degree of interaction between the two as they develop over time (Shanahan & Lomax, 1986). For some L1 researchers (e.g., Flower et al., 1990), reading and writing do not, in fact, constitute two separate skills, but emanate from a unitary but complex base of literate knowledge (see the next section for a description of the *nondirectional hypothesis*). Thus, reading and writing may simultaneously involve the process and the product, the input (what people read) and the output (what people write). Atwell (1984, 1987) characterized the literate person as having a dual identity: that of reader and that of writer. Coexisting harmoniously in the reader–writer's head, these personæ engage in an ongoing transaction whenever the reader–writer must read or create a text (Bridwell, 1980; DeFord, 1981; Perl, 1979; Petersen, 1986; Pianko, 1977; Smith, 1983, 1985).

As pointed out earlier, however, ESL literacy acquisition involves a more complex interaction of skills and knowledge than it does in L1 literacy acquisition because literate students may bring to the ESL writing class a set of well-developed L1 literacy skills (and sometimes literacy skills in other languages as well). At the same time, because students may have underdeveloped linguistic knowledge and academic skills in English, we cannot assume reading–writing relationships to be as clear or predictable for ESL students as they might be for their NES counterparts. Still, Cummins (1981, 1984) presented a convincing case for the transfer of literacy skills from L1 to L2. He maintained that speakers of all languages share a common cognitive/academic proficiency that allows for the interlingual transfer of literate skills and behaviors (cf. Heath, 1986). If such an interdependence model holds true, the development of L2 literacy is liable to be influenced, at least indirectly, by literate knowledge and processes available in the L1.

Support for Cummins' Cognitive Academic Language Proficiency (CALP) model can be found in several empirical studies of L2 learners' reading and composing performance. For example, Clarke's (1978) case study of two adult learners—one a highly proficient L1 reader and the other a weak L1 reader—suggests that learners who read well in L1 also tend to read well in L2, although one would not expect to find equivalent reading proficiency in L1 and L2. In a study of elementary bilingual education students, Goldman, Reyes, and Varnhagen (1984) similarly indicated that learners were able to transfer high-order L1 comprehension skills to narrative comprehension tasks in L2. Mace-Matluck, Dominguez, Holtzman, and Hoover (1983) examined the interlingual transfer of literacy skills among Chinese-speaking ESL students. They reported finding a strong statistical relationship between learners' measured achievement on multiple L1 literacy tasks (prior to studying English) and their newly acquired L2 literacy skills.

In addition to research that has focused broadly on literacy, a number of studies have focused specifically on relationships between L1 and L2 composing skills. Canale, Frenette, and Belanger (1988) examined the L1 and L2 writing proficiency of French–English bilinguals in Canadian high schools. According to their results, measured L1 writing proficiency was a strong predictor of L2 writing proficiency. Edelsky's (1982) qualitative investigation of the composing skills of Spanish–English bilingual children likewise provides convincing support for the transfer of effective writing processes and strategies across languages.

In a study aimed at testing the interlingual relationships among literacy variables and the reliability of the variables, Flahive and Bailey (1993) collected data from 40 college-level ESL students representing 12 language backgrounds. Their variables included self-reported L1 and L2 reading experience, L2 reading achievement, holistic argumentative essay scores, and two measures of ESL grammar/writing style. On the basis of correlational results, Flahive and Bailey concluded that there is "no relationship between the quantity of reading the subjects claim to do and the quality of their [ESL] writing" (p. 133). However, they noted that L1 reading habits appear to carry over to L2 reading patterns. Consistent with both L1 and L2 studies, they reported significant (although weak) correlations between reading achievement and ESL essay scores. Where grammar and writing style are concerned, Flahive and Bailey noted that, "All correlations between L1 and L2 pleasure reading and the various grammar/writing style variables hover around the .00 mark and appear to suggest that pleasure reading ... does not lead to increased grammatical proficiency" (p. 134). At the same time, they reported significant positive relationships between L1 and L2 pleasure reading and measures of ESL reading ability. Their results provide "a small measure of validation for the common L2 pedagogical practice of combining intensive and extensive reading activities within a single reading course" (pp. 137–138). This study further shows that current theories of L2 literacy acquisition are incomplete and in need of integration "into a more generalized theory of language acquisition" (p. 137). Such a theory might more readily address the issue of how L2 *writing* ability develops.

As already noted, however, the transfer of L1 literacy to L2 is by no means automatic (Bossers, 1991; Hulstijn, 1991; McLaughlin, 1987). Cummins (1981) maintained that learners must first attain a threshold level of L2 proficiency before they can be expected to transfer their L1 literacy expertise into their emerging L2 (cf. Alderson, 1984; Carrell, 1991; Raimes, 1987). For example, Cummins (1981) held that the cognitively demanding language processing involved in L2 reading and composing necessitates a certain degree of linguistic control and fluency. Clarke (1978) similarly argued that a threshold level of L2 competence is a prerequisite to selecting and carrying over transferable L1 literacy skills. Cziko's (1978) study of the differences between L1 and L2 text processing likewise shows that only the most proficient L2 students could interpret crucial semantic cues as they read L2 texts.

Such results have significant implications for ESL writing instruction; they challenge assumptions about the interlingual transferability of literacy skills, and they highlight the complex nature of the knowledge systems that L2 students have to manage as they read and write L2 text. Results reported by Carson et al. (1990) exemplify the multiple dimensions of L1 and L2 literacy involved in developing L2 composing skills. Deploying a sophisticated design, Carson et al. collected L1 and L2 reading and writing performance data from 105 Chinese- and Japanese-speaking ESL students enrolled in U.S. universities. They set out to examine relationships between: (a) L1 and L2 reading abilities, (b) L1 and L2 writing abilities, (c) L1 reading and writing abilities, (d) L2 reading and writing abilities, and (e) L2 proficiency, interlingual transfer, and intralingual transfer. Confirming that interlangual transfer can occur, Carson et al. nonetheless pointed out that the pattern and strength of this transfer is related to L1 background as well as educational background and experience. Although L1 reading skills appeared to transfer to L2 for both groups of students, only the Japanese students appeared to transfer L1 writing skills into English. For both Japanese and Chinese students, L1 reading and writing abilities were at least weakly related, as were L2 reading and writing abilities. The authors also claimed stronger relationships between interlingual reading abilities than between interlingual writing abilities. For the Chinese students, the relationship between L1 and L2 writing abilities was not significant.

Although Carson et al. described these results as exploratory, their study underscored that multiple factors related to linguistic proficiency and literacy interact as learners approach the tasks of reading and composing in a second language. As for pedagogical implications, the researchers suggested that L2 reading instruction should exploit L1 reading skills, but that teachers should not assume that these skills will necessarily transfer to the L2. The extent to which writing instruction can exploit learners' L1 writing skills may be confined to certain L1 groups and possibly to lower L2 proficiency levels. In contrast to the claims of Alderson (1984), Cummins (1981), and Cziko (1978), who argued for a threshold level of L2 competence, Carson et al. proposed that, "whereas teachers may be able to exploit L1 literacy relationships in the transfer of L2 literacy practices at lower proficiency levels, they cannot do so reliably at more advanced L2 levels" (p. 261). At more advanced levels, teachers may need to rely more heavily on students' emergent L2 literacy. At lower proficiency levels, interlingual transfer may be more marked, whereas at more advanced levels, intralingual input may be more influential for developing L2 literacy.

Regardless of the position one takes with respect to the threshold of L2 proficiency, teachers of ESL writing will be better equipped to provide effective instruction when they understand that their composition students may require special support in developing literacy-related skills (Eisterhold, 1990). Earlier, it was noted that L1-based formulations of reading–writing relationships should be recognized and appreciated for raising researchers' and teachers' awareness of the need to promote good reading habits and efficient reading skills among their students.[3] However, more recent research (e.g., Carson et al., 1990) has highlighted the need to avoid oversimplifying the complex connections that hold among the multiple factors that make up L2 academic literacy.

READING–WRITING MODELS: TOOLS FOR TEACHERS

This section encapsulates a few of the principal generalizations that can be drawn from the research presented in this chapter. The purpose of the following summary is to present a theoretical synthesis that teachers can use as a framework for assessing research in the field, as well as methods and practices prescribed for the ESL writing classroom. Empirical findings that point to strong connections between reading ability and writing performance have led many researchers to infer that efficient reading skills lay a foundation for the growth of writing proficiency in L1 and L2. Sometimes described as the *directional hypothesis* (Eisterhold, 1990), this input-based view presupposes that the emergence of composing skills must necessarily be preceded by the establishment of sound reading skills, which occurs through practice and abundant contact with print. Although this model has its strong advocates, research in L1 and L2 composition offers at least two alternative means of describing how reading and writing may be related: the *nondirectional hypothesis* and the *bidirectional hypothesis*. The *nondirectional model* presupposes a set of "common underlying processes" that underlie both reading and writing (Eisterhold, 1990, p. 93). Thus, its pedagogical implication is that instruction should focus on constructing meaning in both reading and writing tasks. In the *bidirectional view* (as in the nondirectional model), practice in writing promotes the development of reading skills, just as improved reading proficiency can enhance writing skills. However, the bidirectimonal model holds that the reading–writing connection undergoes qualitative change as learners develop their literacy skills.

The perspective taken in this chapter (indeed, throughout this book) is that ESL writing instruction should be cautiously eclectic (Brown, 1994b; Eisterhold, 1990). However, an eclectic approach by no means implies randomness, arbitrary decision-making, or a lack of theoretical drive. Rather, effective eclecticism requires principled decision-making concerning the differential priorities that writing teach-

---

[3]Stotsky's (1983) survey of L1 studies of reading–writing relationships, for example, leads to the following generalizations: (a) Correlations between reading achievement and writing ability suggest that good writers are also good readers; (b) correlations between writing performance and reading experience/habits suggest that good writers read frequently and extensively; and (c) correlations between reading ability and measures of syntactic complexity in writing suggest that good readers produce more sophisticated texts than do weaker readers.

ers assign to reading and other literacy-oriented tasks and activities. The three reading–writing models outlined earlier can serve as guidelines for striking an appropriate balance between providing input (the directional hypothesis), promoting the construction of meaning (the nondirectional hypothesis), and tapping into learners' evolving and interdependent reading and writing proficiencies (the bidirectional hypothesis). Equipped with the understanding that reading–writing relationships are potentially multidimensional and may change as learners progress, teachers can adjust the weight given to reading tasks and writing practice according to the needs and expectations of their learners (Shanahan, 1984; Shanahan & Lomax, 1986). In a sense, every class of students represents a unique population with particular characteristics such as age, general L2 proficiency, L1 literacy, L2 literacy, academic and professional objectives, and so on. For example, low-level college or pre-university learners with little or no ESL academic literacy may benefit from extensive and intensive reading coupled with abundant practice in writing for fluency. Advanced-level university students may learn more from intensive, discipline-specific reading and practice in writing for accuracy. Therefore, composition teachers should make decisions about materials, classroom activities, and assignments based on these needs. Such decisions should also be informed by the multiple instructional options suggested by the directional, nondirectional, and bidirectional reading–writing models (cf. Harste, 1988; Kroll, 1993).

Although these models may differ in orientation, they do not exist in opposition to one another. In fact, they are highly complementary and share an important fundamental principle: Writing skills cannot emerge by dint of practice alone. In other words, underlying each of these hypotheses is the premise that the ability to compose in L1 or L2 cannot develop without a knowledge of the forms, patterns, and purposes of written language. The principle that real learning depends on the provision of abundant input is virtually axiomatic in the field of language learning and teaching. Nevertheless, instructional practices in L1 and L2 composition have not always followed this principle. An attitude that persists in some institutions and among some educators is that one must *learn to write* before one can *write*. In this view, the most logical and practical way to turn nonwriters into writers is to *teach them to write*. Such an attitude is problematic and misguided, however, because there are aspects of composing that may not be teachable at all. Some researchers (Krashen, 1984; Smith, 1988) have even taken the controversial position that writing is essentially an acquired, unteachable set of skills that develops naturally as a result of extensive interaction with print and of participating in authentic literacy events such as reading for information and further learning (cf. Grabe, 1991; Harste, 1988; Hedgcock & Pucci, 1993; Kucer, 1991; Peregoy & Boyle, 1997).

In keeping with both the nondirectional and bidirectional models, Zamel (1992) discussed tools for maximizing the transactional, synergistic relationship between reading and writing in the writing classroom. Just as reading is constructive and recursive, writing about texts enables us to reexamine texts, thereby allowing us to confront uncertainties, "reflect on the complexities, deal with the puzzlements, and offer approximative readings. By providing us a means for working out a reading, writing allows insights that may have been inaccessible or inchoate at the time the text was read" (p. 472). In this view, apprentice ESL writers benefit from engaging in reading-based writing tasks that encourage them to read like writers (Hairston, 1986; Smith, 1983) and to write like readers (Ede & Lunsford, 1984; Kroll, 1993; Raimes, 1985). According to Beach and Liebman-Kleine (1986), the most effective writers learn "to imagine reader attributes and to use those attributes to assess their [own] writing" (p. 65). Such tasks may include reading for meaning, reading for details, inferencing, prediction, critical reasoning, journaling, and so on (cf. Carson, 1993; Devine, 1993; Gajdusek & van Dommelen, 1993; Harste, 1988; Hughey, Wormuth, Hartfiel, & Jacobs, 1983; McKay, 1984; Peregoy & Boyle, 1997; Sarig, 1993; Zamel, 1992). The Application Activities at the end of this chapter contain sample activities and procedures that exemplify a number of these task types.

SOCIAL ASPECTS OF READING AND WRITING
IN ACADEMIC DISCOURSE COMMUNITIES

The reciprocal connections between reading and writing outlined in the previous sections have a socioeducational dimension that should not be overlooked (cf. McKay, 1993; Vygotsky, 1986; Wertsch, 1987). Literacy acquisition never occurs in a vacuum, and the development of academic literacy skills is no exception. ESL writers in schools, colleges, and universities read and write for specific purposes, all of which involve the attainment of some combination of academic and/or professional goals. Ultimately, academic ESL instruction should enable learners to acquire skills, develop strategies, and master the spoken and written conventions (i.e., discourse patterns) of the academic community in general and of the individual disciplines they will pursue (Lynch & Hudson, 1991; Spack, 1988, 1993). Before they can achieve these objectives, ESL students must first understand that they will read and write for some rather tangible purposes that are grounded in established ways of being and thinking:

> Since any particular discourse is composed of the work of the people who read and write its texts, it follows that discourse in general—and, by extension, literacy—has a *social* as well as a cognitive dimension, a dimension that plays a major role in shaping the literate behavior of readers and writers in any real-world context. (Eskey, 1993, p. 224)

ESL teachers play a crucial role in bringing their learners into such discourses, for they have the responsibility of socializing their students to the demands and challenges of academic institutions (Hill, 1990). This process necessarily involves providing students with the tools that comprise academic literacy. Such writing-related tools would minimally include:

- skills and strategies for reading texts assigned in general education and discipline-specific courses;
- techniques for taking reading notes to be used for subsequent tasks and assignments (e.g., exams, reports, essays, research papers, etc.);
- skills and strategies for selecting topics, as well as drafting, revising, and editing various types of written texts (e.g., exams, reports, essays, research papers, etc.).

One of the obvious means of bringing about academic literacy, of course, is to promote reading as a way into the community of academic readers and writers—what Smith (1988) called the "literacy club" and what Gee (1992, 1996) called a "literacy" or a "discourse." ESL teachers must further demonstrate that reading and writing competence are vital to becoming a member of any educational discourse community (e.g., school, college, university, particular field of study, etc.), and that success therein depends on completing literacy-based tasks. As Johns (1993) pointed out, "Almost every writing assignment in the disciplines requires reading; many reading assignments and examinations require writing" (p. 274; cf. Horowitz, 1986a, 1986b, 1986c). Spack (1993) explained that ESL composition instructors have an essential responsibility to assist their students in acquiring general knowledge about the purposes served by writing in these domains. She further asserted that writing instruction must move ESL students "back and forth along the continuum to grow as writers as they build enough local knowledge to enable them to perform effectively" (p. 183). That is, students refine their writing abilities through their classroom experiences and through immersion in a field of expertise.

ESL composition teachers can play an important part in helping their students become members of any number of institutional and/or discipline-specific clubs or discourses by acquainting learners with the enterprises and literate practices of people who are already part of those communities (Goldstein, 1993). Expert members of these communities (e.g., professors) as well as novices (e.g., peers) can serve ESL students "as their unsuspecting surrogates in the trial and error of learning" (Smith, 1988, p. 22) via their written products. ESL teachers must expose their learners to the texts that real academic writers (i.e., textbook writers, researchers, students) *write* for the academy and that real academic readers (i.e., researchers, teachers, students) *read* for the purposes of learning and acquiring expertise in a given field. In doing so, teachers can reveal to their ESL learners that "text is in fact the link between reading and writing as the complementary halves of literacy. ... Text is where reader and writer meet and interact" (Eskey, 1993, p. 223). As such, text constitutes a transactional medium through which a kind of social behavior takes place, for a text allows its writer to communicate a message to its reader, provided the reader can understand the core principles of how meaning is constructed by members of the literate audience envisioned by the writer (cf. Petersen, 1986). Mastering the interpretation of text (i.e., learning to read and make sense out of someone else's writing) is a significant step toward achieving membership in the community of readers for whom that text is meaningful. Indeed, achieving such mastery may guarantee membership in some literacy clubs (Smith, 1988). Mastering the construction of text (i.e., learning and observing the conventions of a particular *genre* or *discourse type*) may similarly grant the apprentice writer admission to the community of writers in that discipline or field of knowledge (see the next section for discussions of *genre*).

Eskey (1993) situated the sociolinguistic and psycholinguistic aspects of the reading–writing relationship with respect to literacy clubs (such as academic institutions) by describing two of the ESL writing teacher's principal jobs. The first of these is motivating learners to develop reading and composing skills that accord with the conventions of *our* literacy club and its related discourse communities. This responsibility entails demonstrating literate skills, "introducing ... students to the universe of texts in English," and identifying how and why certain texts are valued (Eskey, 1993, p. 230). The second job of the ESL instructor consists of facilitating learners' acquisition of comprehension, problem-solving, and production skills, such as "word and phrase recognition, reading rate development, grammatical sentence writing, and organizing discourse in accordance with the established conventions of some particular genre" (Eskey, 1993, p. 231).

Thus, Eskey emphasized the pedagogical imperative to show ESL learners that reading and writing can help them acquire and display knowledge, as well as become participants in a literate community of students, teachers, and scholars. As more seasoned members of the literacy club, ESL teachers are perhaps the most accessible models of literate behavior, or surrogates, that their students can expect. In this role of surrogate or facilitator, ESL composition teachers can make their learners aware of the social, personal, and educational uses of written language, bringing students into the community of people (expert and novice) who know how to read and write. They can do this by incorporating into their syllabi materials that exemplify the kinds of texts that are used, valued, and created by academic readers and writers for the purposes of acquiring and creating new knowledge. It is only by understanding and adopting the behaviors and values of the academic discourse community that ESL students can join the ranks of academic readers and writers.

ENGLISH FOR ACADEMIC PURPOSES

The English for Academic Purposes (EAP) movement aims specifically to characterize the genres, standards, behaviors, and values of academic disciplines and their participants. Broadly speaking, EAP is a term that can be applied to "any course, module, or workshop in which students are taught to deal with academically related language and subject matter" (Brown, 1994b, p. 127). Since its genesis in the 1960s and its evolution through the 1970s, EAP pedagogy has relied heavily on needs and task analyses for curriculum design (cf. chap. 3). EAP research, which proliferated in the 1980s, has examined how non-ESL faculty rank the importance of linguistic and critical skills in their classrooms, what approaches to writing are required of students in particular majors and disciplines, and which task types (e.g., summary, analysis, critique, classification, etc.) prevail in those disciplines and subdisciplines. These findings have enabled both teachers and researchers to identify the components of academic literacy and develop tools for helping their students achieve it in EAP courses (Johns, 1990; Prior, 1995).[4]

In terms of ESL writing instruction, an EAP orientation involves the production of texts that are acceptable to academic readers (chiefly faculty in the disciplines, but also students' NES and NNS peers). Thus, achieving academic literacy has a pragmatic dimension in that successful academic writers must be skilled at meeting the standards and requirements of their readers. To generate acceptable texts, students must master the mechanical aspects of composing sentences, paragraphs, and larger units of discourse that correspond to the dominant genres of the academy and/or a specific field. At the same time, "learning to write is part of becoming socialized to the academic community—finding out what is expected and trying to approximate it" (Silva, 1990, p. 17). As argued herein, reading is an obvious and accessible means of effecting this socialization. It is by reading and understanding that apprentice writers become experienced members of their target disciplinary communities, developing discursive schemata and views of what constitutes appropriate writing. Therefore, EAP pedagogy emphasizes genres, formats, and standards (none of which is necessarily static or fixed), as well as "the socially determined nature of writing options, preferences, and conventions" that pervade the academy and its many disciplines (Leki, 1995b, p. 43).

Although EAP research initially focused on the products of academic writers, its emphasis has shifted toward the readers and writers of academic texts and how they comprehend and compose such texts (Johns, 1991; Lynch & Hudson, 1991). This transition parallels in many respects the development of the process orientation in composition instruction, as outlined in chapter 1. Although some tension has arisen between proponents of science- and technology-based writing on the one hand (Braine, 1988; Johns, 1988a) and humanities-based writing on the other (Spack, 1988), EAP practitioners generally recognize the importance of situating texts as well as reading and composing processes in their socioeducational contexts (Silva, 1990). Recent studies clearly demonstrate that writing tasks in academic

---

[4]We should acknowledge that some researchers and teachers do not feel that ESL students should be taught academic literacy or forced to become members of the academic discourse community. For example, Bizzell (1987) argued instead that academic institutions and discourse communities should adapt to the diversity of cultures that ESL learners represent (cf. Leki, 1995b).

disciplines are "cued, produced, and evaluated through complex, largely tacit, social and intellectual processes" (Prior, 1995, pp. 48–49). Because of this complexity, EAP pedagogy is no longer confined to taxonomic, rule-oriented descriptions of disciplinary genres, nor to the mere specification and presentation of academic writing tasks. EAP practitioners are increasingly called on to avoid static conceptualizations of communicative competence that suggest well-structured knowledge representations and instead to develop the communicative flexibility that students need to participate in dynamic interaction in specific contexts. Prior (1995) maintained that, by examining academic writing tasks as "speech genres" that emerge in real situations with real participants, we can help students "to encounter the dialogic forces shaping academic activity and discourse, to see the situated interpretive and interactional work that generates meanings and texts, and to sense how that work is socially mediated or socially impeded" (p. 77).

$\boxed{\Rightarrow AA\ 2.5}$

READING AND GENRE IN ACADEMIC WRITING

A major practical issue in preparing academic ESL learners concerns how composition instruction can help students become readers and writers of the particular kinds of texts that they identify with specific literacy clubs or discourses, such as the discourses of computer scientists, engineers, physicists, biologists, sociologists, historians, journalists, literary scholars, educators, and so on. Smith (1988) held that it is critical for teachers to provide their learners with materials "that are relevant to the kind of writer [students] are interested in becoming" (p. 26), noting that text comprehension and production are always connected to real purposes, real writers, and real audiences (cf. Swales, 1990). The social dimensions of text comprehension and production are especially pertinent to the discipline of writing instruction because, "in the real world where readers and writers mingle, individual texts do not stand alone." Texts form "a *genre* or ... the *discourse* of some particular group of readers and writers who read and write the same kinds of texts, that is, the discourse of everything from personal letters to linguistics or physics" (Eskey, 1993, p. 223).

The rules of use and usage, which are necessary for the comprehension and production of specific text types as well as for teaching them, "are best acquired by taking part in real, socially grounded communicative events like reading or writing for some authentic purpose or writing in a real genre for a real audience" (Eskey, 1993, p. 224).[5] Claims about strong or even weak links between what learners read and write have potentially far-reaching implications for language teaching in

---

[5]For a thorough description of the distinctions between *rules of usage* and *rules of use*, please see Widdowson (1983).

general and for writing instruction in particular. Smith (1988) offered the following genre-related pedagogical recommendations:

> To learn how to write for newspapers you must read newspapers; textbooks about newspapers will not suffice. For magazines, browse through magazines rather than through correspondence courses on magazine writing. To write poetry, read it. For the typical style of memoranda that circulate in your school, consult the school files. (p. 20)

Although not uncontroversial, Smith's directive constitutes a call for authenticity in text selection—a call echoed by a number of second language researchers (e.g., Brinton, Snow, & Wesche, 1989; Hedgcock & Pucci, 1993; Kucer, 1985, 1991; van Lier, 1996). Perhaps more important, Smith's proposal underscores the need for teachers and students to recognize that all texts are not created equal (Biber, 1988; Swales, 1990). As previously noted, the construction and meaningful interpretation of nearly any kind of text involves a complex interaction of features, rules, and layers of meaning that even the most experienced reader-writer may be unable to perceive or discern on a conscious level: "Even arbitrary rules, descriptions, and definitions evade us when it comes to … subtle matters as *style,* the intricate *registers* that depend upon the topic of discussion and the audience addressed, and the *schemas* [*sic*] appropriate to the particular medium" (Smith, 1988, p. 19).

Such observations imply an interaction between genre-specific reading and writing—a theme that has only recently been explicitly addressed among researchers. Specific questions have emerged concerning the specific links between what learners read and how they write. For example, let us suppose that a learner exposes him or herself to large quantities of writing in a specific genre—say, book reviews in applied linguistics journals. Let us further assume that he or she has a desire or need to gain information encoded in that genre and that he or she consequently learns to read and comprehend such texts efficiently. Let us even further assume that he or she is driven to compose such texts perhaps because of a class assignment or because he or she aspires to publish such a piece. Will this learner have at his or her disposal latent knowledge regarding the underlying and surface features of the book review genre (e.g., rhetorical stance, organizational patterns, grammatical conventions, lexical choice, etc.)? If the answer to this latter question is yes, then the learner's writing should somehow manifest evidence of that knowledge. In other words, he or she should be more proficient in producing book review samples than peers who have not exposed themselves to substantial quantities of this type of writing.

Unfortunately, providing empirical evidence to support a link between reading genre and learners' abilities to write in a particular genre poses serious challenges for researchers. Few efforts have been made to examine relationships among the numerous genre-related factors outlined earlier. Hedgcock and Atkinson (1993) reported on a preliminary study aimed to test the hypothesis that extensive reading of specific text types in L1 and L2 is tied to writers' ability to produce texts of a particular genre. Their L1 results show that the academic expository writing scores of university freshman students were significantly related to a set of 14 reading habits variables. These variables involved the frequency of students' contact with textbooks, fiction, newspapers, and so on at various stages of their formal education. Essentially, these findings suggest that the students who read more, who read voluntarily, and who read a variety of texts for pleasure and for school tended to be better writers of English. Also revealing was the finding that the following three variables were significantly (although not strongly) related to the students' measured writing performance: (a) frequency of fiction reading in elementary school, (b) frequency of textbook reading in elementary school, and (c) frequency of fiction reading while enrolled in university courses. The researchers conclude that writers' L1 composing proficiency "can partly be accounted for by learners' extensive reading experience, with some indication that experience with specific text types in the early school years may be particularly important" (p. 332).

In contrast, results of the same study revealed no significant relationships between preferred reading genre and the ESL writing performance of a large group of non-native university learners. Although identical information concerning L1 and L2 reading habits was collected from these students, the authors could not find any evidence that reading in a specific genre was connected to the students' ESL composing proficiency. They suggested that extensive exposure to specific kinds of written texts may, in fact, have little traceable impact on the L2 writing performance of ESL learners. They alternatively proposed that the influence of reading genre is perhaps too difficult to measure given current conceptualizations of L2 literacy development (cf. Flahive & Bailey, 1993; Stahl & Hayes, 1997). Although our present understanding of genre-specific reading as a contributor to ESL writing development is not sufficient to suggest definitive implications for the teaching of composition, inconclusive research results should not overshadow the extensive and convincing empirical findings that point to reading as an essential, positive contributor to ESL students' emerging composing skills at various stages of L2 literacy development.

SUMMARY AND IMPLICATIONS

This chapter has described major aspects of L1- and L2-based research on interactions between reading habits and skills on the one hand and the development of writing proficiency on the other. Although the theoretical formulations that have emerged from the empirical studies (i.e., the directional, nondirectional, and bidirectional hypotheses) represent somewhat different conceptualizations of literacy development, they all suggest that the source of composing skills essentially resides in print matter. L1 and L2 literacy studies further indicate that skilled writers generally tend to demonstrate more efficient reading skills than weaker writers. Proficient L1 and L2 writers are also more likely to have read extensively for school and/or for pleasure than their less proficient counterparts. However, studies of L2 reading and writing patterns have revealed that literacy does not automatically transfer from L1 to L2. Moreover, the development of L2 writing skills may depend on a constellation of interdependent factors such as L2 proficiency, L1 and L2 reading ability, L1 and L2 writing proficiency, and exposure to particular genres of writing.

Despite somewhat inconclusive findings, ESL writing instructors have much to draw from current literacy research, particularly from research that views reading and writing as social behaviors. The skills of comprehending, using, and creating text are ways of achieving membership in academic communities, which are made up of readers, writers, teachers, and scholars. As such, the acquisition of literacy skills can and should be viewed as a process of apprenticeship to discourses where people read, construct, and share different kinds of texts for real purposes. The inferences drawn from literacy research thus suggest the following implications for the teaching of writing to ESL students:

- ESL teachers should adjust the relative weight given to reading and writing assignments based on their students' L2 proficiency levels, needs, and expectations.
- L2 writing skills cannot be acquired successfully by practice alone. Some aspects of composing are difficult to teach and must be acquired through sustained exposure to multiple varieties of text.
- ESL learners need instruction to become successful writers of English. Neither extensive exposure to reading materials nor large quantities of writing practice alone is sufficient—*both* are necessary.
- Just as reading facilitates the development of writing skills, so writing can help build proficiency in reading. Therefore, teachers should therefore consider writing activities that help students prepare for, respond to, and comprehend reading selections more effectively.
- Academic ESL instruction should include reading and writing tasks that will prepare learners for the demands of the wider academy *and* for their individual disciplines.
- ESL teachers should expose their students to their own processes and practices of engaging in academic literacy events.
- ESL teachers should strive for authenticity in selecting texts and developing composing tasks.

Reflection and Review

1. Consider your own history as a reader and writer in your L1. Which of the three hypotheses outlined by Eisterhold (1990; the directional, nondirectional, and bidirectional models) best account(s) for your development as a writer? What specific evidence would you use to support your claim?

2. If you have experience reading or writing in a second or third language, would you say that your L2 writing skills can be explained by the same model you cited to explain your L1 writing skills in Item 1? Why or why not? If you do not have L2 literacy experience, ask a non-native speaker of English (perhaps a classmate or another ESL learner you know) to describe for you the major sources of knowledge that have contributed to his or her ability to compose in English. Which of Eisterhold's (1990) hypotheses would be most consistent with the views expressed by your non-native informant?

3. What kinds of texts do you read for pleasure? For information? For your courses? In what ways do you think this reading has contributed to your ability to compose academic and other kinds of texts? If you do not consider yourself an extensive reader, what do you think prevents you from reading voluntarily or for personal enjoyment?

4. Reflecting on your recent experiences as a learner and academic writer, describe the types of texts you have most often produced for your courses (e.g., summaries, reports, reviews, essays, annotated bibliographies, research papers). Have you had explicit instruction in how to construct such texts? If not, how did you learn to compose them? If you were asked by a peer how to compose such texts, what instructions would you give?

5. Given Smith's (1988) metaphor of the "literacy club" and Eskey's (1993) description of a discourse as a community of readers and writers, consider the clubs or discourses to which you belong. For example, would you consider yourself a member of the "club" of TESL students in your department? Would you consider yourself a member of the discourse of ESL teachers at your institution? Are you a member of a volunteer organization, a parent, or a bird watcher? If so, can you identify the specific literate behaviors or skills that you and other members of these discourses demonstrate? What discourses would you *like* to belong to? Why? What skills will you have to acquire to be regarded as a reader or writer of those discourses?

6. In your opinion, why might the notion of genre be an especially important consideration for teachers of ESL writing? For example, what are some of the pedagogical advantages of addressing the specific kinds of texts that students read (and are expected to read) for pleasure and for academic coursework?

Application Activity 2.1: Encouraging Extensive, Self-Initiated Reading

Directions.   Imagine you are teaching a college-level ESL reading/writing class in your community. Briefly identify the educational, vocational, and/or professional needs of the students, as well as their level of L1 and L2 literacy. In a small group or in your journal, brainstorm ideas for:

a. motivating students to read for pleasure in English;
b. helping students to find sources of accessible, interesting English texts in the community.

Application Activity 2.2: Maximizing Reading–Writing Relationships in the Classroom: Writing From Texts Using Reading Journals

Writing journals are not necessarily synonymous with reading journals. Although a reading journal may be included as part of a writing journal, it may also stand alone. The reading journal's primary function is to serve as a vehicle for ESL writers to respond to assigned and/or self-selected readings; it can thus serve as a logical component of a voluntary or mandatory reading program in the composition classroom. To promote students' written fluency, critical thinking skills, engagement with the texts they read, and latent knowledge of how written language communicates meaning, Zamel (1992) presented a number of approaches to giving students "experiences with the dialogic and dynamic nature of reading" (p. 472). Several of these approaches are summarized in the following task.

Many teachers discourage using reading journals as evaluative tools. Rather than marking entries individually or collectively, teachers frequently prefer to respond orally or in writing to their students' journal entries. Thus, many teachers request that students compose a minimum number of entries based on a range of prompts, assigning a full mark to students whose entries are complete. Obviously, reading journals are an ideal vehicle for teachers to use for responding personally to their students' reflections on course readings.

Directions.   Individually or with a classmate, examine one or more of the following classroom tasks, which are proposed by Zamel (1992). After you consider how you might put them into practice in a real or hypothetical ESL writing course, assess their potential effectiveness. Identify the instructional advantages and practical challenges that might be involved.

- Ask students to maintain reading journals or logs where they record and elaborate on what they read for school or for pleasure (e.g., textbooks, literary texts, newspapers, newsmagazines, etc.).
- Give students the opportunity "to write about what they find interesting/significant/moving/puzzling" to help them realize that "their written reflection makes ... understanding possible" (p. 474).
- Ask students to keep double-entry or dialectical notebooks where they copy or summarize passages of interest to them in one column and then respond to them in the other. Responses can also take the form of the images and associations that a passage or text evokes.
- Ask students to write entries that they might normally include as cryptic marginal notations in the original text. According to Zamel, "this form of response allows students to consider, weigh, and interpret their reading and gives rise to reactions that they may not have been aware of" (p. 477).
- To make students aware of their associations with texts *before* they read them, ask students to write journal entries about an experience featured in a text they are about to read. This helps them construct and anticipate connections they would not otherwise identify.
- Similarly, ask students to consider and weigh their own ideas about an issue before they read a text to enable them "to approach the reading from a position of authority" (p. 478).
- To show students that readers use predictions to construct meaning, ask them to write speculatively about what will happen in a text and to compare these predictions with those of their peers and with the original text. "Written predictions of this sort literally transform student writers into authors of the text" (p. 479).
- Sequence journal entries around readings so that students address texts from different perspectives. Encourage students not only to view texts but also to *re*view them using their newly acquired knowledge.

Reading journals should be nonevaluative; students should not receive a grade for their entries, except for completing a minimum number of them. Teachers frequently opt to respond to some or all of their students' entries.

Application Activity 2.3: Writing-to-Read
Task Development

Directions. You have selected a brief text for your intermediate-level reading/writing class (e.g., a short story such as Shirley Jackson's "The Lottery," a poem such as Robert Frost's "Stopping by Woods on a Snowy Evening," an essay such as M. Scott Peck's "Stages of Community Making," a chapter or excerpt from a content textbook, etc.). Individually or with a partner, develop prompts/tasks and instructions for one or more of the following:

1. Double-entry journal entries.
2. Marginal annotation.
3. Write-before-you-read assignments.
4. Prediction activities.
5. Viewing reading from different perspectives.

(Please see Application Activity 2.2 for descriptions of these activity types.)

Application Activity 2.4: Writing From Texts— A Sample Assignment Sequence

Spack (1993) wrote that ESL composition instruction should enable students to "write from and about written texts and gathered data" (p. 187). The following assignment outline, adapted from Spack's article, could be based on a reading selection required in the ESL composition course or content courses in students' majors. It is intended to serve as a guideline, not as a self-contained or prescriptive set of instructions. Readers are also referred to the chapters in Carson and Leki (1993) for additional classroom tasks and assignments designed to train students to write from texts.

Directions.   Individually or with a partner, select a sample text that would be appropriate for use in a low, intermediate, or advanced level ESL reading–writing class. Using the schema outlined next as a starting point, design a lesson sequence that would address the specific needs of the students you have in mind:

1. Assign a write-before-you-read activity. Ask students to compose a free writing, journal entry, or sequence of journal entries about an issue, idea, or experience featured in the reading selection you are about to assign or that students individually or collectively elect to read.

2. Assign the text as homework. If possible, allow class time for students to begin the reading in class. Before students begin, instruct them to annotate the text in whatever way they choose. If students are unfamiliar with annotation processes, provide them with sample techniques.

3. Ask students to compose reading journal entries using one or more of the procedures suggested by Zamel (1992; see Application Activity 2.2). To further students' engagement with the text, consider asking them to express agreement or disagreement with the contents of the reading selection.

4. To aid students in exploring their understanding of the text, request that they compose a summary of the reading, which they will bring to class to share with small peer groups.

5. Plan and supervise peer-group discussions of the summaries. This task will not only send students "back into the text" (Spack, 1993, p. 191), but will also dramatize that the exchange of ideas, reactions, criticisms, and opinions is an integral part of intellectual life and academic discourse (cf. Blanton, 1993). Students will see that texts are the currency of academic discussion and debate. Moreover, by reading the summaries of their peers, they will be able to look at the reading selection with a degree of distance that they had not previously experienced.

6. Introduce the essay assignment in writing and ask students to analyze the directions individually or in small groups. With the students, explicitly identify the audience of the essay. Discuss the strategies they will use to meet the expectations of the audience (e.g., rhetorical approach, evidence, length, citation style, etc.). The writing assignment should be designed so that it requires students to delve deeply into the text and reflect on it critically.

7. Ask students to draft a version of the essay to be presented to their peers (and possibly to you). If it is practical, set aside some class time for this.

8. Plan and supervise peer review sessions or teacher conferences (see chap. 6 for specific recommendations concerning peer response). As a prelude to the session, ask students to review their annotated reading selections and their pre- and while-reading journal entries. Peer or teacher response should focus on the extent to which the writer has fulfilled the assignment, made use of the reading selection, and constructed the essay to meet audience expectations. Following the feedback session, students should make sure that they understand the feedback so that they can incorporate it into a subsequent draft. The revision cycle then continues at the teacher's discretion (see chaps. 3 and 4).

Application Activity 2.5: Text Analysis

In contrast to writing-to-read tasks and assignments that feature student interaction with substantive and autonomous texts, text analysis activities frequently involve shorter texts and require learners to read intensively rather than extensively. The following text analysis task, based on a content reading assignment in Brinton, Snow, and Wesche (1989), asks students to examine the rhetorical structure of an excerpt from a university-level textbook. As part of a series of similar assignments involving multiple skills, a major purpose of this task is to sensitize students to paragraph structure. This task precedes a writing assignment in which students will be asked to incorporate the forms and styles they identify in the passage.

Step 1—Simulation and Practice

Directions.

1. Complete the following sample reading task as if you were an ESL student.
2. When you are finished, compare your responses to those of a classmate.
3. After you share your results, devise a follow-up activity that could lead to a writing assignment (e.g., summary, library investigation, essay) in an intermediate or advanced ESL writing class.

TEXTBOOK PASSAGE FOR ANALYSIS:
DEFINITION STRUCTURE

The following passage is from a popular university linguistics textbook. Please read the passage and then answer the questions that follow.

Speaking, Writing, Signing: Modes of Linguistic Communication

Speaking, writing, and signing are the three primary modes of linguistic communication, each with advantages and limitations. For example, speech is the only mode of linguistic communication possible when visibility is hindered. It is also the only mode in which the communicator's hands and eyes are left free to do other things. People signing to one another must be in view of one another and, in effect, facing one another. Speech has limitations, too, some of which are shared by signing. Both speech and signing have an evanescent character and vanish upon being uttered. Neither spoken nor signed utterances can be retrieved after they have been uttered unless they were tape-recorded or filmed. Writing, on the other hand, has evolved to meet other needs. It can be preserved for thousands of years, as with the words of Homer, Plato, Aristotle, and Jesus—all of whom were public speakers whose words were written down by others. Writing has another advantage over speech and signing in that it can transcend space. One can send a written message anywhere on earth. With technology, of course, this advantage of writing over speaking and signing is decreasing.

In this book we focus on language as it is represented in spoken and written communication. It is important to keep in mind that, historically and developmentally, writing is a secondary mode of linguistic communication. This can be a challenge to students, whose principal focus and principal context for discussing language heretofore has been written language, and for all literate people, who are familiar with the extraordinary power and influence of the written word. (Finegan, 1994, p. 18)

Questions to Consider

1. What is the primary purpose of this passage?
2. Can you locate the following elements in the paragraph?

    a. Topic sentence

    b. Transitions

    c. Concluding sentence or statement

3. Can you identify one or more of the author's supporting points?
4. What kind of evidence does the author use to develop those points?

Step 2—Authentic Task Development

Directions.   Select an authentic reading passage from an academic source and prepare a reading–writing exercise similar to the one above. Authentic sources would include content textbooks, scholarly articles and papers, articles and opinion pieces from the campus newspaper, student writing, and so on.

Clearly, many adaptations of this task could be applied to a wide range of text types, including literary passages, research materials, student compositions, and so on. Many text types have not been mentioned specifically in this chapter due to space limitations. Some of these include (in alphabetical order): advice books, almanacs, biographies, business letters, business reports, classified advertisements, college handbooks, conference and seminar handouts, diaries, fables, *festschrifts,* graffiti, job application forms, jokes, legal briefs, legal summonses, legends, letters of reference, local news reports, memos, myths, personal letters, product advertisements, proverbs, recipes, religious tracts, sermons and homilies, service manuals, society columns, and travel narratives (Grabe & Kaplan, 1996). Specific reading-based approaches, methods, tasks, and assignments appropriate for use in the ESL composition classroom can be found in numerous publications related to L1 and L2 reading instruction. Readers are encouraged to consult one or more of the following resources for teaching: Beach and Liebman-Kleine (1986); Benesch (1988); Bogel et al. (1988); Bowen, Madsen, and Hilferty (1985); Bridges (1986); Brinton, Snow, and Wesche (1989); Brookes and Grundy (1990); Carrell, Devine, and Eskey (1988); Carson and Leki (1993); Celce-Murcia (1991); Connor and Farmer (1990); Dubin, Eskey, and Grabe (1986); Dyson (1989); Ede and Lunsford (1984); Flower et al. (1990); Grabe and Kaplan (1996); Graves (1990); Gunderson (1991); Hashimoto (1991); Johnson and Roen (1989); Kantz (1990); Lindemann (1987); McCarthy and Carter (1995); Moran and Lunsford (1984); Newkirk (1986); Peregoy and Boyle (1997); Peterson (1989); Stahl and Hayes (1997); Tate and Corbett (1988); Tierney and Pearson (1983); and Williams (1996). Recent ESL reading textbooks also can provide excellent models for creating reading-to-write and writing-to-read tasks and assignments (e.g., Spack, 1990, 1994).

Syllabus Design and Lesson Planning in the ESL Writing Class

Questions for Reflection

- In what ways can/should the design of a writing course accommodate the students' backgrounds and needs? The requirements and culture of the educational institution?
- To what extent are composition courses like or unlike other courses in terms of how they are designed and organized? What features do you think makes the planning of a writing course distinct from other types of courses?
- Recalling your experiences as a student, think about syllabi you have received in some of the courses you have taken. What made the syllabi useful for you? What was missing from the weaker ones? What elements do you consider to be essential in a course syllabus? Why?
- In your opinion, what are the essential components of a successful lesson in a composition course? What types of activities should form the basis of such a lesson? How should they be organized? What skills should be practiced and why?

SYLLABUS DEVELOPMENT: PRINCIPLES AND PROCEDURES

This chapter outlines a concrete approach to planning instruction in the ESL composition class and provides basic tools for developing effective lessons. Rather than addressing global principles concerning the design of entire curricula,[1] we concentrate our discussion chiefly on the day-to-day planning tasks of writing teachers: constructing course syllabi, sequencing components of a writing cycle, and designing lessons. The first section addresses the needs assessment process in detail because understanding the unique characteristics of ESL writers is essential to shaping effective L2 composition instruction.

---

[1]Comprehensive sources on curriculum design include Brown (1995), Pratt (1980), Richards and Rodgers (1982), and Stufflebeam, McCormick, Brinkerhoff, and Nelson (1985).

NEEDS ASSESSMENT:
A TOOL FOR SYLLABUS DESIGN

In broad terms, needs assessment consists of "procedures for identifying and validating needs, and establishing priorities among them" (Pratt, 1980, p. 79). Because of the particular constraints involved in teaching writing to non-native speakers (NNSs) of English, we need a systematic way of inquiring into the diverse background features, skills, schemata, and expectations of ESL writers so that we can take this information into account when planning instruction. Generally, some of this information (e.g., institution type, immigration status) is obvious to teachers and requires no data collection. However, specific demographic and proficiency-related characteristics of the learner population may only be available by eliciting specific information directly from the students in our classes. Although many other effective needs analysis tools exist (Brown, 1995; Reid, 1995a), this section concentrates on those that are easy to construct, practical to administer, and simple to analyze within the context of an individual program or course: written questionnaires and informal interviews. Instead of presenting a stock "one-size-fits-all" questionnaire or interview format, we offer the variables in Fig. 3.1 and the explanations that follow as elements to consider in constructing a needs analysis instrument (or set of instruments) tailored to your particular institutional setting.

Understanding the Learner Population

Figure 3.1 provides a general starting point for identifying students' instructional requirements by requesting information about factors known to influence the effectiveness of L2 composition instruction. This information should ultimately be used to design course syllabi and classroom tasks.

Institution Type.   For the same reasons that we should not make pedagogical decisions without considering the diversity of learners in our classrooms, we should be mindful of the types of students described in the research literature (Browning, 1996; Raimes, 1991; Silva, 1993). One of the most obvious characteristics to consider is the type of institution in which students receive their ESL instruction. For example, we can generally assume that college- and university-level ESL writers have had more experience with English and have developed more extensive academic literacy skills than high school ESL writers simply by virtue of the length of their formal schooling. Likewise, students in institutions of higher education, by virtue of their having elected to continue their studies beyond compulsory secondary education, may have varied educational and career goals in mind.

Within the broad range of postsecondary institutions, we also find diverse types of students. Whereas the ESL populations of U.S. high schools and community colleges serve a high proportion of immigrant students depending on geographical

Institution type (Check one)

- ☐ Secondary school
- ☐ Community college
- ☐ College/University-based intensive ESL program
- ☐ Four-year college
  - ☐ Freshman/Sophomore
  - ☐ Junior/Senior
- ☐ Research university
  - ☐ Freshman/Sophomore
  - ☐ Junior/Senior
  - ☐ Graduate/Professional

Non-U.S. educational experience (Check highest level of education completed outside the U.S., if applicable)

- ☐ None
- ☐ Primary/Elementary school
- ☐ Secondary/High school
- ☐ Adult school
- ☐ Vocational/Technical/Trade school
- ☐ Community college degree
- ☐ College/University degree
- ☐ Graduate degree/diploma
- ☐ Other: _____

U.S. educational experience (Check highest level of education completed in the U.S., if applicable)

- ☐ None
- ☐ Primary/Elementary School
- ☐ Secondary/High School
- ☐ Vocational/Technical/Trade school or Community college
- ☐ College/University degree
- ☐ Graduate Degree/diploma
- ☐ Other: _____

L1 literacy (Check appropriate cell for each item)

High Mid Low
☐ ☐ ☐ Reading expertise
☐ ☐ ☐ Writing expertise

L2 proficiency & literacy (Check appropriate cell for each item)

High Mid Low
☐ ☐ ☐ General ESL proficiency
☐ ☐ ☐ Reading expertise
☐ ☐ ☐ Writing expertise

Immigration status (Check one)

- ☐ Immigrant/Refugee (Permanent resident)
- ☐ International (Student visa holder)

Traditional/Nontraditional status (Check one, if applicable)

- ☐ Traditional (No interruption in higher education experience)
- ☐ Non-traditional/Returning (One or more interruptions in higher education experience)

FIG. 3.1. Inventory of institutional
and educational variables.

location, 4-year colleges and research universities may also attract a high proportion of international students. Many 4-year and research institutions maintain steady populations of both types of student, although it is common for institutions in some areas to be dominated by either immigrant or international students with nonpermanent resident status. Community colleges often have higher numbers of immigrant students because these institutions offer low-cost education and numerous opportunities for students to transfer to 4-year colleges and research universities upon completion of basic education requirements (cf. Ching, McKee, & Ford, 1996; Flachman & Pluta, 1996). We make a distinction between immigrant and international students here because immigrant students (some of whom may be the children of refugees or refugees themselves) may have permanent resident status in the United States. In contrast, international students usually enter the United States on student visas, complete their college or university studies, and subsequently return to their home countries.

Further distinctions are to be made between students taking courses in intensive English programs (IEPs) and their counterparts in traditional degree programs. IEPs are frequently housed on college and university campuses, but may not award students college or university course credit (with the occasional exception of certain advanced-level courses). Many IEPs offer both academic and nonacademic ESL courses for international and/or immigrant learners. Academic track IEP courses are often geared toward providing students with the linguistic and academic skills to matriculate as regular students and enter traditional degree programs (Gaskill, 1996). Meanwhile, nonacademic courses frequently serve international students who intend to spend only a short time in the United States to improve their English proficiency and then return to their home countries. Clearly, the teaching of ESL writing in IEP courses needs to be geared specifically toward students' educational, professional, and personal goals.

At the community college, 4-year college, and research university levels, ESL students may be assessed and placed into pre-academic, basic, or remedial courses designed to bring their oral/aural, reading, or writing skills to a level at which they can enroll in content and English courses with NES students (cf. Garlow, 1996; Murray, 1996; Rose, 1983). Frequently, students assigned to these courses are identified as weak in specific skill areas and are allowed to take courses that count toward a degree or certificate only after they (a) pass these courses, (b) pass an in-house ESL test, and/or (c) achieve a minimum score on the Test of English as a Foreign Language (TOEFL). The implications for the teaching of writing in these circumstances are clear: Instruction must furnish students with the skills required to succeed on tests and function effectively in subsequent ESL, mainstream English, and content courses in the disciplines. In a number of institutions, passing these courses entitles students to make the transition from the ESL track to the regular or native track (where no distinction is made between ESL and NES students and where classes are made up of both types of learners).

Other institutions may offer ESL- or NNS-stream composition and/or literature courses that parallel NES courses in terms of curriculum and assessment criteria, but that are designed specifically with NNS learners' needs in mind. These courses, like their NES counterparts, enable students to earn credit toward a degree; they are sometimes taught by instructors who have ESL training or who at least have experience working with NNS writers. In NNS-stream courses that parallel NES courses, instruction is largely determined by the NES curriculum and is guided by the principles and techniques featured in the equivalent NES course. In some such cases, there may be conflicts between philosophies and approaches to the writing processes that students must practice and master (cf. Atkinson & Ramanathan, 1995; Garlow, 1996).

Prior Educational Experience. In addition to the numerous factors influencing the extent and type of writing instruction offered and required by schools, colleges, and universities, ESL students' formal educational backgrounds must also be considered. The inventory of student variables shown in Fig. 3.1 includes two broad categories aimed at capturing this information: non-U.S. and U.S. educational experience. For each of these categories, students' level of education completed (or, alternatively, years of formal schooling) offers only a rough indicator of their experience and expertise as classroom learners, note takers, discussion participants, readers, writers, test takers, and so on, in both L1- and English-medium environments. ESL teachers need to bear in mind, of course, that their students' formal education outside the United States may have been quite different from any training they may have received in the United States due to the wide diversity of educational systems and philosophies in non-U.S. cultures. This information can be of immediate relevance to writing teachers because many immigrant and nonimmigrant ESL students come from educational traditions in which school-based texts exemplify rhetorical patterns that are fundamentally distinct from those of U.S. schools (cf. chap. 1).

Moreover, in some non-U.S. educational models, writing processes may not be explicitly taught; students trained in those traditions may sometimes view composing as incidental to the learning of discipline-specific subject matter. Such students may thus be unfamiliar (and possibly uncomfortable) with the numerous ways in which texts and composing processes are used and taught in U.S. academic settings (cf. Horowitz, 1986b, 1986c; McKay, 1984; Raimes, 1985; Reid, 1984a, 1984b; Scollon & Scollon, 1981; Shen, 1989). Knowing about students' U.S. educational backgrounds can be equally informative because teachers may need to accommodate their learners' familiarity with composing skills and strategies to prepare them effectively for writing at a more advanced level. For the university freshman composition instructor, for example, it is important to understand the extent to which his or her ESL students are prepared to undertake the expository and/or argumentative writing that is often required in freshman-level courses (Atkinson

& Ramanathan, 1995; Parker, 1985; Russell, 1990; Tarvers, 1993; Williams, 1996). Students with a U.S. high school and/or community college background may already be familiar with these English-based genres, although their level of proficiency in producing them is bound to vary (Sasser, 1996). Students with no U.S. educational experience may come into the freshman writing class with little or no explicit awareness of these pervasive rhetorical forms or how to reproduce them.

Language Proficiency and Literacy. Along with information regarding the type and extent of students' formal schooling, indications of their general ESL proficiency as well as L1 and L2 literacy skills can offer ESL writing teachers vital information about where composition instruction should begin and how it should proceed (Eisterhold, 1990). Regardless of their level of L1 literacy, adult ESL learners have at least two bases of knowledge from which to draw in building their L2 proficiency: L1 knowledge and L2 input. If they have acquired a level of L1 literacy, L2 learners can also "draw on their literacy skills and knowledge of literacy practices from their first language (*interlingual transfer*), and they can also utilize the input from literacy activities—reading and writing (*intralingual input*)—in their developing second language" (Carson, Carrell, Silberstein, Kroll, & Kuehn, 1990, p. 246). Some researchers have maintained that L2 learners make use of both of these knowledge bases as they develop L2 literacy skills (Canale, Frenette, & Belanger, 1988; Cummins, 1981; Edelsky, 1982; Mace-Matluck, Dominguez, Holtzman, & Hoover, 1983). Others have argued that the transfer of literacy skills from the primary language to the L2 is not automatic and that the relationship between the two literacies is complex and in need of extensive research (Bell, 1995; Hedgcock & Atkinson, 1993; McLaughlin, 1987). Nonetheless, it is intuitively appealing to assume that reading and writing input influences the development of both reading and writing proficiency in a given language. For developing L2 writers, of course, the situation involves multiple dimensions of knowledge and skills: "One must take into account not only the learner's L2 ... proficiency, but also the possibility of interaction of first language literacy skills with second language input" (Carson et al., 1990, p. 248). Obviously, these interactions cannot possibly be captured in a crude instrument such as a questionnaire, although a rough measure of students' current L1 and L2 reading and writing skills can offer teachers basic information about their students' literacy profiles (cf. chap. 2), as can a characterization of students' learning styles and study habits (Reid, 1995a, 1995b).

Immigration Status. An additional background factor that is set apart as a separate item in Fig. 3.1 concerns students' immigration status. Although this is admittedly a technical piece of demographic information, it can be a tremendously significant determinant of an individual student's educational pathway and consequently has implications for ESL writing instruction. Ann Johns (personal communication, April 1996) has pointed out that immigrant students' linguistic and educational histories, instructional needs, and career plans may differ widely from those of international students, who, as already noted, generally intend to return to their home countries upon completion of their studies in the United States.

As a supplement to information about students' prior educational experience, language proficiency, and literacy skills, immigration status can tell teachers a great deal about their students' socioeconomic backgrounds as well as the educational and professional futures they may envision for themselves. It was indicated earlier that immigrant students have (or may be in the process of obtaining) permanent resident status in the United States. In some cases, these students have lived in the United States for extended periods, in contrast to their nonimmigrant counterparts who generally enter the United States on temporary student visas and do not intend to make the United States their permanent home. Immigrant students also may have immigrated as refugees or may be the children of refugee parents. Such students may consequently be members of sizable and well-established ethnic and linguistic minority communities.

In many ethnolinguistic minority communities in the United States, ESL students' L1 is the language of the home as well as the discourse of social and religious institutions such as community and religious organizations (cf. Skutnabb-Kangas & Cummins, 1988).[2] Although this situation may promote the development of bilingual proficiency among some learners, for others it poses serious challenges in the educational setting (see Ediger, Ching, & Poole, 1996; Hakuta, 1986; Skutnabb-Kangas & Cummins, 1988; Wong-Fillmore, Ammon, McLaughlin, & Ammon, 1985). That is, some immigrant students who have resided for many years and have attended school in the United States achieve a highly functional level of linguistic proficiency and academic literacy in English, enabling them to advance through ESL courses fairly quickly and transition into NES-track courses. These students may complete their postsecondary education while maintaining, and even strengthening, their bilingualism and cultural ties to their home communities (Hakuta & D'Andrea, 1992).

For many other immigrant students, achieving bilingualism and biliteracy can be considerably more difficult and frustrating. Those for whom ties to a cohesive home ethnic and linguistic community—in which English is seldom or never

---

[2]Such communities can be found in urban, suburban, and even rural areas throughout the United States and Canada. For example, Chinese-speaking communities of long standing have thrived for generations in large cities such as San Francisco and New York City. Likewise, Chinese immigrants have recently become entrenched in suburban areas such as Monterey Park, California, and outlying areas of Houston, Texas, to name but two considerably large communities. Similarly, the ethnic population of areas in and around Anaheim, California, is dominated by Vietnamese and other Southeast Asian immigrants. In addition, significant populations of Spanish-speaking immigrants from Mexico and Central America now reside in large and small cities as well as rural areas across the Southwest and other regions of the United States. Space restrictions, of course, do not permit a thorough or comprehensive survey of the dramatic shifts in ethnolinguistic demographics. Our purpose in presenting these examples is to remind teachers of the diversity of linguistic, cultural, and socioeconomic features associated with immigrant ESL students.

used—may find that the school, college, or university campus is the only place where English is the primary medium of communication (cf. Hakuta, 1976). Consequently, they may have limited opportunities to use English for purposes other than those directly related to formal education and may therefore require substantial instructional support to compensate for these limitations. International ESL students enrolled in colleges, universities, and IEPs frequently report an analogous sense of social and linguistic isolation from English-speaking students and the wider community, often because both international and immigrant students tend to socialize and find solidarity with peers from the same ethnolinguistic background. A result of this tendency is that ESL students may use the L1 in their social interactions nearly everywhere but the educational setting.

This situation can pose problems of a slightly different nature for immigrant students than for international students. Immigrant students are faced with having to use English not only to complete their formal studies, but to seek and secure employment and pursue a career and livelihood in an English-speaking workplace in the United States. Moreover, the majority of immigrant students currently enrolled in educational institutions struggle with economic and social hardships that their international peers may never experience. For example, the majority of international students come from developed or developing countries and have the economic resources to cover the cost of their U.S. training, thanks either to government sponsorship or family resources. Immigration laws, in fact, require student visa holders to demonstrate proof that they possess these financial means and that they maintain full-time status throughout their course of study.

The circumstances of many (if not most) immigrant students contrast sharply with those of international students. Because of the need to contribute financially to their family income and even to support families of their own, immigrant learners enrolled in ESL programs at all levels of education may hold part- or full-time jobs. These financial and family-related obligations may place heavy demands on ESL students, for whom educational achievement may also be a palpably strong social value in their respective ethnic communities. Not only may resident students face ever-present financial and educational pressures and hardships, but they may have to confront problems associated with being members of ethnolinguistic minority communities that do not enjoy equal, let alone privileged, social status with respect to the dominant Anglo culture.

These divergent experiences clearly set the resident student population apart from the international student population and suggest the need for ESL teachers to adjust pedagogical assumptions accordingly. The content and assignments in a writing course designed for international students may be largely inappropriate for immigrant students. For example, consider a syllabus in which American culture and literature serve as core content, in conjunction with writing tasks that involve students in making comparisons between the cultural practices of the United States and their home culture. Although such a curriculum would probably serve the needs of learners who are new to the U.S. cultural and educational environment, it would be of marginal relevance to ESL students who have lived and studied in the United States for quite some time and for whom the home country is a distant memory. Recognizing and understanding the current personal, social, and economic conditions of immigrant and international students can help ESL teachers develop a sensitivity to the constraints their students must overcome in their attempts to improve their linguistic and academic skills, as well as their composing proficiency (Valdes, 1992).

Traditional and Nontraditional Students. An additional factor that is frequently overlooked but that can influence the character of learning and teaching in a given ESL setting has to do with learners' status as so-called *traditional* or *nontraditional* students. Traditional students (both NES and NNS) are described as such if they have experienced few if any interruptions in their progress from secondary school to (and through) higher education. That is, traditional students are those who, on completion of secondary school, proceed directly to a community college, 4-year college, or research university (and from there perhaps to more advanced study). Because of this rapid progress from a secondary to a postsecondary institution, traditional students are, by definition, young adults in their late teens or early 20s when they begin their postsecondary education.

Nontraditional or *returning* students, in contrast, may have experienced one or more interruptions along their educational pathways. These interruptions can include substantial periods of full-time employment (and sometimes the pursuit of an entire career) and/or considerable time devoted to caring for children or elderly family members. Thus, these students, whose numbers are increasing rapidly in all types of educational institutions, represent a variety of age groups (Peterson, 1995; Stewart, 1993; Williams, 1996). Moreover, many nontraditional students reinitiate their formal studies while working part or full time, and may likewise have personal, financial, and family commitments to fulfill. These circumstances can sometimes have a direct and obvious impact on students' participation, motivation, confidence level, and performance in a composition course. For example, consider a returning immigrant student who undertakes part-time coursework toward an undergraduate degree after having successfully completed her ESL composition requirements 10 years before. Such a student may have decided to return to college for compelling personal or economic reasons, including no longer having young children to care for and a desire to pursue a career outside the home. A student in this situation might understandably need help readjusting to the academic environment. It might also take time for her to reactivate reading and writing skills that have not been practiced in a long time. With a sensitivity to such circumstances, teachers can anticipate the academic, linguistic, and social obstacles faced by their students and appreciate the challenging experiences that might strongly influence their students' progress as writers.

A. Student background information.
Name:
Native country: _____
Native language(s):   _____

B. Classroom work styles.
DIRECTIONS: This portion of the survey will help your instructor understand the ways in which you prefer to complete class assignments. Think about your most recent experiences in college or university classes. For each statement below, place an 'X' in the cell that most accurately describes your habits and preferences. Please be frank: Your honest responses will give your instructor valuable information.

1 = Strongly agree   3 = Somewhat agree   5 = Disagree
2 = Agree   4 = Somewhat disagree   6 = Strongly disagree

		1	2	3	4	5	6
1.	In my native country, I had many opportunities to work with a partner or a small group.	☐	☐	☐	☐	☐	☐
2.	In the U.S., I have had many opportunities to work with a partner or a small group.	☐	☐	☐	☐	☐	☐
3.	In general, I enjoy working with a partner or a small group.	☐	☐	☐	☐	☐	☐
4.	When I work with a partner or a small group, I usually do a better job on assignments.	☐	☐	☐	☐	☐	☐
5.	When I work with a partner or a small group, I usually concentrate better and learn more.	☐	☐	☐	☐	☐	☐
6.	I am comfortable working with partners who are also nonnative speakers of English.	☐	☐	☐	☐	☐	☐
7.	I prefer working with a partner or with a group when the teacher assigns a role to each group member.	☐	☐	☐	☐	☐	☐
8.	I hope we will do a substantial amount of pair and group work in this course.	☐	☐	☐	☐	☐	☐

C. Strengths, styles & preferences.
DIRECTIONS: This portion of the survey is designed to help you and your instructor understand the ways in which you prefer to prepare writing assignments in English. Think about your most recent experiences in classes where you wrote academic papers. For each statement below, place an 'X' in the cell that most accurately describes your habits and preferences. Please be frank: Your honest responses will give your instructor valuable information.

1 = Strongly agree   3 = Somewhat agree   5 = Disagree
2 = Agree   4 = Somewhat disagree   6 = Strongly disagree

		1	2	3	4	5	6
1.	I consider myself a good academic writer in my native language.	☐	☐	☐	☐	☐	☐
2.	I consider myself a good writer of academic English.	☐	☐	☐	☐	☐	☐
3.	I know how to use source material (e.g., textbooks, scholarly books, journal articles, newspapers, newsmagazines, on-line tools such as the WWW, etc.) effectively in my writing assignments.	☐	☐	☐	☐	☐	☐
4.	One of my major strengths as a writer of English is producing interesting ideas.	☐	☐	☐	☐	☐	☐

Learner Preferences, Strategies, and Styles. A final but crucial dimension of the needs assessment process involves accounting for learners' predispositions toward the multiple aspects of classroom instruction and independent learning. The information targeted in Fig. 3.1 is primarily demographic, whereas the learner variables included in the writing styles questionnaire (Fig. 3.2) address aspects of learners' preferences, strategies, and styles that are subject to considerable change over time and that may be most productively measured locally in the classroom context. Research on learner strategies and styles (which is, unfortunately, too extensive to consider in detail here) consistently shows how these highly personal and dynamic learner-internal variables affect learning processes, both within the classroom and beyond (Oxford, 1990; Reid, 1987, 1995a, 1995b). This

		1	2	3	4	5	6

5. I am skilled at organizing my ideas and putting them together logically. ☐☐☐☐☐☐

6. I have learned about academic writing mostly through reading. ☐☐☐☐☐☐

7. When I write academic assignments, I am a good typist and an efficient computer user. ☐☐☐☐☐☐

8. I rearrange my ideas a lot when I am planning to write. ☐☐☐☐☐☐

9. When I revise a paper or draft, I often make a lot of changes. ☐☐☐☐☐☐

10. As I revise a paper, I like to add new material. ☐☐☐☐☐☐

11. When I write and revise a paper, I think carefully about what my reader wants to know from me. ☐☐☐☐☐☐

12. Before I revise a paper, I ask a classmate or friend to give me feedback on it. ☐☐☐☐☐☐

13. My papers usually have very clear and direct thesis statements. ☐☐☐☐☐☐

14. I use clear and succinct transitions between paragraphs. ☐☐☐☐☐☐

15. The paragraphs of my papers usually contain plenty of examples and/or explanations. ☐☐☐☐☐☐

16. I try hard to connect each of my paragraphs to my thesis. ☐☐☐☐☐☐

17. My conclusions synthesize my thesis and the evidence I've presented in the paragraphs of my papers. ☐☐☐☐☐☐

18. When I turn in papers, they have mostly minor grammatical errors. ☐☐☐☐☐☐

19. My papers show that I have a strong command of English vocabulary. ☐☐☐☐☐☐

20. When I turn in papers, they have few errors of spelling or punctuation. ☐☐☐☐☐☐

21. When I write an academic paper, I am comfortable using references, quotations, footnotes, bibliographic sources, etc. ☐☐☐☐☐☐

22. Generally, I learn a lot from the comments I get back from my instructor. ☐☐☐☐☐☐

23. I enjoy sharing my writing with other students and learn from reading the writing of my classmates. ☐☐☐☐☐☐

Please complete the statements below as honestly and as fully as you can.

a) My greatest strengths as a writer of English include ...

b) The aspects of my writing that I would like most to improve in this course include ...

FIG. 3.2. Writing styles questionnaire for classroom use
(adapted from Kinsella & Sherak, 1995).

work also suggests ways in which teachers can diagnose their students' styles and preferences, raise their students' awareness of productive and unproductive strategies, and help their students add new strategies to their existing repertoires.

The questionnaire in Fig. 3.2, inspired by several instruments presented in Reid (1995a), was developed by an instructor who administered it on the first day of an advanced university EAP writing course for international graduate students in political science. The prompts are clearly geared toward nonimmigrant students with limited experience in U.S. classrooms. Items are specifically aimed at inducing students to report their perceived expertise as readers and writers, in addition to their views toward group work, drafting procedures, feedback, and revision. The instructor was able to use his students' responses to address these issues explicitly in the course and to plan instruction to accommodate the reported needs and preferences of the class.

By regularly considering formally or informally gathered self-report data about their students' work patterns, study habits, drafting styles, task-type preferences, and so on, teachers can design syllabi, plan lessons, and construct activities and assignments that capitalize on students' strengths and overcome their weaknesses. Instruments used to collect this information are perhaps most suitably and productively developed by adapting and combining the styles and strategies resources already available.[3]

⇒ AA 3.1

SETTING AND MEETING GOALS
FOR LEARNING AND TEACHING

Goals are frequently recognized as global targets around which instructional programs and course syllabi are designed. Brown (1995) defined them as "general statements concerning desirable and attainable program purposes and aims based on perceived language and situation needs" (p. 71). The goals for a particular program and its sequence of courses should address the specific needs of the student population and the requirements of the educational institution as identified by regular, systematic needs analyses (cf. Frodesen, 1995; Reid, 1995a, 1995b). A summary of goals for a pre-mainstream, advanced academic ESL reading/writing course series, for example, might look something like this: "... students will be able to identify implicit relationships in academic English between parts of a concept: in a flow chart, in a table, and in an outline, as well as in the prose describing a chart or table in an essay" (Brown, 1995, p. 77). Goals such as these ideally reflect cognitive, linguistic, and academic skills that can be described, practiced, and assessed in the context of an instructional program and the courses it comprises.

In most ESL settings, instructional goals are preestablished by administrators and institutions; the role of individual teachers is to accomplish these goals in the planning and execution of the courses they teach. However, this does not mean that teachers cannot play a part in shaping program-level goals or in using them to their advantage in developing their own syllabi and lesson plans. Further, explicit goals do not necessarily have to be confining. In fact, they can assist teachers in the following ways:

---

[3]Reid's (1995a) work contains a wealth of similar instruments designed for classroom use, some of which specifically target the teaching of composition (e.g., Carrell & Monroe, 1995; Reid, 1995a). Other useful sources include Oxford (1990), Oxford and Ehrman (1993), and Oxford, Holloway, and Horton-Murillo (1992).

1. Formalized goals articulate the purposes of the course and/or educational program;
2. Goals focus on what the course or program intends to accomplish, indicating the skills that students will acquire on completion of the course;
3. Goals allow for the formulation of more precise and achievable instructional objectives;
4. Goals are dynamic—they evolve as a function of the changing needs of the students as their skills develop. (Adapted from Brown, 1995, pp. 72–73)

In the sections that follow, we look at procedures for constructing course syllabi and designing lessons. By planning instruction to meet specific learning objectives formulated on the basis of a solid needs analysis, teachers can bring about the realization of broader programmatic goals.

FROM GOALS TO OBJECTIVES: THE SYLLABUS AS A FRAMEWORK FOR INSTRUCTION

Whereas goals typically constitute general statements of the purpose of a curriculum, *objectives* are more specific statements describing "the particular knowledge, behaviors, and/or skills that the learner will be expected to know or perform at the end of a course" (Brown, 1995, p. 73). The term *instructional objective* is used here to describe the purposes of a course as outlined in a syllabus and as a tool for devising units and lessons.[4] Thus, objectives are fairly precise. According to Mager (1975), instructional objectives specify the following essential characteristics: (a) performance (what the learner will be able to do), (b) conditions (parameters within which the performance is expected to occur), and (c) criteria (the quality or level of performance that will be considered acceptable). The following example illustrates how these components can be spelled out succinctly in a course description: "By the end of the course, the students will be able to write the full forms of selected abbreviations drawn from pages 6–8 of the course textbook with 80 percent accuracy" (Mager, 1975, p. 74). The instructional objectives outlined in Fig. 3.3 represent a small sample of the types of functions that ESL writing syllabi might include at various proficiency levels and in various institutions.

Not all curriculum design experts, language educators, or rhetoricians advocate setting *a priori* instructional objectives. A principal objection to explicit objectives relates to their negative association with behavioral psychology; the charge is that they somehow trivialize classroom teaching by forcing instructors to focus only on narrowly defined skills and written products (Hillocks, 1995; Tumposky, 1984; van Lier, 1996). A further complaint is that explicit objectives limit teachers' freedom

---

[4]For extensive critical discussions of instructional objectives and their implementation, see Findlay and Nathan (1980), Finocchiaro and Brumfit (1983), Nunan (1991), Richards and Lockhart (1994), and Steiner (1975).

Course Type and Level	Sample Objectives as Outlined in Course Syllabus
Grades 9–12 ESL: Intermediate/High to Advanced	• Identify and summarize in writing main ideas of paragraphs and larger units of written discourse, including textbooks and literary passages. • Compose paragraph-length answers to specific questions in connected prose form. • Compose original expository and narrative essays (up to 500 words in length) on personal and academic topics.
Adult/Vocational: Low to Low Intermediate	• Transcribe simple words in dictation. • Compose lists of words that relate to a theme or semantic category. • Complete simple forms and documents, including bank deposit and withdrawal slips. • Use simple illustrations and diagrams to compose simple descriptive sentences.
Preacademic Intensive ESL: Low to Low Intermediate	• Take legible notes on familiar topics. • Respond in complete sentences to personal and academic questions. • Compose simple letters, paraphrases, and summaries of biographical data as well as work and school experiences. • Compose descriptive, narrative, and expository paragraphs of 100 words or more based on simple model texts.
Community College/University ESL: Intermediate to Advanced	• Take detailed notes on familiar and unfamiliar topics. • Respond in connected written discourse to text-based questions. • Compose summaries of biographical data, work, and school experiences. • Compose paraphrases and summaries of extended academic prose (texts of up to 10 pages in length). • Compose descriptive, narrative, and expository essay-length texts (up to 500 words in length).
Graduate-Level ESL: TOEFL Score = 600 or higher	• Take detailed notes on familiar and unfamiliar topics. • Respond in connected written discourse to text-based questions. • Compose summaries of statistical and graphic data. • Compose paraphrases and summaries of extended academic or technical prose (texts of up to 20 pages in length). • Compose descriptive, expository, and argumentative texts of 1,500 words or more.

FIG. 3.3. Sample course objectives: ESL writing skills.

and constrain their decision-making. These objections are weakened, however, when objectives are seen not as rigid and prescriptive targets, but as flexible guidelines: As Brown (1995) maintained, "… objectives are most effective when a variety of different types are used and when the level of specificity for different objectives is allowed to diverge" (p. 95). The explicit presentation of instructional objectives in a course syllabus enables teachers to: (a) transform student needs into teaching points that can be organized into a teaching sequence, (b) identify target skills that underlie instructional points, (c) decide on the level of specificity for the teaching activities in the syllabus, (d) adopt or adapt teaching materials that appropriately accommodate student needs and expectations, (e) map out a blueprint for assessing student performance and progress, and (f) evaluate their own teaching effectiveness (cf. Frodesen, 1995).

THE NUTS AND BOLTS
OF SYLLABUS DEVELOPMENT

Conducting a needs assessment can be an informative and rewarding process leading to the development and establishment of clear, achievable course objectives. These objectives and their operationalization, of course, need to be formalized in writing on the course syllabus. It is useful to think of a course syllabus as a document comprising two main parts. First, it is a contract between the instructor and the students—a summary of course objectives and how they will be met (Tarvers, 1993; Tate & Corbett, 1988; Williams, 1996). Second, a syllabus serves as a planning tool: It structures and sequences objectives, units, lessons, assignments, classroom procedures, and assessment procedures for the instructor and students (Nunan, 1991; Raimes, 1983a). The checklist in Fig. 3.4, although not exhaustive, offers a framework for providing students with all the information they will need about course objectives and content, workload, participation requirements, policies, assignments, and performance expectations. Figure 3.4 also serves as an advance organizer for discussion in the sections that follow. A sample syllabus for a community college composition course appears in Appendix 3A.

THE COURSE SCHEDULE: PRIORITIZING,
SEQUENCING, AND PLANNING
FOR MULTIDRAFTING

Laying out a sequence of reading materials, classroom activities, and assignments can be one of the most challenging tasks facing novice and experienced teachers. Before describing specific techniques for meeting these challenges, we offer a few guiding principles to assist in laying some of the groundwork for writing a syllabus and course outline. Figure 3.5 presents an overarching schema and suggested procedures for incorporating overlapping phases of the writing process into a course outline (cf. chap. 1). The stages leading from prewriting through publishing are not mechanical, autonomous steps, but potentially overlapping and recursive phases and subprocesses. We do not wish to oversimplify or trivialize the complexity of individual writers' evolving composing processes, but suggest this model as a broadly based approach to sequencing classroom tasks.[5]

To operationalize this writing process schema, we must first and foremost establish student and program goals as our highest priority, organizing our material and tasks accordingly (cf. MacDonald, 1991). Second, it is crucial that we under-

---

[5]Hillocks (1995) offered a persuasive argument challenging conventional views of the so-called *process* model: "While the general model of the composing process is useful, it cannot begin to account for variations in process that appear to be dependent on a variety of factors" (p. xix).

1. **Descriptive information**
   - ☐ Course name and number
   - ☐ Prerequisites and other requirements
   - ☐ Instructor's name, office location, hours, telephone number, and e-mail address
2. **Course goals/objectives and content**
   - ☐ Program-level and course goals
   - ☐ Course objectives, both short- and long-term (see program-level and course goals)
   - ☐ Core course content, including aspects of the composing process to be presented and practiced
   - ☐ Aspects of English rhetoric, textual analysis, grammar, etc., that will be directly addressed in class
   - ☐ Description of what constitutes *progress* toward the achievement of course goals/objectives (see Item 8)
   - ☐ How much reading will be covered in class and in writing assignments
3. **Reading materials**
   - ☐ Titles of course texts and where to find them
   - ☐ List of reading assignments, their sequence, page numbers, and deadlines (if possible)
4. **Writing assignments**
   - ☐ Number and description of writing assignments, with due dates
   - ☐ Description of how many assignments will involve drafting in class, teacher and peer feedback, etc.
   - ☐ Indication of how many assignments will involved timed (in-class) writing
   - ☐ Policies on late and revised papers, group projects, etc.
   - ☐ Presentation requirements (e.g., preferred style sheet, word-processing conventions, length limitations, etc.)
5. **Instructional procedures**
   - ☐ Class time devoted to workshops, peer response sessions, class discussion, lecture, in-class writing, etc.
   - ☐ Expectations concerning student participation in classroom tasks and activities, group work, peer response, etc.
6. **Course requirements**
   - ☐ Summary of compulsory assignments and their deadlines
   - ☐ Description of assessment criteria, including how student work will be evaluated
   - ☐ Explanation of policies regarding attendance and participation, missing/late assignments, etc.
7. **Evaluation and grading procedures**
   - ☐ Explicit description of evaluation criteria and how they will be applied to each assignment
   - ☐ Breakdown of how final course grades will be determined (if applicable)
   - ☐ Justification of grading procedures, if necessary
8. **Course schedule or timetable**
   - ☐ A meeting-by-meeting calendar of events and topics, including (if possible) the sequence of reading and writing assignments

FIG. 3.4. Syllabus checklist.

stand how our planning decisions (materials selection and sequencing, choice of assignments, etc.) will help our students meet the course's instructional objectives (see chap. 4). If textbooks and assignments are prescribed by departmental or program policy, our syllabi will still not write themselves; our teaching will be most effective when we can justify (to ourselves and our students) our planning decisions with direct reference to course objectives. Third, flexibility is essential: As Tarvers (1993) aptly reminded us, "A ruthless sense of realism must go into planning [a] course schedule" (p. 42) because no timeline can be etched in stone (cf. Williams, 1996).

With these general precepts in mind, we can begin to lay out the work of a quarter or semester with the goals of the institution and our students (as operationalized in the course objectives) as a clear target. It is useful to start the process with an academic calendar or planner showing the exact number of class meetings and holidays; cancellations due to personal and professional commitments should then be noted, and any required makeup meetings should be built into the schedule. Class days should also be reserved for timed writings, midterms, examinations, and the like to give a clear picture of exactly how many meetings can be planned for teaching.

Prewriting

- Text-based tasks (see Chaps. 2 & 4);
- Writing from texts, e.g., reading journals (see chap. 2, Application Activities 2.2 & 2.4);
- Brainstorming, mapping, cubing, etc. (see chap. 4);
- Free-writing or zero-drafting (see chap. 4).

⇓

Planning & drafting

- Allow for extensive (as opposed to intensive) writing for discovery (cf. Elbow, 1981b; Murray, 1978, 1987; Zamel, 1982, 1983, 1985), both in class and out. Promote abundant production of texts that address the task(s) at hand (Kroll, 1991);
- Encourage students to plan as they go along and to understand the evolving purposes of their writing;
- Continue to supply content- and theme-based input in the way of readings, discussions, etc., to supplement students' emerging ideas and plans;
- Allow enough time in the drafting and planning phase for students to exchange ideas, share their plans, and elicit new information for further development of a schema for the writing task.

⇓

Rewriting & revising

- Situate the writing task in a transactional space; give students practice envisioning the audience, getting a clear picture of who the reader will be, how the reader's expectations will have to be met, etc. (cf. Zamel, 1982);
- Provide students with practice incorporating peer and expert feedback into their evolving drafts (see Chaps. 5 & 6);
- Continue to supply content- and theme-based input in the way of readings, discussions, etc., to supplement students' emerging ideas and plans.

⇓

Feedback, incubation, & revision

- Demonstrate productive and supportive ways in which students can respond to the writing of their peers (see chap. 6);
- Conduct peer response sessions in a safe environment in which students act as readers, not as evaluators (see chap. 6);
- Emphasize the benefits of reading and responding to the work of others; point out that the greatest contribution of peer feedback may not be to the writer's work, but to the reader's;
- Demonstrate procedures and technique for evaluating peer and expert feedback, and for applying that information to students' changing drafts;
- Build in time for incubation between iterations of steps in the process. As Zamel's (1982) student said, "The more days go by, the more ideas come. It's like fruit; it needs time to ripen" (pp. 200-201).

⇓

Editing & polishing

- Build time into the teaching sequence for peer, teacher, and self-editing of mature, developed pieces of writing (see Chaps. 5, 6, & 7).

⇓

Publishing

- Provide opportunities for students' "final" products to be distributed, shared, and appreciated by others.

FIG. 3.5. Writing process schema for course planning.

Next, it is a good idea to schedule due dates for graded writing assignments (especially if those deadlines are prescribed by the program or department) and work backward to include deadlines for drafts, peer feedback sessions, editing workshops, student–teacher conferences, and so on. The sample syllabus and course outline in Appendix 3A show how this can be done. Be sure to allocate adequate time for multidraft assignments and revised papers, particularly in the beginning of the term when writing assignments tend to take longer. Extra class periods may be necessary early on to discuss preliminary drafts, practice peer response techniques, and revise assignments in class. Likewise, build into the course timetable adequate time for you and your students to read and respond to assignments when you require students to review their peers' work and when you need to annotate or evaluate student papers. Allow as much time between sessions as is practicable to make the multidraft approach worthwhile. This may necessitate initiating a new writing assignment while the preceding one is still in progress. For example, it may be time-efficient to collect a set of short papers for feedback or evaluation while students are working on an extended essay or research paper.

Once the core assignments are in place and the deadlines for preliminary work (drafts, feedback, etc.) are established, the course outline has at least a skeletal form that allows for the planning of reading assignments, discussions, lectures, student presentations, peer response workshops, and so on. If reading figures prominently in the course objectives (as chap. 2 argues it should), reading selections should be assigned with great care so that they correspond logically to the themes and rhetorical patterns to be featured in the syllabus, as well as the writing assignments and rhetorical tasks that are based on them (McKay, 1994; Peterson, 1995). Generally, reading selections in anthologies and rhetorics (see chap. 4) are presented as units, topically linked, and connected to specific writing tasks (e.g., expository or argumentative essays). Examples of themes included in recent ESL and NES composition textbooks include affirmative action, educational policy, gender issues, human sexuality, language policy, multiculturalism, and racism. Where such textbooks are not part of the curriculum, a thematic approach may still be used as the basis for syllabus design, with a thematic unit revolving around an identifiable topic or context (Omaggio Hadley, 1993; Purgason, 1991; Shrum & Glisan, 1994). As with writing assignments, reading assignments should be allotted generous time; lengthy reading selections may need to be divided into several smaller parts to enable students to complete them and provide for effective discussion in class.

Finally, lay your plan out so that you and the students can see the chronology of the entire term. Before finalizing the course schedule, check to see that sufficient time has been allocated for especially labor-intensive reading selections and writing assignments. For multidraft assignments, track the sequence you have sketched out to ensure enough time for the necessary iterations of drafting, feedback, revision, and editing (cf. McKay, 1994). Wherever possible, reserve a class period in a thematic unit or writing cycle as a flex day that can be used for unexpected needs that might arise, such as extending an especially productive peer feedback workshop, continuing an engaging discussion of a text or student composition, discussing a pervasive problem in students' writing, or holding teacher–student writing conferences.

⇒ *AA 3.2*

LESSON PLANNING:
PRACTICES AND PROCEDURES

Identifying Lesson Objectives

In the same way that the instructional objectives specified in a syllabus identify what knowledge and skills students will acquire at the end of a course, effective lesson objectives describe the observable behaviors that students will demonstrate at the end of a class period or unit (Prabhu, 1992; Raimes, 1983a, 1983b; Shrum & Glisan, 1994). If instructional objectives are clearly specified in the syllabus, identifying lesson objectives should be an easy task when it comes to planning individual class periods. Lesson objectives should emanate directly from instructional objectives (and at least indirectly from program or course goals). For example, consider this instructional objective for a low to low-intermediate, preacademic ESL writing course: "Compose descriptive, narrative, and expository paragraphs" (outlined in Fig. 3.3). A corresponding *lesson* objective derived from this course objective might read "Draft a 200- to 250-word paragraph in which each student describes his or her dormitory room, apartment, or house." The anticipated outcome is described in terms of an observable student behavior as well as a written product that students can work with and that can ultimately be evaluated. The statement is also worded with action verbs such as *draft* and *describe,* as opposed to verbs such as *learn* or *understand*, which are difficult to observe (Shrum & Glisan, 1994; Steiner, 1975). Although many experienced and skilled teachers plan and execute productive lessons without writing out their objectives in detail, effective teachers *do* have a clear purpose in mind when they select and organize classroom tasks. As Purgason (1991) pointed out, "Each activity needs to have a reason. A teacher must think through why that activity is important to the students and what they will be able to do when they finish it" (p. 423). Consequently, it is advisable for both novice and experienced teachers to articulate lesson objectives routinely in their planning. Objectives help teachers unify the components of their lessons: "In synthetic terms, lessons and units of work will consist, among other things, of sequences of tasks, and the coherence of such lessons or units will depend on the extent to which the tasks have been integrated and sequenced in some principled way" (Nunan, 1989, p. 10).

Sequencing and Organization

A lesson plan can take many forms depending on the time constraints and personal style of the individual teacher. Regardless of what it looks like, a lesson plan provides the teacher with a script for presenting materials, interacting with students, and leading students through structured and unstructured activities. Much more than a mere step-by-step chronology of a classroom event, however, a lesson plan is a practical, tangible, and potentially dynamic tool for meeting student needs as operationalized in course objectives. It serves as a vital link between curricular goals and the learning we wish to bring about among our students. In this sense, the lesson is where the known (instructional objectives, texts, etc.) meets the unknown (the learners in our composition classes). As Hillocks (1995) pointed out, mapping out instruction is initially an exploratory endeavor: "At the beginning of a year or term, our students are likely to be new to us. We cannot begin planning, except with general outlines, until we know what students do as writers" (p. 132). Because we cannot possibly anticipate every aspect of what happens in our classrooms, we can think of lessons as opportunities for experimentation. Not all lessons or activities will succeed. However, we can be prepared for this outcome by expecting the unexpected. We can also improve our teaching effectiveness by reflecting on what works well and what does not work so successfully with the students in our own classes (Bailey & Nunan, 1996; Brown, 1994b; Prabhu, 1992; Richards & Lockhart, 1994). Hillocks (1995) offered sound planning advice in noting that "the thoughtful teacher, in searching for ways to help students learn more effectively, will plan real trials (what researchers call quasi-experiments), determine what effect they have, even as the trial goes forward, and consider new options as a result" (p. 125).

Most teachers, even those seasoned and self-assured enough to conduct entire lessons with no written notes, are aware of the benefits of advance planning, coupled with a willingness to depart from their plans when necessary (Bailey, 1996). A written lesson plan, whether a general list of activities or a meticulously detailed sequence of procedures, can offer the following short- and long-term advantages:

1. A plan familiarizes the teacher with the lesson content and tailors activities and tasks to the students' needs and learning styles. It also assists the teacher in making decisions about content, materials, sequencing, and time allocation.

2. A plan gives the teacher a script or blueprint for the class period, allowing him or her to face the students confidently and concentrate on the material rather than on what to say and do next.

3. A plan provides the teacher with a record of what material has been covered and what skills have been practiced or learned, as compared to the course's instructional objectives and outcomes of the needs assessment. A detailed plan can also inform testing and student performance assessment.

4. A plan offers the teacher a record for reflection on his or her materials selection, task development, and presentational skills. That is, it scaffolds the process of postlesson evaluation, prompting the teacher to diagnose the causes of problems and pinpoint successful features of materials and activities.

5. A plan can be a managerial tool, providing a peer or supervisor with a guide for observation and evaluation; it can also help a substitute teacher take over the class with ease. (Adapted from Brown, 1994b; Omaggio Hadley, 1993; Purgason, 1991; Richards & Lockhart, 1994.)

The Mechanics of Lesson Planning

In purely mechanical terms, a lesson plan can be handwritten or word processed on standard paper and formatted in any number of ways. Likewise, it can be printed out on note cards. In fact, for some teachers, it is enough to write out lesson notes before class to put them into their heads; in this way, they do not need a written plan during the lesson. Whatever form a lesson plan takes, it should be readable, convenient to refer to in class (if necessary), and usable as a future record of what took place. Rather than proposing a rigid or prescriptive model for planning ESL writing classes, we would like to offer the following general outline and conceptual framework as options for many possible designs for daily lessons.[6] The outline in Fig. 3.6 includes practical and procedural aspects of the planning process that many teachers consider essential in constructing a lesson. Appendix 3B contains an example of an authentic lesson plan that follows this format. Figure 3.6 focuses principally on logistical elements, whereas Fig. 3.7 focuses on pedagogical moves and instructional procedures.

Although most of the items in Fig. 3.6 are self-explanatory, a few are worth some discussion here. In addition to reviewing the lesson's objectives, making a note about the work that students did during the previous class and have done for homework can give us a realistic feeling for what kinds of reading, writing, or discussion tasks students are ready for next. This process is invaluable in managing time effectively. Preparing a list of equipment (e.g., an overhead projector, markers, etc.), materials, page numbers, and so on before class can prevent the need to spend valuable class time getting organized. Having a prepared checklist of student work to return and/or collect can likewise save time, as can dispensing with announcements in an efficient way. Some teachers routinely write these on the board or an overhead transparency for students

---

[6] Brown (1994a), Cross (1991), Hunter (1984), Hunter and Russell (1977), MacDonald (1991), Matthews, Spratt, and Dangerfield (1985), Nunan (1991), Purgason (1991), and Richards (1990) provided a wide range of guidelines for constructing lesson plans.

to read on their own; others prefer to make announcements at the end of class when they will not have to be repeated for late-comers.

The core lesson elements in Fig. 3.6 refer to techniques for successfully executing the steps outlined in Fig. 3.7. The first of these core elements is time management—perhaps the single most pervasive challenge for teachers in carrying out their lesson plans (Brown, 1994b). For this reason, a useful practice is to anticipate the time each activity in a lesson will take and add several additional minutes to that total; this gives teachers a way of estimating what can reasonably be accomplished in a single class period. A general rule to follow is that open-ended activities such as unstructured discussions of texts, pair/group activities, and peer response workshops frequently take much longer than teachers predict, partly because of the numerous unexpected questions that can emerge. The same can often be said of untested classroom tasks (see chap. 4).

Overall objectives
□ Brief summary of lesson objectives

Work previously completed
□ Summary of reading, writing, and discussion completed in the previous class

Materials
□ Textbooks(s)
□ Handouts (e.g., worksheets, feedback guides, copies of student writing, etc.)
□ Materials for student writing (e.g., writing paper, blue books for in-class writing, etc.)
□ AV materials (e.g., OHP transparencies, video player, computer projection screen, etc.)

Class management
□ Assignment(s) to be collected
□ Assignments to be given and explained before the next meeting
□ Class business, announcements, reminders, etc.

Lesson sequence (These are elements to consider in applying the steps in Fig. 3.7)
□ Time allocation for tasks and activities
□ Variety of activity types (writing, reading, discussion, pair/group work; balance of teacher-fronted vs. student-centered interaction)
□ Transitions between tasks, integration of activities, and general flow
□ Clear and explicit directions for all tasks and activities
□ Easy procedures for setting up pair/group tasks

Contingency plans
□ Ideas for alternative tasks or activities in case there is extra time or something doesn't work

Reflection/Self-evaluation (To be done following the lesson)
□ Observations to keep in mind before planning the next class
□ Notations on successful tasks and techniques
□ Comments on tasks and techniques to modify before trying them again

---

FIG. 3.6. Lesson plan outline/checklist.

Lesson Phase	Teacher Actions	Student Actions
1. Activation of prior learning	• Helps students recall what they have learned or practiced in previous lesson	• Report on prior learning
	• Asks students to demonstrate new knowledge and skills	• Demonstrate new knowledge and skills through practice
2. Preview/warm-up	• Previews new lesson, connecting new material to what was just reviewed or practiced	
	• Guides students in anticipating lesson content by capturing their interest and stimulating thought about the topic and task	• Respond to teacher's prompts
3. Lesson core: Instruction, procedures, participation	• Presents lecture, writing task, or activity	• Responds to teacher's presentation (e.g., by taking notes, asking questions, etc.)
	• Communicates lesson objectives to students	
	• Models task or activity, guiding students to practice new concepts	
	• Asks students to complete the task or activity individually or in groups	• Observe modeling; ask questions
	• Provides opportunities for students to practice using new knowledge/skills independently	• Undertake the task or activity individually or in groups
	• Encourages student involvement, participation, and interaction	• Complete the task or activity independently
		• Elicit teacher's assistance to complete the task, as needed
	• Checks students' understanding of material and concepts at hand	
4. Closure	• Prompts students to reflect on what they have learned or practiced	• Discuss or describe what they have learned or practiced
	• Link new learning to prior learning	• Discuss relationship of new learning to prior learning
5. Follow-up and preparation for next lesson	• Presents additional tasks or activities to practice same concepts	• Complete additonal tasks or activities

FIG. 3.7. Conceptual framework for lesson sequence.

Related to the issue of time management is the principle that lessons should involve some degree of variety in terms of task type and interactional styles (Gower & Walters, 1983; Nunan, 1991; Omaggio Hadley, 1993; Richards & Lockhart, 1994; van Lier, 1996). In an ESL composition course, it is entirely appropriate that a significant amount of class time be dedicated to the practice of writing and the discussion of writing processes. At the same time, teachers need to recognize that allocating large chunks of time to writing in class can become an unproductive use of instructional resources (teacher expertise, class discussion, peer interaction, etc.). Similarly, because many composition courses are not only writing courses but also reading courses (cf. chap. 2), it is reasonable that a substantial portion of class time be dedicated to responding to, analyzing, discussing, and writing about required reading selections. Likewise, class meetings should reflect a careful balance between teacher talk and student talk, with pair/group work, class discussion, and lecture appropriately balanced. Classroom activities should also be linked explicitly to one another and the instructional objectives so that students can see that lessons are internally coherent and connected to overall educational goals. Of course, the use of transitions requires skill on the part of the teacher, but they are a necessary part of the teaching process. Making explicit transitional links is easier when classroom tasks of all types have a discernible purpose and are introduced with clear, easy-to-understand directions and procedures (see chap. 4).

Whenever possible, lesson plans should involve careful and systematic thought about how classroom activities will be set into motion by the teacher and students. It is also sometimes necessary to have a contingency plan in the event that you have extra time or have to abandon something you had planned due to some unexpected circumstance. This alternate task or activity does not necessarily require elaborate advance preparation; it could involve something as simple as asking students to (a) compose a journal entry on the day's topic of discussion, (b) do a focused free writing on the reading assignment completed for homework, or (c) begin the next reading selection or homework exercise. The point here is that, although these are straightforward solutions to the problem, they may not seem so straightforward when you reach the end of your lesson plan with 10 or 15 minutes to spare.

The postlesson reflection phase of instructional planning should not be seen as an addendum, but as an integral part of meeting course objectives and promoting one's own professional development. There are simple yet productive steps that teachers can take in evaluating a lesson plan once the class has ended. For example, decide whether you would repeat the same procedures if you were to teach the lesson a second time or if you would make changes. "Ask yourself how well students responded to the activities you planned and try to diagnose the causes of problems you encountered" (Omaggio Hadley, 1993, p. 489). In addition to recording what worked and what did not work so well, it is extremely helpful to note how long each activity took for future reference. Many teachers use their postlesson observations and evaluation as a starting point for planning the next class period. This practice provides the teacher and his or her students with a sense of continuity from one meeting to the next, facilitating the process of tracking the class' progress through the syllabus. Comprehensive and systematic self-assessment tools can be found in Brown (1995) and Richards and Lockhart (1994).

We now turn to the central pedagogical task of lesson planning: Laying out the actual procedures involved in teaching a group of students something about writing and providing them with some meaningful writing practice in the course of a class period. The framework in Fig. 3.7 presents a general outline for the lesson sequence (i.e., that part of the class period focused not on logistics, but on teaching, learning, interaction, and the production of written discourse). After whatever preliminary business precedes the actual lesson (see Fig. 3.6 and the explanation that follows it), the sequence ideally begins with a procedure in which students are given an opportunity to recall what they have learned or practiced previously. This phase does not necessarily require an elaborate or comprehensive review; it might involve a 5-minute task in which students write a brief summary of the preceding day's discussion or a reading selection, compose a three-sentence reaction to the instructor's feedback on their last essay assignment, or complete a simple quiz on the text to be discussed in groups that day. These are straightforward techniques for reactivating students' knowledge and awareness to facilitate the introduction of new knowledge and promote the practice of new skills.

The preview phase is sometimes indistinguishable from the activation phase, although the preview phase tends to direct students' attention to what lies ahead. An activity that might logically follow on the heels of the summary task described earlier would be a read-aloud of students' summaries in small groups. A follow-up to students' three-sentence responses to comments on their essays might be an introduction to strategies for incorporating teacher feedback into a revised writing, whereas a discussion of the reading quiz answers would be a good way to use that exercise productively to initiate a more detailed analysis of the text. Depending on students' understanding of the material at hand, this portion of the lesson could last 5 to 15 minutes before giving way to the lesson core, where new material is introduced and practiced.

At this point, the teacher might briefly expose his or her objectives to the students before getting into the heart of the lesson. In the case of the discussion summaries and subsequent read-aloud activity, the teacher might initiate students on an essay draft focused on the text that sparked the original discussion. One option would be to brainstorm essay topics; another would be to have students begin writing based on a choice of prompts. To use students' three-sentence reactions to essay feedback and his or her subsequent introduction to incorporation strategies, the teacher might instruct the class to begin working on revised drafts while he or she briefly discusses revision plans with individual students. Following a correction of the reading quiz and a discussion of the solutions, the teacher might scaffold a class or group activity in which students perform a detailed analysis of the text. In all of these hypothetical situations, students are actively involved in tasks that require them to recycle familiar knowledge, practice new skills, and acquire new knowledge.

Like the activation and preview segments, the closure phase may require little time. Closure should also lead naturally and logically to the follow-up. In each case, closure might involve prompting students to identify what they have practiced and why, and clarifying for them the purposes that their work will serve. For the students who began composing first drafts in class, a natural extension of this task would be to complete the drafts and elicit peer responses to them at the next class meeting. Students who were given instruction on incorporating feedback and who conferenced with the instructor might be asked to complete their revisions and reflect on the value of the feedback process. In the case of the students who practiced with text analysis, the teacher might assign a brief written analysis for the next class; he or she might also ask them to apply the same analytic techniques to a different but related text in preparation for a class discussion. In all of these scenarios, the conclusion of each lesson requires the application of previously introduced skills and knowledge and lays the groundwork for future learning.

At this juncture, it is worth reiterating several related points made earlier in this chapter. The first is that, as with designing course syllabi, constructing lesson plans and putting them into action requires considerable flexibility if the teacher is to achieve course goals, meet instructional objectives, and avoid persistent frustration. The second point concerns the planning framework described in the preceding section and schematized in Figs. 3.6 and 3.7. This design is intended to provide a general heuristic for designing lessons and making them successful—it should not be applied zealously or rigidly. Although some type of structure is necessary in planning and teaching writing classes, that structure should be adjusted to accommodate the wide-ranging needs of students and the unexpected events that are inevitable in any classroom (Bailey, 1996; Brown, 1994b). To paraphrase Hillocks' (1995) notion of lesson planning, the most effective teacher of writing is the one who designs lessons as trials, expects them to produce unanticipated results, and applies those results in subsequent teaching. It is through this process that we discover "new options" (p. 125).

SUMMARY

Curriculum design and implementation constitute complex tasks for many composition teachers. To make these tasks more manageable, this chapter has explored principles and procedures for constructing syllabi, course outlines, and lesson plans as a function of identifiable student and institutional needs. We present the following summary statements as a general synthesis of the principles we have covered:

- A clear understanding of learners' backgrounds, needs, expectations, styles, and strategies, as well as institutional requirements (as identified in systematic and ongoing needs analysis) is crucial to the formulation of achievable course goals and instructional objectives.
- Effective course outlines and lesson plans are those that accommodate multiple, recursive writing processes by allowing adequate time for multidrafting, feedback, revision, and exploration of new content.
- Maintaining a clear sense of instructional objectives in constructing daily lesson plans enables the teacher to effect coherent instruction by connecting tasks within lessons and linking each lesson to past and future lessons.
- Flexibility is essential in all aspects of instructional planning.

⇒ AA 3.3

⇒ AA 3.4

Reflection and Review

1. In what ways can student background variables (e.g., primary language, nature and length of prior education, educational and career goals, immigration status, etc.) affect their potential performance in ESL and non-ESL writing courses? How can (or should) a systematic characterization of students' backgrounds inform writing instruction?
2. Describe the roles played by goals and objectives in the planning of syllabi, course outlines, and lesson plans. What advantages are offered by linking goals and objectives to course content and classroom tasks?
3. In what ways can a syllabus and course outline assist the teacher in planning writing instruction? How can they assist students in their writing skill development and general learning?
4. Explain specific methods for operationalizing process-oriented tasks in a syllabus or lesson plan.
5. What are the particular benefits of composing lesson plans and reflecting on their effectiveness in a systematic manner?
6. What are the principal components of a writing lesson and why are they important?

Application Activity 3.1: ESL Writer Profile

Directions.

1. Using the background and situational variables in Fig. 3.1 and the learning styles and strategies variables in Fig. 3.2 as starting points, devise a questionnaire that you could administer to a prospective group of student writers at an institution that you are familiar with, where you teach, or where you would like to teach. You may wish to add specific items that pertain to the population and institution you have in mind. Your purpose in this task is to develop an instrument (or prototype) that you could use in your own classroom teaching and/or action research. Ask for feedback on your questionnaire from your instructor, a colleague, a classmate, and/or possibly an administrator or teacher in the program. Following your revisions, administer the questionnaire to one or more classes of ESL writers, tally the frequency data, and compose a demographic profile of the sample. In your report, suggest an instructional approach that you believe would be appropriate and effective for that group of writers.
2. As in the preceding task, use the background and styles variables outlined in Figs. 3.1 and 3.2 as starting points for developing a questionnaire or interview protocol that you will use to conduct a small-scale case study of an apprentice ESL writer. Secure permission from your student to audiotape one or more interviews

that focus on his or her background as a language learner and writer. In your analysis of the data, discuss how your student's primary language, educational experiences, immigration status, and so on, have influenced his or her progress as an ESL writer. Also try to capture his or her perceptions of the usefulness of the composition instruction he or she has received. Suggest possible instructional implications based on the student's views of the effectiveness of the training he or she has received in writing courses.

Application Activity 3.2: Syllabus Assessment

Directions. Using the syllabus development tools and checklists in Figs. 3.3 and 3.4, examine the sample syllabus in Appendix 3A or a syllabus and course outline for a writing course at your institution or a local school or college. Based on the criteria outlined in this chapter and in Figs. 3.4 and 3.5, discuss orally or in writing the strengths and weaknesses of the syllabus in light of what you know about the institution and the learner population. What are the course goals and instructional objectives? To what extent do course content and organization seem to meet goals and objectives? If you were to teach the course, what changes would you make to the syllabus and why?

Application Activity 3.3: Assessing Lesson Plans

Directions. Compare the lesson plan formats suggested in Figs. 3.6 and 3.7 to the sample lesson plan in Appendix 3B. Alternatively, compare these to one of your own lesson plans or one written by a colleague. Based on the criteria presented in this chapter, assess the strengths and weaknesses of the lesson plan in light of what you know about the course and the students. To what extent does the lesson plan address instructional objectives? What changes would you make to the lesson plan? Why?

Application Activity 3.4: Working With Lesson Plans

Directions.

1. Using the lesson plan formats suggested in Fig. 3.5 and/or Fig. 3.7, compose a simple lesson plan for a writing course that you teach or are familiar with (perhaps by virtue of observational visits). Alternatively, write a plan for one of the following hypothetical situations:
   a. an introductory lesson on writing paragraph-length comparisons for a high school ESL class;

b. a lesson for an advanced-level university IEP course on summarizing outside sources (e.g., textbook chapters, scholarly articles and essays, etc.) in short research papers;

c. a review lesson on paraphrasing and quoting in academic writing for community college ESL students in a prefreshman composition reading/writing course;

d. a lesson on supporting assertions and arguments with evidence for a university composition course made up of NES and NNS students.

2. After writing (and, if possible, teaching) a lesson or unit using the suggested format, explain the revisions you would make to the format. Should any sections be added or omitted? What changes in the format would make the plan easier to use?

APPENDIX 3A: SAMPLE SYLLABUS AND COURSE OUTLINE*

English 110A
Syllabus and Course Outline

English 110A — Fall Semester   Instructor: _____
MWF 11:00 — 12:30

English 110A is a composition course for learners who have achieved the required score on the College Language and Critical Skills Test or completed the prerequisite ESL or Basic Skills courses. This course emphasizes reasoning, clarity, and logical organization in composing out-of-class and in-class essays of various types (e.g., description, narration, illustration, summary, factual, process, comparison, persuasion, etc.). Through extensive reading and writing exercises, students will learn to develop ideas related to a variety of topics and to put those ideas together in coherent, academically appropriate form.

A word about the composing process
Becoming an academic writer involves much more than completing essay assignments and turning them in on time; writing can be an excellent way to sharpen our thinking skills and to discover new ideas. Please consider this course not only as an opportunity to improve the quality of your formal writing, but as a means of enhancing your reasoning skills.
Please keep in mind that writing does not always start out with an outline, nor does it always end up in a nice, clean, grammatically accurate package. Indeed, writing is for many writers an ongoing process that requires constant rethinking and plenty of revision. As a result, we may sometimes need help from others (e.g., other students, an instructor) who can respond to our work and offer new perspectives and ideas. Although we spend a lot of time writing by ourselves, we can make our writing more meaningful by sharing it with others, and by reading and responding to the writing of others. This means using our class activities and assignments as a means of becoming better *readers* as well as *writers*. Much of our time will therefore be spent reading and responding to the work of published authors and to the work of your peers.

Required textbooks and materials
1. Goshgarian & Krueger, 1997, *Crossfire: An argument rhetoric and reader* (2nd ed.)
2. Axelrod & Cooper, 1997, *The St. Martin's Guide to Writing* (5th edition),
3. A one-inch, three-ring binder to serve as your 110A Portfolio (see below)
   Note: These materials are available for purchase at the College Bookstore.

---

*This is a syllabus for a community college freshman composition course open to both NES and NNS students who had completed their ESL requirements.

Requirements and student responsibilities

1. **Attendance** is mandatory. Students need to attend every class session. As per Department and College policy, an excess of three hours of absence will result in exclusion from the class. I will note late arrivals; two late arrivals will count as an hour of absence.
2. **Late work** is not acceptable except under extenuating circumstances (i.e., illness, personal and family emergencies, as defined in the Student Handbook).
3. **Participation** in class discussions and feedback sessions is expected of all students and will be considered in the course grade.
4. **Word processing** is required for all essay assignments that I respond to (usually second drafts) and evaluate (final versions). Of course, you are welcome to submit either handwritten or word-processed Journal entries and essay drafts. Students who have not completed the College Computer Literacy Workshop and received a Computer Lab Pass should do so by the end of the third week of class (this is a departmental policy explained on your registration card).

Grading policy

Your course grade will be determined according to the following weighted scale:

1.	Your choice of two essays from Essays 1-4 to be included in your 110A Portfolio (see below)	50%
2.	Journal	15%
3.	Quizzes & Textbook Exercises	15%
4.	Midterm Exam (Timed Essay)	10%
5.	Final Exam (Timed Essay)	10%

Essays will count for graded credit when the *final version* is submitted to me (this will mean up to three in most cases). In Week 14, you will select two of the four essays for inclusion in your 110A Portfolio (which is due in Week 15); the essay portion of your course grade will be based on the quality of these two essays (which will be rated by the instructor and two other instructors).

Journal entries will be required on a weekly basis. You will make separate entries of at least two pages per week. I will give you a number of topics to choose from; these will focus on selections from *Crossfire*, other course readings, class discussions, and your own writing processes. Please consult the "English 110A Journal Guidelines" for details.

Quizzes will cover reading assignments from both *Crossfire* and *St. Martin's Guide to Writing*.

Textbook exercises will consist of written assignments in *Crossfire* and *St. Martin's Guide to Writing*, group activities, and in-class writing tasks (i.e., impromptu essays, reading responses, etc.).

Midterm & Final Exams will consist of a combination of in-class writing and subsequent revision. Topics and criteria will be given one week in advance of each exam, as per department policy.

Important procedural requirement: You are required to maintain a Portfolio, a one-inch, three-ring binder in which you will organize: 1) your essays, drafts, and feedback sheets; 2) your Journal entries; 3) your quizzes and textbook exercises; and, 4) your midterm exam (I will add your final exam to your Portfolio at the end of the semester before I return it to you). Please see the "English 110A Portfolio Guidelines" for specific instructions.

Course Outline

This outline lists readings from *Crossfire (CF)* and *St. Martin's Guide to Writing (SM)*; daily homework assignments will be given the class day before they are due. Reading and writing assignments listed below are due *on the day indicated*. The decimal number after each essay number reflects the number of the draft (for example, the second draft of Essay 1 is Essay 1.2, etc.)

Week	Day	Topics & Class Activities	Assignments Due
1	M	Introduction to course; In-class writing (Essay 1.1)	
	W	Student interviews; Begin Essay 1.1 revision (Essay 1.2)	Read SM 1-33
	F	Student interviews (cont'd.); The writing process	Read SM 34-64; CF 245-250 (Gaiter)
2	W	Discuss Gaiter essay;	Read CF 1-18; Review SM 1-64
	F	Complete Gaiter discussion; Misconceptions about writing; Correct SM exercises	Read SM 65-98
3	M	Misconceptions about writing; Constructing paragraphs; Practice in-class writing	Read SM 164-166, CF 258-263 (Steele)
	W	Write about Steele; SM Exercises	
	F	Paragraph development; Discuss Steele	Review SM 91-98; Read CF 314-320 (Conniff)
4	M	Paragraph development; Freewriting and journalling	Read SM 167-172; Review Conniff story
	W	Revision strategies; Discuss Conniff; Brainstorm topics for Essay 2 in Journal	Prepare further questions on Conniff for group discussion
	F	Freewriting; Brainstorming & discussion; Begin Essay 2.1	Submit Journal entries
5	M	Peer response training and workshop	Complete Essay 2.1; Read SM 235-258
	W	Introduce Smith story; Peer response (cont'd.)	Essay 2.2; Review SM 235-258 for Quiz
	F	QUIZ on SM; Discuss Smith story	Read CF 474-482 (Smith); Journal entry on Smith
6	M	Analyze Essay 2.3; Discuss Smith story (cont'd.)	Essay 2.3
	W	Discuss Tannen essay; Introduce Farrell story	Read CF 204-210 (Tannen); Journal entry on Tannen; Read SM 419-430
	F	Discuss Farrell story; Examine conventions of written language (SM 422-426)	Read CF 189-193 (Farrell); Journal entry on Farrell; Read SM 422-426; 483-485; Review SM 92-97; 419-430; 481-492
7	M	Freewriting; Discuss essay exam strategies; Discuss sample essay exam questions	Review SM 92-97; 373-383; 413-416; 763-776; Journal entry on male-female differences
	W	Essay exam strategies—Thesis statements; Simulation exercise	Review Smith, Tannen, & Farrell for Midterm
	F	MIDTERM EXAM (Timed essay)	Read SM 384-405; Begin CF 268-271 (Burke)
8	M	Freewrite on Burke essay; Group workshops on pronouns, verbs, punctuation	Review SM 235-258; 373-430; 481-492 for Quiz; Rewrite Midterm Essay using guidelines in SM 44-45
	W	Analyze Midterm Essays for rhetorical patterns; Grammar workshops— agreement, relative clauses, punctuation	Journal entry on Burke; Review SM 235-258; 373-430; 481-492 for Quiz
	F	Editing practice (Worksheet); Group workshops—grammatical patterns, mechanics	Review SM 235-258; 373-430; 481-492 for Quiz
9	M	QUIZ on grammar & mechanics	Journals and Portfolios due; Review Burke
	W	Discuss Burke; Sentence editing (Worksheet)	Read CF 523-533 (Schor); Prepare selected SM exercises (TBA)
	F	Freewriting on Burke; Sentence editing—Faulty predications (Worksheet)	Journal entry on Schor essay; Read SM 282-292
10	M	QUIZ on Schor essay; Discuss Schor	Complete SM 401-402 Exercises; Read CF 263-274 (Murray)
	W	Correct SM (401-402) Homework; Discuss Schor essay (cont'd.)	Journal entry on Murray essay; Review SM 441-465
	F	Brainstorm Essay 3 topics; Begin drafting Essay 3.1	Review SM 259-272; 145-162; Complete SM exercises (TBA)

11	M	Continue drafting Essay 3.1 in class	
	W	Correct assigned SM exercises; Peer review of Essay 3.1 for immediate revision	Essay 3.1
	F	Peer editing of Essay 3.2	Essay 3.2; Read CF 649-655 (Mead)
12	M	Self-analysis of Essay 3.3; QUIZ on Mead story	Essay 3.3; Journal entry on Mead
	W	Discuss Mead; Analyze sample student essays	Read CF 656-663 (Carson); Journal entry on Carson
	F	Analyze sample student essays (cont'd.); Freewriting on Carson essay; Discuss Carson essay	Write response to sample student essay; Read SM 778-780; 567-570; 441-472
13	M	Textual analysis; Discuss Carson essay (cont'd.)	100-word summary of Carson essay; Review SM 447-462
	W	Impromptu essay on Carson essay; Introduce Swift story	Read CF 606-613 (Swift); Journal entry on Swift
14	M	Analyze & discuss impromptu essay; Discuss Swift story	Review for SM Quiz (Handout provided);
	W	QUIZ on selected SM sections; Discuss & plan Essay 4	Read CF 614-619 (Jefferson)
	F	Draft Essay 4.1 in class	Read CF 620-636 (Thoreau); Journal entry on Thoreau story
15	M	Peer review of Essay 4.1; Begin revising Essay 4.1 (Essay 4.2)	Essay 4.1
	W	Preview Final Exam topics; Plan Final Exam strategies	Essay 4.2
	F	Draft Final Exam (Timed Essay — Version 1) in class	Assemble 110A Portfolio
16	M	FINAL EXAM (Revised Final Exam Draft based on instructor comments)	

APPENDIX 3B: SAMPLE LESSON PLAN*

ES 420 Lesson Plan   Week 02: First meeting

OBJECTIVES
- Consolidate students' familiarity with features of academic writing;
- Review and practice academic reading strategies;
- Increase students' familiarity with issues related to immigration policy to build their schemata for the first writing assignment;
- Practice skills for understanding writing assignments and professors' expectations;
- Introduce and practice drafting strategies while initiating the first writing assignment.

WORK PREVIOUSLY COMPLETED
- Students (Ss) have read Textbook Chapter 3 on writing strategies;
- Ss have read and taken notes on a selection of 3 brief immigration articles: "Anti-immigrant initiative sparks fuss," "Measure protects American workers," & "Anti-immigrant mood moves Asians to organize";
- Ss have been introduced to basic principles of academic writing and bibliographic research.

---

*This detailed 2-hour lesson plan is designed for an advanced university EAP writing course for students in political science and policy studies. This lesson takes place in the second week of the term, at the beginning of a thematic unit on U.S. immigration policy.

MATERIALS
- Immigration articles (see above);
- OHP Transparencies;
- Worksheet: "Planning according to the professor's assignment";
- Handout: "Paper #1 Guidelines" (Choice of prompts for first revised essay);
- Students' timed writings (in-class essays) from Week 1 and photocopied model essay;
- Students' reading journals.

CLASS MANAGEMENT
- Homework for next class period (Display on OHP Transparency):
  - Read Textbook, Chapters 4-5;
  - Review Style Manual, Chapter 13 (Bibliographic References);
  - Read and take notes on new article, "Immigration backlash" — Prepare for possible reading quiz;
  - Review instructor comments on Week 1 timed writing.
- Announcements:
  - Class meets in multimedia computer lab next week;
  - Please fill out computer lab questionnaire.

LESSON CORE
1. Attendance and other business [5 min.]
   - Take roll while Ss copy assignments from OHP;
   - Make announcements (see above).
2. Review basic principles of academic writing [10 min.]
   - Ask Ss to report what they remember from last week's lecture on academic writing style and the role of research;
   - Review main points by going over lecture outline on OHP transparency.
3. Discuss immigration articles and reading strategies [20 min.]
   - Ask Ss to take out the 3 articles assigned for today, along with their notes;
   - Ask Ss to select one of the articles and to write at least 3 complete sentences summarizing the author's hypothesis or main argument. Allow 5 minutes for this activity;
   - Ask several Ss to read their summary statements aloud; compare summary statements, noting the different perspectives taken;
   - Elicit Ss' help in reviewing the core issues treated in each article;
   - Ask Ss to describe how taking notes helped them to understand the articles. On OHP transparency, list the advantages of taking notes while reading (e.g., note-taking focuses attention on main points as well as details, aids recall, promotes comparison with other texts, provides a record for research and exam preparation);
   - Point out the need to practice this reading strategy; remind Ss that this skill will help them develop their writing skills.
4. Planning according to the professor's assignment [45 min.]
   - Assign Ss to triad groups;
   - Distribute handout, "Planning according to the professor's assignment." Nominate a S to go over directions;
   - Assign each group to only one or two sample assignments (The worksheet includes three authentic assignments from various policy studies courses);

- Tell Ss that we will record their ideas on the OHP once they're done;
- Allow groups to work for 10 minutes, then bring the class together for plenary synthesis. Make sure to reiterate these points:

  These policy studies assignments require complex papers, not simple essays. Each assignment also involves a different approach to the material. Always remember that you want to do these things when you undertake a writing assignment: a) Prove to the professor that you understand the course material, and b) show that you can form an educated, objective opinion about it.
  Item #1 ("Identify"): Look for words that say what you need to do in your assignment.
  Item #2 ("Suggest"): Try to *narrow* your focus so that you know what documentation to include and how to present it.
  Item #3 ("Write"): Here is where you further narrow your focus, specify the information you will use, decide on what library research you will do. You'll need to make practical decisions and plan your time. How do you get started? Review past readings, make connections, begin taking notes, look at previous assignments completed by classmates, etc. Here are some ideas for getting started:

Free-write	Map
Make lists	Cube
Brainstorm	Outline
Cluster	

  Item #4 ("Go back"): It's a good idea to check the assignment periodically to make sure you're on-track and to see that you're fulfilling the assignment's goals.

5. Assign Paper #1 [20 min.]
   - Distribute "Paper #1 Guidelines" handout; ask Ss to read the directions and selection of prompts before discussing their options;
   - Ask Ss to take out their reading notes on immigration readings covered so far, as well as the "Pro-immigration" and "Anti-immigration" notes taken in class last week;
   - If time allows, ask Ss to do a 5-minute free-write in their journals on the essay prompt that interests them most;
   - Ask Ss to bring the assignment sheet and their notes to class next time for brainstorming/drafting.

6. Return timed writings from Week 1 [10 min.]
   - Return Ss' papers; ask them to read the comments as well as the model essay (on handout);
   - Ask Ss to consider the strengths and weakness of their timed writings and how they can prepare for the next one, scheduled for Week 3;
   - Refer Ss to the Textbook, Chapter 4, on timed writing strategies.

| CHAPTER 4 | Text Selection, Materials Development, and Task Construction in the ESL Writing Class |

Questions for Reflection

- Based on your experience as a student, what aspects of textbooks have you found particularly valuable to your learning? What elements have you found to be unhelpful and/or uninformative? Why?
- If you have had experience as a classroom teacher, identify what features you seek and value in a textbook. In your view, what distinguishes a good textbook from a poor one? Why?
- In what respects might the expectations for an ESL writing textbook differ from those we might have for other types of textbooks? Why?
- Under what conditions can or should a composition teacher supplement a textbook with his or her own reading materials, classroom tasks, and assignments? Justify your response.
- In your opinion, what types of in-class and out-of-class activities and exercises are most productive for inexperienced writers? For experienced writers? Why?
- Discuss techniques and procedures for making writing tasks successful.

INTRODUCTION

This chapter elaborates on the procedures of instructional design introduced in chapter 3. Specifically, it examines elements of materials selection, essential steps in supplementing textbooks, and construction of classroom tasks and formal writing assignments for the ESL writing class. These are also crucial teaching tasks that go hand in hand with designing syllabi, course outlines, and daily lesson plans.

TEXTBOOK SELECTION CRITERIA
AND TYPES OF ESL COMPOSITION TEXTS

Because of the overwhelming quantity of published materials available for ESL writers, evaluating textbooks can be an intimidating experience for classroom teachers who are given this responsibility. Although there are a number of excellent resources for evaluating and selecting textbooks for various types of language and content courses (e.g., Brown, 1995; Dubin & Olshtain, 1986; Omaggio Hadley, 1993; Sheldon, 1988; Skierso, 1991; Williams, 1983), few of these resources specifically target the needs of L2 writing teachers. Therefore, the following sections offer general classification and evaluation procedures geared toward the particular needs of ESL composition teachers. This model of textbook evaluation is divided into two broad categories: instructional needs and textbook features. When combined, the components within these categories should provide teachers with useful criteria for undertaking an efficient selection process.

Instructional Needs: Considering Students' Backgrounds and the Institutional Profile

Clearly, as argued in chapter 3, decisions about how and what to teach in a composition course should be directly informed by the makeup of the learner population, student needs, and institutional goals. Systematic and ongoing needs assessment should obviously be a primary source of data for both course design and materials selection, so that teachers can choose materials that best accommodate goals and objectives (Dubin & Olshtain, 1986; Skierso, 1991). Before attempting to evaluate textbooks, teachers should therefore study their students' backgrounds and the requirements of their programs and institutions by reviewing the findings of a recent needs assessment. In particular, it is invaluable to know about students' prior educational experiences (both in the United States and elsewhere), general proficiency in English, primary language literacy, and ESL literacy skills. It is likewise important to know students' immigration status and the proportion of traditional to nontraditional students (see chap. 3).

A knowledge of these factors, along with programmatic goals, is crucial to a fair assessment of the level of difficulty, thematic content, classroom tasks, writing assignments, and pedagogical orientation of composition textbooks. Equally important is a consideration of a textbook's appropriateness for use in a particular academic program or educational institution. For example, a literary reader/rhetoric, in combination with a standard reference guide or style manual, might be a wholly suitable option for a college/university freshman composition course or an advanced-level IEP course designed to introduce nonimmigrant students to U.S. academic writing. However, this would not be an appropriate choice for a basic, intermediate-level academic skills course in a community college or for a graduate-level EAP writing course for students in the social sciences. For the low-level students, the material might be too difficult because such learners are likely to need more extensive practice in reading and interpreting academic prose and in composing simple texts. In contrast, the reader/rhetoric and style manual combination might match the linguistic proficiency and literacy skills of the social science graduate students, but the literature-based content might be unsuitable for addressing their specialized academic needs as future writers in the social science discourse community. For these reasons, effective textbook selection should start with an accurate profile of the learner population and institutional requirements.

Textbook Types and Features

Effective materials selection depends fundamentally on striking a good match between the attributes of the textbook (and other course materials) on the one hand and the student profile and institutional goals on the other (Sheldon, 1988; Skierso, 1991). One can rely to some extent on general criteria for predicting such a match, but these criteria are most effectively applied with the specific characteristics of textbook types in mind. Because of the numbing array of books and other resources aimed at NES and NNS writers, we first identify the prevalent textbook genres currently available before surveying selection criteria.

Manual, Rhetoric, Reader, Reference Guide, or Combination?   Because of the rapid pace with which instructional approaches and materials have evolved, it would be misleading to represent the following categories as mutually exclusive or static. In fact, the textbook categories characterized in this section overlap significantly: Many textbooks intentionally incorporate the central features of two or more genres. The purpose here is to provide a general but meaningful sketch of dominant textbook types.

• A *manual* may very broadly describe a textbook that aims to teach writing skills, strategies, and processes in a sequential (and sometimes comprehensive) way. ESL manuals or textbooks are frequently geared toward beginning- and intermediate-level writers who are presumed to have little or no experience with prewriting, drafting, feedback, or revision procedures. Some textbooks of this type include reading passages, although many are made up chiefly of tasks and activities designed to give students practice in composing increasingly substantial and complex texts (e.g., paragraphs, essays, research papers, etc.) representing a variety of rhetorical modes (e.g., description, narration, comparison, argument, etc.). Many manuals and textbooks are intended to serve as the primary (or sole) textbook for an entire composition course or course sequence; some are intended exclusively for ESL writers at various levels of proficiency,[1] whereas other titles are aimed at

---

[1]See Dumicich and Root (1996); Frank (1990); Kadesch, Kolba, and Crowell (1991); Latulippe (1992); Leki (1995a); Smalzer (1996); Swales and Feak (1994); and Turkenik (1995).

NES- and NNS-track basic (i.e., "remedial" or premainstream) writers.[2] A common type of manual or textbook is geared toward college freshman composition courses; such a book may be indistinguishable from a *rhetoric*. Generally intended for NES writers, many of these texts also contain grammar sections directed explicitly at ESL writers and promote the extensive use of technological resources.[3]

• *Rhetorics*, often used in conjunction with readers and/or reference guides, typically explicate major rhetorical forms, present sample texts exemplifying particular rhetorical patterns, and offer procedures to show students how to reproduce these patterns in their own academic writing. Stand-alone rhetorics are rarely used in ESL composition courses, even at advanced levels, although they are sometimes used in NES composition courses (often along with a reader). Manuals and readers for both ESL and NES writers increasingly incorporate rhetorical content into a single textbook.[4]

• Composition instructors frequently use *readers* as primary source content at all levels of language proficiency and literacy. A sizable number of readers for both NES and ESL learners are literary anthologies containing short fiction, poetry, drama, personal essays, journalistic writing, editorials, political writing, humor, and numerous other published texts.[5] Readers for both student populations generally include excerpts from authentic sources, although those aimed at NES students may contain entries that are both more numerous and more extensive.[6] An increasing number of readers also feature student writing samples as primary content. These textbooks may contain pre- and postreading activities for treating the literary selections both in and outside of class, frequently providing writing prompts and even complete assignments. Depending on the role of literature in the curriculum, some instructors use a reader in conjunction with a reference manual and/or a rhetoric.

• A *reference guide* is a handbook or spiral-bound volume that contains explanations and examples of grammatical, rhetorical, stylistic, mechanical, bibliographic, and even typographical conventions.[7] Many reference guides additionally

---

[2]See Kirszner and Mandell (1996) and Reynolds (1993).

[3] See Anson and Schwegler (1997); Axelrod and Cooper (1993); Day, McMahan, and Funk (1997); Kennedy, Kennedy, and Holladay (1997); Mangelsdorf and Posey (1997); and Meyers (1997).

[4]Smalley and Ruetten (1995) is just such an ESL course text, combining grammar and rhetoric. Recent NES texts likewise attempt to serve the multiple purposes of rhetoric, reader, and handbook (e.g., Axelrod & Cooper, 1997; Collette & Johnson, 1997; Daiker, Kerek, Morenberg, & Sommers, 1994; Dawe & Dornan, 1997; Ramage & Bean, 1997; Smith, 1997; Tibbetts & Tibbetts, 1997).

[5]ESL readers include Brooks and Fox (1995) and Spack (1994).

[6]Examples include Behrens and Rosen (1997), Goshgarian and Krueger (1997), and Rosa and Eschholz (1995).

[7]Reference guides should not be confused with editing guides, whose use is discussed in chapter 7.

contain exercises for classroom use and/or self-study.[8] Whereas such materials are generally not featured as core textbooks, teachers may require that their students use them as resources in drafting, revising, and editing their writing assignments. Commonly used in mainstream writing courses, reference guides are sometimes built into manuals, generally as appendixes. Reference guides often have numbering systems that teachers can use to refer students to particular topics, rules, examples, and exercises. A growing number of reference guides also provide supplementary sections written specifically for ESL writers.[9]

Textbook Selection Criteria.   Given the staggering range of textbooks and other resources available for teaching writing,[10] it is easy to see why a "one-size-fits-all" approach to materials selection is not likely to produce satisfactory results. Nonetheless, this section describes several overarching features to consider, regardless of the type of book you are considering. It then proposes a more specific set of criteria to be applied selectively by considering particular students and course goals (Fig. 4.1).

It is sometimes possible to eliminate from consideration materials that fail to meet most or all of your general requirements. We suggest asking the following yes/no questions as part of your preliminary screening:

Does the textbook ...

1. Cover topics that you want to address and/or need to include in your course?
2. Present examples of the types of written discourse that you want your students to read, practice, and reproduce?
3. Contain clear, well-constructed activities, tasks, and exercises that will help your students practice the composing skills you have targeted?
4. Provide an adequate number of useful and productive discussion topics/questions and other classroom activities?
5. Provide explanations, strategies, suggestions, and supplemental material that will help you present new material to your students effectively?

If you are unsure about any of these issues, review the questions from your students' point of view: How confidently can you predict that the book's content and tasks

---

[8]Titles designed for NESs include Aaron (1997), Beason and Lester (1997), Dodds (1997), Mulderig (1995), Kennedy, Kennedy, and Holladay (1997), and Lunsford and Connors (1992).

[9]See Hacker (1995).

[10]To keep teachers informed of newly released writing textbooks, the journal *Writing Program Administration* annually publishes an annotated guide to recently published materials (mainly texts for NSs, but ESL and developmental titles are also now included). Also check textbook reviews that regularly appear in the *TESOL Quarterly,* the *Journal of Second Language Writing, English for Specific Purposes, College Composition and Communication,* and *Research in the Teaching of English.* These resources can help you select a few textbooks to request directly from publishers for careful evaluation.

4 = Outstanding   2 = Satisfactory   0 = Totally lacking
3 = Good   1 = Unsatisfactory

Textbook features & Evaluation criteria

	Rating
	4 3 2 1 0

Bibliographic features

1. Authors' qualifications to produce a writing textbook for your student population and institutional setting.   ☐ ☐ ☐ ☐ ☐

2. Availability of accompanying materials, including instructor's manual, workbook, sample assignments, software, etc.   ☐ ☐ ☐ ☐ ☐

3. Completeness (How easily can the course be taught using only the students' version and accompanying materials?)   ☐ ☐ ☐ ☐ ☐

4. Cost-effectiveness (How reasonable is the price of the material given the instructional benefits it offers?)   ☐ ☐ ☐ ☐ ☐

Instructor's manual and accompanying materials

1. Completeness of instructor's manual (Does it include sample syllabi, lesson plans, activities, assignments, teaching techniques, answer keys, etc.?)   ☐ ☐ ☐ ☐ ☐

2. Flexibility and teachability (Does the manual offer guidance on how to present lessons in different ways, according to your particular situation?)   ☐ ☐ ☐ ☐ ☐

3. Feedback and evaluation tools (Does the manual offer guidance on responding to and evaluating student writing?)   ☐ ☐ ☐ ☐ ☐

4. Professional quality, appropriateness, and user-friendliness of student workbook, software, etc.   ☐ ☐ ☐ ☐ ☐

5. Fit between textbook and supplements (Are the workbook, software, etc. designed for easy use alongside the core textbook?)   ☐ ☐ ☐ ☐ ☐

Goals, objectives, and approach

1. Audience appropriateness (Does the text address your student population in terms of age, cultural background, educational experience, writing proficiency, etc.?)   ☐ ☐ ☐ ☐ ☐

2. Match with student needs and expectations (How well does the text address your students' instructional needs, as determined in your needs assessment?)   ☐ ☐ ☐ ☐ ☐

3. Match with instructor's philosophy and approach (How well does the overall design of the text reflect your methodology and instructional practice?)   ☐ ☐ ☐ ☐ ☐

4. Match with institutional expectations (Does the text accommodate the learning and teaching objectives of your department or institution and its methodology?)   ☐ ☐ ☐ ☐ ☐

Content

1. Appropriateness and interest level (Does the text's subject matter include topics, issues, tasks, and skills that will appeal to the interests of your students, encourage their engagement in the course, and promote their own progress as writers?)   ☐ ☐ ☐ ☐ ☐

2. Authenticity (Does the material feature discourse types and styles that accurately represent and explicate the kinds of writing that students will need to read, understand, and reproduce?)   ☐ ☐ ☐ ☐ ☐

3. Variety (Does the material offer an adequate assortment of text types such as literary and academic samples, model essays, etc.)?   ☐ ☐ ☐ ☐ ☐

4. Individualization (Is the book's material varied enough to allow you to individualize your selection of texts and tasks to your students' and institution's needs?)   ☐ ☐ ☐ ☐ ☐

5. Editorial quality and accuracy (Are the texts and explanations in the book well written, academically sound, and factually accurate?)   ☐ ☐ ☐ ☐ ☐

	4	3	2	1	0

Overall design and organization

1. Feasibility (Can the quantity and type of material in the text be covered in the time frame specified in your syllabus?) ☐ ☐ ☐ ☐ ☐

2. Sequencing and progression (Do chapters or units present topics, themes, skills, discursive categories, and tasks in a logical, transparent, and coherent manner?) ☐ ☐ ☐ ☐ ☐

3. Grading (Are the materials and tasks graded according to students' proficiency levels, existing knowledge, and learning needs?) ☐ ☐ ☐ ☐ ☐

4. Schema-building, review, and recycling (To what extent do the text's content, tasks, and assignments facilitate practice of new reading and writing skills while giving students opportunities to practice previously-introduced skills?) ☐ ☐ ☐ ☐ ☐

5. Skills integration and recursion (How extensively are reading tasks interwoven with writing tasks to promote recursive phases of students' writing processes?) ☐ ☐ ☐ ☐ ☐

6. Flexibility (How easily can you reorder chapters, activities, assignments, etc. to fit your syllabus and your students' changing needs? How suitable is the book for students with disparate learning styles?) ☐ ☐ ☐ ☐ ☐

7. Currency (How recent is the material? Does it reflect current composition theory and practice?) ☐ ☐ ☐ ☐ ☐

Apparatus (i.e., tasks, activities, exercises, assignments)

1. Potential for engagement and participation (Do activities and exercises lead to internalization of content and skills by encouraging students to participate actively in reading, discussion, feedback, and composing tasks?) ☐ ☐ ☐ ☐ ☐

2. Promotion of critical thinking (Do classroom tasks and writing assignments promote students' interpretation, application, analysis, synthesis, and evaluation skills?) ☐ ☐ ☐ ☐ ☐

3. Promotion of independent skills development (Do reading and writing tasks and assignments enable students to develop autonomous skills, techniques, and strategies?) ☐ ☐ ☐ ☐ ☐

4. Clarity of presentation (Are the instructions to activities, tasks, exercises, and assignments transparent, easy to understand, and explicit about intended outcomes?) ☐ ☐ ☐ ☐ ☐

5. Feedback tools (Does the text offer models for peer and instructor feedback on student writing? Are they clear and easy to use?) ☐ ☐ ☐ ☐ ☐

Layout and physical attributes

1. Useful front and back matter (Are the table of contents, index, glossary, references, and answer keys well located, clearly organized, and easy to use?) ☐ ☐ ☐ ☐ ☐

2. Layout and visual appeal (Are margins wide enough for note-taking? Are text, white space, and shadowed sections balanced to promote readability? Are figures, tables, and illustrations adequately sized, clearly reproduced, and appropriately positioned?) ☐ ☐ ☐ ☐ ☐

3. Textual enhancements (Are the font and type size readable and appealing? Does the text include highlighting or boldface type to signal key lexical items, etc.?) ☐ ☐ ☐ ☐ ☐

4. Physical features (Do your students prefer a hard or a soft cover? Does the cover have an attractive appearance? Are the format, dimensions, and weight of the book appropriate for the book's intended use? Are the paper and binding of durable and lasting quality?) ☐ ☐ ☐ ☐ ☐

Cumulative value

Overall quality, effectiveness, and suitability (In view of student needs, teaching and learning objectives, institutional expectations, time constraints, your instructional beliefs, etc., to what extent is the book (and accompanying material) pedagogically sound, appropriate, and cost-effective?) ☐ ☐ ☐ ☐ ☐

FIG. 4.1. Textbook assessment guide.

(Note: It is not intended for you to use all of the items in the list. In your textbook evaluation, please select the most relevant items to customize your own assessment checklist.)

will enable your students to achieve your learning objectives? If your answer to one or more of these questions is "no," you might legitimately eliminate the book from further appraisal.

Once you have winnowed prospective selections to a field of two or three books, you can incorporate a more detailed and comprehensive checklist into your evaluation process. The textbook assessment guide displayed in Fig. 4.1 is designed to facilitate both analysis (i.e., systematic examination of the material's content and presentation) and judgment (i.e., deciding whether to accept or reject the material based on relevant criteria; also see Fig. 4.2 for additional ideas on textbook selection). As with many of the other tools and checklists in this book, this guide can be adapted, abbreviated, or expanded depending on the user's individual preferences. Each of the items can also be weighted according to your specific priorities. For example, instructors in search of self-contained materials for a content-based college ESL course may place the highest value on a textbook that contains extensive readings, discussion activities, writing assignments covering related contemporary themes, sample syllabi, and lesson plans. If their primary objective is to supply students with multiple reading and writing opportunities, teachers might weigh content-related criteria more highly than the importance of the instructor's manual or layout features.[11]

Under less-than-optimal conditions, evaluating instructional materials can certainly be "a subjective, rule-of-thumb activity" (Sheldon, 1988, p. 245). However, the use of simple yet systematic materials assessment tools can streamline the process of selecting resources that best meet the needs of students and teachers. A final point to be made here is that effective materials assessment is an ongoing process—one that should take place while the materials are being used as well as after the instructional period has ended (Brown, 1995).

$\boxed{\Rightarrow AA\ 4.1}$

SUPPLEMENTING COURSE TEXTS
WITH ORIGINAL MATERIALS AND TASKS

Many composition teachers seek textbooks or textbook packages that meet all of their instructional needs. Unfortunately, few find exactly what they are looking for. A textbook and its accompanying materials can rarely meet all of a teacher's criteria simply because students', teachers', and institutions' needs vary so widely. According to the dominating conventional wisdom in the field, "there is no such thing as a perfect textbook" (Brown, 1995, p. 166). Moreover, teachers generally want and

---

[11] See Skierso (1991) for a detailed explanation of how to design and use a weighted scale.

Key:
S = Schemata   SA = Social awareness   R = Rhetorical knowledge
L = Linguistic control   WS = Writing strategies

Task types/Functions (according to proficiency level)	Aims				
	S	SA	R	L	WS
Beginning					
• Extract information from written text	√				
• Basic analysis of authentic texts for rhetorical patterns			√		
• Practice using basic rhetorical metalanguage (e.g., topic, thesis, etc.) for describing and analyzing authentic texts			√		
• Brainstorm	√				√
• List	√				√
• Free- or speed-write	√				√
• Cluster ("mind-map") & "cube"	√				√
• Practice sentence-combining				√	
• Write on free and focused journal topics (see chap. 2)	√				√
• Compose simple sentences and paragraphs using models			√		√
• Compose deductive/expository paragraphs on self-selected topics			√		√
• Read and respond to other students' writing (See chap. 6)		√			
• Rewrite and revise					√
• Practice with basic mechanical conventions (e.g., capitalization, indentation, etc.)				√	
• Practice basic editing (e.g., for coherence, grammar, mechanics) (See chap. 7)				√	√
Intermediate					
• All of the task types/functions listed under the Beginning heading	(√)	(√)	(√)	(√)	(√)
• Practice drafting based on the outcomes of prewriting tasks (e.g., brainstorming, listing, free-writing, etc.)					√
• Reproduce multiple text types (e.g., summaries, letters, portions of academic texts, etc.)	√		√		√
• Reproduce paragraph- and essay-length texts following specified rhetorical patterns (e.g., narration, description, comparison, process analysis, etc.)			√		√
• Predict the needs and expectations of an academic reader		√			
• Develop independent prewriting and drafting skills					√
• Respond to the content and form of other students' writing (see chap. 6)		√			
• Practice with more extensive revision (i.e., multi-drafting)					√
• Practice with self-checks for producing revised texts (see chap. 7)			√	√	√
• Practice with more finely-tuned editing for a range of rhetorical, grammatical, and mechanical conventions (see chap. 7)			√	√	√
Advanced					
• All of the task types/functions listed in under the Intermediate heading	(√)	(√)	(√)	(√)	(√)
• Practice identifying, analyzing, and reproducing multiple written genres	√	√	√	√	√
• Expand understanding of a critical reader's expectations (i.e., broaden awareness of academic audience)		√			
• Draft and revise essay-length texts with specific purposes and audiences in mind	√	√	√		√
• Reproduce new text types that will lead to discipline-specific (i.e., non-ESL) writing	√		√		√
• Practice with inductive writing and other rhetorical approaches as complements to deductive text structure			√		√
• Develop confidence and personal voice					√
• Read and review other students' writing; practice applying this experience to one's own writing (see chap. 6)		√			√
• Use self-selected or self-generated checklists for independent revision and editing (see chap. 7)			√	√	√

FIG. 4.2. Task types and functions for the ESL writing class.

93

need to adapt supplemental instructional materials to changing student populations, learning needs, and individual interests. For these reasons, it is essential for teachers to develop basic skills in supplementing and adapting published course texts and in devising techniques for deploying these materials effectively in the classroom.

Locating and Adapting Supporting Materials

The process of supplementing a core textbook or materials package typically begins when an instructor inevitably notices a gap in existing course materials or perceives a mismatch between those materials and students' needs and capabilities (or between the materials and course goals). Consider the hypothetical case of an intermediate-level community college ESL writing course (i.e., a course that precedes an advanced writing course, which in turn would be a prerequisite to mainstream or NES freshman composition). The coursebook is a manual with short, thematically organized reading selections of about 1,000 words in length; writing practice tasks and assignments lead students through multiple drafts of paragraphs exemplifying common academic patterns (e.g., description, exposition, comparison, etc.). After teaching students fundamental techniques of description and reading students' descriptive paragraphs, the instructor determines that the students need more work with reading descriptive texts—in addition to further practice in using descriptive language in their own writing. There are neither further models in the coursebook nor any additional practice assignments. Rather than moving on to another rhetorical pattern, the instructor opts to present a descriptive passage from a popular novel, using it for textual analysis in class (see chap. 2) and as a departure point for an elaborated writing assignment. Without compromising his or her syllabus or course objectives, the instructor integrates this additional practice into lesson planning, treating the supplemental descriptive text as an extension of the corresponding activities in the textbook.

Discerning such gaps or mismatches in the coursebook may thus necessitate locating alternative materials and evaluating them following a process similar to (although perhaps less elaborate than) the one described in the preceding sections. To fill a gap or reconcile a mismatch, teachers can turn to obvious and almost innumerable authentic sources, including:

- competing textbooks and their supplements (i.e., textbooks, materials, and software designed for equivalent courses and similar students);
- textbooks from outside ESL and composition, but related to the topics covered in the writing course (i.e., textbooks used in other academic disciplines, such as the humanities, sciences, social sciences, and the professions);
- authentic academic texts (e.g., scholarly articles, research reports, essays, etc. from academic journals);
- literature (e.g., fiction and nonfiction prose, biography, poetry, drama, essays, reviews, etc.);

- journalistic and periodical literature (e.g., articles and reviews from newspapers, newsmagazines, literary and artistic periodicals, special interest magazines, etc.);
- sample student writing;
- popular media (e.g., film and music recordings, television and radio broadcasts, etc.); and
- recordings and/or transcriptions of planned and unplanned oral discourse (e.g., speeches, lectures, debates, discussions, and conversations).

Formerly, teachers might have had to conduct searches in libraries, bookstores, newsstands, and departmental resource files. In the current electronic age, however, a growing number (if not a majority) of university, college, and even secondary school instructors (as well as their students) have access to the Internet and CDs in their offices, campus computer labs, libraries, classrooms, student centers, coffee houses, and homes (Anderson, Benjamin, Busiel, & Paredes-Holt, 1996). Thus, locating supplemental material is much less of a challenge than selecting and presenting it in a pedagogically sound way.

Features of Task Design: Balancing Process and Product, Content, and Form

This section outlines principles and procedures for constructing pedagogically effective tasks for the writing class, some of which incorporate authentic text types listed in the previous section.[12] Referring to three specific components related to learning processes and their outcomes, Doyle (1983) defined a *task* in terms of:

> a) the products students are to formulate, such as an original essay or answers to a set of test questions (i.e., target tasks), b) the operations (or processes) that are necessary to produce these products, such as memorizing and classifying (i.e., learner tasks), and c) the givens, the resources available to students while they are generating the product, such as a model essay. (p. 162)

For Doyle, academic tasks reflect "the answers students are required to produce and the routes that can be used to obtain these answers" (p. 162). This view of the task as a procedural unit not only parallels social constructionist views of academic literacy (Coe, 1987; Johns, 1993), but also incorporates essential learning and composing processes (cf. chap. 2). Thus, Doyle's (1983) definition of task integrates process and product so that we can avoid an artificial separation of these two crucial elements of academic training.

---

[12]For a discussion of procedures for incorporating authentic texts and promoting reading skills in the L2 writing class, see chapter 2.

From an analytic perspective, a task minimally contains verbal input data (e.g., a reading passage from one of the multiple sources listed earlier, a dialogue, etc.) or a nonverbal stimulus (e.g., a picture sequence), along with an activity related to the input. A task also exposes "what learners are to do in relation to the input," the task's implicit or explicit goals, as well as teacher and learner roles (Nunan, 1989, p. 10). McKay (1994) outlined four global aims that can be used to identify and either adapt or develop meaningful tasks for the composition classroom. These aims include developing students' schemata, social awareness, knowledge of rhetorical patterns, and control of the conventions of written language. We have added a process element to this list: writing strategies. The items shown in Fig. 4.2, categorized according to the principal learning and strategic goals they are intended to achieve, are designed to offer ideas for constructing tasks appropriate for beginning-, intermediate-, and advanced-level ESL writers. Specific sample tasks are presented later. Underlying these task types and functions is the purpose of equipping students with both learning and composing strategies that will help them undertake "real academic assignments" (Horowitz, 1986a) in disciplinary contexts outside the ESL writing class (McKay, 1994).

The Mechanics of Task Design and Implementation

Before constructing and integrating a new task or assignment into a lesson or unit of work, the teacher should first consider the extent to which the exercise will (a) enable students to practice one or more aspects of the composing process (viz., prewriting, drafting, revision, editing, etc.), and (b) test their developing composing strategies (cf. Cooper, 1975). The checklist items in Fig. 4.3 target both general and specific features to bear in mind in selecting content matter (if applicable), narrowing pedagogical expectations, writing directions and procedures, and operationalizing the task. Elements of this checklist can be used selectively for devising both day-to-day in-class and out-of-class tasks as well as more formal writing assignments (i.e., those that will be evaluated and/or require extensive advance planning).

Admittedly, it would be difficult to ensure that all of our classroom tasks and activities meet each of these expectations. However, it is crucial for teachers to remind themselves that meaningful writing assignments (even day-to-day practice activities) "can't be made at random" (Tarvers, 1993, p. 71) and are often more difficult for students to undertake than teachers think (White, 1994; Williams, 1996). In summary, then, writing tasks that engage students and lead to the enhancement of their composing skills rely fundamentally on thoughtful planning and contextualization, in addition to concrete, accessible, and engaging content (Bereiter & Scardamalia, 1987; Chastain, 1988; Clayton, 1993; Leki & Carson, 1994; Paulson, 1992; Peterson, 1995; Raimes, 1983a, 1983b; Reid & Kroll, 1995; Thorne, 1993; White, 1994; Williams, 1996). The sample tasks and assignments described next are aimed at various writing proficiency levels and correspond to one or more phases of the writing cycle. They are designed to reflect the basic properties of sound pedagogical tasks and serve as departure points for devising your own materials, exercises, and assignments.

$\Rightarrow AA\ 4.2$

Does the written task or assignment outline provide explicit information about the following?

1. Practical and mechanical requirements

☐ Timetable for drafts, feedback, graded version, etc.

☐ Format/Rhetorical form (e.g., essay, editorial, summary, lab report, review, etc.)

☐ Suggested length

☐ Presentation conventions (e.g., typing, spacing, etc.)

☐ Documentation, if any (i.e., use of primary bibliographic sources)

☐ Succinct, unambiguous, and easy-to-follow directions and procedural descriptions

2. Discourse context and core content

☐ A topic, subject, or range of options that will interest and appeal to students of all proficiency levels, motivating them to convey existing and/or new knowledge

☐ A topic that covers a wide enough band of course content to engage all students without unfairly privileging some students over others (i.e., a topic, issue, or question that can be written about with ease by using resources presented and covered in the course)

☐ A task that necessitates the production of connected written discourse and presents options that will generate written products that are comparable in terms of complexity, length, and rhetorical mode

☐ A task that requires cognitive and linguistic skills that tap into students' current schemata and competencies, takes them beyond their current level of expertise, and diversifies their rhetorical and stylistic repertoires

☐ Description of the assignment's purpose(s) and the skills that students will demonstrate by completing the assignment

☐ A task that represents or approximates the writing that students will be required to do in their respective disciplines (in school and/or in the workplace)

☐ Justification of the task as a tool for addressing students' educational needs and goals

☐ Intended audience and audience expectations

☐ Identification of the *text's* purpose (i.e., why writers of that type of text compose such texts)

3. Resources

☐ Texts that students can consult for ideas, inspiration, and assistance

☐ Reference to relevant class discussions, workshops, and lectures

☐ Helpful and relevant prewriting, drafting, and revision strategies and tools

☐ Outside help such as peers, writing center tutors, librarians, word-processing and composing software, etc.

☐ Roles that instructor and peer feedback will play in the revision process (if any)

☐ Adequate time for successful completion of the assignment

4. Assessment criteria (if applicable)

☐ Specific elements that will determine the success of the assignment (e.g., topical focus, essential content, adherence to rhetorical patterns, stylistic and grammatical features, length, etc.; please see chap. 8)

☐ Standards to be applied in evaluating the product and the process (e.g., extent of feedback incorporation, departmental or program-wide requirements for word-processing, grammatical accuracy, etc.; please see chap. 8)

FIG. 4.3. Writing assignment checklist.

Developing Materials and Tasks Using Models and Other Authentic Texts

Chapter 2 underscores the essential role played by extensive and intensive reading in the development of ESL composition proficiency. It also describes numerous tools for building instruction on authentic texts and reading techniques. This section focuses more specifically on the use of such texts as the basis for writing exercises and formal composing assignments. It begins with a brief description of the model text as a pedagogical tool and its possible roles in materials development. Models can take the form of both published, professional texts (or excerpts thereof) as well as sample texts written by students or other novice writers (cf. the so-called "product" approaches discussed in chap. 1). Another variety of model is the schematic drawing or diagram of a particular text type sometimes used in combination with a sample text to illustrate topic and discourse structure in a visual medium. A deductively organized expository paragraph, for example, can be sketched out as in Fig. 4.4 (cf. Raimes, 1983b).

The study of models has not been a primary feature of process-oriented writing instruction for reasons that should be addressed before considering their use in any kind of composition course. A serious and justifiable objection to the use of models is that they can lead students to attend mainly (if not exclusively) to rhetorical and/or grammatical form far too early in the composing process, thereby short-circuiting productive invention, drafting, and revision processes (Spack, 1984). If not used judiciously as a complement to a wide range of reading and composing activities, excessive reliance on models can create the impression that writing involves following simple rhetorical formulæ or merely pouring content and ideas into a prefabricated mold—in much the same way that a baker pours batter into a tin to produce muffins of uniform size and shape (Raimes, 1983b). More serious is the real danger that the imitation of models can inhibit writers, preventing them from developing their own voices and productive compositional skills (Eschholz, 1980; Taylor, 1981). It is thus essential to avoid using models mechanically or prematurely. Instead, we should

Topic Sentence:

For maintaining ideal weight and general health, a vegetarian diet is a satisfactory option for many people.

SUPPORTING POINT 1

SUPPORTING POINT 2

FIG. 4.4. Sample model of a deductive paragraph.

Purpose:	Draw students' attention to conventions of pronoun and possessive adjective agreement
Target proficiency level:	Beginning to low-intermediate
Materials:	Sample passage (preferably from an authentic source) with pronouns and possessive adjectives deleted
Procedure:	See directions to students.

Directions to students: *Please read the following paragraph, which is taken from a column by Anna Quindlen, an American writer who often begins her essays and stories with an anecdote like this one. Once you understand the passage, fill in the blank spaces with the appropriate pronoun or possessive adjective.*

> At dusk the deer come down the hillside like bridesmaids, stately in their single file, their eyes straight ahead, their path sure. From the crest of the mountain they cut a diagonal to just above the barn, then disappear into the stand of pines near the center of a field of high grass. Each night for a month, they do this at exactly five minutes to 5, the sky to one side of them turning from hot pink to ashes of roses as they descend. Now, they are nowhere to be seen. (Quindlen, 1988) Note: The missing pronouns and possessive adjectives have been left as in the original text.

	Variation: Controlled composition
Purpose:	Give students guided practice with basic descriptive writing techniques and conventions
Target proficiency levels:	Beginning to intermediate
Materials:	• Model text drawn from published materials or an appropriate student-generated sample • Corresponding photo, drawing, or sketch (optional)
Procedure:	Present the same passage as is, but ask students to rewrite it as a narrative in the past by changing the verb forms (cf. Raimes, 1983b).

FIG. 4.5. Sample task based on a model paragraph.

incorporate them into our teaching as "a resource rather than an ideal" (Watson-Reekie, 1982, p. 12). When thoughtfully presented, carefully constructed model-based exercises involving textual analysis can help ESL writers to understand how rhetorical and grammatical features are used effectively by NES and NNS writers in authentic discourse contexts (Frodesen, 1991; McKay, 1994).

In beginning-level writing courses, model-based tasks may be tightly controlled and should thus be used in combination with many other types of productive tasks. Watson-Reekie (1982) categorized model-based tasks according to focus and emphasis. Focus may consist of grammatical aspects in the model (e.g., verb tenses, relative clauses, pronoun use, etc.), its dominant rhetorical pattern (e.g., deductive vs. inductive, argumentative, etc.), or its communicative function (to describe, narrate, convince, etc.). Paragraph-length exercises such as the one in Fig. 4.5 can activate learners' awareness by directing their attention to sentence- and paragraph-level features of written discourse during prewriting and/or drafting phases. Meanwhile, emphasis may involve tasks aimed at comprehension and analysis of the model often for the purpose of initiating the production process (albeit under restricted conditions). One of the most basic forms of these tasks is to require students to imitate and reproduce model forms by undertaking some kind of structural manipulation. The instructional aim of these tasks (sometimes called *controlled compositions*) is to enhance students' confidence and fluency in the use

Purpose:	Give students guided practice with basic descriptive writing techniques and conventions
Target proficiency levels:	Beginning to intermediate
Materials:	• Model text drawn from published materials or an appropriate student-generated sample
	• Corresponding photo, drawing, or sketch (optional)
Procedure:	Introduce, analyze, and discuss model paragraph as appropriate. See directions to students.

Directions to students: *Please read the paragraph below, which was written by an ESL student about a teacher who was nominated for an award. In the paragraph, the writer describes her teacher and explains why she respects and admires her; she sums up by noting how her teacher has influenced her life. In this assignment, you will compose and revise a similar paragraph about a person you know.*

A teacher who earned my respect and admiration

One of the people I most respect and admire is Eliana Todorov. I met Eliana soon after I arrived in the U.S. and began my junior year of high school. Eliana was my English teacher. Because of her background as an immigrant and her teaching style, she impressed me very much. First, even though I could understand very little English and speak only a few words at first, Eliana was always patient and encouraging. For example, she promised me and the other students that she would help us speak, read, and write English well as long as we worked hard in class and at home. She fulfilled her promise by speaking slowly and clearly, by repeating things when we couldn't understand her, by giving us plenty of practice, and by inspiring us to learn. Second, in our English classes, she led lively and interesting discussions about the stories we read. Often, the students did the talking, while she smiled and listened carefully. Usually, we didn't even realize we were learning so much because we were so interested in the stories and what they meant. Third, Eliana never corrected our mistakes in class; instead, she held private conferences with us to let us know about our progress and how we could improve our speaking and writing skills. Her words were always positive, and she told us often that she was proud of our improvement and hard work. Finally, I admire Eliana because she showed us every day how important it was to believe in our abilities, even when we were discouraged. She told us of her experience as an immigrant from Russia who struggled with English through high school and then the university in the U.S. She found English very difficult at first and couldn't speak it at all, but she learned the language so well that she was able to become an English teacher. In fact, she is the best English teacher I have ever had. Even though I am now in college, I remember her inspiring words and actions because they give me confidence that I will continue to improve my skills and enjoy my learning. (Edited and reprinted with permission.)

Now, think of a person who has influenced you in a similarly positive way. Imagine that this person has been nominated for a special award and that you have been asked by a committee to write a statement of support for him/her. The committee has sent you a list of items to mention and questions to answer. Draft a paragraph in

of word-, sentence-, and paragraph-level patterns and conventions (e.g., new vocabulary, the use of pronouns as referring expressions for full noun phrases introduced earlier in the discourse, or verb tense inflection, as in Fig. 4.5). Obviously, this kind of task should be used sparingly and judiciously to avoid boredom and prevent excessive attention to discrete-level concerns when the development of global fluency is of much greater concern to both students and teacher (MacGowan-Gilhooly, 1991).

Completion exercises based on similar authentic passages may be more helpful and pedagogically sound if designed to guide rather than control (Watson-Reekie, 1982). That is, text-based tasks that ask learners to comprehend *and* do something meaningful and authentic, are more likely to promote their awareness of linguistic and discursive patterns. Often referred to as *guided compositions* (Raimes, 1983b), "structured process" tasks (Applebee, 1986, p. 105), or "the environmental mode" *which you respond to these items in the order in which they appear. In preparing your second draft, you may wish to rearrange the information.*

1. Name one of the people you most respect and admire.
2. When and where did you meet this person?
3. What was this person's profession or job at the time you met him/her? What was your relationship to him/her?
4. Describe at least two reasons for which you respect and admire this person. Try to give specific details or examples.
5. State one of this person's qualities that you try to imitate in your life. Describe why this person is still influential in your life.

Variation: Picture-based guided composition.

Purpose:	Give students guided practice with basic descriptive writing and speculative techniques based on a visual stimulus
Target proficiency levels:	Beginning to intermediate
Materials:	• Photo, drawing, or sketch with easily identifiable images, objects, and/or characters • Corresponding model text drawn from published materials or an appropriate student-generated sample (optional)
Procedure:	Give students copies of a photo, drawing, or sketch. Following a discussion of the image, ask students to write their answers in paragraph form to a set of factual and/or speculative questions. For example, imagine a photo of a woman running down a sidewalk carrying a backpack and an overcoat over her arm. Suitable questions/prompts might include the following: 1. Who is the woman? 2. What is she wearing? 3. Describe her facial expression and her apparent mood. 4. Where is she? 5. What is she doing? Why? 6. Where is she going? Why? 7. What do you think is going to happen next?

FIG. 4.6. Sample guided composition exercise.

(Hillocks, 1986, p. 122), these exercises simultaneously challenge and reassure learners as they generalize the syntactic and rhetorical features apparent in the model. For example, a model-based exercise might require students to answer a set of focus questions or prompts (about a well-defined topic or a picture, as in Fig. 4.6) or complete individual sentences that combine to form a coherent narrative or summary that parallels the model (as in Fig. 4.7). Alternatively, students can be given the first sentence(s) of a model text (as in Fig. 4.7), a paraphrase, or a summary and then be instructed to construct the rest of the parallel text.

⇒ *AA 4.3*

Promoting Fluency With Prewriting Tasks

Controlled and guided tasks such as those presented in the previous section are geared primarily toward beginning- to intermediate-level ESL writers for whom a degree of structure and focus is useful for initiating the writing process. Involving learners in such simple, narrowly defined activities can break down barriers to putting pen to paper or applying one's fingers to the keyboard. Guided and open-ended tasks can also offer students practice in the mechanics of writing, easing their sometimes inevitable fear of getting started (Elbow, 1973, 1981b; Raimes, 1983b). Eventually, of course, all writers need to develop strategies and skills for writing fluently (MacGowan-Gilhooly, 1991). This section examines several types of tasks and exercises aimed at building the fluency of writers at the beginning,

---

Purpose: Give students practice with techniques and descriptive
                                 conventions for giving directions
Target proficiency levels: Beginning to low-intermediate
Materials: • Partially completed sentences presented in
                                   sequence (see below)
                                 • A model text following the format sketched in the
                                   partially completed sentences
                                 • A corresponding picture or map (optional)

Directions to students: *Imagine that you have arranged with a classmate to study for an upcoming exam at your home. Your classmate, a new student, is unfamiliar with your campus and the surrounding neighborhood, so s/he asks you to write detailed directions for him/her in an e-mail message. Your friend asks for specific directions and landmarks because you can't easily re-create a map on e-mail. Complete sentences 1-5, then put them together in paragraph form in a note to your classmate, like the one shown below. Remember to mention details and landmarks that will help him/her find your home easily.*

1. My house/apartment/dormitory room is _____ from campus.
2. You can reach it easily by _____ (walking, cycling, driving).
3. To find it, you'll first _____ (give directions).
4. Look for _____ (give the address) on the _____ side of the street.
5. The house/building _____ (give a description of the building and how to gain access).
6. In case you get tied up or have trouble finding it, _____.

Example: Directions from campus to home

Hi, Sam —
My apartment is about 1-1/2 miles from campus. You can reach it easily by walking or riding your bike. To find it, you'll first take University Boulevard north six blocks, then turn right on 17th Avenue (just past the convenience store). After you turn right on 17th Avenue, go two blocks up the hill to Hannum Lane, where you'll turn left next to a two-story house with a hedge in front. Look for 1726 on the left side of Hannum; it's on the right-hand side of a one-story white house. My building is a three-story, converted brick house with a center door. There's a stairway on the right side leading to my apartment (#4). In case you get tied up or have trouble finding it, you can call me at 555-6214. (Edited and reprinted with permission.)

Variation: Paragraph completion
Purpose: Give students practice composing topically focused
                                 but open-ended texts
Target proficiency levels: Beginning to intermediate
Materials: • A prompt consisting of a topic sentence or thesis
                                   statement such as those listed below
                                 • Model texts drawn from published materials or an
                                   appropriate student-generated sample (optional)
Procedure: Instruct students to begin writing based on a single
                                 prompt or a selection of two or three after studying
                                 one or more models that represent a similar rhetorical
                                 pattern. Alternatively, delay analysis of a model until
                                 after students have composed a first draft, then use
                                 selected samples of students' texts for analysis,
                                 expansion, and revision.

Directions for students: *You have begun corresponding with an e-mail penpal on another campus. S/he has just sent you a message telling you something about him/herself and has requested a reply from you. Draft a one-paragraph response (of 150 to 200 words) that begins with one of the following sentences:*

• The wisest/most foolish decision I ever made was ...
• The most rewarding experience I ever had as a student was ...
• I have chosen to pursue a college degree because ...
• The most serious problem facing this campus/city/state/country is ...
• As a writer, I feel that my greatest strengths/weaknesses include ...

FIG. 4.7. Sample paragraph completion exercise.

intermediate, and advanced levels of ESL proficiency. Of course, these tasks should not be viewed as isolated from one another or as representative of a single, normative approach to teaching composition. Rather, as emphasized in chapter 3, effective writing units and lessons are made up of multiple tasks of varying types. This diversity is essential for building options for recursion into a writing cycle that involves one or more iterations of reading, thinking, invention, drafting, feedback, revision, and so on. (cf. Fig. 3.4). Variety also ensures that instruction includes tasks and interactional patterns that accommodate students' multiple learning styles, strategies, and preferences (Reid, 1995a, 1995b; van Lier, 1995, 1996).

Unstructured Prewriting.   Unstructured prewriting tasks such as freewriting, brainstorming, and listing are hallmarks of process-oriented approaches to writing instruction. Now familiar to many teachers and student writers, these teaching and learning tools are designed to build writing fluency and creativity by stimulating thought and invention under uninhibited conditions (Spack, 1984). When teachers use such unstructured activities to help students develop new knowledge or organize existing knowledge in novel ways, these strategies can "become gateways to open competencies and to better writing" (Tarvers, 1993, p. 78).

For example, *freewriting* (sometimes called *speed writing*) is recommended as a means of releasing students from the compulsion to write correctly (Macrorie, 1980, 1984). Elbow (1973) offered the following description of the technique:

> The idea is simply to write for ten minutes (later on, perhaps fifteen or twenty). Don't stop for anything. Go quickly without rushing. Never stop to look back, to cross something out, to wonder how to spell something, to wonder what word or thought to use, or to think about what you are doing. If you can't think of a word or a spelling, just use a squiggle or else write, "I can't think of it." Just put down something. The easiest thing is just to put down whatever is in your mind. If you get stuck it's fine to write "I can't think of what to say, I can't think of what to say" as many times as you want: Or repeat the last word you wrote over and over again; or anything else. The only requirement is that you never stop. (p. 3)

If you elect to try freewriting with your students, we suggest much shorter sessions (of 3–5 minutes) in which freewriting is focused on a relevant theme or topic and leads directly into a goal-oriented activity such as responding to a reading selection, brainstorming, discussion, or essay planning. Using freewriting productively in an ESL writing class thus requires planning, practice, patience, and perseverance. Clearly, it would not be appropriate to evaluate freewriting. In fact, many teachers do not even collect freewriting so that the process remains a private activity in which students envision *themselves* as the primary audience for these preliminary texts. Other teachers incorporate freewriting into pair and group sharing sessions geared toward probing more deeply into the ideas generated and expanding on them in discussion and writing. We should point out that many NNS writers are initially uncomfortable with freewriting. In fact, some resist the procedure entirely because it contradicts their innate predispositions as planners (cf. Reid, 1995a, 1995b). Thus, teachers should respect their students' divergent learning styles by offering freewriting as but one of numerous options for building writing fluency.

Brainstorming is a related invention technique designed to allow writers to explore different facets of a topic or issue, either privately or collectively. Quite simply, brainstorming can consist of

> producing words, phrases, ideas as rapidly as possible, just as they occur to us, without concern for appropriateness, order, or accuracy. As we produce free associations, we make connections and generate ideas. Brainstorming can be done out loud in a class or group, or individually on paper. (Raimes, 1983b, p. 10)

The basic precept driving the technique is "to list all the ideas that come to mind when a writer thinks about a subject" (Tarvers, 1993, p. 78). In many cases, brainstorming sessions can follow directly on the heels of a freewriting exercise. Prompts may derive from reading selections or models, may lead toward responding to a preplanned essay question, or may be directed at constructing a new topic for writing. During class-wide and group brainstorming sessions, the teacher can assume the role of facilitator and scribe. That is, he or she prompts and probes by asking questions such as, "What do you mean?", "Can you give an example?", or "How are these ideas related?", recording these ideas on the board or an overhead projector transparency.

Regardless of the short-term objective of the brainstorming or stimulus (e.g., reading passage, textbook topic, picture, personal experience, formal essay question), the teacher can encourage students to produce relevant vocabulary, make comments, ask questions, and make free associations at a rapid pace.[13] "The ideas should come quickly and the suggesters shouldn't worry about grammar, spelling or syntactic completeness. Those come at a much later stage" (Tarvers, 1993, p. 79). The outcomes of a brainstorming session (recorded on the board, a transparency, or in students' handwritten notes) can then be used as a randomly ordered set of resources for further freewriting, listing, or more structured prewriting activities.

Like brainstorming, *listing* involves the unmonitored generation of words, phrases, and ideas; it offers yet another way of producing concepts and sources for further thought and exploration. Listing is distinct from freewriting and brainstorming in that students are encouraged to generate only words and phrases so that these can be subsequently classified and organized (even if only in a sketchy way). Consider the case of an academic ESL writing course in which students are first asked to develop a topic related to modern college life and then to compose an editorial piece on the subject. One of the broad topics that emerged in freewriting

---

[13]See Raimes (1983b) for a more extensive discussion of classroom brainstorming techniques and procedures.

and brainstorming sessions was "The benefits and challenges of being a college student." This simple stimulus generated the following list:

1. *Benefits*
   independence
   living away from home
   freedom to come and go
   learning responsibility
   new friends
2. *Challenges*
   financial and social responsibilities
   paying bills
   managing time
   making new friends
   practicing good study habits

This list is obviously preliminary, and its items overlap considerably. Nonetheless, such a list can offer students concrete ideas for narrowing a broad topic to a manageable scope and selecting a meaningful direction for their writing.

Structured Prewriting. Like their less structured counterparts, structured prewriting tasks help students explore topics, generate ideas, gather information, relate new knowledge to existing knowledge, and develop strategies. Structured tasks, however, tend to be more systematic and heuristic in design; they are often aimed at focusing students and preparing them to undertake planning. That is, they scaffold processes and procedures without specifying sequences, contents, or outcomes in an a priori fashion (Hughey, Wormuth, Hartfield, & Jacobs, 1983). Thus, many structured prewriting tools and devices lend themselves particularly well to procedures leading to drafting and composing more formal or extensive writing assignments. Although we characterize these techniques in terms of how they can be presented and practiced in the classroom, most are also designed to be incorporated into the reflective writing that students do outside of class—namely, in their journals or logs (see chap. 2).

Loop writing is a somewhat overlooked technique that piggybacks directly on the freewriting technique introduced earlier, although it involves more focus and systematic recycling. Elbow (1981b) noted that the looping process "is a way to get the best of both worlds: both control and creativity" (p. 59). In loop writing, students are given a broad or narrow subject related to the theme at hand (e.g., tradition, education, social values, etc.); they are then instructed to keep this topic in their minds as they freewrite. If their writing goes off track, they are encouraged to write what comes to their minds until their thinking returns to the focus topic. After the freewriting session, students read their texts and then summarize them in a single sentence. In some cases, students can merely extract a sentence they have already written; at other times, they have to construct a new one. This summary sentence constitutes the first loop in the process. The second loop begins by asking students to freewrite again, this time focusing on the summary sentence as the departure point. Next, students are instructed to complete another iteration of freewriting and summarize the new writing in a single sentence, which subsequently becomes the stimulus for a third loop, and so on. The summary sentences can be compared, expanded, or even discarded as a means of capturing the gist of the writer's thoughts and ideas on the topic. As with any invention or prewriting task, loop writing should be modeled so that students can practice the procedure on their own (Elbow, 1973, 1981b; Spack, 1984). Furthermore, its effectiveness and appeal should be monitored because, like freewriting, it may not be suitable for all (or even most) novice writers.

Clustering (or *branching*) is a structured technique based on the same associative principles as brainstorming and listing. However, it is distinct because it involves a slightly more developed heuristic (Hillocks, 1995). Clustering procedures vary considerably, although their fundamental objective is to equip students with tools for arranging the words, ideas, memories, and propositions that are triggered by a single stimulus (i.e., a piece of information or a topic). As with the other techniques described so far, clustering can first be modeled and practiced in class so that students can eventually incorporate the tool into their own repertoire of invention and planning strategies. The procedure is simple, although its steps are self-defining and can result in a complex representation of relationships and mediated connections. Figure 4.8 shows part of a cluster diagram generated by a pair of students in a second-semester NES/NNS composition course in which they had been asked to plan and draft a collaborative essay. After leading students through a thematic unit on the role of technology in modern society and its institutions, the instructor and students jointly developed the prompt for a revised argumentative essay that would include some library research.

Although the sample in Fig. 4.8 was sketched by a pair of students working together, similar diagrams can easily be developed by individual writers and entire classes. An advantage of a cluster diagram is that it provides a visual medium in which students can classify and cluster ideas and concepts captured in words and phrases. It also stimulates thought about the relationships among elements in a cluster and the connections between clusters, sometimes naturally leading to more structured and formalized planning procedures.

Similarly, *cubing* provides a tool allowing writers to select an effective and appropriate way of approaching a topic, or to combine methods of understanding and treating a topic. In procedural terms, cubing requires students to examine an idea or proposition from six perspectives, each corresponding to one of the six sides of a cube. In cubing, students are encouraged to look quickly at their topic and construct a statement corresponding to each side, or rhetorical perspective, so that

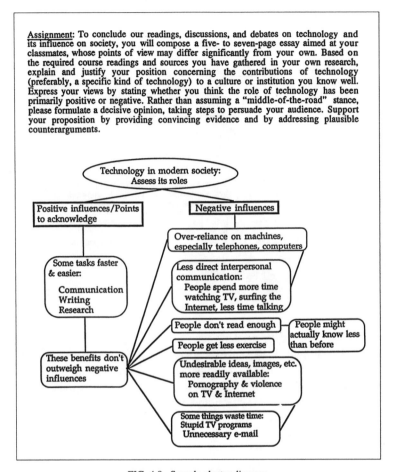

Assignment: To conclude our readings, discussions, and debates on technology and its influence on society, you will compose a five- to seven-page essay aimed at your classmates, whose points of view may differ significantly from your own. Based on the required course readings and sources you have gathered in your own research, explain and justify your position concerning the contributions of technology (preferably, a specific kind of technology) to a culture or institution you know well. Express your views by stating whether you think the role of technology has been primarily positive or negative. Rather than assuming a "middle-of-the-road" stance, please formulate a decisive opinion, taking steps to persuade your audience. Support your proposition by providing convincing evidence and by addressing plausible counterarguments.

FIG. 4.8. Sample cluster diagram.

they generate multiple approaches from which to choose before undertaking planning or drafting. As Fig. 4.9 shows, each side of the cube corresponds to a rhetorical angle and set of focus questions, which are not unlike the classic journalists' questions (i.e., who, what, why, where, when, and how; Tarvers, 1993).

To illustrate the use of cubing, consider how the technique could be applied to a topic such as bilingualism. We could describe bilingualism as a state of linguistic and cultural knowledge that is doubly rich when compared with monolingualism. We could further compare bilingualism to monolingualism by noting the particular intellectual and social advantages of knowing two languages and cultures. To analyze bilingualism, we could point out that it consists of two sets of linguistic and cultural skills, as well as expertise in how and when to use them. We could

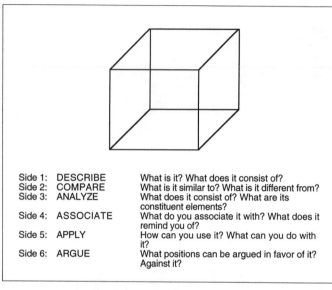

Side 1:	DESCRIBE	What is it? What does it consist of?
Side 2:	COMPARE	What is it similar to? What is it different from?
Side 3:	ANALYZE	What does it consist of? What are its constituent elements?
Side 4:	ASSOCIATE	What do you associate it with? What does it remind you of?
Side 5:	APPLY	How can you use it? What can you do with it?
Side 6:	ARGUE	What positions can be argued in favor of it? Against it?

FIG. 4.9. Cubing diagram.

associate bilingualism with a talent such as knowing how to play a musical instrument (i.e., bilingualism can expand the ways in which one can express oneself). Likewise, bilingual skills can be applied in any social, professional, or educational setting where knowing a single language is not enough. Finally, we could argue that bilingualism is a desirable state of knowledge because it doubles (or multiplies) one's prospects for communicating, granting one access to two or more linguistic and cultural communities. Clearly, thinking carefully about a single issue or problem from multiple angles offers the writer a range of rhetorical directions to follow before planning a piece of writing.[14]

A related technique aimed at developing perceptual skills involves providing students with stimuli that help them "break out of old patterns and find new ways of viewing their subjects" (Tarvers, 1993, p. 80). Topics and foci for such *perspective-taking* activities can range from the wholly concrete and pedestrian to the abstract. Consider the following tasks and prompts, which might be used effectively at nearly any proficiency level:

• Write a detailed one-paragraph description of a familiar object, such as the dashboard display in your car, your computer keyboard, a radio alarm clock, or the control panel on your microwave oven. Compare your description to the real thing and record the differences. What did you miss and why?

---

[14]Neeld (1986) described similar but more elaborate heuristic techniques based on adaptations of classical *topoi*.

- In a single paragraph, describe from memory a familiar place such as your room, the classroom, a coffee shop that you frequent, and so on. Afterward, visit the place you described and add any important details you might have missed. Next, revise your paragraph as if you were writing it for someone who is blind.
- Select a familiar place such as your room, the classroom, or your favorite place to study in the campus library. Describe the location from the point of view of an insect that has landed on a light fixture.
- Select a place you frequent but where you do not spend extended periods of time, such as a local convenience store or your gym. Describe this place from the perspective of the person behind the counter.

For assignments requiring more sophisticated rhetorical patterns than description, teachers can ask students to play devil's advocate by arguing *against* a position they have selected to defend by contrasting their position to that of a classmate, or by identifying the precedents for their own points of view. These tasks can be undertaken in freewriting sessions, in students' writing journals, or even in texts that students submit for the instructor's feedback.

Planning and Drafting Heuristics

Both planning and drafting are addressed in this section because, as research on L1 and ESL composition has consistently shown, planning does not necessarily precede drafting, nor does drafting only begin after a definitive plan for a piece of writing has been formalized (cf. chap. 1). In fact, many effective NES and NNS writers plan as they move through the numerous stages that comprise their drafting processes (Emig, 1971; Flower & Hayes, 1980; Perl, 1979; Rose, 1980; Zamel, 1983). To accommodate the discovery-making processes entailed in making and revising plans as a piece of writing evolves, preliminary planning should take shape flexibly, with reference to whatever structural frameworks or strategies are most effective for student writers. Therefore, we discourage the formal outlining that once characterized both L1 and ESL writing textbooks and instead suggest offering students generous opportunities for drafting—a process in which they can experiment with tools for planning.

That is not to say that outlines and variations on them are not productive for some writers, experienced and inexperienced. Based on textbooks of the traditional and current-traditional paradigms, generations of academic writers might certainly have been led to believe that the only kind of planning (or prewriting, for that matter) consisted of the formal outline, with Roman and Arabic numerals neatly aligned and headings spelled out in complete sentences. In some educational settings, students may still be required to produce and submit such traditional outlines along with lengthy essays and research papers. Teachers who find themselves in this situation might find it useful to present the formal outline as a distinct rhetorical form that follows on a complete piece of prose, rather than a linear structure that must necessarily precede it (Peterson, 1995; Tarvers, 1993; Tate & Corbett, 1988). We offer this suggestion for both practical and pedagogical reasons. Practically speaking, student writers may need to supply outlines along with the writing they do outside the composition course. Moreover, a post hoc outline can serve as a useful advance organizer for readers (e.g., lengthy texts in many disciplines require a table of contents). Meanwhile, the exercise of preparing an outline can give the writer a sense of the hierarchical and linear structure of the themes, propositional content, and rhetorical links that bind the prose text on which the outline is based. Therefore, our point is not to discourage the use of outlines, but to situate them more appropriately as rhetorical and analytic tools to be applied after drafting, rather than as indispensable prewriting heuristics or planning devices.

Informal outlining (i.e., taking notes and sketching out a rough plan for a piece of writing), of course, derives from the classic outline and naturally flows from prewriting and invention procedures. After a brainstorming, listing, clustering, or cubing session, for example, students may have developed enough raw material with which to lay out a plan (however vague) for a piece of extended discourse. Taking a list, cluster, or cube diagram, writers can be shown how to exclude extraneous or unrelated ideas, narrow elements that cohere and can be explicitly linked, and arrange them in ways that exhibit some sort of logic (e.g., chronological, spatial, thematic, categorical, etc.). What emerges from this process may amount to a simple and sketchy list of topics and subtopics that make sense only to the writer. However, as a preliminary scaffold for a developing text, this is all the writer may need to begin the composing process, although significant changes to this plan are likely to occur once he or she begins to produce sentences and paragraphs. The sample plan shown in Fig. 4.10 illustrates how one student writer structured a written draft in which he would compare university studies in the United States to those in Japan, his home country.

University studies in the United States
In general: Rigorous
Application and admission: Personal essay, high school grades, SATs, teachers' recommendations
Professors' expectations: Generally high (students have several assignments, papers, tests, etc. throughout the semester)
Student attitudes: Generally mature and serious
Other points: Tuition can be costly, and high school studies may not be too difficult, so students have to study hard

University studies in Japan
In general: Rigorous only for some students
Application and admission: By entrance examination
Professors' expectations: Generally low (students may only have to take one exam at the end of the year)
Student attitudes: Generally not very serious
Other points: Public universities are not expensive; university entrance exams are very competitive, so getting accepted may be the hardest part

---

FIG. 4.10. Sample student essay plan.

The fairly symmetrical plan shown in Fig. 4.10 evolved from a list that included subtopics, each with specific notes about examples. Obviously, this plan could be rearranged and expanded with further details, although many details might come to the writer's mind during the composing phase. Furthermore, the writer has noted other points that seem important but that haven't been fitted squarely into the plan. In drafting the essay, however, the writer discovered a way to unify the other points as an informative organizing principle that reflected the thesis, which concerned the characteristics that distinguish university studies in the United States from those in Japan.

A variation on this approach to planning, *zero-drafting*, involves creating more text material and reorganizing it. Murray (1985, 1986) recommended this planning technique as a way of reducing students' inhibitions about generating extended prose. Zero-drafting essentially consists of extended freewriting that is done in multiple iterations, much like loop writing. In contrast to loop writing, however, each iteration may focus on a distinct subtopic or rhetorical angle (see the descriptions of cubing and perspective-taking procedures described earlier in this chapter). According to Tarvers (1993), "the goal is simply to get a couple of sheets of writing together, so that the writer can begin working; they're private, safe places to put down ideas" (p. 87). After several focused freewriting sessions, the writer has assembled multiple chunks of text that he or she can shuffle or discard based on the topic and purpose of the writing task. The resulting series of roughly hewn texts may be disjointed and far from what the writer anticipates even as a preliminary product. Nevertheless, these sketchy writings can allow him or her to formulate a structure or work plan that emerges from extended discourse, rather than a series of key words and phrases (as in the informal planning process described earlier).

It is important for teachers to realize that, whereas some writers are comfortable with idea development and planning strategies, others may find them unnecessary and/or unsuitable for their particular drafting styles. That is, not all writers need to execute direct planning strategies by writing ideas, plans, or outlines on paper or computer screen. In fact, some students may have developed internal planning skills that enable them to begin drafting confidently without a written plan (Carrell & Monroe, 1995; Jensen & DiTiberio, 1989). Therefore, planning techniques should be presented and practiced as options; they should not be forced, nor should they become obligatory elements of a writing cycle or syllabus.

Regardless of whether our students are extensive or minimal planners, it is beneficial to provide them with as many opportunities for drafting in class and in the computer writing lab as possible. By doing so, we can model planning and other processes that might reasonably take place as students draft and redraft their texts. For many writers, revision and feedback incorporation might be part of drafting and redrafting processes (see chaps. 5, 6, and 7). We have already suggested tasks and procedures for drafting using journals (see chap. 2). Class time can also be used productively for more focused and structured types of assignments, such as multidraft essays and timed writings. Designating time for in-class drafting is especially valuable for inexperienced writers, who may have an especially difficult time getting started or maintaining momentum on their own. The social context of the classroom can provide the necessary motivation to overcome these obstacles; in-class writing also enables writers to avail themselves of their peers and the instructor if they need help or inspiration (Rose, 1980, 1985).

Some composition specialists recommend leading inexperienced writers through one or more multiple drafting sequences, the phases of which are conducted primarily in class. The purposes of such an extended exercise include providing students with concrete practice and dramatizing how expert writers benefit from multidrafting. For example, it has often been reported that Ernest Hemingway rewrote the final page of *A Farewell to Arms* nearly 40 times before he was satisfied with the passage. Clearly, few composition teachers have this amount of time available to them. However, it is possible to compress a drafting sequence into manageable stages. Tarvers (1993) suggested planning five drafting sessions along these lines:

1. Zero-draft;
2. Shaping draft (students focus on organization, audience, and voice);
3. Style draft (students focus on paragraphing, syntax, and diction);
4. Editing draft (students focus on grammatical, mechanical, and formatting features; see chaps. 6 and 7); and
5. Final draft (students submit the text for inclusion in their portfolios and/or for the instructor's evaluation).

Of course, a multistage drafting sequence such as this should not be seen as a prescription for rigid sequencing (cf. chap. 3). For example, this plan can be reduced or expanded according to students' proficiency level, specific features of the writing task, and amount of class time available. These tasks also lend themselves to the incorporation of teacher and peer feedback (see chaps. 5 and 6), in addition to the introduction of new reading selections and/or model texts.

Finally, to stimulate student writers to generate more specific or complex ideas and encourage them to expand and sharpen their drafting skills, teachers can incorporate focusing and elaboration tasks based on existing drafts. The tasks outlined in Fig. 4.11, inspired by what Murray (1986) called *messing around with texts*, can help writers see their drafts and the written products of others as fluid and evolving, rather than as immovable and confining.

These mid- and between-draft tasks can give students practice in devising alternative ways of moving through the drafting process toward a product that meets their expectations, as well as the expectations of their target audience. Clearly, not all of these tasks will effect changes in what students eventually submit for evaluation, but they offer teachers and students versatile methods of working with drafts.

Imitation & incorporation
Ask students to select a brief passage from the draft of a peer or a related course reading that they particularly like (five sentences or possibly a paragraph). Help them identify why they like the passage by analyzing its content and form. Next, ask them to apply one or more of these techniques or stylistic features into the draft they are currently developing. Optionally, suggest that students include a note to you about what they have done when they submit the draft for your comments.

Text expansion
Ask students to imagine that their editor was very pleased with one or more aspects of their latest piece of writing (e.g., a forceful argument, an appealing set of details, etc.). The editor has asked them to expand on these strengths and insists on a new draft in which these strengths are enriched. Help students think of sources for enhancing these strengths (e.g., a thesaurus for improving word choice and clarity, metaphors to make details and images more vivid, etc.).

Text compression
Instruct students to cut their texts or a particular passage by a significant proportion (e.g., 25%, 50%, 70%) to balance it more appropriately or to meet space restrictions. Assist students with techniques for preserving their original meaning, structure, and voice while conforming to a fiercely enforced limitation. Remind students that writers in many fields are required to meet such demands.

Rhetorical reorganization
Ask students to reorganize major or minor elements of their current drafts. For example, they might rearrange the supporting points of an argument, present its weaknesses before its strengths, or describe objections before introducing solutions. Help students to decide on a structure that works most effectively.

In-progress rhetorical analysis
After a brief incubation period (e.g., one or several days), instruct students to sketch a strategy diagram or informal outline of their drafts. Ask students to analyze these skeletal representations of their texts and to examine how well they express their original intentions. This exercise can highlight gaps that students might not have seen otherwise. To expand on this activity, ask students to share their diagrams/outlines with a peer who evaluates them for logic, clarity, and completeness.

Recasting
Specify a new audience for your students, then ask them to recast their drafts (or a portion thereof) to accommodate this different group of readers. For example, whereas their original draft may have been directed at an audience of their peers, suggest that they recast their texts to appeal to a group of professionals in their field, a university admissions committee, or a scholarship panel. Discuss appropriate changes in perspective, register, tone, and voice.

FIG. 4.11. Focus and elaboration tasks.

Constructing and Evaluating Formal Tasks and Assignments

This final section specifically addresses issues related to the design and implementation of formal writing tasks and assignments, which may differ from the task types so far covered in one or more respects. The term *formal* is used to refer to tasks and assignments designed explicitly to elicit writing that will be used to evaluate students' performance and progress. Formal assignments may likewise involve one or more of the subtasks introduced in the preceding sections, as well as one or more cycles of revision (including feedback incorporation). Clearly, all of the elements presented in the Writing Assignment Checklist (Fig. 4.3) apply equally well to formal assignments as they do to those that lead up to them. Because formal assignments may require substantial forethought, however, several additional points concerning their planning and presentation are worth treating in more detail.

Issues of topic and scope are obviously of eminent importance in planning composition instruction and evaluating student performance. As Raimes (1983a) pointed out, a well-designed assignment can stimulate a range of varied and productive classroom activities, writing tasks, and feedback techniques. To bring about these desirable outcomes, however, the task needs to stimulate thought and scaffold procedures that writers can use to carry it out. It should also establish guidelines with which writers can compare their emergent texts to the assignment's parameters. Based on their extensive analyses of processes leading to the design and assessment of effective writing prompts, Kroll and Reid (1994, 1995) proposed a number of straightforward categories for teachers and evaluators to use in developing fair and meaningful assignments.[15] They suggested addressing the following questions in shaping the composition assignments given in our courses:

- For what *reason*(s)/*purpose*(s) will the writing be assigned?
- How will the assignment fit into the *immediate context*, and in the *overall objectives* of the class? That is, how *authentic* is the prompt?
- In what ways will the content of the prompt be *accessible* to students as it *integrates* classroom learning with long-term goals?
- Who are the *students* who will be responding to the assignment, and what are their *needs*?
- How will the writing processes *engage* the students and *further their knowledge* of the content and skills being taught?
- What knowledge should the students be "*demonstrating*" in their written products? (Kroll & Reid, 1994, p. 21)

It is also worth reiterating the importance of targeting the rhetorical approaches, structures, or modes that are most logical and appropriate for addressing a given topic or prompt. As McKay (1994) urged, writing assignments should collectively (if not individually) "reflect a range of rhetorical development so that students can experiment with different patterns ..." (p. 201).

Related to the issue of topical and rhetorical range is the question of choice. In other words, assignment writers need to weigh the advantages of giving students a single prompt or offering them two or more options or topics. A convincing argument can be made for assigning a single prompt because it gives students practice with tasks that approximate the kinds of academic assignments that are common outside of ESL and English departments (McKay, 1994). This is also a

---

[15]Readers are encouraged to consult these sources for a more detailed set of procedures and guidelines.

viable pedagogical choice when working with beginning- or intermediate-level writers who may work best with a confined topical area and a limited set of rhetorical and grammatical patterns. A single question or prompt is also appropriate when introducing intermediate- and advanced-level writers to unfamiliar rhetorical patterns, particularly when the course syllabus involves unfamiliar content. However, there are important advantages to providing students with a choice. The first and most obvious of these is that students may be more interested in and motivated by a prompt they have selected from a short menu. A related benefit for both the teacher and students is that the texts produced by students are likely to represent a wider variety, making peer feedback more appealing and teacher response a bit less monotonous. At the same time, it is worth recalling one of the criteria listed in the checklist in Fig. 4.3: When students are presented with two or more options, the prompts should be designed and written so that students' texts can be fairly compared on the basis of complexity, length, and rhetorical mode.

As most experienced writing teachers know, "It takes time to design writing assignments that help students reach their writing goals" (Tarvers, 1993, p. 76). Furthermore, it requires skill and experience to construct assignments that capitalize on students' strengths and help them develop ways of overcoming their weaknesses. Nonetheless, we can alert ourselves to common pitfalls and take steps to avoid them. According to Kroll and Reid (1995), one of the most common pitfalls is posing a task that is "too broadly focused for successful student writing within the classroom context" in which it is assigned (p. 29). A related danger concerns flawed and/or underspecified content while another concerns problematic, ambiguous, and/or opaque language. The authentic sample assignments shown in Figs. 4.12 and 4.13 are designed to avoid the pitfalls identified by Kroll and Reid (1995) and exemplify many of the criteria listed in Fig. 4.3.

$\boxed{\Rightarrow AA\ 4.4}$

SUMMARY

This chapter explored principles of textbook selection and supplementation, materials development, and task design, with specific reference to practical approaches and techniques. In keeping with the theme of flexibility introduced in chapter 3, this chapter outlined specific recommendations for designing materials and tasks in ways that recognize the diverse needs of ESL writers, teachers, and educational institutions. Although we have emphasized the importance of systematic planning and execution, we have also attempted to illustrate the value of offering students abundant variety and opportunities for carrying out diverse writing processes in the composition classroom. Our major precepts can be summarized in the following generalizations:

English Studies 420 — Content Writing
Paper 1: Assignment and Guidelines

Directions: Please read the information on this sheet
carefully.

Topic: U.S. Immigration Policy

Background information: Immigration policy and reform
have long been debated in the U.S. Recently, anti-
immigrant sentiment appears to have escalated as federal
and state governments have proposed initiatives to crack
down on illegal immigration and to reduce the current
level of legal immigration into the U.S. For example,
California's Proposition 187, approved by voters in
November 1994, aims to discourage illegal immigration by
denying children of illegal immigrants access to public
education and by refusing to provide health care to
persons who cannot prove their legal status. Although
this initiative is has been challenged in the courts, it
represents but one of movements in numerous states to
curb the influx of new residents, legal and illegal.

Assignment: Based on your own knowledge and the course
readings (see below), analyze current U.S. immigration
policy and speculate on how it might change in the near
or distant future. Because many societies are currently
grappling with immigration issues, you may wish to
include in your analysis comparisons to immigration
policies (or reform movements) in other countries. You
will not be *required* to make comparisons, however.
Identify a problem (or set of problems) in U.S.
immigration policy or in proposed legislation (e.g.,
Proposition 187) and propose a solution. In describing
your solution, outline the specific ways in which your
solution would ameliorate the problem(s) you have
focused on.

Suggestions for getting started: You have already begun
to read about this topic in the course readings; you may
have also composed one or more Journal entries related
to this issue. Review the material you have read as well
as your personal reflections, then consult the list
below to locate more information on the topic. You are
also encouraged to check *The Economist, The New Republic*
and *The New York Times* for recent news items related to
immigration policy/reform.

- As with syllabus design and lesson planning, decisions concerning materials selection and task construction need to be grounded in the teacher's assessment of students' needs and abilities as well as his or her particular approach to writing instruction;
- Textbook evaluation and selection are facilitated by applying both coarsely grained and finely tuned criteria that take into account textbook type;
- Textbooks almost invariably require supplementation and adaptation, which are processes requiring a careful balance of process to product, content to form; and
- Meaningful and productive prewriting tasks and composing assignments can derive from a wide range of authentic models and systematic instructional procedures, none of which should be applied rigidly.

Reading materials/Sources (NB: More recent articles will
be made available.)
  Holmes, Steven. "Anti-Immigrant Mood Moves Asians to
    Organize." *The New York Times,* 3 January 1996.
  Ocasio, Linda, "The Year of the Immigrant as
    Scapegoat," *NACLA Report on the Americas* 29/3
    (November/December 1995): 14-17.
  Rosin, Hanna. "Strange Days." *The New Republic,* 6
    November 1995, 11-12.
  "Welcome to America: The Immigration Backlash," *NACLA
    Report on the Americas* 29/3 (November/December
    1995): 13.
  Wright, Robert. "TRB from Washington: Star Search,"
    The New Republic, 22 January 1996.

Timeline:
  25 January   Bring notes from your reading to class
                    for brainstorming session
  30 January   Exchange Paper 1.1 (=First draft) with
                    classmates; bring one photocopy of
                    your paper to class
  1 February   Critique your classmate's paper in
                    class
  6 February   Submit Paper 1.2 (=Revised draft) to
                    instructor for feedback
  8 February   Individual conferences with instructor
  13 February   Bring newly revised paper to class for
                    proofreading
  15 February   Submit Paper 1.3 (=Second revised
                    version) for instructor's evaluation.

Evaluation criteria:
The "Evaluation criteria for revised writing
assignments" will be used in assessing the final version
of Paper 1. Special attention will be paid to the
following:

Δ A title that reflects your thesis or proposition.
Δ An introductory paragraph (or series of paragraphs)
  that previews your entire paper.
Δ A thesis or proposition stated clearly in your
  introductory section.
Δ Logically ordered paragraphs developed with specific
  and convincing evidence.
Δ Clear distinctions between your ideas and those of the
  authors you cite.
Δ A concluding paragraph (or series of paragraphs)
  summarizing your main points and describing the
  significance of your paper.
Δ A brief bibliography that follows one of the Style
  Manual models.
Δ Adherence to formal conventions of grammar, diction,
  spelling, and mechanics.

FIG. 4.12. Sample formal essay Assignment 1.
(Note: This is the first formal [revised] assignment given in a graduate-level
EAP course for students in political science and policy studies.)

Reflection and Review

1. Compare the principal foci of the textbook genres described in this chapter (viz.,
   manual, rhetoric, reader, and reference guide). Which of these genres is
   likely to be most suitable for your current or future students? Why?

Linguistics 120 — Introduction to Linguistics
Essay Assignment 1

Directions: Identify one of the principal findings or
concepts from Chapter 7 on language typology that most
intrigued or surprised you (e.g., pronoun marking
systems across languages, the noun phrase accessibility
hierarchy, cross-linguistic differences in color
terminology, etc.). Consider how and why your learning
about this research might affect your future learning
(including your formal and informal education, as well
as your professional training).

In an essay of 750 to 1,000 words, please:

1. Describe how your understanding of this finding or
   concept has helped you to understand linguistics as a
   field of inquiry;
2. Explain your learning process;
3. Discuss your reaction to that learning and its
   application to your future learning (in linguistics
   and/or other fields).

Focus on one finding or concept only. Although you are
encouraged to refer to the textbook and Reserve readings
when necessary, please do not merely review typological
research. This is not a bibliographic essay, so please
avoid the temptation to quote sources or to overuse
them. (Remember, I know these sources pretty well!)

Assessment criteria: As per the syllabus, I will assign
numerical grades based on how completely you address the
assignment. Here are my specific expectations:

1. Demonstration of your awareness of the linguistic
   principle under study;
2. The accuracy with which you characterize the
   findings and the guiding theory;
3. Clear and explicit connections between the
   linguistic facts and your personal learning process;
4. Adherence to university-level standards of academic
   English (i.e., grammatical and readable prose,
   accurate spelling and mechanics, APA bibliographic
   style, etc.).

The collection of sample essays on Reserve at the
Library will give you a good idea of how to organize and
express your thoughts.

Essay presentation: Your text should be word-processed,
double-spaced (with 1-1/2" margins), spell-checked, and
headed with your name, section number, and essay title
in the upper left hand corner (no cover sheets, please).

FIG. 4.13. Sample formal essay Assignment 2.

(Note: This is an assignment given by the instructor of an undergraduate linguistics course at a research university.)

2. Discuss the practical and pedagogical justifications for supplementing and/or
   adapting a course textbook.
3. Identify the pedagogical and cognitive benefits of incorporating a variety of
   task types and assignments into the ESL writing curriculum. What do
   students stand to gain from undertaking varied composing processes and
   procedures?
4. Assess the benefits and disadvantages of using models (of one or more types)
   in the teaching of ESL writing.

5. For what theoretical and practical reasons have the boundaries between prewriting and writing, process and product, fluency and accuracy, and so on become blurred? Why is it important for composition teachers to be aware of these relationships?

Application Activity 4.1: Practice Textbook Evaluation

Directions. Select a textbook or set of textbooks being used in an ESL writing course at your institution or an institution in your community. Based on what you know about the institution and its population of writers, decide which of the criteria in Fig. 4.1 might be useful in constructing a manageable textbook evaluation instrument. In consultation with a teacher in the program or a classmate, put together an appropriate set of criteria, which you then apply to the textbook(s) in question. You may wish to substantiate your evaluation with a written prose commentary of no more than one page in which you describe particular features not covered in the evaluation instrument.

Application Activity 4.2: Writing Task Analysis and Assessment

Directions. Locate one or more samples of an authentic in-class or out-of-class task or exercise by requesting one from your instructor, a colleague, or an instructor at an institution near you. Analyze the task in terms of the functions outlined in Fig. 4.2 and the checklist components listed in Fig. 4.3. (You may also wish to use the materials in Figs. 4.5–4.7 and 4.11–4.13 as reference points.) If you feel the task merits revision or further development, modify it according to the outcomes of your analysis. Justify your proposed revisions.

Application Activity 4.3: Writing Task Adaptation

The tasks and prompts shown next, all aimed at composing notes or letters, are designed for both ESL and NES writers. Although they are clearly not designed to serve as academic writing assignments, they might serve as exercises for practicing functions that could be part of more extensive academic tasks (e.g., spatial description, narration in the past, writing observations and requests, etc.).

Directions. Individually, in groups, or as a class, examine the sample writing tasks by addressing the focus questions listed. Next, select one of the prompts and revise it for a specific population of writers with which you are familiar. You may wish to rewrite the directions so that the task addresses a particular rhetorical or grammatical function. Finally, compose a small-scale in-class or out-of-class task of a similar nature that would be appropriate for your target group of ESL writers. The following are focus questions:

1. For what population of writers would the task/prompt be most appropriate? Why?
2. What writing skills and strategies do you think the task/prompt targets?
3. Given the type of writers you have identified, assess the potential effectiveness of the task/prompt.

Sample Writing Tasks.

• Imagine that you are vacationing at a posh resort. Write a postcard to a close friend in which you boast about your luxurious accommodations, the beautiful surroundings, and your many recreational activities. Tell your friend one thing that you especially like about the place and maybe one thing that you are unhappy about.

• Compose a brief e-mail message to a friend whom you have not heard from in several months. Give him or her an update on recent events and describe your daily routine of classes, work, study, exercise, and so on. Ask him or her about recent events in his or her life and request a reply.

• Write a handwritten or e-mail message to a professor requesting an appointment to discuss an assignment.

• Imagine that your housemate or spouse has displayed some unpleasant and messy habits lately, including leaving food and personal effects around your home. Draft a note explaining how you feel about this behavior and ask him or her to show more consideration.

Application Activity 4.4: Writing Assignment Critique

The following sample writing assignments were drawn from a variety of authentic sources, some of which include high school, college, and university courses outside of ESL or English.

Directions. Individually or with a classmate, examine the sample prompts/questions, identifying their specific flaws and weaknesses based on the criteria presented in this chapter. Decide which of the assignments you think could be salvaged after some careful revision, then rewrite two or more of the prompts so that they conform to guidelines that you find acceptable.

1. Out-of-class essay assignment for an undergraduate freshman composition course:
   Critique the college's affirmative action policy.
2. Timed essay exam item for an undergraduate geology course:
   Describe tectonic plate movement. (Do not exceed 500 words.)

3. In-class paragraph topic for an intermediate-level IEP reading/composition course:
   Define *friendship*.
4. Overnight essay assignment for a university undergraduate course in comparative philosophy:
   Do you believe in fate or free will? Explain.
5. Take-home exam item for a community college U.S. history course:
   Using a contemporary federal political issue, demonstrate in one to two typewritten pages what aspects (if any) of the separation of powers doctrine should be changed.
6. Library research assignment for a history of science course at a liberal arts college:
   Write a five- to six-page biographical report on a 20th-century chemist, physicist, or astronomer who has strongly influenced an applied science such as genetics, engineering, computer science, atmospheric science, and so on. Use at least three separate sources. Please be sure that your paper is adequately researched and well written.

Application Activity 4.5: Constructing a Writing Assignment

Directions.

1. Individually or with a partner, select a topic or content stimulus from each of the four ESL proficiency levels listed next.
2. Compose a writing assignment or prompt centered on that topic or content stimulus. Please be specific about procedures, techniques, and apparatus (see Fig. 4.3, Writing Assignment Checklist).
3. Explain the functions and genre(s) that your task would help learners to practice. Specify the goal(s) that your task would achieve.

The following list includes four ESL proficiency levels:

1. *Low ESL proficiency topics/stimuli*
   Objects visible in the classroom
   Numbers
   Dates
   Weather or seasons
   Colors
   Biographical data
   Family relationships
2. *Low-intermediate ESL proficiency topics/stimuli*
   Class demographic information

Personal preferences (e.g., foods, films, etc.)
Health
Travel/transportation
Leisure activities
Career goals
Popular culture
Reasons for studying English
A strange, interesting, or humorous event

3. *High-intermediate ESL proficiency topics/stimuli*
Current events
Facts and topics related to personal interests
Reactions to an academic or nonacademic reading
An admired person/role model
A pivotal moment or event

4. *Advanced ESL proficiency topics/stimuli*
Social problems
Comparison of two opposing points of view
Position on a controversial issue

(Omaggio Hadley, 1993; Tarvers, 1993)

<table>
<tr><td>

CHAPTER

5

</td><td>

Teacher Response to Student Writing: Issues in Oral and Written Feedback

</td></tr>
</table>

Questions for Reflection

- From your own experiences as a student writer, what memories do you have of teacher responses to your texts?
- What types of feedback have you as a writer found most helpful? Most problematic?
- Do you feel that the types of responses (in both content and form) that you have received would also be appropriate for ESL student writers? Why or why not?
- As you think about responding to student writing in your present or future teaching, what questions and concerns come to mind? What do you feel you need to know or do to give your students effective feedback?

PERSPECTIVES ON TEACHER RESPONSE

As discussed in chapter 1, approaches to teaching composition (whether to NES or ESL writers) have changed dramatically over the past quarter century. Despite all of these changes, however, one element has remained constant: Both teachers and students feel that teacher feedback on student writing is essential. Another constant in the area of teacher response has been debate over how to provide the most effective feedback. At what point(s) in the writing process should a teacher intervene, if at all? Should the teacher's feedback be written or oral? Should notes be written in the margins or at the end of the paper? Should teachers respond to students' ideas or their errors, and on which drafts? Should all problems in a student paper be addressed or only some of them? Are complete sentences or correction symbols most effective? Finally, and most important, what types of feedback are of most help to students in the short- and long-term improvement of their writing?

Does Teacher Feedback Help?

Prior to process-oriented instruction, teacher feedback was fairly straightforward. The student would write a paper; the teacher would return it with a grade, errors marked in red, and perhaps a summary comment about what the student had done wrong (or right); and then the student would then write a new paper and repeat the process (cf. Hairston, 1982). Presumably, the teacher hoped that his or her feedback would help the student avoid mistakes and show improvement on the next paper. Early teacher-response research in both L1 and L2 composition was virtually unanimous in concluding that such feedback did little or nothing to help students improve their writing, either in the short or long term, because it was too capricious, too idiosyncratic, too vague, and/or too focused on students' surface-level errors (for L1 research, see Hillocks, 1986; Knoblauch & Brannon, 1981; Sommers, 1982; for L2 studies, see Krashen, 1984; Leki, 1990a; Zamel, 1985).

L1 Research on Teacher Response.   Over the past several decades, a large body of scholarly work on teacher feedback in L1 composing has been produced. This work has included major reviews (e.g., Hillocks, 1986; Knoblauch & Brannon, 1981), book-length treatments (e.g., Anson, 1989; Freedman, 1987), opinion essays including lists of suggestions for effective teacher response (Brannon & Knoblauch, 1982; Greenhalgh, 1992; Hodges, 1992; Lees, 1979; Mallonee & Breihan, 1985; Moxley, 1989), and a wide variety of studies of teacher response (e.g., Beach, 1979; Beason, 1993; Connors & Lunsford, 1993; Hillocks, 1982; Land & Evans, 1987; Sommers, 1982; Sperling, 1994; Sperling & Freedman, 1987; Whichard et al., 1992). Although the methodologies of these studies have ranged widely (from a case study of one student to an examination of 3,000 marked student papers), the body of research together with the opinion and review essays have yielded some general observations and suggestions:

1. Teacher feedback is often problematic, tending to be overly negative, prescriptive, vague, inconsistent, and confusing;
2. Teacher response to student writing is much more successful when it is provided on preliminary and intermediate, rather than final, drafts; and
3. Teacher response may often appropriate (i.e., take over) student texts by being too directive or prescriptive.

Problems With Teacher Response.   An often-cited article by Knoblauch and Brannon (1981) reviewed several dozen research studies contrasting the effects of praise versus criticism, oral versus written commentary, marginal versus end commentary, and grammatical/mechanical correction versus substantive commentary. They came to the discouraging conclusion that, "for all practical purposes, commenting on student essays might just be an exercise in futility. Either students do not read the comments or they read them and do not attempt to implement suggestions and correct errors" (p. 1). Several years later, Hillocks (1986) again reviewed dozens of studies, concluding that "teacher comment has little impact on student writing" (p. 165).

In discourse analytic examinations of teacher commentary, a number of problems have been identified. Sommers (1982) criticized teacher commentary in her study of the responding behaviors of 35 teachers. She found that handwritten comments were "arbitrary and idiosyncratic" (p. 149), contradictory, and too general. She also observed that this feedback fails to prioritize suggestions in terms of their relative importance and that it can "be interchanged, rubber-stamped, from text to text" (p. 152). Sommers argued that such feedback is appropriative, confusing, frustrating, and ultimately ineffective. In a more recent large-scale study of 3,000 marked student papers, Connors and Lunsford (1993) noted a "large number of short, careless, exhausted, or insensitive comments" (p. 215). They further argued that the commentary provided by the teachers in their study was "formalist," "authoritarian," and "antithetical to the reading strategies currently being explored by many critical theorists" (p. 215).

Teacher Intervention at Preliminary Stages of the Writing Process. Despite these grim conclusions, some of the same reviewers as well as various other researchers have argued that teacher feedback on preliminary drafts (i.e., papers that will subsequently be revised) does help students write better revised papers (Freedman, 1987; Hillocks, 1986; Knoblauch & Brannon, 1981; Moxley, 1989; Sommers, 1982). For example, a descriptive study by Beason (1993) showed that students did indeed address teacher comments in their revisions, although the author did not examine whether those changes actually improved the quality of student texts.

Appropriation of Student Texts
Through Teacher Commentary

Many L1 composition researchers have criticized writing teachers for appropriating students' writing through their own feedback, warning them of the dangers of the practice. Sommers (1982) claimed that "teachers' comments can take students' attention away from their own purposes in writing a particular text and focus that attention on the teachers' purpose in commenting" (p. 149). One particular pedagogical practice that leads to such appropriation, according to Sommers, is the indiscriminate mixing in the same essay draft of comments intended to lead to substantive revision and comments about specific errors in grammar and usage. Sommers claimed that such comments "encourage students to believe that their first drafts are finished drafts, not invention drafts, and that all they need to do is patch and polish their writing" (p. 151). Sommers' arguments have led to the widespread pedagogical practice, often explicitly taught to new teachers, of responding only to students' ideas and organization on early drafts and saving feedback on grammar and usage until the final stages of the writing process (cf. Tsui, 1996).

In a companion piece to Sommers' article, entitled "On Students' Rights to Their Own Texts: A Model of Teacher Response," Brannon and Knoblauch (1982) further described the phenomenon of teacher appropriation, arguing that it is demotivating to students:

> By making elaborate corrections on student writing, teachers appear to be showing the discrepancy between what the writing has actually achieved and what ideal writing ought to look like.... But this correcting also tends to show students that the teacher's agenda is more important than their own, that what they wanted to say is less relevant than the teacher's impression of what they should have said.... One consequence is often a diminishing of students' commitment to communicate ideas that they value and even a diminishing of the incentive to write. (pp. 158–159)

To avoid such appropriation, Brannon and Knoblauch advised teachers to "serve as a sounding board" to help writers clarify their intentions, to "see confusions in the text" and to "explore alternatives that [they] may not have considered." They further proposed some general questions that both teachers and student writers can use to evaluate and discuss texts, including, "What did the writer intend to do?", "What has the writing actually said?", and "How has the writing done what it is supposed to do?" (p. 162).

RESEARCH ON TEACHER RESPONSE IN L2 WRITING

Although there has been fairly extensive examination of error correction in ESL writing, there has been surprisingly little research on other sorts of teacher commentary in L2 writing. A number of articles suggest procedures and techniques for responding to ESL compositions, but the majority of these appear to be based largely on L1 research and/or on individual teachers' experience and intuitions. Many L1 studies have serious methodological flaws and are not directly applicable to L2 writing instruction. It is also worth noting that, in a recent collection of articles on second language writing (Leeds, 1996), the only article included on teachers' written response to ESL writing is one that was published over a decade ago (Zamel, 1985). Further, the little research that has been reported is largely unpublished or appears in small, relatively inaccessible journals or PhD dissertations (Tannacito, 1995; cf. Silva, 1993). The research that has been completed on response to L2 student writing has typically taken one of three forms: (a) studies of teacher error correction, (b) studies of teachers' responding practices and (sometimes) the effects of teacher response on subsequent student writing, and (c) surveys of student reactions to teacher feedback.

Studies of Error Correction in L2 Writing

As discussed in chapter 7, research in general has not demonstrated that direct correction of errors by teachers is effective in helping students improve either the accuracy or substance of their writing. Rather, researchers and practitioners have suggested that a variety of indirect, self-discovery techniques can help students learn to monitor and self-correct their own errors (Bates, Lane, & Lange, 1993; Fathman & Whalley, 1990; Ferris, 1995a, 1995c; Hendrickson, 1978; Lalande, 1984). In this way, novice writers can become independent self-editors of their own work, able to function outside of the writing and language classroom (Bates et al., 1993; Lane & Lange, 1993). So far research has suggested that indirect techniques such as noting the location of errors helps students improve their overall accuracy, both on subsequent drafts of the same paper and later assignments (Fathman & Whalley, 1990; Ferris, 1995a, 1997; Lalande, 1982; Robb, Ross, & Shortreed, 1986).

Studies of Teachers' Response Practices

Several studies have examined L2 writing teachers' responding techniques. These studies have included analyses of marked student papers (Cumming, 1985; Zamel, 1985), think-aloud protocols and teacher interviews (Kassen, 1988), and surveys (Ihde, 1994). In her analysis of 15 ESL teachers' responses to 105 student texts, Zamel (1985) noted that research findings agree with the major conclusions drawn concerning the response patterns of L1 writing teachers:

> ESL writing teachers misread student texts, are inconsistent in their reactions, make arbitrary corrections, write contradictory comments, provide vague prescriptions, impose abstract rules and standards, respond to texts as fixed and final products, and rarely make content-specific comments or offer specific strategies for revising the texts ... the teachers overwhelmingly view themselves as language teachers rather than writing teachers. (p. 86)

Like L1 researchers, Zamel recommended that ESL writing teachers avoid mixing substantive comments for revision with grammatical corrections on the same draft, "replace vague commentary and references to abstract rules and principles with text-specific strategies" (p. 95), be flexible in their standards, lead students through several revision cycles rather than simply responding to texts as final products, and establish priorities in their responses.

In a similar but smaller study, Cumming (1985) examined how 10 experienced ESL teachers responded to one ESL student paper, also concluding that most teacher response focused on surface errors. Kassen (1988) studied seven teachers of intermediate French, examining their written comments, think-aloud transcripts, and interview data, again finding that sentence-level concerns were the teachers' primary focus. Ihde (1994) surveyed 50 American and French teachers of ESL and EFL to examine their written feedback practices. The teachers reported that they used a range of techniques to mark papers (including circling, correction symbols, and direct correction), few of them used summary methods (e.g., verbal comments about error patterns), and most of them required students to rewrite their papers.

Thus, the results of the few published studies that directly examined teacher commentary on L2 writing appear to support the critiques of Zamel (1985) and the L1 researchers she cited. That is, writing teachers in general, and particularly ESL writing teachers, are more concerned with providing feedback on error and other sentence-level concerns than with responding to global issues of content and organization.

A recent study by Ferris, Pezone, Tade, and Tinti (1997) analyzed the comments given by one university ESL teacher on 111 papers written by 47 different ESL students (one to three essays per student). In categorizing over 1,500 marginal and end comments, they found that the teacher's comments fulfilled a variety of objectives (to ask for information, make requests/give directives, give information, praise, and give verbal feedback about problems with grammar/mechanics), took several different syntactic forms (questions, statements, imperatives), sometimes included lexical or syntactic hedges to soften a criticism, and were mostly text-specific comments. They also found significant variation in the teachers' commentary across different essay assignments, points in the semester when feedback took place, and students' proficiency levels. They concluded that, "description of teacher response to student writing must go well beyond simple discussions of whether a teacher should respond to 'content' or 'form'" (1997, p. 175) and that "the substance and form of teacher commentary can vary significantly depending upon the genre of writing being considered, the point in the term at which the feedback is given, and the abilities and personalities of individual students" (p. 176).

Studies of the Effectiveness of Teacher Feedback

Experimental studies have examined the effects of different types of feedback on student writing. Cardelle and Corno (1981) examined the progress of 80 beginning- and intermediate-level students of college Spanish. These students were randomly assigned to one of four treatment groups: praise, criticism, praise plus criticism, and no feedback. A combination of praise plus criticism reportedly produced the best effects, as measured by students' posttest scores on both grammar and comprehension. The authors suggested that instructors "provide specific written feedback ... that identifies student errors, guides the student toward a better attempt next time, and provides some positive comment on work particularly well done" (p. 260). Cardelle and Corno also stressed that positive commentary alone (absent any criticism or identification of salient errors) is not sufficiently motivating to college-level second language learners to produce improvement; although criticism alone led to some improvement, it was not as effective as criticism and praise combined. It should be noted, however, that Cardelle and Corno's subjects were NESs studying Spanish in college classes and that ESL writers may have different motivations and concerns (cf. chap. 1; Hedgcock & Lefkowitz, 1994, 1996).

Content Versus Form.   In an experimental design that focused on the issue of content versus form in teacher feedback, Fathman and Whalley (1990) randomly assigned 72 ESL students to one of four treatment groups: no feedback, grammar feedback alone, content feedback alone, and grammar plus content feedback. Students were asked to write a paper and then produce a revised version after receiving one of the four treatments. The first drafts and revisions were then scored separately for grammar (operationalized in terms of the number of errors) and content (as determined by a holistic rating). Although students in all four groups improved in both grammar and content, the biggest improvements were seen in the content group (for content) and the combined group (for both grammar and content). An interesting finding was that students in the no-feedback group produced longer rewrites (based on the number of words) than did any of the other three treatment groups, suggesting that teacher feedback may inhibit the quantity, if not the quality, of student revisions.

The results of this study are also important in addressing the question of when to provide certain types of feedback. As discussed previously, both L1 and L2 scholars had advised teachers to avoid mixing attention to content and form on preliminary drafts of student papers (Brannon & Knoblauch, 1982; Sommers, 1982; Zamel, 1985). However, Fathman and Whalley (1990) concluded that when grammar and content feedback are provided simultaneously, the content of revised texts improves approximately as much as when writers receive content feedback alone. Moreover, a focus on grammar "does not negatively affect the content of writing, suggesting that students can improve their writing in situations *where content and form feedback are given simultaneously....* Grammar and content feedback can be provided ... at the same time without overburdening the student" (pp. 186–187, italics added).

Corrections and Rule Reminders
Versus Meaningful Commentary

Kepner (1991) studied the responses given to the journal entries of intermediate-level college Spanish students. She concluded that, "written error corrections combined with explicit rule reminders" are not effective in improving either students' accuracy or the quality of their ideas. However, she found that consistently providing students with "message-related comments" promotes the development of L2 writing proficiency in terms of both "ideational quality and surface-level accuracy." (1991, p. 310). Kepner further noted that substantive teacher comments in the target language "may serve as a model of correct L2 for the student, while communicating personalized encouragement as well as higher-order questions and meaningful, content-related comments designed to promote critical thinking in the emerging L2 writer" (p. 310).

A discourse analytic study by Ferris (1997) related specific teacher comments to changes made in students' revised drafts (cf. Ferris et al., 1997). In all, 110 pairs of first drafts and revisions written by 47 ESL students (three to six papers per student) on several different assignments were examined. It was found that many of the teacher comments on the first drafts influenced substantive changes in the revisions, and that most of these changes improved the quality of the papers. It was also found that certain types of teacher commentary (positive and "give information" comments) most often led to no change in the revisions and that other types (e.g., requests for information) sometimes led to changes that had negative or mixed effects on the revised essays. The author noted that the results suggest "two conflicting but coexisting truths: That students pay a great deal of attention to teacher feedback, which helps them to make substantial, effective revisions, and that students sometimes ignore or avoid the suggestions given in teacher commentary" (Ferris, 1997, p. 330).

L2 Students' Opinions and Preferences for Teacher Feedback Types

A number of surveys of student opinions and preferences concerning teacher commentary have been undertaken by both L1 and L2 composition researchers. Leki (1990a) reviewed L1 student survey research on reactions to teacher response and painted a rather grim picture: Survey respondents report disregarding their teachers' feedback, having difficulty understanding it, and even feeling hostility toward their teachers' perceived attempts to appropriate their writing. Early L2 surveys (e.g., Cohen, 1987; Leki, 1991b; Radecki & Swales, 1988) have reached similar conclusions. For instance, Cohen (1987) concluded that "the activity of teacher feedback ... may have a more limited impact on the learners than the teachers would desire" (p. 36).

Feedback on Feedback: Preferences for and Reactions to Teacher Feedback

In ESL writing research, surveys of student opinion about teacher feedback have followed two general lines of inquiry. In the first, students have been asked about the types of teacher feedback they prefer to receive (Hedgcock & Lefkowitz, 1994; Leki, 1991b; Radecki & Swales, 1988). The earlier two studies found that students generally preferred feedback on grammar more than on content. However, Hedgcock and Lefkowitz (1994, 1996), who studied L2 writers' preferences and predispositions concerning teacher feedback as well as the types of teacher response they had received, reported that ESL students claim to prefer comments on ideas and organization on earlier drafts and feedback on grammar in later drafts. The authors suggested that their ESL students' reported preferences may have been "a direct reflection of the priorities they thought their instructors were already observing" (1994, p. 155). In other words, as process-oriented, multiple-draft approaches have taken hold in ESL composition pedagogy, some instructors have changed their teaching and responding strategies and have communicated these shifting priorities to their students.

In the second line of student survey research (Cohen, 1987; Cohen & Cavalcanti, 1990; Ferris, 1995b; Hedgcock & Lefkowitz, 1994, 1996), ESL students have been asked about feedback they had been given on their writing. On what aspect(s) of writing had their teachers focused? What had the student writers done in response to commentary they received, and how had they resolved any problems with their teachers' feedback? Again, Cohen's (1987) study offered the most discouraging results: Although most students reported paying attention to their teachers' suggestions, a full 20% did not. Further, the students appeared to utilize "a limited repertoire of strategies for processing teacher feedback" (p. 65). The more recent studies, however, indicate that students appreciate their teachers' responses to their writing, that they find it helpful, and that they claim to pay a great deal of attention to it. Ferris (1995b), who replicated Cohen's (1987) study, noted that students reported a variety of problems in understanding their teachers' comments, but that they employ a wide variety of strategies for resolving these problems (e.g., asking the teacher, tutor, or peers for help; consulting a grammar book or dictionary, etc.). Also, like Hedgcock and Lefkowitz (1994, 1996), Ferris (1995b) reported that students viewed feedback on content and organization to be of great importance, particularly on preliminary drafts.

$\Rightarrow$ *AA 5.1*

PROCEDURES AND TECHNIQUES
FOR WRITTEN RESPONSE

What Should Teacher Feedback Cover?

As discussed earlier, teacher response to student writing needs to cover all facets of students' texts, including issues of content, organization, style, grammar, and mechanics. However, for a variety of reasons, it is neither necessary nor desirable for a teacher to respond to every problem on every draft of a student essay. On early drafts, students most likely will be generating, focusing, and organizing their ideas. A teacher's responses should help them do this by giving them feedback that will lead them to develop their ideas fully and present them effectively. Responses should assist the writer in revising the content of his or her papers. Because major portions of the paper may be changed or moved (or are yet to be written), excessive attention to word- or sentence-level concerns is premature and may even short-circuit the writer's attention from substantive revision to microlevel correction.

However, on later drafts, student writers must be encouraged to proofread, edit, and correct their papers (see chap. 7 for a discussion of rationales, strategies, and procedures for helping students achieve greater degrees of grammatical accuracy in their writing).

Although this discussion separates the issues of responding to student content from response to lexical and syntactic problems (as does most research), it is important to point out that the oft-cited distinction between content and form is largely artificial. For instance, consistent verb-tense errors (form) can cause confusion for the reader about the time frame or immediacy of the action (content). Inaccurate lexical choices (form) can cause major problems in the overall comprehensibility of a text, causing the reader to be unsure of what the writer intended to say (content). Nonetheless, because teachers' strategies for detecting and marking lexical and syntactic errors tend to be different from responding to content issues, the techniques that can be used warrant a separate discussion.

Responding to Content and Organization

Bates et al. (1993) suggested the following general guidelines for responding to the content of ESL students' texts:

1. Write personalized comments;
2. Provide guidance or direction when necessary;
3. Make text-specific comments; and
4. Balance positive and negative comments.

Writing Personalized Comments. When responding to a student's text (whether orally or in writing), it is helpful to think of teacher feedback as the continuation of a dialogue between reader and writer. Many teachers address the student by name at the beginning of an end note; some even sign their own names, as at the end of a personal letter. It can also be appropriate to respond personally to points in the text (e.g., "I like this example," "I'm confused by your argument here," etc.). Finally, a teacher's feedback over the course of several drafts and over the term of the writing class should acknowledge the ongoing relationship with the student and his or her writing (e.g., "You have really cleared up this point since your last draft!").

Providing Guidance or Direction. As previously discussed, a great deal of attention has been given to the alleged appropriation of student texts by teachers through overly directive or prescriptive assignments, advice, and feedback (Brannon & Knoblauch, 1982; Moxley, 1989; Sommers, 1982). In response to this line of argument, both L1 and L2 composition teachers have been trained to avoid directives and prescriptions in their responses to student texts, specifically through stylistic means such as indirectness (e.g., "Can you add a specific example here?")

and hedging (e.g., "An example might help here"). In particular, writing teachers are encouraged to ask their students questions to encourage them to think, rather than give them orders with which they are expected to comply.

Both L1 and L2 scholars have begun to scrutinize these arguments and suggestions, finding that student writers are often uncomfortable with and confused by their teachers' apparent abdication of authority (Delpit, 1988; Newkirk, 1995; Sperling, 1991). In an article entitled "The Myths of Appropriation," Reid (1994) argued that research that characterizes teacher response as "obtuse, negative, and appropriative" (p. 281) fails to acknowledge the larger sociocultural context in which the texts and teacher responses are produced—namely, the writing class. Noting that ESL writers differ from NES writers in their "linguistic, content, contextual, and rhetorical schemata" (p. 282), she asserted that "teachers should accept their responsibility as cultural informants ... in the ESL writing classroom" (p. 275).

Many ESL writers come from cultural traditions in which the teacher's authority is highly valued and respected, and most L2 writers lack confidence in their abilities (Ferris, 1995b). If composition teachers do not give students clear and direct feedback and instructions about how to correct and improve their texts, ESL students may feel that their instructors are incompetent or lazy or that there must be nothing wrong with their papers because they were not told what to fix (cf. Hedgcock & Lefkowitz, 1996). This can result in confusion and resentment on the part of the students. Indirect or inductive response strategies may further confuse students who are not as familiar with English pragmatic patterns. For instance, rather than interpreting a teacher's question in the margin as a request or suggestion, the student may misunderstand the intent of the question or ignore it altogether. These issues pose a dilemma for ESL writing teachers who wish to be clear and helpful without appropriating authorship from student writers. Instructors should be careful to explain their responding practices and strategies to their students (cf. Ferris, 1995b; 1997)—for instance, by telling them that questions in the margins or an endnote are intended to help the writer's thinking but do not always need to be answered within the text. However, the most important questions for ESL writing teachers to consider as they provide feedback are: (a) Will my students understand the intent and substance of my comments and corrections? and (b) Will my feedback help my students meet their writing goals in this paper/course? Only within the context of positive answers to the prior two questions should issues of appropriation be considered.

Making Text-Specific Comments.   A number of researchers (e.g., Fathman & Whalley, 1990; Sommers, 1982; Zamel, 1985) have argued that teachers' comments on student papers are more helpful if they are text-specific. That is, feedback that is directly related to the text at hand, rather than generic comments that could be attached to any paper, tends to produce more effective revisions. Bates et al. (1993) offered the comment "I liked the example about your sister" as an example of a text-specific response and "Good example" as an illustration of a generic comment (p. 24). Although it makes sense that text-specific comments are generally clearer and more helpful to students, we would like to make a few observations about this advice:

1. In a recently completed study, Ferris et al. (1997) found that it was harder than it had first appeared to classify comments as either text-specific or generic. For instance, if the generic comment "Good example" is written in the margin next to the example being praised, it is most likely clear to the writer which specific point is being commented upon. Another example occurred frequently in end notes: "You have a lot of verb tense errors in this draft. I've underlined some examples on the first page." It could be argued that this comment is text-specific (because it refers to a particular error pattern and describes erroneous linguistic forms in the text) or generic (because the same comment could be written on any paper containing verb tense errors). Perhaps the key criterion needs to be whether the comment is clear and helpful to the student, rather than whether it conforms to researchers' notions of what is text-specific.

2. There are also arguments to be made in favor of more general summary comments in written feedback, in which the teacher communicates principles that will carry across drafts and throughout the writing class. After all, teacher feedback on student papers is an important form of communication and instruction, not merely a fix-it manual for a particular essay draft (Kepner, 1991). If every comment on a paper is self-consciously text-specific, it is possible that the novice writer will fail to internalize the concepts being communicated and will not see their relevance to subsequent writing assignments (cf. Aljaafreh & Lantolf, 1994). An example of an end note that provides a balance of text-specific and summary comments is provided in Fig. 5.1.

Balancing Positive and Negative Comments. Much has been written about the importance of placing comments of praise side by side with constructive criticism. L1 critiques of product-oriented response have characterized such re-

---

Julie—

 You have a well-developed draft, with some good examples of your own friendships. However, you need to discuss Viorst's essay more in order to relate it to your own experiences. Your intro and conclusion could both be strengthened. See Guidelines, *pp. 109 & 114 for some suggestions on this.*

 Also, you have many major grammar mistakes. Sentence fragments (incomplete sentences) are the most serious.

FIG. 5.1. Example of an endnote with text-specific and general comments.

sponse as too negative and discouraging to students (Connors & Lunsford, 1993; Sommers, 1982). Studies of L2 students' reactions to teacher feedback have found that L2 writers remember and appreciate encouraging remarks made by their teachers (Cardelle & Corno, 1981; Ferris, 1995b; Hedgcock & Lefkowitz, 1994). However, Ferris noted that a significant minority of her participants described critical comments as being positive, some saying that all of their teachers' comments were positive in that the responses all helped the student writers to improve. This suggests that, although ESL students appear to enjoy and appreciate positive feedback, they expect to receive constructive criticism and are not necessarily offended by it. Some researchers and teachers (e.g., Cardelle & Corno, 1981) argue that providing too much praise, especially at early stages of the writing process, may actually discourage students from revising (e.g., "My teacher liked this part, so I shouldn't change it"). Worse yet, premature praise may confuse novice writers and possibly lead them to resent receiving low marks ("My teacher said lots of nice things about my essay, so why did I get such a low grade?"). The wisest course of action is to provide some praise for students' efforts, but not abandon the teacher's crucial instructional role in the name of equally balancing positive and negative comments.

$\boxed{\Rightarrow AA\ 5.2}$

What Forms Should Teacher Feedback Take?

Types of Feedback.   According to a longitudinal, descriptive study of written teacher commentary (Ferris et al., 1997), responses to students' ideas and organization can take several general forms:

1. Asking for further information.
2. Giving directions, suggestions, or requests for revision.
3. Giving the student new information that will help him or her revise.
4. Giving positive feedback about what the student has done well.

Figure 5.2 provides examples of these types of feedback. These feedback types can also be presented in a variety of linguistic forms (questions, statements, imperatives, or exclamations) and can be softened through the use of a variety of *hedges* (e.g., "Please," "Maybe," as well as modals such as "could," "might," etc.). Moreover, the types of feedback provided can and should vary according to the nature and goals of the student text, the strengths and weaknesses of the individual student, and the shared knowledge of the teacher and student. For instance, Ferris et al. (1997) found that comments and questions requesting further information were more common on papers that discussed writers' personal experiences, whereas comments that provided information to the student writer were found more

Asking for specific information:
What was your friendship like before her illness?
Direction/suggestion or request for revisions:
Can you summarize Barna's essay a bit more in your intro?
Giving information to the student:
Neusner's point here is that college is easy, forgiving, and fun—unlike the real world. This is a different argument from what you discuss here.
Positive feedback:
You have an interesting perspective on Ho's ideas.

FIG. 5.2. Examples of feedback types (from Ferris et al., 1997).

frequently on text-based writing assignments (i.e., papers in which students responded to another author's text). The study also found differences in the amounts and types of feedback given to stronger and weaker writers (i.e., more questions were addressed to the former and more imperatives to the latter). It was further noted that the teacher wrote progressively fewer comments of any single type as the semester continued, perhaps reflecting the fact that in-class instruction and discussion, commentary on earlier papers, and student progress had been occurring, thus making it less necessary for the teacher to offer direction about various issues. With respect to this same point, Reid (1994) commented that:

> A researcher outside the social context of my classroom who examines just my written responses … may classify my comments as erratic, useless, and/or appropriative. The researcher may miss the rationale and the result of the communicative negotiation between the student and the teacher, made within the established and mutually understood content and context of the classroom. (p. 281)

Location of Feedback. Teachers' written responses to student papers can take the form of marginal and/or terminal comments. In Connors and Lunsford's (1993) large-scale study, it was found that some teachers give only marginal comments, some only end comments, and some a combination of both. They also reported that some teachers provide a summative comment at the beginning of the paper to focus the student's attention prior to rereading, noting that such up-front comments were relatively rare in their sample. Reviews of research (Knoblauch & Brannon, 1981; Leki, 1990a) have noted that there is no conclusive evidence that either marginal or terminal comments are preferable or more effective. Based on our own experience, we suggest the following guidelines:

1. If only one form of commentary (marginal or terminal) can be given (e.g., due to an overwhelming number of papers and severe time constraints), a comprehensive and clear end note is perhaps preferable. Because the teacher has more room

to write at the end of the paper than in the margins, the feedback is likely to be clearer and less cryptic, easier to read, and more thorough. In addition, an end note allows the teacher to read the entire paper and select and prioritize the points he or she wants to make in the commentary.

2. That said, however, we strongly recommend a judicious combination of marginal and terminal comments when time permits. Marginal comments have the advantage of immediacy and proximity—the teacher's response can be given at the exact point in the essay where the issue occurs. Foregoing marginal comments forces the teacher to be either too general in the end note (e.g., "You need to explain your examples more clearly") or resort to awkward instructions to direct the student to the relevant part of the text (e.g., "The second sentence in the third paragraph on page two seems out of place and should be moved or deleted"). Figure 5.3 outlines a procedure for teachers to use for combining marginal and terminal comments effectively in responding to student papers.

The Mechanics of Feedback. As teachers have become more conscious of developing effective response procedures, a variety of techniques have been proposed to provide feedback to students. These techniques have included audiotaped oral feedback (as opposed to written comments on papers), comments inserted into the students' computer files (by means of a floppy disk passed back and forth between student and teacher), and comments sent via e-mail. Clearly, all of these techniques have their advantages. In the case of audiotaped commentary, students are provided with listening comprehension practice; in addition, student writers who are more comfortable processing information via auditory rather than visual modes may find such feedback more helpful than written commentary (Reid, 1993b). However, some students may find oral responses frustrating and confusing due to weak aural skills or a more visual learning style. Teacher feedback given on the computer, whether

---

1. Read the entire paper through at least once without writing anything on the paper.
2. Read the paper through again, paying attention to the most important issues of content and organization that you might address.
3. Compose your end note, which should be comprehensive, but selective. Address the points you want to make clearly, but don't overwhelm the student by attempting to address every single problem in the chapter. Focus on the most important issues.
4. Go back and add marginal comments that highlight specific examples of the general points you made in the end note.

FIG. 5.3. Procedure for combining marginal and terminal comments.

via floppy disk or e-mail, has the same visual advantages as handwritten commentary, with the added benefit that the teacher's handwriting will not interfere with students' mental processing of the written message (Ferris, 1995b). Further, providing feedback on the computer can encourage students to become comfortable with technology that can help them improve their writing (see chap. 9 for a more extended discussion of the uses of computers for writing instruction).

With all of these alternative responding techniques, convenience and the availability of technology may be the deciding issues for classroom teachers. Some teachers may find it easier to take a stack of papers with them wherever they go, working on them as they have time. Because of the limitations of time and space associated with audiotape and computer formats, many teachers may find these options to be practical for only a small proportion of their students' assignments. For the composition teacher who has several large classes of students submitting papers every week, convenience is a significant consideration. Furthermore, in many teaching situations, students may not have audiotape players or computers available to them or have equal access to them. However, if we assume that all students have adequate access to technology, the teacher's decisions about whether to use these tools will likely rest on student preferences and learning styles (i.e., for oral vs. written feedback) and on the teacher's preferences and needs as well.

The Tools of Handwritten Feedback.   For the reasons discussed previously, a majority of teacher response is likely to be of the pen-and-paper variety. Even with this more traditional mode of responding, teachers have several choices to make: Will they use pen or pencil—and what color pen? Will they use a separate response sheet or write directly on the paper? Will they use some sort of rubric, coding sheet, or checklist for responses, or will they simply provide verbal comments? Again, research findings do not point to an advantage of a single method over another. Some practitioners insist that using a red pen seems punitive and can inhibit students or make them anxious; others argue that the tone and substance of the response (and the overall relationship between teacher and student) is far more significant than the color of ink used (cf. Hedgcock & Lefkowitz, 1994). As far as response sheets, rubrics, and checklists are concerned, it can be argued that such forms provide teachers and students with a consistent framework and terminology to provide and process feedback. However, it also can be argued that response checklists can limit and inhibit teachers from providing personalized responses appropriate to the student and the assignment given. In Ferris et al. (1997), when a teacher switched from writing end notes directly on the student paper to using a response form (Fig. 5.4), she produced significantly fewer (and shorter) comments (although not necessarily less effective ones). Perhaps more important, if students do not learn or understand the checklist or rubric, the forms can actually be distracting and counterproductive.

Student name:_____ Essay # _____ Draft # _____

1. General comments on content/organization (see essay text for more specific comments):
2. Comments on editing problems. Your most frequent and important errors are underlined (or circled, if there is a spelling error). Your most frequent errors are in the following categories:

Error Type   Frequent Errors

1. Article & nouns
2. Verb forms
3. Punctuation & sentence structure
4. Word form
5. Prepositions

Editing assignments from textbook: _____
Grade (Final drafts only): _____

FIG. 5.4. Example of a teacher response form.

Responding to Students' Grammatical, Lexical, and Mechanical Errors

When and How to Respond to Grammatical Errors.   As discussed earlier and in chapter 7, many process writing advocates feel strongly that teachers should only make comments about ideas and organization on preliminary drafts of student papers. However, several studies of error treatment and its effects on ESL writing suggest that, contrary to the suggestions given by some L1 and L2 researchers, ESL writers do not appear to be adversely affected by feedback on grammar given on preliminary drafts of their compositions (Fathman & Whalley, 1990; Robb et al., 1986). In fact, given the strong preferences that L2 writers have expressed for receiving grammar feedback, its complete absence may actually be upsetting and demotivating (cf. Hedgcock & Lefkowitz, 1996). Given these conflicting arguments, teachers can respond in one of two ways:

1. They can follow the advice of Zamel (1985), Sommers (1982), and others by responding only to student writers' ideas and organization on early drafts, but mitigating the possible negative affective factors of this practice (provided they carefully explain their strategies and accompanying justifications to students).
2. They can blend content and grammar responses on all drafts, but vary the format and emphases of the responses. For instance, on first drafts, they can respond

primarily to content but make a general end comment about the writer's grammar problems (see Fig. 5.5). On later drafts, when the student's ideas are more solidified, the teacher can provide specific sentence-level feedback while still making general comments on the student's ideas (Fig. 5.6).

Irene:

Again, an outstanding essay. Very good examples; excellent analysis of Neusner's arguments. Your final paragraph is a bit of a surprise, since you hadn't mentioned your view about "irresponsible professors" (or supported it with examples) before. This material probably belongs earlier in the essay, during your analysis of Neusner's other points.
In editing, pay special attention to articles and punctuation.
Very good first draft!

FIG. 5.5. First draft end note with general grammar comments.

Irene:

*You've done an excellent job of revising your essay. **The ordering of your arguments makes a lot more sense now, but now you should work on writing a stronger conclusion.***

You need to proofread and edit your draft carefully, looking specifically for the following problems:

- *Missing articles in front of singular count nouns.*
- *Unnecessary "extra" commas—each time you use a comma, ask yourself whether it's really needed in that spot.*
- *Review the comma rules we discussed in class and ask me if you need any help with this.*
- *Be sure to spell-check and proofread for typos before turning in your final draft.*

On the first page of your essay, I've underlined some examples of nouns that are missing articles and of unnecessary commas. I've also circled some spelling/typing errors. You will need to go through your paper carefully after you're done revising and find remaining article, comma, and spelling mistakes.

I have seen real improvement already this semester. Keep up the good work!

FIG. 5.6. Second draft end note with specific grammar feedback
and general comments on content.

As for how to give students feedback about their grammar problems, suggestions abound in the literature. Teachers can choose from checklists of grammar/editing symbols (e.g., Lane & Lange, 1993) or verbal feedback to mark both the location and type of error made. Alternatively, they can merely identify the location of the error by means of underlining or circling the error and/or making checkmarks in the margin (Fathman & Whalley, 1990; Hendrickson, 1978; Hyland, 1990; Keh, 1990). Another option is simply to give general verbal feedback in the margins or end comment about the patterns of error on which the student should focus during editing activities (see Figs. 5.5 and 5.6, as well as the techniques outlined in chap. 7).

$\Rightarrow$ AA 5.3

TEACHER–STUDENT WRITING CONFERENCES

Another important means of giving feedback and instruction to writing students is through one-to-one writing conferences. Over the past several decades, the writing conference has emerged as a popular teaching tool. There are several reasons for its popularity. One is the perception that writing conferences save teachers time and energy otherwise spent in marking student papers. Another is the immediacy and potential for interaction and negotiation that the conferencing event offers. Finally, with the consideration given in recent years to students' learning styles (e.g., Reid, 1995b), it is argued that writing conferences offer a more effective means to communicate with students who are auditory, rather than visual, learners. Some writing instructors feel so strongly about the value of writing conferences that they have suggested doing away with all other forms of in-class instruction to make time for them (e.g., Carnicelli, 1980; Garrison, 1974).

Research on Teacher–Student Writing Conferences: Empirical Trends

A number of studies have examined different aspects of conferencing, including attitudes toward and advantages of teacher–student writing conferences, the discourse of writing conferences, the outcomes and effects of the conferences, and the differing roles and behaviors of teachers and students during the conferences. Early researchers looked at students' and/or teachers' attitudes toward conferencing (Carnicelli, 1980; Sokmen, 1988; Zamel, 1985), concluding with strong endorsements of writing conferences as pedagogical tools because students can ask for on-the-spot clarification and because "dynamic interchange and negotiation" can take place (Zamel, 1985, p. 97).

Other studies have examined the actual discourse of writing conferences, finding predictable characteristics of conferences (Freedman & Katz, 1987), and qualitative differences in the conferences of high- and low-achieving students (Freedman & Sperling, 1985; Walker & Elias, 1987). Three studies (Goldstein & Conrad, 1990; Jacobs & Karliner, 1977; Patthey-Chavez & Ferris, 1997) have linked conference discourse with subsequent revisions of the essay under discussion. These studies have identified qualitative and quantitative differences between high and low achievers (Jacobs & Karliner, 1977) and among ESL students from various cultural backgrounds (Goldstein & Conrad, 1990). These differences manifest themselves in both the nature of the conferences and their apparent effects on student revision. Patthey-Chavez and Ferris (1997) also looked at drafts of subsequent student essays (beyond the revision of the draft discussed in the conferences) to assess the degree to which concepts discussed in the conferences had been appropriated and extended by the student writers. Like Jacobs and Karliner (1977), they found quantitative and qualitative differences in the conferences of high- and low-achieving students. However, they also found that even the low-achieving students showed progress following their conferences with the teacher.

Conferencing Techniques: Suggestions and Criticisms

Early process-oriented concerns, particularly the desire to avoid appropriating students' texts or dictating the terms of the revisions, led to specific suggestions and guidelines for conducting teacher–student writing conferences. For instance, Murray (1985) encouraged teachers to allow students to take the lead in conferences by eliciting student writers' responses to their own writing before offering any feedback or evaluation—a procedure characterized by Newkirk (1995) as being *indirect*. Similarly, Harris (1986) presented a list of nondirective strategies to guide teachers in their one-to-one interactions with students.

However, some composition theorists have expressed concern that in empowering students to retain ownership of their writing, we force them into roles for which they are not prepared and with which they are not comfortable (e.g., Bartholomae & Petrosky, 1986; Delpit, 1988; Newkirk, 1995; Silva, 1997). In ESL writing research, scholars have argued that nondirective approaches to teaching and responding to student writing leave L2 writers ill-prepared to deal with demands for either linguistic accuracy or for the reading, writing, and thinking skills expected by subject-matter professors (Eskey, 1983; Ferris, 1995b, 1997; Horowitz, 1986c; Johns, 1995a).

Although most previous research on response to ESL student writing has examined teachers' written feedback, it is safe to assume that students may have problems with adequate comprehension of oral feedback even though the conferencing context allows them increased opportunities to request clarification. Goldstein and Conrad (1990) pointed out that, "ESL students bring with them diverse cultures and languages ... that potentially affect how students conference or how their teachers respond to them" (p. 459). For instance, some students may have strong inhibitions against questioning or arguing with a teacher in any situation, especially a one-to-one conference. Meanwhile, others may feel that teachers' comments or corrections are to be incorporated verbatim into their texts because of instructors' superior knowledge and authority.

Implementing Writing Conferences: Issues and Options

If a teacher wants to incorporate writing conferences into the writing class, there are several practical issues to consider. The first is whether to provide feedback to all students in this manner. Some students would no doubt enjoy the opportunity to discuss their writing face to face with their teacher, both to get individual attention and clear up any problems. Meanwhile, others might prefer written feedback because (a) they find one-to-one discussions with their teacher intimidating, (b) they prefer seeing feedback in writing, or (c) they might forget what they have discussed with the teacher during the conference. There are several options for sorting through these issues. A teacher can ask the students at the beginning of the term whether they prefer written or oral feedback or some combination of both. For students who are unsure, the teacher can provide written feedback on one assignment and oral feedback on the next. For students who feel nervous about conference dynamics, ideas to relieve their anxieties might include conferencing with pairs of students (also adding a peer feedback dynamic to the mix) and allowing students to audiotape or take notes during the conference.

Logistics: When, Where, and How Often?   Along with the question of whom to conduct conferences with, a teacher must decide when, where, and how often to hold such conferences. Options range from holding conferences every week or at every class session (the "Garrison Method," in which students write during class and come up to the teacher's desk for a conference whenever they feel the need), to holding them at regular intervals (e.g., seeing each student during office hours on a 3- or 4-week rotation), to requiring students to come in at least once during the class for a conference, to making conferences completely optional and holding them only at the student's request. Decisions about frequency and time frames will be influenced by logistical issues such as scheduling and office space. If a teacher has an office and holds regular office hours, this can be the best way to hold conferences; some instructors occasionally cancel classes to hold conferences with hard-to-schedule students. However, many part-time ESL instructors have neither an office nor office hours. If teachers in this situation want to hold one-to-one conferences, they most likely have to do so during class time—a situation that requires careful planning especially because the other students need to be occupied while the teacher holds individual discussions. Alternatively, as discussed in chapter 9, the computer writing lab can be an ideal setting for one-to-one teacher–student interaction because students work at individual computer terminals and the teacher can move around the room and hold brief conferences as the need arises and inclination leads.

What Topics Should Conferences Cover?   Once the teacher has resolved logistical issues, it is important to prepare and plan for conferences. What to discuss during conferences will vary according to the context of the conference. For instance, if the conference is student-initiated, the student may well have a particular question to discuss or problem to resolve. If the teacher has scheduled a conference, options for topics to discuss range from a holistic reaction to the student's latest paper to a specific discussion of a particular writing problem or a teaching point covered in class. For instance, in a study by Patthey-Chavez and Ferris (1997), one of the teachers had as a specific goal in her conferences the introduction of the rhetorical construct of anticipating counterarguments—something she was about to discuss with the whole class. Options for conferences also vary depending on how much time is allotted for conferences. In the Garrison Method, for instance, the teacher quickly reads something the student has just finished writing (e.g., a thesis statement, a conclusion, etc.) and gives immediate feedback on that piece of text. However, a longer conference can cover various aspects (ideas, grammar, etc.) of an entire paper. If the teacher has an opportunity to prepare ahead of time for a conference, he or she might want to make notes on particular issues to discuss with the student that have arisen during class or that he or she has noted in previous papers. Alternatively, if discussing a particular essay, the teacher may want to read through the essay and make a few notes or checkmarks in the margins as reminders of items to discuss.

How Should Conference Dynamics Be Shaped?   Another pedagogical issue concerns the dynamics of teacher–student writing conferences—specifically, the relative proportion of talk by teacher and student as well as instructor directiveness (or lack thereof). Studies that have examined this issue have suggested that teacher–student conferences are most *successful* (with success not always operationally defined) when the writer makes a significant contribution to the conference, meaning that he or she participates fully in the discussion rather than sitting passively as the teacher dispenses criticism and advice. Also, researchers have suggested that when teachers avoid being overly directive in the conference setting, students can participate more fully, negotiate meaning more effectively, and ultimately produce texts that result from their own thought processes (presumably influenced by the teacher's input), rather than from verbatim reflections of the teacher's oral feedback. Specific ways to encourage students to participate and avoid being overly directive include asking questions (e.g., "What do you think about this paper?" and "Can you explain in another way what you were trying to say here?"), actively eliciting student participation ("Do you have any questions or issues to bring up?"), and allowing occasional silences so that the student can formulate and articulate his or her thoughts.

As already noted, however, a nondirective approach can be confusing, frustrating, and even threatening to some ESL students depending on their cultural expectations and language ability. Teachers of L2 writers can be sensitive to such problems either by explaining why they are asking questions rather than issuing commands or rephrasing questions and comments so that they are linguistically and pragmatically clear to students. For example, if a student has written an essay draft on her mother's influence on her life, the teacher can give essentially the same feedback in any of the following three ways:

1. *Directive:* "You need to add an example here that shows exactly how your mother influenced your decision to go to college."
2. *Non-Directive:* "How did your mother influence you?"
3. *In-Between:* "Maybe you could add an example or story here that could help me understand your mother's influence on you."

Although the third option is clear about what the teacher advises, it is less specific (i.e., the student can decide what kind of example to provide) and more tentative (*"Maybe* you could ...").

How Should Conferences Be Followed Up? Finally, as with written teacher feedback and peer feedback, it is helpful to build some sort of accountability into the conferencing event so that the student does not regard it as merely an opportunity to have a nice chat with the teacher. The teacher can ask the student to write a brief journal entry or paragraph to be included with the student's next revision summarizing what was discussed in the conference and what the student did (or did not) find helpful in subsequent writing. It is important to stress, however, that by *accountability* we do not mean that the student must incorporate every single word or suggestion uttered by the teacher into his or her next draft, but rather that the student should consider the teacher's instructional feedback carefully.

Problems With Teacher Feedback and the Need to Explain Response Practices. Surveys of student reactions to teacher feedback (Cohen, 1987; Cohen & Cavalcanti, 1990; Ferris, 1995b; Hedgcock & Lefkowitz, 1996) have sometimes asked respondents to describe problems they have experienced in understanding their teachers' feedback and to explain the steps they take to resolve any misunderstandings. Students frequently report difficulties in deciphering teachers' handwriting, decoding correction symbols (circles, arrows, symbols, etc.), and understanding the purpose of the teacher's questions, which are often criticized for being both too general and too specific. Further, students often note that, even when they understand their teachers' feedback, they disagree with or are offended by it. Likewise, students report a range of strategies for resolving problems with their teachers' commentary—from consulting a grammar book to asking the teacher for help. The strategies they select may vary due to the different populations of students and contexts in which they were surveyed or interviewed.

These problems and concerns highlight an important point about response to student writing, whether written or oral. The teacher should have clear-cut strategies for response and should communicate them effectively to the students. Like any other form of human communication, teacher feedback on student writing is likely to be misunderstood at times. Teachers can minimize and alleviate misunderstandings by taking the following steps:

1. Explain, from the beginning of the course, the philosophy of response to be used throughout the term. For instance, if the teacher has elected not to comment on or mark grammar problems until later drafts, students should be informed;

2. Explain and discuss the types of response to be given. For example, if correction symbols or other abbreviations will be used, they should be described and illustrated for the students. Any checklist or set of correction symbols should be provided to the students, preferably with each essay draft;

3. If the teacher plans to write questions on the draft to guide the revision process, it should be explained how writers are expected to deal with those questions. For example, are they supposed to provide an answer in the text or are they merely to stimulate the student's thinking?

4. If possible, the teacher should review an annotated student paper orally with the whole class (on an overhead projector transparency or in a handout) prior to responding to students' drafts;

5. The teacher should state and restate that students are encouraged to ask questions if they do not understand or agree with their teacher's feedback. When returning marked student papers, the teacher should include in his or her lesson plan time for interaction and questions about the marks and comments on the papers; and

6. Students should be encouraged to analyze and reflect on their teacher's feedback by writing journal entries and/or in self-assessment sheets in which they summarize and respond to the commentary on their papers.

We may assume—erroneously—that our students will naturally come to us if they have questions about or disagreements with our feedback. Nonetheless, some students may be reticent do do so, feeling that it shows disrespect by implying the instructor has been unclear. The teacher needs to set the tone for open discussion by acknowledging that there inevitably will be occasional breakdowns in communication, welcoming questions about (and challenges to) their feedback and providing time and structure for students to process and respond to teacher commentary.

SUMMARY

L1 and L2 studies of teachers' written feedback on student writing have examined a variety of theoretical questions:

- At what point(s) in the writing process should a teacher intervene (if at all)?
- What is the difference between appropriation and intervention in responding to student writing?
- Should feedback related to content and organization be given separately from comments/corrections on form (grammar, spelling, punctuation, etc.)?
- What types of feedback (praise/criticism, direct/indirect, etc.) bring about the most significant improvements in students' writing?

Scholars and teachers concerned with response to student writing have likewise examined a number of practical issues:

- When is written feedback more effective than oral feedback?
- Are marginal comments more helpful than end comments, or are both necessary?
- Should correction symbols or verbal commentary be used?
- What problems do ESL students experience in understanding teacher feedback, and how should teachers address these problems?

Teacher response to student writing is important at all levels and in all instructional contexts. However, responding effectively to student writing is a skill that can elude even experienced teachers. Like any other form of interpersonal communication, teachers' written responses to their students' writing vary considerably according to the needs, personalities, and abilities of the participants (i.e., the teacher and student) and according to the context (i.e., the course, institutional goals, constraints of the particular assignment, point in the course at which the feedback is being given, etc.). Because of this variation, we must understand the underlying issues and considerations that constrain our responses. Providing written feedback on student writing is a skill that can improve with practice and reflection. To gauge our effectiveness, of course, we must rely on information from our students and on continuous assessment of ultimate outcomes.

$\Rightarrow AA\ 5.4$

$\Rightarrow AA\ 5.5$

$\Rightarrow AA\ 5.6$

$\Rightarrow AA\ 5.7$

Reflection and Review

1. To what extent has research on teacher intervention in L1 composition influenced teacher response practices in the teaching of ESL writing? What are the similarities and differences between feedback processes in the two contexts?

2. Despite disparate research findings on the effectiveness of teacher response in L2 composing, several consistent patterns have emerged in the literature. What are these patterns, and which do you feel are (or will be) the most releva⁻ ᵗ to you in your current (or future) teaching situation? Explain.

3. What educational and psychological factors do you think underlie the general conclusion that a combination of feedback techniques deployed at specific junctures in the composing process produce the most satisfactory results in terms of students' written products?

4. What arguments can you propose for and/or against the content–form dichotomy? How can such a dichotomy be useful while also misleading to composition teachers?

Application Activity 5.1: Surveying Teachers and Students About Responding Practices

Directions.

1. Contact the teacher of an intermediate or advanced ESL writing class in your community (at a high school, community college, university, or intensive English program). Ask the teacher if you can visit the class, administer a survey to the students, and interview him or her later about the results (see Appendix 5A).

2. Using the survey developed by Cohen (1987) and adapted for multiple-draft contexts by Ferris (1995b), prepare enough copies of a survey form for the class you will visit.

3. Attend the class, give instructions, and administer and collect the surveys.

4. Analyze the survey responses, following the procedures discussed in Cohen (1987) and (Ferris, 1995b).

5. Interview the teacher about the survey results to discover whether the students' perceptions are accurate (at least in the teacher's view).

6. Compose an analysis of your survey results and teacher interview, comparing your findings with those of the published research surveyed in this chapter.

Application Activity 5.2: Analyzing Teacher Feedback—1

Appendix 5B contains a marked first draft of a student text along with the original prompt.

Directions. Read the paper and teacher commentary, considering the following questions:

1. To what extent is the feedback personalized?
2. Does the feedback provide adequate guidance and direction for the student writer?
3. To what extent is the feedback text-specific?
4. Is there an appropriate balance of positive and critical commentary?

Remembering this chapter's discussions about these four criteria, write a one- to two-page analysis of the teacher feedback in the sample in Appendix 5B. Be as specific as you can about the strengths and weaknesses of the teacher response. What inferences can you make from the student text and the teacher feedback regarding the specifications of the task, characteristics of this teacher's class, and relationship between the teacher and student?

Application Activity 5.3: Responding to Student Errors

The following student text portion contains several significant error patterns. Practice different techniques for responding to student errors by completing the following steps.

> There are a lot of events that had lead me to understand something. But the most sufficient one was when I enter Barbizon, the school of modeling. At Barbizon, the teachers taught me a lot of things such as how to model, do commercial, fashion show, make-up, and etc. After graduating from Barbizon, I learned how to make more friends and how to overcome my shyness. This event had led me to understand that shyness and low self-esteem can really put one down.

Directions.

1. Make three copies of the text portion.
2. On one copy, annotate the errors using the checklist in Bates et al. (1993), reproduced in chapter 7 (Fig. 7.4).
3. On another copy, choose an "indirect" marking technique (underlining, circling, or checkmarks in the margin) and mark the text using that technique.
4. On the third copy, provide general verbal comments about the error patterns.
5. Compose a brief prose response in which you analyze the experience of marking the text in the ways noted in this chapter. Which did you find most comfortable? Most difficult? Explain why.

Application Activity 5.4: Responding to Student Papers

Appendix 5C contains four copies of a student essay, "A Good Friend," which was written in an ESL freshman composition course in response to the same prompt as the one shown in Appendix 5B.

Directions.

1. Make your own handwritten comments and annotations on "A Good Friend—1."
2. Compose a one- to two-page justification of your own feedback, taking into account the principles covered in this chapter.

Application Activity 5.5: Analyzing Teacher Feedback—2

Three novice teachers were asked to provide written feedback on the same essay that was annotated in Application Activity 5.4. All three marked papers ("A Good Friend," versions 2–4) are provided in Appendix 5C.

Directions.

1. Write a brief but well-organized commentary in which you compare and contrast the three teachers' responses with one another and with your own responses from Application Activity 5.4, speculating on the potential effectiveness of each response in helping this L2 student writer to revise her essay.

2. Analyze each of the following three sets of teacher comments on the same paper, focusing on these questions:

   a. What are the teacher's apparent goals and strategies in responding to the first draft?
   b. What, in your opinion, are the strengths and weaknesses in the teacher's feedback?
   c. In what way(s) does this feedback relate to the philosophies and strategies discussed in this chapter?

Application Activity 5.6: Self-Analysis of Response Patterns

Appendix 5D contains three student papers written in class by advanced university ESL students.

Directions.

1. Write marginal and end comments on the three essays as if you were going to return the papers to the students for further revision. Because the essays were written in class, you should approach them as first drafts.

2. Code each of the three papers according to the instructions given at the end of Appendix 5D and then complete an analysis form for your feedback on each paper.

3. Compose a prose response in which you reflect on your experience in responding to the paper and analyzing your responses. What did you focus on? What principles guided you? What struggles did you have? What do you think you still need to learn/practice to respond effectively to student writing?

Application Activity 5.7: Examining Research on Teacher Response

Read one of the two pairs of studies in the following list on responding to student writing. Write an analysis of the two, considering the following questions.

Directions.

1. Compare and contrast the data-collection procedures and the analysis methods used to examine the teacher commentary. What problems, if any, do you notice with either study?

2. Examine the conclusions and pedagogical applications reached in each study. Do you feel that these conclusions were justified given your responses in item 1? Which study did you find most convincing? Why?
Articles to compare:
Pair A: Sommers (1982) and Connors and Lunsford (1993).
Pair B: Zamel (1985) and Fathman and Whalley (1990).

APPENDIX 5A: COMPOSITION SURVEY[*]

Composition Survey

1. How much of each composition do you read over again when your instructor returns it to you?

1st/2nd Drafts
All of it____   Most of it____   Some of it____   None of it____

Final Drafts (the one that receives a grade/score)
All of it____   Most of it____   Some of it____   None of it____

2. How many of the instructor's comments and corrections do you think about carefully?

1st/2nd Drafts
All of them____   Most of them____   Some of them____   None of them____

Final Drafts
All of them____   Most of them____   Some of them____   None of them____

3. How many of the comments and corrections involve:

1st/2nd Drafts	A lot	Some	A little	None
Organization	____	____	____	____
Content/Ideas	____	____	____	____
Grammar	____	____	____	____
Vocabulary	____	____	____	____
Mechanics	____	____	____	____
(e.g., punctuation, spelling)				
Final Drafts	A lot	Some	A little	None
Organization	____	____	____	____
Content/Ideas	____	____	____	____
Grammar	____	____	____	____
Vocabulary	____	____	____	____
Mechanics	____	____	____	____
(e.g., punctuation, spelling)				

4. If you pay attention to what your instructor wrote, how much attention do you pay to the comments and corrections involving:

1st/2nd Drafts	A lot	Some	A little	None	Not Applicable
Organization	____	____	____	____	____
Content/Ideas	____	____	____	____	____
Vocabulary	____	____	____	____	____
Mechanics	____	____	____	____	____
(e.g., punctuation, spelling)					
Final Drafts	A lot	Some	A little	None	Not Applicable
Organization	____	____	____	____	____
Content/Ideas	____	____	____	____	____
Grammar	____	____	____	____	____
Vocabulary	____	____	____	____	____
Mechanics	____	____	____	____	____
(e.g., punctuation, spelling)					

5. Describe what you do after you read your instructor's comments and corrections (e.g., Do you look up the corrections in a grammar book? See a tutor? Rewrite your paper?)
1st/2nd Drafts
Final Drafts

6. Are there ever any comments or corrections that you do not understand? If so, can you give any examples?

7. What do you do about those comments or corrections that you do not understand?

8. Are any of your instructor's comments positive? If so, can you give an example?

9. Do you feel that your instructor's comments and corrections help you to improve your composition writing skills? Why or why not?

10. How would you rate yourself as a learner?
Excellent____   Good____   Fair____   Poor____

11. How would you rate your skills in writing compositions?
Excellent____   Good____   Fair____   Poor____

---

*From Ferris (1995b)

APPENDIX 5B: SAMPLE ESSAY ASSIGNMENT AND STUDENT ESSAY WITH TEACHER COMMENTARY FOR APPLICATION ACTIVITY 5.2

Assignment: Write an essay in which you draw from your own experience to express a personal viewpoint. Describe in detail an event or experience (or series of events or experiences) that has led you to learn, believe, or understand something.
Audience: Your classmates and instructor.
Purpose: To help your audience understand why the experience was significant to you. (Adapted from Spack, 1990, p. 37.)

```
          My Experience at Modeling School

     There are a lot of events that had lead me to
                                       ?
understand something.  But the most sufficient one was

when I enter Barbizon, the school of modeling.  At

Barbizon, the teachers taught me a lot of things such

as how to model, do commercial, fashion show, make-up,     you could
and etc.  After graduating from Barbizon, I learned how     develop this
                                                            more later in
to make more friend and how to overcome my shyness.         the essay

This event had lead me to understand that shyness and

                    low self-esteem can really put one down.
what made
you go to                The first day when I entered Barbizon, I was very
Barbizon?
              shy.  I looked around the room and I was the only

Asian.  This really make me felt uncomfortable and even

more nervous.  At first I wanted to quit because I was

scare and I didn't have any confidence in myself but I
              quit        wanted
didn't because I really like to model.  When my teacher

told me to model for her, I didn't want to because I

was scare and nervous but I have to.  I can still

remember the first time when I was on the ramp.  My

heart was beating very fast and I didn't know what I

was doing.  I looked around the room and it seem like

everyone was looking at me.  I can feel that my face

was blushing, and after I finish modeling, it was like

a relief.  I was so happy that I got it over with.

     As time pass, I make some new friends and I

learned that no matter what I do, I have to have

confidence in myself.  I was still a little bit scare
```

because when everyone _have_ to line up to model, I

always wanted to go last. I was always afraid to model *Why?*

in front of a lot of people because I was afraid that

they might laugh at me. When my friends felt that

Good

there _is_ something wrong, they always _try_ to cheer and

encouraged me. They also said, "I know you can do it,

I have confidence in you" As a result, I really

changed because I _know_ that in order to become a model,

I would have to get rid of my shyness and ~~I must~~ have

more confidence in myself.

Toward the end of the training, I was not that shy

anymore. When my teacher told us to model, I was

almost always the first person to go up the ramp and

model. This time when I was on the ramp my heart was

not beating that fast anymore. I ~~even~~ knew what I was

doing and I even felt happy that I _have_ a chance to

model. After I got off the ramp, my teacher said I did

a good job and she was proud of me. *(A real one? Or at Barbizon?)*

Another time was when I _have_ to do a commercial.

I only _have_ 15 minutes to study the script. Then each

person _will_ take _turn_ to do their commercial. This

time I was not that nervous because I _know_ I _can_ do it.

Also, with the support ~~from~~ *of* my friends, I even _have_

more confidence in myself. As a result, I did a pretty

good job and I didn't _forgot_ my line. Now, I do

believe that when you are not shy and have confidence

in yourself, then you will be able to do ~~a~~ better. At

first I didn't really notice I [had] changed until my <u>friends</u>
told me and said I have improved 150(%). She told me
[percent]
when she first met me I was very shy and nervous, but
now I am not.

   In conclusion, entering Barbizon really <u>lead</u> me to
understand that if you have confidence in yourself,
there is nothing you can't do.   I also feel proud of
myself because I finally <u>achieve</u> <u>something</u>.   This [what?]
really <u>make</u> me happy and gave me a lot of
encouragement.   Now, I believe that low self-esteem and
lack of confidence can really put one down.   I'm very
glad that I went to Barbiz<u>on it</u>'s a great experience.

[How did it put you down?]

Sue —
This is an interesting topic, a well-told story with
clear organization. You could develop it further by
answering a couple of questions:
① Why do you think your confidence & self-esteem
was so low?
② How has the improved confidence from modeling
influenced other parts of your life?
When you are editing your 2nd draft, check your verb
tenses. I've underlined some examples.

APPENDIX 5C: SAMPLE ESSAY ASSIGNMENT AND STUDENT ESSAY WITH TEACHER COMMENTARY FOR APPLICATION ACTIVITY 5.4

Assignment: Write an essay in which you draw from your own experience to express a personal viewpoint. Describe in detail an event or experience (or series of events or experiences) that has led you to learn, believe, or understand something.
Audience: Your classmates and instructor.
Purpose: To help your audience understand why the experience was signifi-

Version 1   A Good Friend

I think having a good friend is very important. A
good friend can be either a male or a female. I
believe having a good friend can help and guide you to
be successful in life. Some says "You can tell a
person by knowing a person's friends." In other words,
most close friends are alike to each other. So if a
person is hanging around with some bad friends, a
person is most likely to be bad. However, if a person
is hanging around with some good friends, a person is
most likely to be good. After all, we human loves to
copy others.

I have a good friend named Yi Hwa Kang. When I
think of her, I feel so proud to be her friend. I'm
glad we are good friends to each other. She first came
to the United States five years ago and I have known
her ever since. She came to the United States righ
after her father's death by liver cancer. Since some
of her mother's relatives were in the United States,
they decided to move. When she first came to America,
like most other immigrants she didn't know how to speak
any English or know much about anything else. However,
she was willing to do anything to be successful. She
had strong will power and determination.

My good friend's strong will power and
determination brought her to graduate in top ten
percent and earned her honors entrance to California

156

State University of San Diego last fall. She attends
school with full scholarship which includes some of her
living expense. She accomplished so much, I sometimes
felt embarrassed comparing myself to her. In a way
that help me to improve myself. I didn't want to fall
behind and I wanted to stay at least at level as her in
every way. So during our high school we did many
things together. We learned how to play tennis and
joined school tennis team. We learned how to play
violin and joined school orchestra. We were also in
choir for straight two years. Other school activities
like science and year book clubs were all fun.
Throughout the years of knowing her, I learned that if
you really want your goals to come true, you can
achieve theme only if work hard enough. Also she
taught me to live my life fully, meaning try everything
because you only live once.

If she was a kind cf person who didn't care about
her school work and had no eagerness to learn and to
achieve, I wonder if we could have ever been good
friends to each other. If she was not, I don't think I
would have worked hard as I did when I was attending
high school.

Version 2   A Good Friend

I think having a good friend is very important. A
good friend can be either a male or a female. I
believe having a good friend can help and guide you to
be successful in life. Some says "You can tell a
person by knowing a person's friends." In other words,
most close friends are alike to each other. So if a
person is hanging around with some bad friends, a
person is most likely to be bad. However, if a person
is hanging around with some good friends, a person is
most likely to be good. After all, we human loves to
copy others. *You need a main idea/thesis statement.*

I have a good friend named Yi Hwa Kang. When I
think of her, I feel so proud to be her friend. I'm
glad we are good friends to each other. She first came
to the United States five years ago and I have known
her ever since. She came to the United States righ
after her father's death by liver cancer. Since some
of her mother's relatives were in the United States,
they decided to move. When she first came to America,
like most other immigrants she didn't know how to speak
any English or know much about anything else. However,
she was willing to do anything to be successful. She
had strong will power and determination. *Excellent coherence with word repetition*

My good friend's strong will power and
determination brought her to graduate in top ten

percent and earned her honors entrance to California
State University of San Diego last fall. She attends
school with full scholarship which includes some of her

why did you feel embarrassed?

living expense. She accomplished so much, I sometimes
felt embarrassed comparing myself to her. In a way
that help me to improve myself. I didn't want to fall

what helped you to improve yourself?

behind and I wanted to stay at least at level as her in
every way. So during our high school we did many

This sounds competitive. Did you do these things because you liked them or because your friend did them?

things together. We learned how to play tennis and
joined school tennis team. We learned how to play
violin and joined school orchestra. We were also in
choir for straight two years. Other school activities
like science and year book clubs were all fun.

This needs more development.

Throughout the years of knowing her, I learned that if
you really want your goals to come true, you can
achieve theme only if work hard enough. Also she
taught me to live my life fully, meaning try everything

How? Give a specific example.

How did she teach you that success comes from hard work?

because you only live once.

     If she was a kind of person who didn't care about
her school work and had no eagerness to learn and to
achieve, I wonder if we could have ever been good
friends to each other. If she was not, I don't think I
would have worked hard as I did when I was attending
high school.

Student,

You are obviously very proud of your good friend, and it shows in your writing. Your description of your friend is good. Also, your essay is well organized, moving from friendship in general to your friend specifically and how her accomplishments make you proud of her and try harder for yourself. For your next draft, I have some suggestions which will help you develop your analysis further. Don't worry about editing issues. We'll cover those in the next draft (there aren't too many – good for you.) Feel free to stop by during office hours if you have further questions.

   ① How did your friendship make you try harder?
   ② Why did you try harder? Were you trying to keep up with your friend out of friendship or competition?
   ③ What did you come to learn or understand as a result of your friendship? (Look back at essay assignment.)

Version 3   A Good Friend

connect
How is a friend
important to

I think having a good friend is very important. [A good friend can be either a male or a female.] I believe having a good friend can help and guide you to be successful in life. Some says "You can tell a person by knowing a person's friends." In other words, most close friends are (alike) to each other. So if a person is hanging around with some bad friends, a person is most likely to be bad. However, if a person is hanging around with some good friends, a person is most likely to be good. After all, we human loves to copy others.

Is this the main idea?

another word might be less confusing

Better give that example shows how you are friends.

I have a good friend named Yi Hwa Kang. When I think of her, I feel so proud to be her friend. I'm glad we are good friends to each other. She first came to the United States five years ago and I have known her ever since. She came to the United States right after her father's death by liver cancer. Since some of her mother's relatives were in the United States, they decided to move. When she first came to America, like most other immigrants she didn't know how to speak any English or know much about anything else. However, she was willing to do anything to be successful. She had strong will power and determination.

Better give an example

nice transit

What did she do to achieve this?

My good friend's strong will power and determination brought her to graduate in top ten

percent and earned her honors entrance to California
State University of San Diego last fall. She attends
school with full scholarship which includes some of her
living expense. She accomplished so much, I sometimes
felt embarrassed comparing myself to her. In a way
that help me to improve myself. I didn't want to fall
behind and I wanted to stay at least at level as her in
every way. So during our high school we did many
things together. We learned how to play tennis and
joined school tennis team. We learned how to play
violin and joined school orchestra. We were also in
choir for straight two years. Other school activities
like science and year book clubs were all fun.
Throughout the years of knowing her, I learned that if
you really want your goals to come true, you can
achieve theme only if work hard enough. Also she
taught me to live my life fully, meaning try everything
because you only live once.

If she was a kind of person who didn't care about
her school work and had no eagerness to learn and to
achieve, I wonder if we could have ever been good
friends to each other. If she was not, I don't think I
would have worked hard as I did when I was attending
high school.

explain how by detailing a specific event, not just mentioning activities you shared

did this come before she went to college?

* modal needed

Cindy — Really free of grammar errors on the first draft!
and the main idea that friends copy each other is basically
one I follow, but I'm from what you write not sure why. Could
you: (1) Describe specific actions and events about your friend. These
are events you saw and affected you. (2) Use your friend's influence
on you to explain how this effected your life overall.
See a tutor or me to get help — this is not easy!
(3) I underlined some grammar mistakes you can fix alone

161

Version 4   A Good Friend

you have several ideas here, I'm not sure which one is your thesis

I think having a good friend is very important. A good friend can be either a male or a female. I believe having a good friend can help and guide you to be successful in life. Some says "You can tell a person by knowing a person's friends." In other words, most close friends are alike to each other. So if a person is hanging around with some bad friends, a person is most likely to be bad. However, if a person is hanging around with some good friends, a person is most likely to be good. After all, we human loves to copy others.

Maria—Is all this detail supporting your main idea? Is it all necessary?

I have a good friend named Yi Hwa Kang. When I think of her, I feel so proud to be her friend. I'm glad we are good friends to each other. She first came to the United States five years ago and I have known her ever since. She came to the United States (righ) after her father's death by liver cancer. Since some of her mother's relatives were in the United States, they decided to move. When she first came to America, like most other immigrants she didn't know how to speak any English or know much about anything else. However, she was willing to do anything to be successful. She had strong will power and determination.

My good friend's strong will power and determination brought her to graduate in top ten

In what ways did Yi Hwa help you to improve yourself? How did you improve?

percent and earned her honors entrance to California State University of San Diego last fall. She attends school with full scholarship which includes some of her living expense. She accomplished so much, I sometimes felt embarrassed comparing myself to her. In a way that help me to improve myself. I didn't want to fall behind and I wanted to stay at least at level as her in every way. So during our high school we did many things together. We learned how to play tennis and joined school tennis team. We learned how to play violin and joined school orchestra. We were also in choir for straight two years. Other school activities like science and year book clubs were all fun. Throughout the years of knowing her, I learned that if you really want your goals to come true, you can achieve theme only if work hard enough. Also she taught me to live my life fully, meaning try everything because you only live ouce.

If she was a kind of person who didn't care about her school work and had no eagerness to learn and to achieve, I wonder if we could have ever been good friends to each other. If she was not, I don't think I would have worked hard as I did when I was attending high school.

Maria, I really like your topic about friends. As you write your second draft, please consider the following —

1. Firmly state your main idea. I'm not sure if your thesis is a) "friends are important," b) "friends are alike," or c) "A good friend can guide you."

2. Look again at the support for your main idea. Most of your supporting details only describe your friend Yi Hwa Kang. Remember the question also asks _how_ the experience (your friendship) has led you to learn, believe, or understand something. Please add more details to answer this question.

3. Some of your sentences seem short & "choppy." Try to vary your sentence lengths as you revise.

—Teacher

163

APPENDIX 5D: SAMPLE ESSAYS
AND CODING PROCEDURE FOR APPLICATION
ACTIVITY 5.6

Essay Prompt

In "A Mason-Dixon Memory," Clifton Davis (1993) tells of a recent event that triggered a significant childhood memory. Have you had an experience that brought a former incident to mind? Write an essay in which you describe both experiences, explaining clearly how the more recent one caused you to remember the earlier incident. Also, discuss what was significant about (or what you have learned from) your comparison of the two experiences.

Sample Essays

ESSAY 1

Clifton Davis tells of a recent event that triggered a significant childhood memory. The recent event was a story of Dondre Green. He was not allowed to play golf at the Caldwell Parish Country Club because it was reserved for whites only. Dondre Green is a blanck and the management didn't let Negroes to enter their private club. About 32 years ago when Clifton Davis was 13 years old same thing had happened to him. Only that time it was not being able to go to Glen Echo Amusement Park in Maryland because he was a black.

As I was reading A Mason-Dixon Memory by Clifton Davis I was also triggered by a memory. I came to the United States 7 years ago. I guess I've been fortunate and lucky that I didn't have to face those terrible situations like Dondre Green and Clifton Davis. However, my friend from high school had to go through injustices like Dondre Green and Clifton Davis. When she first came to the United States just like many new immigrants she didn't know how to speak English very well. However, do to different school systems back in her country she was well taught compared to her classmates in the United States. She knew so much more and one day she went to her school counselor and asked him to change her classes to little bit more challenging ones. She also told him that she is getting all good grades and turned in every homework assignments as well. However, the counselor took a look at and said "No". My friend was very surprised and wanted to know why. The only reson she got was that she is not good at English like other whites kids in class. The counselor strongly forced the world "whites". She didn't know what the counselor was trying to say but quickly found out that he didn't want her to be in class where only whites were believed to achieve good grades. The counselor didn't even wanted my friend to give the harder class a try. He didn't even give her a chance. Even through she learned everything back in her country she had to waste one high school year because of the counselor at that school. I suddenly remembered my high school friend's story as I was reading about Dondre Green and Clifton Davis.

My high school friend, Dondre Green and Clifton Davis were treated wrong because of their color. They were not even given a chance or rights. I think this is very wrong. Who are we to say some of us are better than others. Who are we to say I'm better than you because I have lighter skin color. Some says that the United States is referred to as "The Melting Pot" because so many different races are intertwined and making this country one. The United States is not just for whites, but for all those who works hard and wanting to be successful. For those who has willingness to make their dreams come true. Everybody should be given a chance no matter what skin color they have because underneth the skin color we are all same.

ESSAY 2: "Passing Away"

There are a lot of events that had happen in my life, but the most memorable is when I loose someone. Recently my grandmother had just pass away because of cancer. When I heard this, I couldn't believe it because I don't want to loose my grandmom. My grandmother death had brought back a very sad memory, which is my uncle death just a few years ago My uncle die because he was caught in a fire which brought tears to everybody. In just a couple of years I had lost two relative already and it's very hard for me for me to take.

The moment my mom told tohat my grandmom pass away tears were just running down my eyes and I was very shock. On the day of my grandmom funeral everyone was so sad and the only thing I could heard was my crying. I try not to cry so much, but I just couldn't help it especially, when they brought my grandmom in for us to see. When I saw my grandmom body I started to cry even more and I say to myself that you can not leave me, I really love you. As I was crying another memory just pop up in my mind and that's my uncle death because so far—this is the second funeral I been to in my life and both are my relative.

I remember just a few ago when it was close to father's day and one of my uncle was remodeling his house and a lot of my other relative was also helping. One day while they are eating their lunch outside, two of my uncle was still in the house cleaning Suddenly the house was caught on fire and because of the gasoline in the house it was burning very fast and my two uncle was trap in there. By the time the fire truck and ambulance got here my two uncle was 60% to 70% burn. A few days later, one of my uncle did and I was very sad because all of his children are young and the oldest was only ten years old. My uncle wife was also pregnant during that time and didn't even know. During that whole summer his family, friends, and relative were very sad. Loosing my uncle was a very sad thing that happen in my life and now, loosing my grandmother is like making the world seem hopeless.

Now every time I think of my grandmother I will always think of my uncle. Loosing them both is a very painful thing for me. From this two experiences, I learn that loosing someone is very painful, but I still have to continue my life because I know they will always be there for me.

In conclusion, my grandmother death had brought back a very sad memories because I'm loosing someone Every time I think of my grandmom I will also think of my uncle because I'm not able to see them anymore. Now, I learn that loosing someone is very painful, but I know that they will always be in my heart. When I think of my grandmom and uncle tears will always be in my eyes and I can't control it, but I know I really love them.

ESSAY 3

The parents-children relationship is the most memorable experience for many people. For me it has been valuable "package" of experiences that I'm happy to carry with me. Besides many important things I've learned from my parents I also learned that forgiveness in the right place and time can teach the child much better lesson than the punishment.

One day when I got home from school I found out that my little daughter had done something bad. She is 3 years old and she had often watched me using the perfume. Sometimes I put the perfume on her little nose as well. So, when I came home that day I found that she had emptied the entire bottle of my French perfume. I became very upset especially because it was a very special gift from my husband. I started explaining to my little girl that she shouldn't have done so, that she should've ask me if she wanted and so on.

But then I looked at her. She stood infront of me with her lips curved down and her eyes were full of embarrassment. I stoped for a moment because I suddenly remembered myself feeling the same kind of embarrassment when I was 6 or 7 years old.

The entire story started when my family moved to a new home. We had some friends over from other city to see our new place. After lunch it was decided to take a walk and look arround in the city. As my father locked the door I asked him if I can hold the key. He wasn't shure about my idea and then I became stubborn. I wanted to show up myself infront of the guests as a responsible "big kid"; so, I finally got that key. I remember we had a great time visiting the old buildings and museums in my city which was builded in 12th century.

When we returned home my father asked me for the key. I proudly put my arm into my pocket but—Ops!—it wasn't there. I checked the other pocket too but the key wasn't there either. Then I started to look arround. I was pretty shure it had to be arround here somewhere. The guests smiled, looked at me and then at my father. My face and ears starte to turn red. I felt as embarrassed as I could be. My father still he didn't say a word looked at me sadly but lovingly.

Very slowly, I can remember it even now, 20 years later, my father put his arm into his pocket and took out the key. Luckily he noticed that very moment when I accidently dropped the key from my pocket. Of cource, my father knew all the way from the beginning that I might loose the key. I think it was very smart of him that he let me have my own experience teach me the lesson. I was expecting the punishment but it didn't happen. Instead I understood that to be able to be responsible is much harder than just take the responsability.

So, as I was standing there and looking at my little daughter's embarrassment, I thought I could still benefit from that story of a little key. I didn't say any more words to my little girl. I just picked her up and huged her. I wanted her to feel the same overwhelming feeling of forgiveness that I had felt in my childhood.

Procedure for Coding Comments

1. Number all comments in the text. Analyze comments in the order in which they appear.
2. Count the number of words in each comment, noting totals in the first column of the coding form.
3. For multisentence comments, use your judgment as to whether to categorize the propositions separately or treat them as a single point. (The same applies for compound sentences joined by dashes.)
4. Categorize both the "Comment Type" and "Linguistic Form" of each comment by checking the appropriate cell in the table. Examples of each type are given next.
5. For each comment, also indicate whether it included a hedge (e.g., "maybe," "might," "could," etc.). In the appropriate cell, note the hedge.
6. For each comment, determine whether or not it was text-specific. If so, check the appropriate cell.
7. For end notes, apply the same procedure, except that you should number each sentence as a separate comment. However, see Step 3 as to "compound sentences joined by dashes."

Analytic Model for Teacher Commentary

A. Comment length (number of words)
   1 = Short (1–5 words)
   2 = Average (6–15 words)
   3 = Long (16–25 words)
   4 = Very Long (26+ words)
B. Comment Types
   1 = Ask for information/Question
      EXAMPLE: Did you work out this problem with your roommates?
   2 = Request/Question
      EXAMPLE: Can you provide a thesis statement here? What did you learn from this?
   3 = Request/Statement or imperative
      EXAMPLE: This paragraph might be better earlier in the essay.
      EXAMPLE: Mention what Zinsser says about parental pressure.

4 = Give Information
EXAMPLE: Most states do allow a waiting period before an adoption is final. Do you feel that all such laws are wrong?
EXAMPLE: Iowa law favors parental rights. Michigan and California consider the best interests of the child.
5 = Positive Comment
EXAMPLE: A very nice start to your essay! You've done an impressive job of finding facts and quotes to support your arguments.
6 = Grammar/Mechanics Comment
EXAMPLE: *Past or present tense?
EXAMPLE: *Don't forget to spell-check!
C. Hedges
0 = No hedge
1 = Hedge included:
LEXICAL HEDGES, e.g., "Maybe," "Please," "might," etc.
SYNTACTIC HEDGES, e.g., "Can you add an example here?"
POSITIVE SOFTENERS, e.g., "You've raised some good points, but..."
D. Text-Specific Comment
0 = Generic comment (i.e., a note that could have been written on any paper)
EXAMPLE: Nice intro.
1 = Text-specific comment
EXAMPLE: Why is the American system better for children, in your opinion? (Adapted from Ferris, 1997, p. 321)

Coding Form (Duplicate for Additional Papers)

Comment #	Length	Type	Hedge	Text-Based
1				
2				
3				
4				
5				
6				
7				
8				
9				
10				
11				
12				
13				
14				
15				

Building a Community
of Writers: Principles
# of Peer Response

Questions for Reflection

- Beyond the specific context of composition courses, what types of experiences have you had with peer feedback and collaboration, whether in academic or nonacademic settings?
- What types of experiences have you had with receiving one-on-one oral feedback from a teacher or other authority figure? How have you felt about these experiences?
- Do you enjoy collaboration with peers? Do you find it helpful? Why or why not?
- Considering your own previous experiences with oral feedback (whether from peers or from an authority), what are the potential benefits of implementing oral feedback in a composition class? The possible drawbacks? In what ways (if any) do you think these considerations might differ for L2 students?

PEER RESPONSE: KUDOS AND CRITICISMS

The brief history of peer response in the L2 writing class, both as a pedagogical technique and a research concern, has been somewhat tumultuous. Advocates are almost lyrical in their praise of peer response, citing a variety of advantages and benefits of this approach (e.g., Mittan, 1989). However, critics claim that peer feedback activities are, at best, limited in their influence on student writing (Connor & Asenavage, 1994). At worst, they are potentially harmful to students because of novice writers' ineptitude in providing useful responses and because of L2 students' lukewarm, if not downright hostile, feelings toward peer feedback (Carson & Nelson, 1994; Leki, 1990b; Zhang, 1995).

In this regard, the literature on peer response in L2 writing is more comparable to that of computer-assisted writing instruction (see chap. 9) than to discussions of teacher feedback (chap. 5). As discussed in chapter 5, written teacher feedback has most typically been regarded by L1 and L2 researchers as a necessary evil—burdensome to writing teachers and limited in its effectiveness for helping student writers improve. There are few enthusiastic proponents of written teacher response, although recent surveys of ESL student opinions on teacher feedback have found that L2 writers feel instructor feedback is both necessary and helpful (Ferris, 1995b; Hedgcock & Lefkowitz, 1994; Zhang, 1995). Also, as previously discussed, there have been surprisingly few detailed examinations of written teacher feedback (Ferris et al., 1997). In contrast, peer response, like computer-assisted writing instruction, has vocal, forceful proponents *and* detractors as well as a rapidly increasing number of detailed studies on the nature and influence of peer response.

Benefits of Peer Response

Theoretical Frameworks.   Arguments in favor of peer response have been based on several related schools of thought. First, because peer response activities can take place at various stages of the writing process (prewriting/discovery/invention, between-draft revision, and editing), they fit well with the increased emphasis on processes in composition teaching (Connor & Asenavage, 1994; Emig, 1971; Flower & Hayes, 1981; Zamel, 1982, 1985, 1987). A second theoretical basis for peer response "is the notion of collaborative learning which derives from the social constructionist view ... that knowledge is essentially a socially justified belief" (Carson & Nelson, 1994, pp. 17–18). According to social constructionists, new ideas or paradigms are "constructs generated by communities of like-minded peers" (Bruffee, 1986, p. 774). Support for collaborative learning and social constructionism is derived, in turn, from the Vygotskyan view that "cognitive development results from social interaction" (Carson & Nelson, 1994, p. 18; cf. Mendonça & Johnson, 1994; Vygotsky, 1962/1986). Finally, in the L2 context, group work in general and writing response groups in particular have support from second language acquisition (SLA) claims about the importance of interaction for L2 development (e.g., Long & Porter, 1985; Mangelsdorf, 1989; Mittan, 1989; Pica, 1984).

Practical Benefits.   Both L1 and L2 teachers and researchers have claimed that peer feedback activities in the classroom offer numerous advantages. For novice writers in general, whether NESs or NNSs, the following benefits have been suggested:

- Students can take active roles in their own learning (Mendonça & Johnson, 1994);
- Students can "reconceptualize their ideas in light of their peers' reactions" (Mendonça & Johnson, 1994, p. 746);
- Students can engage in unrehearsed, low-risk, exploratory talk that is less feasible in whole-class and teacher–student interactions;

- Students receive "reactions, questions, and responses from authentic readers" (Mittan, 1989, p. 209; but see Leki, 1990b; Newkirk, 1984, for counterarguments to this assertion);
- Students receive feedback from multiple sources (Chaudron, 1983; Mittan, 1989);
- Students gain a clearer understanding of audience (reader) needs by receiving feedback on what they have done well and on what remains unclear (Mittan, 1989; Moore, 1986; Witbeck, 1976);
- Responding to peers' writing builds the critical skills needed to analyze and revise one's own writing (Leki, 1990b; Mittan, 1989); and
- Students gain confidence and reduce apprehension by seeing peers' strengths and weaknesses in writing (Leki, 1990b; Mittan, 1989).

In addition to the benefits of peer feedback for all student writers, Mangelsdorf (1989) argued that there are specific benefits of peer response for L2 students' linguistic development because peer interactions build communication skills and provide important opportunities for students to test and revise their L2 hypotheses.

Finally, it has been suggested that peer response activities can reduce the writing teacher's workload and can impart to the teacher important information about individual students' reading abilities and their understanding of what constitutes good writing (but see Mittan, 1989, p. 211 for a counterassertion). Mittan (1989) called this last point

the ultimate benefit of the peer review process for the teacher. Regardless of how I judge the quality of [a student's] finished essays, [the] peer review can show me some of her knowledge about good writing.... Indeed, I have found that students whose writing is consistently average or even poor very often write the most thoughtful and helpful peer reviews. This is true empowerment: encouraging students to demonstrate and use their knowledge and expertise rather than punishing them for their as-yet unpolished performance. (p. 212)

Criticisms of Peer Response

Practical Limitations. As previously noted, peer response as a pedagogical tool is not without its detractors. Leki (1990b) noted several potential problems with peer feedback, derived both from the comments of 20 ESL students and from her own and other writing teachers' experiences:

- Students sometimes focus too heavily on "surface concerns" (p. 9) or editing, neglecting larger revising issues;
- Students can provide vague, unhelpful comments;
- Students may be hostile, sarcastic, overly critical, or unkind in their criticisms of their classmates' writing;
- Students feel uncertain about the validity of their classmates' responses;

- In peer group discussions, students may struggle with their own listening comprehension skills or with the peer's foreign accent; and
- Lack of L2 formal (rhetorical) schemata may lead to inappropriate expectations about the content and structure of peers' texts, which can then result in counterproductive feedback that leads writers further away from U.S. academic expectations.

Cultural Issues. Carson and Nelson (1994) raised concerns about peer response and writing groups that are based on larger cultural issues rather than specific pedagogical problems. Drawing a distinction between collectivist cultures (e.g., Chinese and Japanese) and individualist cultures (e.g., United States), they pointed out that, although both collectivist and individualist cultures utilize collaborative learning, they typically do so for opposing purposes. In collectivist cultures, "a primary goal of the group is to maintain the relationships that constitute the group, to maintain cohesion and group harmony among group members" (Carson & Nelson, 1994, p. 20). However, "writing groups, as they are frequently implemented in composition classes in the U.S. function more often for the benefit of the individual writer than for the benefit of the group" (p. 22). The result of these differing cultural expectations for group work may be that, for students from collectivist cultures, "the impetus/motivation behind their responses is likely to come from a need for a positive group climate rather than a need to help an individual writer" (p. 23). In a subsequent study of the interactions of several Chinese ESL students in a writing group, Carson and Nelson (1996) found that "the Chinese students were reluctant to initiate comments and, when they did, monitored themselves carefully so as not to precipitate conflict within the group" (p. 1). In a similar vein, Allaei and Connor (1990) cautioned that culturally mixed writing groups may experience problems due to differing expectations and communication patterns.

Affective Factors. Zhang (1995) took a critical look at the so-called affective advantage of peer feedback for ESL students. In a survey of 81 college/university ESL students, he found that the respondents overwhelmingly preferred teacher feedback over peer or self-feedback. Based on these results, he argued that L2 practitioners should exercise caution in applying the findings and recommendations of L1 composition researchers and teachers to the teaching of ESL writing, noting that "the L2 student and the L1 student may enter the writing process with distinctly different conceptualizations and priorities about input or intervention at the revision stage" (p. 218; cf. Silva, 1993, 1997).

Research on L2 Peer Response

Descriptions of Student Interactions in Peer Response Sessions. Several researchers have undertaken discourse analytic descriptions of the types of communicative moves and stances utilized and adopted by students during peer feedback activities. In the earliest study, Mangelsdorf and Schlumberger (1992) asked 60 ESL freshman composition students to respond to an essay written by another ESL student to examine "the stances the students took toward the writer of the text, the characteristics of these stances, and what these stances suggest about the students' assumptions concerning written classroom discourse" (p. 235). They found that the students' stances fell into three categories with some overlap: interpretive (23%), prescriptive (45%), and collaborative (32%). The researchers also looked at the types of comments made by the student reviewers on content, finding five distinct categories of response: no comment, generic comment, critical evaluation, critical evaluations and suggestions (the largest category, comprising 41% of the comments), and critical evaluations and extended suggestions. They also found that reviewers' stances were related to the types of discourse features on which they focused (thesis, organization, diction) and that students who adopted collaborative stances ultimately earned the highest final grades in their composition classes.

In contrast to the decontextualized design of Mangelsdorf and Schlumberger (1992), Mendonça and Johnson (1994) taped and transcribed the oral interactions of six pairs of advanced ESL graduate students. The students had written research papers related to their major fields of study; four of the six dyads consisted of students in the same field, whereas the students in the other two pairs were in different disciplines. In their analysis of the peer review negotiations, the researchers identified five major categories of interactions (with related subtypes): question, explanation, restatement, suggestion, and grammar correction. These interactions could be initiated by either the writer or reader. They found that explanations and restatements were the most common types of interaction. They also found that most interactions were reader-generated and that types of interaction differed somewhat between the students whose partners were in the same academic field and those whose partners were pursuing a different major.

The two most ambitious studies, by Lockhart and Ng (1995) and Villamil and de Guerrero (1996), build on the previous two. Lockhart and Ng analyzed transcripts of interactions between 27 dyads of ESL students to identify the stances taken and the language functions and topics discussed during peer review sessions. Four reader stances (authoritative, interpretive, probing, and collaborative), five language functions (summarize essay, express intention, give suggestion, give opinion, and give information), and three topic/content categories (writing process, ideas, and audience/purpose) were identified. In general, Lockhart and Ng found that "different approaches to reviewing a writer's text [were] linked to the stances assumed by the readers" (p. 645). They suggested that these stances may be influenced by the student's previous experiences with writing classes, particularly with regard to giving and receiving feedback, the student's attitudes about writing, the writer's role in the peer response session, participants' personalities, the structure of the response task, and the nature of the text under discussion.

Villamil and de Guerrero (1996) also studied 27 pairs of ESL college students, analyzing transcripts of two peer review sessions per dyad. Through their analysis of the peer interactions, they identified seven social-cognitive activities ("Reading, assessing, dealing with troublesources, composing, writing comments, copying, and discussing task procedures"), five mediating strategies ("Employing symbols and external resources, using the L1, providing scaffolding, resorting to interlanguage knowledge, and vocalizing private speech"), and four aspects of social behavior ("Management of authorial control, affectivity, collaboration, and adopting reader/writer roles") (p. 51). Although the two studies focus on different aspects of student–student interaction, both conclude that peer review is "an extremely complex interactive process" (Villamil & deGuerrero, 1996, p. 51) and that there are many different factors that influence this process (Lockhart & Ng, 1995).

The Effects of Peer Feedback on Student Revision.   Several studies have examined the relationship between peer feedback and subsequent revision. Research questions have included whether students consider and act on their peers' comments when revising (Connor & Asenavage, 1994; Mendonça & Johnson, 1994; Nelson & Murphy, 1992, 1992/1993, 1993), what sorts of revisions students make after receiving peer feedback (Berger, 1990; Connor & Asenavage, 1994; Huang, 1994; Resh, 1994), and whether peer feedback leads to high-quality end products (Hedgcock & Lefkowitz, 1992; Resh, 1994).

Studies examining the extent to which writers address peer feedback in their revisions report conflicting findings. For instance, in a study of two peer response groups ($N = 8$), Connor and Asenavage (1994) indicated that few of their students' revisions (about 5% of total changes) responded to peer commentary and that the vast majority of the revisions derived from other sources (teacher feedback and the writer's own textual adjustments). In contrast, Mendonça and Johnson (1994) reported that their 12 participants utilized peer feedback in 53% of their revisions. However, there are two important distinctions between the two studies: (a) The participants in the Connor and Asenavage study were college freshmen, whereas those in the Mendonça and Johnson study were graduate students, meaning that there were likely significant differences between the two participant groups in terms of age, L2 proficiency, prior education, experience with and expectations about collaboration, and, most important, critical thinking, reading, and writing skills; (b) the participants in the Connor and Asenavage study received teacher feedback in addition to peer feedback prior to revision, whereas those in the Mendonça and Johnson study received only peer feedback. Given the multiple sources of feedback in the former study, it is not surprising that students would utilize all of them, nor is it particularly shocking that they would appear to pay more attention to teacher feedback. In contrast to both studies, Nelson and Murphy (1993) reported a mixed finding: Analyses of the responses given and the revisions made by four intermediate ESL students in an ongoing (10-week) response group determined that students sometimes, but not always, utilized peer comments in revising their drafts, and that the extent to which they did so appeared to be based on group dynamics. That is, writers were more likely to incorporate their peers' suggestions when the former had interacted with the group (rather than just listening passively) and when they had adopted a cooperative, rather than defensive, stance toward peer suggestions.

Several studies have examined the types of revisions made by student writers in response to peer commentary. Both Berger (1990) and Connor and Asenavage (1994) used Faigley and Witte's (1981) taxonomy of revisions to categorize the types of revisions made in response to feedback from various sources (peers and self in the earlier study and peers, teacher, and self/other in the later report). Berger found that the majority (over 65%) of her 46 participants' revisions fell into the broad subcategory of surface changes, regardless of feedback source (peer or self-evaluation). Connor and Asenavage found that one of their two groups made more surface changes, whereas the other made more text-based changes. They suggested that the difference may result both from a greater focus on surface issues during the peer feedback session of the first group. The findings of both studies, indicating that ESL students tend to focus on surface changes while revising, are consistent with other studies of L2 revision regardless of whether peer feedback is involved (see Ferris, 1997, for a review; cf. Fig 6.1).

A longitudinal case study by Huang (1994) examined students' progress in effective peer response and revision. Huang tracked four EFL students in Taiwan over two semesters, finding that students' feedback became more substantive and collaborative over time and that the two weaker students made more progress in revision skills, shifting from surface to text-based revisions, whereas the stronger writers did not appear to change their revision strategies. Huang also noted that students' personalities and writing abilities affected their behavior and interaction within the group, specifically observing that the weaker writers tended to relinquish control of their texts in peer response sessions, whereas the stronger writers reacted more assertively and sometimes defensively.

Other studies have examined whether peer response activities have a beneficial effect on writers and their written products. In a dissertation case study, Resh (1994) examined the effects of responding to other students' texts on three student writers, concluding that the activity of responding to peers' papers does predict and influence the writers' own future revision behaviors. In an experimental study of college French L2 students, Hedgcock and Lefkowitz (1992) found that texts written by students who revised collaboratively received higher scores than those who revised after receiving teacher feedback instead.

$\Rightarrow AA\ 6.1$

Student Opinions About Peer Feedback. Studies of student reactions to peer feedback and preferences regarding peer response versus other forms of

I. Surface Changes (Mechanics) [i.e., corrections of errors]
   A. Punctuation
   B. Spelling
   C. Capitalization
   D. Pluralization
   E. Word form corrections other than pluralizations (e.g., subject–verb
      agreement, tense changes)
   F. Substitutions (e.g., fewer for less)
   G. Corrected typographical errors (e.g., the for hte)
   H. Corrections on bibliographic format
II. Stylistic Changes
   A. Lexical changes—Stylistic word substitutions (e.g., several for a few; increase
      for grow)
   B. Phrasing
      1. Syntactic (meaning-preserving rewordings; including adding
         or deleting words: e.g., to avoid an awkward construction)
      2. Structural (meaning-preserving sentence restructuring: e.g., "When
         we went outside" for "Having gone outside")
III. Structural Changes
   A. Organization (within paragraphs; within essay)
   B. Paragraphing (moving whole paragraphs; creating new paragraphs
      from existing ones)
IV. Content Changes
   A. Addition of new material (new subject matter or ideas—as distinct
      from simply adding new words to tighten a phrase or sentence, as in IIB)
      to develop subject or clarify points
   B. Deleting material (deleting subject matter or ideas—as distinct
      from deleting words to make a sentence or phrase tighter, as in IC)
   C. Altering an idea, argument, etc. (e.g., changing from pro to con on an issue;
      shifting focus from description to narration)

FIG. 6.1. Coding scheme for revisions (from Yagelski, 1995, pp. 237–238).

feedback have varied both in research design and results. Mangelsdorf (1992) asked 40 ESL students to respond in writing to four structured-response questions ranging from whether they found peer feedback valuable to what types of suggestions they receive from their peers. They found that 55% of the students had overall positive responses to peer review and 69% of the total comments expressed positive reactions to peer review. She also found that 68% of the comments focused on content, "focusing primarily on the positive effect that peer reviews had on clarifying, developing, generating, and comparing ideas" (p. 276). Similarly, Leki

(1990b) asked 20 ESL students to respond in writing to two questions: one concerning the value of reading other students' papers and the other about the helpfulness of peer comments on their own papers. Leki found that the students overwhelmingly felt that reading peers' papers was helpful and that they generally also felt that peer feedback on their own papers was of value. A few students expressed concerns about the tone and quality of the feedback they received from peers (discussed earlier).

Employing a different research design, Mendonça and Johnson (1994) conducted postinterviews with their 12 graduate student participants after peer review sessions and again after revisions were completed. The researchers asked four questions about the students' reactions to the peer feedback, the extent to which they considered feedback from peers and other sources in revising their papers, and their preferences regarding teacher versus peer feedback. Participants all claimed to have found the peer review activity beneficial and felt both peer and teacher feedback to be important. Along similar lines, Zhang (1995) asked 81 college/university ESL students whether they preferred teacher, peer, or self-feedback. In that study, teacher feedback was found to be greatly preferred (94%) over other response forms, whereas peer feedback was preferred (61%) over self-feedback.

In a recent microethnographic study by Carson and Nelson (1996), three Chinese ESL students were interviewed about their impressions after watching videotapes of their own peer response groups over a 6-week period. Carson and Nelson observed five major topics covered in the participants' responses: reluctance to criticize drafts, reluctance to disagree with peers, reluctance to claim authority, feelings of vulnerability, and interaction patterns (e.g., softening criticisms and indirectness). The researchers maintained that the Chinese students' behaviors and perceptions are not optimal for successful peer response groups. Based on their findings, Carson and Nelson asked this rhetorical question: "What happens [to peer feedback] if the students are more interested in maintaining positive group relations than in helping each other with their writing?" (p. 18). The principles outlined in Fig. 6.2 address these and other important practical concerns.

⇒ *AA 6.2*

Principles of Effective Peer Response Activities

Making Peer Response an Integral Part of the Course.   One of the most comprehensive treatments to date on techniques for utilizing peer response is by Mittan (1989), who presented a number of arguments in favor of peer review and some guiding principles for its implementation. Mittan's first principle is to make peer review an integrated part of the writing course rather than something that occurs only in isolated instances. This can be accomplished in several ways: (a) by making clear to the students from the beginning of the course that peer response

1. Make peer response an integral part of the course.
2. Model the process.
3. Build peer response skills progressively throughout the term.
4. Structure the peer response task.
5. Vary peer response activites.
6. Hold students accountable for giving feedback and for considering the feedback they receive.
7. Consider individual student needs.
8. Consider logistical issues, including
   - The size and compositon of groups
   - The mechanics of exchanging papers.

FIG. 6.2. Principles of effective peer response.

will be required, even noting in the syllabus (where applicable) when peer group activities will take place; (b) by utilizing peer review frequently and consistently throughout the term; (c) by using peer review to accomplish a variety of goals; and, (d) by holding students accountable (through grades and feedback) for their responses and for serious consideration of peer feedback in writing and revising their own papers.

Modeling the Process.   Most advocates of peer response in L2 writing stress the importance of teacher input and modeling prior to the first peer response session (Carson & Nelson, 1996; Leki, 1990b; Lockhart & Ng, 1995; Mittan, 1989; Nelson & Murphy, 1992/1993, 1993). Typical suggestions include discussing with students the arguments in favor of peer response, giving them guidelines for acceptable responses in terms of both substance and tone, and having them practice the process via role-play and/or whole-class reading and discussion of sample essays not written by class members. For the more ambitious teacher, Carson and Nelson (1996) suggested asking students to view videotapes of response groups from previous semesters to analyze the types of comments made and the language used to express opinions. Similarly, Lockhart and Ng (1995) suggested that students be given transcripts of peer review sessions to examine. It is also important to point out that teachers implicitly and indirectly (and sometimes unconsciously) model feedback patterns for their students through their own oral and written responses to student papers (Connor & Asenavage, 1994; Lockhart & Ng, 1995; Stanley, 1992). If a teacher focuses intensively on surface errors or writes brief, cryptic comments on student texts, the students will also adopt those priorities and behaviors in responding to one another's writing. However, if the teacher assumes a friendly, interested, collaborative stance in responding to student papers, the students will similarly attempt to follow this model. (See Calkins, 1983, for an excellent ethnographic analysis of the impact of teacher response on peer and self-feedback.)

Building Peer Response Skills Progressively Throughout the Term. Mittan (1989) suggested that the basic format of peer review (Koch, 1982) remain consistent throughout the writing course. That is, the reader should (a) offer a positive response and encouragement to the writer, (b) identify the purpose or main point(s) of the text, (c) direct questions to the writer, and (d) offer suggestions. However, Mittan suggested that as the term progresses, teachers should "raise the ante slightly, asking students to detail why they find a particular passage effective or to explain how a suggested revision will improve the writing" (p. 213). Building students' competence in reading and responding to peers' papers can be accomplished by careful structuring of peer review tasks and by gradually increasing their difficulty.

Of course, along with the notion of building students' skills in peer feedback comes the assumption that teachers are committed to the process and are willing to set reasonable expectations for the activity—and to be patient as students' responding skills develop. Teachers should not expect students to assume full responsibility for providing feedback to one another or to be exempted from the process, if for no other reason than that students simply will not be capable of providing adequate feedback, especially at the beginning of the term. Therefore, instructors should remember that effective responding is a skill that develops with practice and coaching over time (Huang, 1994; Mittan, 1989); even if students initially do not provide particularly effective feedback to peers, they still benefit from reading one another's papers (Leki, 1990b; Mangelsdorf, 1992; Mittan, 1989; Resh, 1994; Stanley, 1992) as well as from the relationships and classroom community that grow through peer review activities.

Structuring the Peer Response Task. Although peer response enthusiasts agree that providing students with guidance for the peer review sessions is critical, some experts disagree about the extent to which teachers should structure peer review activities. Advocates of a less structured approach have argued that, if the teacher is overly directive or prescriptive about the substance or form of peer feedback, students' interactions will reflect the instructor's intentions and priorities rather than their own independent thoughts and reactions—another form of teacher appropriation of the writing process (Elbow, 1973; Lockhart & Ng, 1995; Nelson & Murphy, 1992/1993; see chap. 5 for further discussion of feedback and appropriation). The guidelines for students proposed by Nelson and Murphy (1992/1993), for instance, simply advise students to "describe [their] reactions to the paper" and to "be specific—point to particular items in the paper" (p. 25). Lockhart and Ng (1995) suggested that "guiding questions may help provide a direction and a focus to the interaction," but that once students become comfortable with the process, "they should be allowed greater autonomy to respond according to the needs of the text and the writer" (p. 648).

Others experts, however, have suggested that writing group sessions be carefully structured to build responding skills, vary the peer review tasks, and provide indirect instruction. Even within this faction, there is divergence of opinion. For example, Moore (1986) advocated using the same peer response form throughout the course so that students can feel comfortable with the task and response process. Mittan (1989) suggested instead that teachers should "design a peer review sheet specifically for each peer review session" (p. 215), arguing that this allows a teacher to build on previous peer response sessions, vary the task according to the specifications of the assignment at hand, and respond to students' needs, strengths, or weaknesses. Commenting on the issue of teacher appropriation in response to student writing, Reid (1994) noted that "the teacher's primary responsibility is to provide opportunities for change in the classroom" (p. 277) and that "teachers must intervene to provide adequate schemata ... that will serve as a scaffolding for writing" (p. 286). In the present context, when peer response tasks are carefully structured to meet pedagogical goals, they can serve as a form of modeling and instruction that is qualitatively different from traditional lecturing or even direct oral feedback from the instructor.

Figure 6.3 illustrates a sample peer response form, the advantages of which are explained by Mittan (1989):

Writer's Name: _____ Reviewer's Name: _____

Your purpose in answering these questions is to provide an an honest and helpful response to your partner's draft and to suggest ways to make his/her writing better. *Be sure to read the entire paper carefully before writing any responses.* Be as specific as possible, referring to particular parts of the paper in your answers.

1. What do you like most about the paper? Choose the most interesting idea and EXPLAIN WHY it captured your attention.
2. **In your own words**, state what you think the paper is about.
3. What parts of the paper need to have more detail added so that readers could understand it better?
4. Choose the statement you most agree with:

     ____ Each of your paragraphs discusses only one idea, and everything in the paragraph is related to that specific idea.

     ____ Some of your paragraphs are confusing because they seem to be about more than one idea. I marked them with an X.

     ____ Your writing seems to be all in one paragraph. I can't tell where you start discussing a new idea. Please help!

5. On the back of this page, write a short letter to your partner explaining how his or her writing can be improved. BE VERY SPECIFIC and explain *why* you think these changes will help readers. Begin your letter with your partner's name and sign your own name.

FIG. 6.3. Sample peer review form—completed essay draft.

1. It begins with clear instructions as to the purpose, audience, and procedure for completing the form;
2. It is limited to one page;
3. It follows a format of encouragement, identification of purpose, questions and suggestions, which can be used for all peer response activities and can also be utilized in teacher feedback, thus providing an integrated and consistent framework for response throughout the writing course;
4. The question types and tasks vary from open-ended comments (Questions 1 and 3) to reformulation of the writer's main idea (Question 2), to selecting the most appropriate response from several choices (Question 4), to writing a letter (which Mittan calls "mini-essays in themselves") to the writer. Question 5, the letter-writing task, "stipulates a particular genre and indicates the role of the participants, both of which are familiar and informal" (Mittan, 1989, p. 217).

Appendix 6A also provides several examples of peer response forms written to correspond with different writing assignments in an ESL freshman composition course using *Guidelines* (Spack, 1990, 1996) as the primary text. These forms illustrate how peer response activities can vary as a term progresses and as writing tasks and assignments evolve.

Varying Peer Response Activities.   The most typical version of peer response takes place when students exchange completed drafts and give one another feedback before the writers undertake revision. Yet peer interaction need not be limited to comments on completed drafts. Writing groups can function within a class to perform a variety of tasks. For instance, students can engage in idea-generation or prewriting activities and then collaborate before even beginning a draft. Sample activities are shown in Figs. 6.4 and 6.5. Figure 6.4 displays two common idea-generation activities (listing and freewriting) and shows how peers can help each other find ideas (Strategy 1) and focus them more clearly (Strategy 2).

The activity shown in Fig. 6.5 encourages students to clarify their ideas before committing themselves to an entire completed draft by listing ideas, preparing an informal outline, and drafting an essay introduction. They then show their introduction to a peer to assess how clearly they have expressed their initial ideas.

Peers can also be involved in the writing process at the editing stage, helping classmates to look for grammatical and/or mechanical errors prior to producing a final draft (Ferris, 1995c). Furthermore, after a paper has been completed and polished, many writing teachers like to finish the process with a *publication* or *celebration* stage, in which student writers share their finished products with their writing groups or with the entire class. Although the sharing of papers with a whole group is perhaps more feasible with primary and secondary students because they spend more time in class (Calkins, 1983), students in a college setting can either

STRATEGY 1: MAKING A LIST. To begin, you can list several experiences and concepts that might be good topics for a personal essay. Here are some examples:

EXPERIENCES: CONCEPTS:
Leaving home   Loneliness
Starting at a new school   Self-respect
Learning a new language   Fear

Activity: **Working in a small group**, add five topics to the lists of experiences and concepts. Share your lists with the other groups in the class.

Follow-up: Make a list of topics you might want to write about in your own personal essay. Star the topics that seem most promising.

STRATEGY 2: FREEWRITING. Sometimes writing quickly on a topic will stimulate your ideas and help you identify things to include in your essay.
     Guidelines for Freewriting:
     1. Write quickly and steadily for a brief period of time (5 to 10 minutes is ideal).
     2. Do not worry about mistakes, word choice, style, etc.
     3. Whatever you do—Do not stop writing. If your mind goes blank, write "I don't know what to write. I don't know ..." until a new thought develops.
     Activity:
     1. Choose one of the topics you starred in the "making a list" activity. Freewrite for 5 minutes on that topic.
     2. **Exchange freewrites with a partner. Have that partner underline a word, phrase, or idea from your freewrite that particularly interests him or her.**
     3. Now take the word/phrase/concept **that your partner identified** and freewrite on that for 5 minutes.

FIG. 6.4. Peer collaboration during brainstorming activities.
(Note: Collaborative portions of the activities are shown in **bold**.
Adapted from Spack, 1990, pp. 38–40.)

share their final papers with their writing group or the papers can be compiled into a booklet to be reproduced and shared with classmates.

$\Rightarrow AA\ 6.2$

Finally, there are many other activities within a composition class that can be completed in pairs or groups. For instance, pairs and groups of students can discuss course readings with one another, take turns preparing questions and leading the class through a discussion of an assigned course reading, work together on oral presentations or debates related to course readings or essay topics, and go to the

---

PREWRITING ACTIVITES

1. What reading(s) have you selected to comment on?
2. Write a two- to three-sentence reaction to the essay.
3. Make a list of details, examples, or experiences you might use to support or contradict the ideas in the reading. Write your list below.
   List of possible examples:

4. Following the example of Doxiadis (1990, p. 107), organize your list into an informal outline.
5. Read p. 109 on "The Introduction." Draft an introduction for your essay. Be sure to include the three steps listed on p. 109!

PREWRITING: PEER RESPONSE

Your Name: _____   Writer's Name: _____

Read your group member's introduction draft and write down **brief** answers to the following questions:

1. Which essay(s) has your classmate selected to respond to?
2. What is your classmate's reaction to the essay? How do you know?
3. What ideas or examples from his or her own experience might your classmate be planning to include in his or her paper?

After you have written your responses, compare them with the worksheet that your group member completed. This should give both of you an idea of how clear the introduction is and what still needs to be improved!

FIG. 6.5. Peer response during the initial drafting phase.
(Note: These activities are based on an essay assignment in which students had to select a reading from their textbook [Spack, 1990] and relate the ideas in the reading to their own experiences. Page numbers in the instructions refer to the textbook.)

library together to find sources for a research paper. None of these activities deals specifically with the students' own writing. However, used in conjunction with peer response sessions, they can help build relationships among students, leading to a greater sense of classroom community. Moreover, these activities can give students valuable experience working collaboratively on both written and oral assignments—an important skill that is increasingly needed in subject-matter university courses (Ferris & Tagg, 1996). Collaborative tasks are especially useful for accommodating students from collectivist cultures who expect group work to benefit the group as a whole (not just individual writers; Carson & Nelson, 1994, 1996). In addition, cooperative activities allow for the integration of language skills (listening, speaking, reading, writing) in the L2 writing class, all of which are important for both writing development and second language acquisition in general (Mangelsdorf, 1989).

Holding Students Accountable for Giving Feedback and Considering Peers' Responses.   Mittan (1989) and Leki (1990b) encouraged teachers to read and respond to peer feedback. Mittan went a step further by suggesting that students actually be assigned grades on their peer response sheets. Both authors stressed that the writer and respondent each needs access to the teacher's feedback on the peer responses (e.g., by receiving photocopies of the response form with the teacher's feedback) "so that both may know what is expected" of respondents (Leki, 1990b, p. 17). In addition to providing feedback and/or grades on the quality and substance of the peer feedback, teachers can ask writers to write a brief summary of and reaction to the feedback they have received from peers (e.g., in a journal entry). Alternatively, they can ask students to compose a letter in which they explain how they incorporated peer feedback into their revisions (or discuss why they chose not to do so) when they submit their revised work. All of these techniques help students take the peer review process seriously, consider the peer feedback they give carefully, and think critically about the responses they have received from classmates.

Considering Individual Students' Needs.   Most of the principles and suggestions outlined so far assume a relatively advanced level of linguistic and writing proficiency. Mittan (1989) claimed that peer review activities could be incorporated at all levels and for all age groups. Along similar lines, Berger (1990) suggested that "teachers should adjust their expectations and the amount of guidance they give to [students'] proficiency level, maturity, and backgrounds ... [and] teach much simpler and more specific feedback techniques with a lower level writing class" (p. 30). Nelson and Murphy (1992/1993) reported that peer response activities worked well with intermediate-level students in a university-level intensive English program. Huang (1994) found that weaker writers benefited even more than stronger writers from peer review. Several popular entry-level academic writing textbooks (e.g., Benesch, Rakijas, & Rorschach, 1987; Reid & Lindstrom, 1985; Rooks, 1988) offer a variety of simple, focused peer response activities for students with low levels of English proficiency and limited English writing experience (see Fig. 6.6).

$$\boxed{\Rightarrow AA\ 6.4}$$

Students' prior experiences with collaborative learning and with U.S. writing courses may also affect their reactions toward and behaviors in writing groups (Allaei & Connor, 1990; Carson & Nelson, 1994, 1996). Leki (1990b) noted that,

Sharing Information Before Writing

Get into a group with two or three classmates. Read your personal information forms out loud to each other. You may ask each other for more information. Then write the information about you and your group members in the chart below. Use the information in the chart to write a paragraph called "About My Group."

Name:			
Country:			
Language:			
Hobby:			
Major:			
Other:			

(Adapted from Benesch et al., 1987, pp. 19–21.)

Sharing a Paragraph Draft (General)

Read your paragraph about yourself to a small group of classmates or to a partner. You may read it more than once or you may give it to them to read. Ask them what they think about your paragraph. Do they understand everything? Ask them for at least one more piece of information they would like to see in your paragraph. Then read your paragraph again. Is there anything you want to change? How can you write your ideas more clearly? (Adapted from Rooks, 1988, p. 4.)

Sharing a Paragraph Draft (Specific)

Write a paragraph describing one thing about your country. Your reader will be a classmate from a different country. Then exchange paragraphs with that classmate, read your partner's paragraph, and answer the following questions:

1. What questions did the writer answer (Who? What? etc.). Underline the answers to the questions in the paragraph.
2. What did you find most interesting about this paragraph?
3. What other interesting information could the writer add to this paragraph? (Adapted from Reid & Lindstrom, 1985, pp. 52–53.)

FIG. 6.6. Peer response activities for students at lower proficiency levels.

ironically, students with limited literacy experience in their L1 (i.e., immigrant students) may have an easier time with peer review because their judgments of peers' texts will not be colored by L1 rhetorical schemata. Further, they may have attended U.S. schools for a number of years and have become familiar and comfortable with U.S.-style group work. International students, particularly those who are highly educated and have strong L1 literacy skills, may need some preparatory contrastive rhetoric consciousness-raising (during the modeling phase of the peer response process) before attempting to critique other students' work (see chap. 1).

Some students may object to peer response activities on personal and/or cultural grounds. Learning style research indicates that some students learn best through working individually; such students may be frustrated and resentful at being forced to spend class time in group work and to share their writing with others (cf. Reid, 1995a). Other students, influenced by sociocultural expectations, may feel that the teacher is the only legitimate critic of student writing and that it is inappropriate to offer opinions about or critique other students' work (Carson & Nelson, 1994, 1996). Teachers should certainly be aware of and sensitive to students' feelings, but they can dispel some student objections through careful preparation and modeling, thoughtful matching of participants to pairs and groups, and pointing out the advantages of peer feedback. Not only does peer feedback promote writing development (e.g., many professional writers depend on writers' groups), but it also builds relationships and enables learners to work with peers—activities that will be important throughout their U.S. academic experience (Ferris & Tagg, 1996). A compromise position would be to have students work collaboratively during the first half of the term and then allow them to opt out of peer response sessions later on in the term (in which case they should complete self-evaluation activities while others are working collaboratively).

Logistical Concerns. As Mittan (1989) noted, successful peer review sessions require more than "simply telling students to exchange their papers and comment on them" (p. 212). Before beginning collaborative work in the writing class, teachers must consider several practical questions:

1. How big should the groups be, and how should they be formed? Although writing teachers vary in their preferred group size, the optimal number of students working together is probably between two and four. The advantage of dyads is that students have the time to engage in thoughtful consideration of peers' papers and in substantive in-class interaction; the benefit of having three or four students in a group is a wider range of opinions and perspectives. A group larger than four may be unable to give adequate time to reading and discussing each participant's paper; larger groups also diminish individuals' opportunities to contribute and participate in the discussion due to reduced floor time.

Some would argue that students should be able to select their own peer groups. Nonetheless, there are compelling reasons for the teacher to assign learners to specific groups and to maintain consistent groups throughout the course. Because there is some evidence that peer response is most beneficial if there is a range of writing abilities, teachers can take students' strengths and weaknesses into account when placing students in groups. The teacher also should consider students' first language backgrounds (there are advantages and disadvantages to both homogeneous and heterogeneous L1 groups), gender, and personality in forming groups. Also, if group composition remains the same, students have the advantage of becoming familiar with group members' work and seeing development over successive drafts, enabling respondents to give more specific and helpful feedback. However, if it becomes clear that a particular dyad or group is not working well together, the teacher may need to consider some reconfiguration later in the term.

2. How will students exchange papers? The simplest way for students to read one another's papers is to exchange them in class and read them on the spot. However, problems can occur if some students fail to bring their drafts to class on peer review day; in-class reading of drafts can also be time-consuming. (Although the standard L1 peer review practice is for the writer to read his or her paper aloud to a partner or group, this practice is problematic for some ESL students due to listening comprehension and pronunciation difficulties.) A possible solution to these problems is to ask writers to bring a photocopy of their drafts to class the day before the peer review session so that group members can read writers' papers at home and be prepared to discuss them. Another option that is rapidly becoming easier and more widely available is for students to exchange and comment on drafts electronically (see chap. 9).

3. Should peer feedback be oral or written? Giving students specific questions to answer and requiring them to write their responses emphasizes the importance of the activity and enables the teacher to hold students accountable for their efforts. However, ESL students may sit silently in class, write out answers to the questions, exchange forms with their partners, and never engage in any discussion. A way to avoid this problem is to require students to read drafts and write responses before coming to class (again, both can be accomplished electronically), using class time to engage in oral interaction about their reactions to the papers. If this is not possible, the teacher should monitor peer groups carefully to ensure that students are talking as well as writing. For instance, the teacher can specify how much time students will be given to read the papers, write reactions on the peer response forms, and discuss their reactions.

4. What about time management and crowd control? Any time a teacher engages in group work, he or she relinquishes a certain amount of control over class time and student participation. The teacher should allot time in the syllabus and lesson plans for peer review and should be careful to plan adequate time for the activity, especially if students are reading drafts for the first time in class (cf. chap. 3). It is also helpful, as already discussed, to give students time parameters at the beginning of the session and then remind them when to move along in the responding process ("It's time to switch and talk about your partner's paper now"). Another risk inherent in group work is that some groups may work more quickly or slowly than others. The instructor should be prepared with follow-up activities for group members who finish early and should check in with slower groups to help them to stay on task and pick up their pace if necessary. If the teacher structures the activity clearly, arranges the groups carefully, and is consistently involved in monitoring the groups, this should minimize the noise level and keep students on track.

SUMMARY AND IMPLICATIONS

Our overview of research on peer response activities appears to leave us with almost as many questions as answers. Studies of student opinion generally indicate that ESL students like peer feedback and find it helpful. At the same time, other studies report that students pay more attention to and prefer teacher feedback. Studies of the influence of teacher feedback on student revision are unfortunately few in number, consist of only small participant samples, and report conflicting results. The key to reconciling the contradictory evidence may lie in studies that characterize students' stances and communicative functions as they interact (e.g., Huang, 1994; Lockhart & Ng, 1995; Mangelsdorf & Schlumberger, 1992; Mendonça & Johnson, 1994; Villamil & deGuerrero, 1996), in investigations that carefully consider cross-cultural issues in peer response (Allaei & Connor, 1990; Carson & Nelson, 1994, 1996), as well as in descriptions of student personalities, relative linguistic and literacy abilities, and prior educational experience. Nonetheless, based on the existing evidence, the following generalizations are offered:

- Students adopt a variety of stances during peer response, with the most frequent being an authoritative or prescriptive stance and the most beneficial being a collaborative stance;
- Students discuss a variety of issues during peer review sessions; thus it should not be assumed that peer reviewers are excessively concerned with grammar/surface issues;
- There appears to be a strong relationship between teachers' feedback patterns and the style and substance of peer commentary;
- In some contexts, students do appear to take peer feedback into account when revising, but the research conflicts regarding the extent to which students utilize peers' comments;
- When students do revise based on peer commentary, their revisions tend to consist of surface, rather than text-based, changes (this generalization holds across all L2 revision studies regardless of whether peer response is involved); and
- Students generally like peer response and feel that it is helpful, but they also express concerns about the accuracy and validity of peers' feedback and, if forced to choose, would probably prefer teacher commentary over peer feedback.

Despite some of the potential problems and unresolved questions, carefully designed peer response activities can be extremely beneficial to individual student writers and to the overall classroom climate. Teachers who dismiss peer feedback as a technique because it doesn't work, or wastes time, or because the students don't like it may have inappropriate expectations concerning the procedure (e.g., that it can replace or drastically reduce the need for teacher response) or may not have structured peer review sessions appropriately. Although the cost of peer response as an integrated part of a writing course is high—it takes a great deal of time not easily spared from the typically crowded composition syllabus—the potential benefits are enormous. The principles and practical suggestions outlined in this chapter should help ESL writing teachers to implement this valuable technique more successfully.

Reflection and Review

1. What are some hypothetical arguments in favor of using peer response instead of teacher response or vice versa? What are arguments in favor of implementing both?
2. After reflecting on your own experience and reading the ideas presented in this chapter, what do you think is the single greatest potential benefit for students who participate in peer feedback activities? Can you think of any conditions or circumstances that could prevent this advantage from being realized in a real classroom context?
3. After reflecting on your own experience and reading the ideas presented in this chapter, what do you think is the single greatest potential drawback for students who participate in peer feedback activities? Can you think of any steps that a teacher might take either to prevent or solve this problem?
4. Imagine you are about to teach an ESL writing class and that you have decided to implement peer review as a regular, integrated part of your class. What are your expectations about what your students will gain or be able to accomplish from participating in peer response activities?
5. Do you agree with those who favor a more open-ended, less structured approach to peer response or those who advocate tighter teacher control? (This chapter clearly favors the latter position. Justify your opinion.)
6. What are the advantages and disadvantages of allowing students to choose their own partners or groups versus teacher assignment of groups? (Although this chapter clearly favors the latter position, there are good arguments to be made on both sides.)
7. What are the advantages and disadvantages of peer feedback groups consisting of homogeneous L1 groups? What could be done to optimize the advantages and mitigate the disadvantages?

**Application Activity 6.1: Investigating the Effects
of Peer Response on Revision**

Directions. To conduct a small study based on Mendonça and Johnson
(1994) and Connor and Asenavage (1994), complete the following steps:

1. Find an ESL writing teacher who regularly utilizes peer response activities
as an integrated part of his or her writing class. Ask the teacher if you can visit the
class, observe and tape record the interactions of one writing group or dyad, and
make copies of the group members' papers (both the draft under discussion and the
next revision). Obtain permission from the students to eavesdrop and tape record
the peer feedback session, analyze their papers, and conduct interviews with them
after they have completed their revisions.

2. Visit the class, observe, take notes on, and tape record the peer response
session; obtain copies of the student drafts discussed during the peer response
session.

3. Make arrangements to obtain copies of the student revisions and conduct
postinterviews with the students. The postinterviews should last 15 to 30 minutes
and should be audiotaped for later review. Ask the following questions:

   a. What was your reaction to the peer review activity? Did you like it or not?
   Why?

   b. Were your peer(s)' comments helpful? Did you use them in writing your
   revision?

   c. Did you use other sources to help you revise your draft? If so, which ones?
   (Adapted from Mendonça & Johnson, 1994, p. 750)

4. Transcribe the tape recordings you made of the peer feedback session and
postinterviews.

5. Compare the original drafts and revisions following the procedure described
by Mendonça and Johnson (1994).

Analysis procedure: First, label the parts of the second draft that were discussed
during the peer review (PR). Second, compare the drafts to identify what students
did and did not revise after the peer review. Place the labels R (revised) and NR
(not revised) in the second drafts next to the parts that were or were not modified,
respectively. You should have three categories with the following labels: PR/R,
PR/NR, and R/NPR (revised, no peer review comments). Calculate totals and
percentages for each category on each revision.

6. Analyze the types of revisions made. Use the analysis scheme developed by
Yagelski (1995), which is adapted from Faigley and Witte (1981) and reproduced
in Fig. 6.1.

7. Write a paper in which you present and analyze your findings, comparing
them with those discussed in this chapter.

Application Activity 6.2: Surveying Student Attitudes Toward Peer Response

Directions.

1. Find an ESL writing teacher who regularly utilizes peer response activities as an integrated part of his or her writing class. Ask the teacher if you can visit the class, administer a survey to the students, and interview him or her later about the results.
2. Using the following survey questions (adapted from Leki, 1990; Zhang, 1995), prepare a survey form and make adequate copies for the class you will visit.
3. Attend the class, give instructions, and administer and collect the surveys.
4. Analyze the results. For Questions 1 and 2, simply collate and summarize the students' comments. For Questions 3 and 5, calculate totals and percentages for the responses.
5. Interview the teacher about the survey results. Ask him or her to what extent the students' views match their comments and behavior in class.
6. Write an analysis of your survey results and teacher interview, comparing your findings with those of the published research, as summarized earlier.

Survey Questions.

1. Do you find it useful to read other students' papers during peer response activities? Why or why not?
2. Do you find it useful to hear/read other students' comments on your papers? Why or why not?
3. If you had to choose, would you prefer (check one):
   ☐ Teacher feedback?
   ☐ Peer feedback?
4. If you had to choose, would you prefer (circle one):
   ☐ Peer feedback?
   ☐ Self-feedback?
5. Check the one statement that *best* expresses your opinion about receiving feedback on your papers:
   ☐ a. I prefer to receive *only* teacher feedback.
   ☐ b. I prefer to receive *only* peer feedback.
   ☐ c. I prefer to receive *both* teacher and peer feedback.
   ☐ d. I prefer to receive *no* feedback (and to revise on my own).
(Adapted from Leki, 1990b; Zhang, 1995)

Application Activity 6.3: Designing Peer Response Forms

Directions.   Imagine you are teaching high-intermediate to advanced ESL students in a high school or college English class. Their first two writing assignments are as follows:

1. An autobiographical essay in which they will describe a personal experience and reflect on its significance in their lives.
2. After reading an essay entitled "A Mason-Dixon Memory" (Davis, 1993), they must choose between the following essay prompts:

    a. In "A Mason-Dixon Memory," Clifton Davis discusses a time in his childhood in which his peers supported him, as well as narrating Dondre Green's story in which Dondre's teammates did the same. Discuss a time in your life when your peers either supported or deserted you, examining what you learned from this experience.

    b. "A Mason-Dixon Memory" details two separate instances of discrimination. Describe a time when you or someone you know were discriminated against because of one or more of the following factors: race, language, age, sex, religious beliefs, economic status, sexual orientatioin, or physical handicap. Based on this experience, do you agree or disagree with the author's conclusion that "love will always conquer hatred"?

Tasks.   [Study the examples in Fig. 6.3 and in Appendix 6A for ideas.]

1. For the first essay assignment, design two peer response forms: one that helps the students during the idea-generation or prewriting process, and one that leads the students through commenting on an entire completed draft.
2. Design one peer response form for the second essay assignment, assuming that students will be commenting on each other's completed drafts. In constructing this form, be sure to both build on your previous peer response activities (from #1) and tailor the questions/tasks to the specifications of the second assignment. (You

should be able to do this even without having read Davis' essay—focus instead on the two essay prompts from which students will choose.)

3. Write a one- to two-page analysis of your work in Tasks 1 and 2. Explain your rationale for constructing the peer response forms in the ways that you did, especially discussing how students' peer response skills will build from the first assignment to the second.

Application Activity 6.4: Giving and Receiving Peer Feedback

Directions.

1. Select a writing or teaching project you have been working on recently (e.g., a paper for a graduate course or conference presentation, a lesson plan or syllabus, a set of class materials). Find a partner who is working on the same project or something similar.

2. Using the ideas and examples discussed in this chapter, design a peer response form appropriate for the paper/project you will discuss.

3. Exchange materials with your partner. Before meeting together, read your partner's materials carefully and write answers to the peer response questions you constructed in Step 2.

4. Meet with your partner and discuss your responses to each other's papers. Take notes on and/or audiotape your discussion.

5. Write a reflective essay in which you discuss:
   - the experience of designing response questions for a professional project;
   - the experience of reading and responding to a peer's work;
   - what you thought about your partner's responses (written and oral) to your work. Did you agree with them? Find them valuable? Why or why not?
   - insights you gained about the peer response process from participating in the discussion and from your notes/tape of the discussion; and
   - how this experience relates to your own teaching and to the students you work with (or hope to).

APPENDIX 6A: SAMPLE PEER RESPONSE FORMS

Note: These forms were all written for the same group of students in an ESL freshman composition course. The primary text for the course was *Guidelines* (Spack, 1990). The essay prompts given to the students are also provided.

First Assignment: Write an essay in which you draw from your own experience to express a personal viewpoint. Describe in detail an event or experience (or series of events or experiences) that has led you to learn, believe, or understand something.

Audience: Your classmates and instructor.

Purpose: To help your audience understand why the experience was significant to you.

PEER RESPONSE FORM: Essay Assignment 1

Your name:_____ Writer's name: _____
Essay title: _____

1. What is the main idea of this essay? Try to write it in one sentence.
2. List the experience(s)/event(s)/example(s) the writer uses to communicate the main idea.
   a.
   b.
   c.
   d.
3. In what way(s) was the experience or event significant to the writer? Explain it in one sentence.
4. What did you like best about the essay?
5. List the two most important ways in which you think the essay should be improved.
   a.
   b.

<u>Second Assignment</u>: Write an essay in which you examine the relationship between ideas in the reading and your own ideas and attitudes. Refer to one or more of the readings in Part Two of *Guidelines*.

<u>Purpose</u>: To show how the ideas of (an)other author(s) compare with your own ideas or experiences, or to show how his or her ideas have influenced your own thinking. You must explain and evaluate the author's ideas; direct references to the reading(s) (summary, paraphrase, or quotation) are required.

PEER RESPONSE FORM: Essay Assignment 2

Your name:_____ Writer's name: _____
Essay title: _____

1. What is the main idea of this essay? State it in your own words.
2. What article(s) does the writer discuss in this essay?
   Author/Title:
   Author/Title:
3. What ideas from the writer's own experience are given to discuss the article's ideas?

IDEA FROM THE ARTICLE/IDEA FROM PERSONAL EXPERIENCE

   a.
   b.
   c.
4. What did you like best about this essay?
5. What are the two specific areas that need the most improvement?
   a.
   b.

<u>Third Assignment</u>: Choosing one of the essays from Part III, write an essay in which you analyze the author's argument. You should:

- Determine what the author says;
- Evaluate the strengths and/or weaknesses of his or her argument (including any points you think the author overlooked);
- Take a position in which you either agree or disagree with (or take a mixed position toward) some key idea(s) or issue(s) raised in the reading.

The purpose of the essay is to evaluate the effectiveness of the author's argument. Thus, extensive reference to the reading (summary, paraphrase, quotation) is necessary.

PEER RESPONSE FORM: Essay Assignment 3

Your name:_____ Writer's name: _____
Essay title: _____

1. Which argumentative essay (from the book) does the writer analyze?
2. Does the writer agree, disagree, or take a mixed position toward the essay she or he analyzed? How do you know?
3. In the chart below, summarize (a) the major points from the essay (in the textbook) to which the writer is responding and (b) the arguments the writer (your classmate) uses to agree/disagree with the original author.
   a. Original author's argument   b. Student writer's response to
      analyzed in this essay   each argument
      1)
      2)
      3)
4. List two major areas of improvement the writer should consider for the second draft. Be specific!
   a.
   b.

CHAPTER	Improving Accuracy in Student Writing: Grammar and Editing in the Composition Class
7	

Questions for Reflection

- In your own writing, at what point in the writing process do you begin to focus on the linguistic accuracy of your work?
- What techniques do you use to edit your writing for grammar, word choice, spelling, and punctuation?
- How and where did you acquire the grammatical knowledge that you use to edit your work?
- How effective is your approach to editing your own writing? If it is very effective, why do you think so? If it does not always work, what do you think might improve it?
- What ideas do you have about the best way(s) to help ESL students focus on editing their written work? Are these ideas congruent with your own editing process? Why or why not?

A BRIEF HISTORY OF GRAMMAR IN THE WRITING CLASS

Most writing theorists and instructors would agree that process-oriented pedagogy has greatly improved both L1 and L2 composition instruction. However, although students may be much better at idea generation and revision than they used to be, ESL student papers may contain excessive grammatical and lexical inaccuracies, by the standards of academicians. ESL professionals may understand that L2 acquisition is a process that takes time and that an expectation of perfect papers, even from advanced students, is unrealistic. Other readers of ESL student writing, however, often demand a fairly high level of accuracy.

Because of these realities and because ESL teachers will not always be there to assist their students, writing instructors need to help their students develop and improve their editing skills.

Prior to the advent of process-oriented instruction in ESL composition classes, teacher feedback to second language writing students was often excessively concerned with eradicating student errors (Applebee, 1981; Zamel, 1985) and that feedback was notably unsuccessful in helping reduce error frequency in subsequent student writing (see Truscott, 1996, for a review). However, as process writing techniques—with their emphasis on student writers' ideas and individual writing processes—have achieved widespread acceptance, some teachers swung to the opposite extreme, giving little or no attention to the morphosyntactic or lexical accuracy of students' final products (Horowitz, 1986a). Zamel (1982) reminded us that

> engaging students in the process of composing [does not eliminate] our obligation to upgrade their linguistic competencies.... If, however, students learn that writing is a process through which they can explore and discover their thoughts and ideas, then product is likely to improve as well. (p. 207)

This assertion illustrates the mixed messages delivered and received by teacher educators and some ESL writing instructors in the early to mid-1980s. That is, some experts and practitioners claimed that process-oriented instruction should not overlook the editing phase, but that the accuracy of students' texts will improve simply because they can explore and discover their thoughts and ideas. Because teaching grammar and editing skills to ESL writers can be tedious, difficult, and frustrating, some instructors (including the authors at times) took the principles of the process approach as license to overlook linguistic accuracy in their writing classes. While holding their breath and crossing their fingers, they trusted in the principle that "good writing is involved writing" (Horowitz, 1986a, p. 142) would hold true for their students.

The opposing extremes of obsessive attention to every student error and benign neglect of linguistic accuracy in favor of product-oriented concerns began to find some middle ground in the English for Academic Purposes (EAP) approach to writing instruction, led by Horowitz (1986a, 1986b), Johns (1993), Reid (1989), and Spack (1988), among others (Silva, 1990). This approach essentially represents a compromise position in which the best elements of process approach instruction, such as discovery and prewriting activities, multiple drafting, revision, collaboration, and so on, can be combined with a concern for helping students meet the expectations of a particular academic discourse community in both the content and form of their writing (see chap. 2). As a result, in the 1990s, many experienced teachers feel that attention to both fluency and accuracy in student writing is not only possible but necessary.

RESEARCH ON ERROR CORRECTION
IN L2 WRITING

There have been several lines of research examining error correction in ESL writing instruction. These studies have attempted to answer two important questions: (a) Why should we correct students' written errors (or attempt to teach students to correct them)? and (b) Does such error correction help student accuracy to improve in the short and/or long term?

Why Focus on Editing?

Given process advocates' arguments that we should focus primarily on students' ideas and reviews of research suggesting that error correction is largely ineffectual (Krashen, 1984; Leki, 1990a; Truscott, 1996; Zamel, 1985), it is fair to ask whether teachers should focus on novice L2 writers' grammar problems at all. A possible answer to this question comes from surveys of ESL student writers, which have consistently affirmed the priority that students place on receiving grammar instruction and feedback to improve their writing. As discussed in chapter 5, a growing body of research has investigated ESL students' opinions concerning the written feedback they receive from their teachers. Although the most recent studies suggest an increasing concern on the part of both teachers and students for improving ideas and organization, all of the studies conclude that students feel strongly about the importance of receiving substantial and useful feedback on their grammatical errors. Truscott (1996) argued that "students believe in correction ... but that does not mean that teachers should give it to them" (p. 359). Nevertheless, many teachers would respond that the absence of any form of grammar feedback can frustrate or worry students and consequently interfere with their motivation and confidence as developing writers.

$\boxed{\Rightarrow AA\ 7.1}$

In another line of research known as *error gravity studies* (Janopolous, 1992; Santos, 1988; Vann, Lorenz, & Meyer, 1991; Vann, Meyer, & Lorenz, 1984), university content area faculty have been asked to assess their tolerance for students' written errors by ranking different types of grammatical errors in order of importance. The results of these studies vary with respect to the specific syntactic, morphological, or lexical errors that professors find most egregious, but the results are fairly uniform on two points: In general, university faculty, in general, (a) are less tolerant of typical ESL errors than of typical native speaker errors, and (b) feel that students' linguistic errors are bothersome and affect their overall evaluation of student papers. In response to this research, some would argue that

ESL teachers should focus their attention on educating their subject-matter colleagues about the duration and limitations of the second language acquisition process. Although it might well be easier for professors to modify their requirements than for students to improve their accuracy, few would argue that ESL writing instructors should ignore their students' linguistic difficulties in the hope that their present or future subject-matter professors will eventually overcome their unrealistic expectations.

Students' and professors' opinions aside, perhaps the best argument for providing grammar feedback and developing students' editing skills is that writers must gradually become self-sufficient in editing their own writing. Regardless of a student's academic or career pursuits, there are likely to be points in his or her future at which the ability to produce written work that is as accurate as possible will be important—whether it is a university writing examination, thesis, on-the-job memo, business letter, report, or résumé. It is certainly arguable whether editing feedback and instruction are consistently effective for all students (Truscott, 1996). However, it seems clear that the absence of any feedback or strategy training will ensure that many students never take seriously the need to improve their editing skills (or that they have the knowledge and strategies to edit even when they do perceive its importance).

Does Error Correction Work?   After reviewing a number of studies on error correction in L2 writing, Truscott (1996) concluded that "grammar correction is not effective" (p. 340). However, in examining the studies that he reviewed (Cardelle & Corno, 1981; Carroll, Swain, & Roberge, 1992; Cohen & Robbins, 1976; Fathman & Whalley, 1990; Kepner, 1991; Lalande, 1982; Robb, Ross, & Shortreed, 1986; Semke, 1984; Sheppard, 1992), it is clear that the research goals, contexts, and methods in the various studies were so diverse that it is nearly impossible to generalize from them. In addition, as noted by Cohen and Robbins (1976) and Zamel (1985), teachers' corrections may be ineffectual and inaccurate. Although it is likely and even probable that poorly done error correction will not help students (the same could, of course, be said of poorly done feedback on students' ideas), it is difficult to conclude from the evidence presented that all error feedback produces uniformly disappointing results.

⇒ AA 7.2

Further, there is also some positive, if preliminary, evidence in favor of error correction. Two studies reviewed and critiqued by Truscott (1996) presented positive evidence for the effectiveness of error correction as defined in their respective studies. Fathman and Whalley's (1990) experimental study, which examined the effects of different feedback treatments on four groups of ESL students, concluded that students who received grammar feedback alone or a combination of content and grammar feedback improved the accuracy of their revised essays. Although Truscott correctly pointed out that this study, being experimental, provided no evidence that any improvement seen in student revisions would result in long-term improvements in writers' linguistic accuracy, Fathman and Whalley convincingly demonstrated that when parcicipants had errors located for them (i.e., underlined, but not corrected), they were successful in correcting many of them. In contrast, Lalande's (1982) longitudinal study assessed the effects of a systematic correction method he used with his students, which included a consistent error correction code, extensive student rewriting, and a chart of the types and frequency of errors made by individual students throughout the term. Lalande found that students taught by this method showed significant improvement over those instructed by traditional error correction methods (i.e., comprehensive correction of all errors). Lalande's study was justifiably criticized by both Truscott (1996) and VanPatten (1988) because of its lack of a control group receiving no error correction. Thus, it remains to be seen whether a comparable instructional/research design including a control group would yield similar results.

Two recent studies reported positive effects of error correction. Ferris (1995a) studied 30 ESL students, examining two in-class essays and three out-of-class essays written at regular intervals to see whether the editing approach used by their instructor (described in Ferris, 1995c) caused them to improve their accuracy in targeted categories of error. She observed that 28 of the 30 participants showed at least some improvement (as measured by a reduction in error frequency), although this improvement was not consistent over all error categories or essay assignments. Finally, in a discourse analytic study of the influence of teacher commentary on student revision, Ferris (1997) found that the vast majority of the teacher's verbal comments on grammar (i.e., comments in the margins or in an end note, as opposed to corrections) led to substantive and effective revisions in the participants' later drafts.

To summarize, Truscott (1996) was correct in asserting that the evidence supporting the effectiveness of error correction is scant, if not nonexistent. This conclusion must be heavily qualified by the inadequacy (both in terms of design and instructional methods) and lack of generalizability of the relatively few studies on this topic. According to Truscott (1996), his conclusion that grammar correction is not effective is reflective of real-world experience:

> Veteran teachers know that there is little direct connection between correction and learning. Often a student will repeat the same mistake over and over again, even after being corrected many times. When this occurs, it is tempting for the teacher to say the student is not attentive or lazy; however, the pervasiveness of the phenomenon, even with successful students, argues against any such explanation. Rather the teacher should conclude that correction simply is not effective. (p. 341)

Notwithstanding Truscott's strong position, our own experience, as well as that of our colleagues, suggests that there is tremendous variability in students' ability to benefit from grammar instruction and feedback and to learn self-correction techniques. Although Truscott's gloomy picture of the student making the "same mistake over and over again, even after being corrected many times" surely reflects the occasional experience of most veteran writing teachers, we also can point to many students who have made observable and encouraging progress in error correction after receiving selective, judicious feedback and strategy instruction. In summary, for both researchers and teachers, the answer to the question "Does error correction work?" must rest on three vital factors:

1. Is grammar feedback and instruction carried out selectively, systematically, and accurately?
2. Are individual student differences (including language proficiency, literacy skills, learning styles, motivation and attitude, first language, etc.) adequately addressed?
3. Are studies that assess the effectiveness of error correction designed and executed appropriately?

Only when these issues are addressed systematically in a body of research can Truscott's conclusion be definitively supported or refuted. For the purposes of this chapter, however, we proceed on the assumption—supported by the intuitions of many ESL writing teachers and certainly by those of their students—that grammar and editing feedback and instruction, when thoughtfully and carefully executed, can help many or most students improve the accuracy of their texts. It is the goal of the remainder of this chapter to discuss how such instruction can be implemented effectively. Nonetheless, it is important to note that we agree with Truscott's assertion (echoing that of early process advocates such as Zamel) that error correction can be harmful to students when it diverts teachers' and students' attention from other crucial aspects of the writing process. Figure 7.1 presents practical principles for error correction based on global inferences from the available empirical research.

---

1. Most sentence–level mechanical corrections are best left to the latter stages of the editing process. However, generalized feedback about students' major error patterns in early drafts may be helpful to them.
2. It is important for teachers to be *selective* in addressing students' written errors. Errors that should receive the greatest attention should include **serious** ("global") errors that interfere with the comprehensibility of the text, **stigmatizing** errors that most disturb NES audiences, and the student's most **frequent** errors.
3. Except for students at very beginning levels of language proficiency, **direct** correction techniques (in which the teacher corrects writers' errors) are not effective or appropriate. **Indirect** techniques, such as noting the location and/or type of error and asking students to find and correct their own errors, are most effective for intermediate to advanced students.

FIG. 7.1. Summary of research findings on error correction in L2 writing.

PEDAGOGICAL ISSUES IN ERROR CORRECTION

When Should Errors Be Corrected?

In early discussions of error correction in ESL composition instruction (Hendrickson, 1978; Krashen, 1984), it was suggested that teachers can most effectively help students reduce their written errors by intervening between composition drafts (rather than after a terminal draft) to point out the location of salient errors—a suggestion congruent with that of L1 researchers (Freedman, 1987; Hillocks, 1986; Knoblauch & Brannon, 1981). As discussed previously, there is some preliminary evidence (Fathman & Whalley, 1990; Ferris, 1995a, 1997; Lalande, 1982) that noting error location and/or patterns on intermediate drafts does help students produce more accurate revisions. There is little direct evidence (other than Ferris, 1995a, which reported mixed findings) that such feedback produces long-term improvement. Nevertheless, it has been pointed out in other contexts that correction may be most effective when it is contextualized: "Accuracy, fluency, and overall communicative skills are probably best developed through instruction that is primarily meaning-based but in which guidance is provided through timely form-focus activities and correction in context" (Lightbown & Spada, 1994, p. 323). As this argument applies to writing, form-focused feedback is probably most effective when it is contextualized (i.e., specific to the student's own writing) and when it occurs at a point in the composing process when the writer may be most aware of its importance and therefore likely to attend to it (e.g., prior to the submission of a final draft for the instructor's evaluation).

Many teachers argue that it is pointless and counterproductive to mark grammatical/mechanical errors on preliminary drafts of student papers when presumably the content of the papers will be substantially revised and some of the grammatical errors will disappear as passages are deleted or changed. Others argue that premature attention to errors can cause writers to fixate on sentence-level problems to the detriment of giving full attention to much-needed rhetorical revision. However, as some research has shown, students want and expect to receive feedback on their grammar throughout the writing process and may be frustrated if the teacher fails to provide it (Cohen, 1987; Ferris, 1995b; Hedgcock & Lefkowitz, 1994; Leki, 1991b). In addition, several studies have found that receiving grammar-focused feedback on first drafts does not impede students' ability to progress in their written fluency or to make significant revisions of their content (Fathman & Whalley, 1990; Ferris, 1997; Robb, Ross, & Shortreed, 1986).

As suggested in chapter 5, a compromise position is for teachers to (a) focus primarily on content and organization in their written and oral feedback to students on their preliminary essay drafts, and (b) provide general comments (perhaps in the form of an endnote) concerning major grammatical problems observed in early drafts (e.g., "You have a lot of subject–verb agreement problems in this draft. I've circled some examples on the first page so that you can be aware of them as you revise"). In later drafts, when the writer's text is more fully developed, the teacher can then provide more substantive feedback on grammatical and/or mechanical errors for the writer to focus on during the revision and editing phases of the composing process.

Which Errors Should Be Corrected?

A number of researchers and teachers have suggested that error correction in student writing be selective (Bates, Lane, & Lange, 1993; Ferris, 1992, 1995a, 1995c; Hendrickson, 1980; Lalande, 1982; Robb, Ross, & Shortreed, 1986). In other words, it is neither necessary nor beneficial for teachers to mark each student error with painstaking precision. This observation, of course, begs the question of which errors should be marked or ignored in a writer's paper. One line of research in L2 error correction has focused on the *global/local* distinction (Burt, 1975; Burt & Kiparsky, 1972). Hendrickson (1980) referred to global errors as "those errors that cause a listener or a reader to misunderstand a message or consider a sentence incomprehensible" (p. 159). Examples of global errors in ESL writing provided by Hendrickson "result from inadequate lexical knowledge, misuse of prepositions and pronouns, and seriously misspelled lexical items" (p. 159). He defined a *local error* as "a linguistic error that makes a form or structure appear awkward, but, nevertheless, causes a proficient speaker of a foreign language little or no difficulty in understanding the intended meaning of a sentence, given its contextual framework"; examples include "misuse and omission of prepositions, lack of subject–verb agreement, misspelled words and faulty lexical choice" (Hendrickson, 1980, pp. 159–160).

There are several problems with the global/local distinction that limit its usefulness to ESL writing teachers. The first should be clear from Hendrickson's examples. For instance, some of the same errors appear on both lists (e.g., misuse of prepositions, misspelled words, and lexical choice). Apparently, the same type of error can be either global or local depending on its severity and the context in which it occurs. This problem of definition and illustration can also be seen by tracing the use of the terms *global* and *local* through the literature over the past 20 years. Burt and Kiparsky (1972) introduced the terms, Hendrickson (1978) modified them for the purposes of his research, and Bates et al. (1993) and Lane and Lange (1993) adapted them again for the purposes of identifying and ranking a taxonomy of errors for their teacher and student editing guides. Finally, research in the use of the global/local distinction as a criterion for selective error correction has failed to demonstrate its effectiveness as either a research construct or a practical pedagogical technique (Hendrickson, 1976).

The global/local distinction admittedly has intuitive appeal. Most ESL writing teachers instinctively know the basic difference between errors that interfere with the comprehensibility of a text and those that do not. However, using the terms global and local as a basis for choosing which errors to focus on may not be as easy as it appears. That is, the *globalness* or seriousness of particular linguistic errors varies from writer to writer and possibly even within a single student text. Therefore, teachers have to use their own intuitions and experience to identify and prioritize their students' global errors to address them successfully in the classroom.

Hendrickson (1976) suggested that error correction in writing is most effective when teachers focus on errors that stigmatize or offend NES audiences the most. Stigmatizing errors are typically those that mark the NNS writer, such as article errors, omitted or unnecessary morphological markers (verb tense, plural endings, etc.), and word order problems. Finally, Hendrickson suggested that teachers focus on errors that individual writers make most frequently. Bates et al. (1993) claimed that "... to be beneficial, feedback on errors must be accurate, clear, consistent, and selective, that is, priority given to those errors that most interfere with communication" (p. 16). To varying degrees, these suggestions have been implemented in a number of recently published editing handbooks for ESL student writers (Ascher, 1993; Fox, 1992; Lane & Lange, 1993; Raimes, 1992a).

The preceding discussion implies that selecting and prioritizing errors for feedback and instruction is far from an exact science. The types of errors found in ESL writing vary greatly from one context to another and are affected by a combination of factors, including students' L1s, level of English language proficiency, extent and nature of prior English language instruction or exposure, literacy skills, learning styles, and so on. These factors affect which errors teachers should address as well as how they should be approached—a point that is addressed more extensively in the next section.

Observing the types of errors most frequently made by students in a given context is not the only criterion by which to select errors to treat in a composition course, however. As L2 acquisition researchers point out, morphological, syntactic, and lexical structures and rules are typically acquired in stages and some are more teachable and learnable than others. Further, as Truscott (1996) noted, "There is some reason to think that syntactic, morphological, and lexical knowledge are acquired in different manners. If this is the case, then probably no single form of correction can be effective for all three" (p. 343).

That said, it makes sense for teachers to focus their feedback and instruction on aspects of grammar that can be explained, understood, and generalized to students' particular writing needs. This criterion would seem to rule out treatment of most, if not all, lexical errors, such as incorrect prepositions, nonidiomatic usage, and other aspects of word choice. Teachers might decide to ignore lexical errors because there are no available rules and few strategies for avoiding them other than enjoining students to be careful. Alternatively, teachers can simply strike errors and write the intended word(s) (if indeed the teacher can discern the writer's intention, which is not an easy task), hoping that these corrections will somehow provide the negative evidence discussed by second language acquisition researchers as essential for acquisition (e.g., Long, 1994; White, 1994). Similarly, such selective grammar-based correction would rule out discussion of issues such as which verbs should be followed by gerunds or infinitives (or either) and whether the English definite article is required in front of the names of bodies of water (oceans, seas, and rivers—yes; lakes, creeks, and ponds—no). However, it is possible, although not simple, to present a definition of a singular count noun and then explain the rule that an article or other determiner is always required in front of one. We have seen English reference grammars that present over 40 different rules for the use of the definite article, yet if students grasp and apply only one (singular count nouns require determiners), they will eliminate the vast majority of their article errors. In summary, teachers should not assume that every error students make is treatable, nor that just because there is a grammatical rule to account for it, it is productive to teach it to students.

How Should Written Errors Be Corrected?

With respect to how written errors should be corrected, researchers in both L1 and L2 composition have concluded that direct correction of errors (i.e., correcting the errors for the student) in student writing is ineffective in helping writers reduce error frequency in subsequent compositions (Bates et al., 1993; Hillocks, 1986; Knoblauch & Brannon, 1981; Leki, 1990a; Robb, Ross, & Shortreed, 1986). However, indirect correction methods (e.g., noting the location and/or type of error, asking students to correct errors themselves, etc.) appear to have a more positive effect on long-term student improvement in accuracy and editing skills (Bates, Lane, & Lange, 1993; Fathman & Whalley, 1990; Ferris, 1995a, 1995c, 1997; Hendrickson, 1980; Lalande, 1982; Robb, Ross, & Shortreed, 1986). As noted later in this chapter, a possible exception to the prohibition on direct correction techniques might be in working with students at early stages of L2 proficiency—those whose grammatical competence in the L2 is not sufficiently developed for them to self-correct even when an error is pointed out to them.

⇒ AA 7.3

Considering Differences Among Students

When giving feedback on student errors, teachers also need to take into account their students' backgrounds, especially their previous English language instruction (see chaps. 1 and 3). Many international students in the United States have studied EFL for many years in their home countries and, in many cases, learned English in classes emphasizing formal grammar instruction. Other foreign students come from countries where English language instruction focuses more on oral communicative proficiency; these learners may be able to speak the language fairly well but may not have the metalinguistic or grammatical knowledge that the former group has acquired. Like the latter group of international students, ESL students who are permanent U.S. residents (i.e., immigrants) may have had all of their English language exposure and instruction in settings where grammatical terms and rules were not emphasized.

Although the preceding group profiles are overly general, they illustrate the point that grammar feedback and instruction (like all L2 instruction) needs to be carefully planned for the needs of the target group of students. For instance, one of the authors recently prepared lessons and materials on subject–verb agreement for a grammar training program for university ESL students who are long-term residents of the United States. Although these students are highly proficient in English and in general function well in their university courses, most of them were educated in the U.S. school system and have had little or no exposure to formal English grammar. Thus, in developing materials, it was necessary to start with basic metalinguistic terms (*noun, verb, subject, singular, plural*) before proceeding to rules for subject–verb agreement and strategies for avoiding and correcting errors. Similarly, teachers should be wary of error checklists and correction guides that list common errors and symbols for marking them because such guides often make unwarranted assumptions about students' knowledge of grammar terms and rules. A marking such as *vt* for a verb tense error would bewilder a student who barely knows what a verb is, much less what *tense* is or which of the 12 English tenses he or she should select in this context.

To the degree possible in a given instructional setting, teachers should also consider the role of students' first languages in selecting errors to address and correct. Early research based on the contrastive analysis hypothesis (CAH) and later investigation of Universal Grammar (UG) have both looked at differences between learners' primary and second languages and how those differences might lead to error production in L2 (see Brown, 1994a; Cook & Newson, 1996; White, 1994, for accessible overviews of CAH and UG). Although neither line of research is conclusive in pinpointing differences and predicting problems based on contrasts between learners' L1 and L2, it is clear from these investigations as well as those based on the CAH (see chap. 1) that there are important differences in the morphological, syntactic, lexical, and rhetorical patterns across languages and that these differences affect L2 student texts and writing development.

To the extent that a teacher can be aware of and informed about such differences (e.g., that Arabic does not have an indefinite article, that Chinese does not mark verbs morphologically for tense, etc.), it is possible to have a more complete picture of sources of error in L2 student writing and a clearer idea of how to assist learners. Being informed of cross-linguistic differences can be quite a challenge in U.S. ESL settings, where a variety of L1s may be represented. In such situations, teachers' best informants may be the students themselves. For example, an ESL teacher may know little or nothing about the syntactic structure of Japanese, but may notice that many of his or her Japanese students make similar types of grammatical errors in written English. The teacher can then ask several of the Japanese students for insights on why, based on their knowledge of both Japanese and English, these errors might be characteristic of Japanese ESL students. Literate adult ESL students frequently notice differences between their L1s and English; with some prompting, they may find ways to explain them, producing enlightenment for the teacher and relief for the student ("I'm not the only one making this mistake").

Preparing the Teacher to Respond to Grammar Errors and Teach Editing

The foregoing discussion suggests that ESL teachers do not always know how to recognize and correct errors or teach students to avoid them. As Truscott (1996) pointed out, perhaps the largest practical obstacles to effective error correction and grammar instruction are the teachers. They may fail to recognize an error in a student composition (Cohen & Cavalcanti, 1990) and, when they do, they may lack adequate knowledge of the grammar point, the tools to explain it clearly, or the time to provide effective feedback (Cohen & Robbins, 1976; Zamel, 1985). Thus, as Truscott (1996) noted,

> teachers may well know that an error has occurred but not know exactly why it is an error. If they do understand it well, they might still be unable to give a good explanation; problems that need explaining are often very complex. Even if capable of explaining the problem well, they might still fail to do so; busy teachers grading large numbers of written assignments have serious problems with time and patience. (p. 350)

Truscott's points about these practical problems are well taken, but such problems are not insurmountable. The answers lie in preparation, practice, and prioritizing. Where preparation is concerned, ESL teachers clearly need a thorough grounding in the structures of English grammar, pedagogical grammar, and perhaps in some form of syntactic theory and/or model of acquisition (cf. Beck, 1997). Most well-designed TESOL preparation programs provide at least some of these elements within the curriculum or assign them as prerequisites. However, inservice and preservice teachers whose training program does not include such coursework may need to seek out coursework or obtain teacher reference books to help them develop their knowledge and skills (e.g., Celce-Murcia & Larsen-Freeman, 1983; Master, 1996). Another valuable source of input on teaching grammar can be found in ESL grammar and editing texts (e.g., Ascher, 1993; Fox, 1992; Lane & Lange, 1993; Raimes, 1990, 1992b). Such texts provide a range of insights on both grammatical structures and ways to present them. Regardless of whether a teacher has had extensive coursework in linguistics or English grammar, a library containing a variety of teacher reference and ESL grammar texts can be an invaluable resource for preparing lessons and materials. Given our previous comments about the importance of tailoring grammar instruction and feedback to the needs and prior experiences of the students, a teacher should plan to consult several different texts for ideas and examples before presenting a grammar mini-lesson to a writing class.

An additional element in preparing teachers to cope with students' written errors is practice. Teachers need ample opportunities to (a) analyze student texts to identify error patterns, (b) explain grammar points, and (c) provide learners with editing strategies. If opportunities to develop these skills are not readily available within a teacher preparation program, pre- and inservice teachers wishing to increase their expertise should seek them out under the guidance of a teacher who is experienced and successful in teaching grammar for writers.

$$\boxed{\Rightarrow AA\ 7.4}$$

$$\boxed{\Rightarrow AA\ 7.5}$$

Finally, assuming that teachers have built their knowledge and have practiced providing feedback and grammar instruction, the final key to a successful approach to teaching editing is prioritizing. Dealing with student errors in written work can be tedious, tiring, and frustrating. This is no doubt why researchers have found that teachers are often erratic and even inaccurate in providing grammar feedback on student writing. Consequently, it is vitally important to commit oneself to selective error feedback or correction and to a strategy for building students' awareness and knowledge of their most serious and frequent grammar problems. Presupposed in the notion of prioritizing is time management: A teacher cannot respond systematically or accurately to errors in student papers without allowing adequate time to do so. Similarly, building grammar and editing skills through in-class activities and out-of-class assignments over the duration of a writing course takes careful planning at the syllabus design and lesson planning stages (see chaps. 3 and 4). Figure 7.2 provides an example of a plan for in-class editing workshops developed by one of the authors for an advanced university ESL composition course. This plan was constructed simultaneously with the overall course syllabus.

Techniques for Teaching Editing Skills in the Writing Class

As discussed earlier, most modern researchers advocate an indirect discovery approach toward teaching editing skills to ESL students. Although the goal of helping students become "independent self-editors" (Lane & Lange, 1993, p. xix) is clearly a crucial one, students at beginning to intermediate levels of English proficiency may not have the language skills to monitor their own written products successfully (cf. Jones, 1985). In a general discussion of error production and correction in second language acquisition, Brown (1994a) suggested that there are successive stages in students' ability to recognize and correct their own errors:

Note: This plan was written for in-class editing workshops during a 15-week advanced ESL university composition course. This editing work was carefully integrated throughout the semester within a syllabus featuring prewriting, peer response, discussion of readings, revision, etc. Chapter numbers refer to an editing handbook that was a required text for the course (Ascher, 1992). In addition to the in-class editing workshops, students were individually assigned homework exercises from the text as well as practice editing exercises based on sample student essays.

EDITING PLAN

1. **Week 2**: Introduce general editing strategies; Verbs (Ch. 1)
2. **Week 3**: Essay/Paragraph Coherence
3. **Week 4**: The Complete Sentence (Ch. 2)
4. **Week 6**: Agreement (Ch. 3)
5. **Week 8**: Peer Editing Workshop (Essay 1, Draft. 3)
   Focus: Verb Tenses (Ch. 4)
6. **Week 9**: Peer Editing Workshop (Essay 2, Draft 3)
   Focus: Comma Splices & Run-Ons (Ch. 8)
7. **Week 13**: Peer Editing Workshop (Essay 3, Draft 3)
   Focus: Mechanics (Ch. 9)
8. **Week 14**: General Editing Practice (Ch. 10)

FIG. 7.2. Plan for in-class editing workshops for a 15-week semester.

1. *The random error stage.* The learner has no systematic idea about a given structure. Examples might include spelling one word in several different ways, using same word in several different ways or using verb tenses correctly some of the time, but not predictably.
2. *The emergent stage.* The learner is growing in consistency in production (While the production is not error-free, the errors are least systematic). At this stage, the learner cannot correct errors when they are pointed out by someone else.
3. *The systematic stage.* The learner is even more consistent; production is approaching target forms. Learners can correct their errors when pointed out to them.
4. *The stabilization stage.* The learner has relatively few errors and can self-correct. (pp. 211–212)

Students in Stages 1 or 2 in terms of error recognition/correction ability most likely need different types of intervention than students in Stages 3 or 4. Brown (1994b) and Frodesen (1991) suggested that the types of writing of which low-level students are capable include copying (of model texts and their own teacher-corrected compositions), controlled or guided writing exercises involving manipulation of various syntactic structures, and *dictocomps* (see Fig. 7.3).

A. Controlled Writing Exercise.
Instructions: Change the paragraph into past tense. The first sentence is done for you.

My wife gets up early in the morning. She hates to get up in the morning. She has to get dressed quickly to catch an early bus to work. I go to work later, and I drive my car. She doesn't have much time for breakfast, so she just has a cup of coffee when she gets to work. I have a bowl of cereal and fruit before I go to work. I understand why my wife doesn't like mornings. (Paragraph adapted from Fox, 1992.)

Beginning of past tense paragraph: *My wife got up earlier in the morning than I did.*

B. Guided Writing Exercise.
Instructions: You just read a paragraph about a man and his wife getting ready for work in the morning. Now write a paragraph about what you did this morning. Answer the questions to get ideas for your paragraph.

• Did you get up early or late?
• Did you have a lot of time or did you have to hurry?
• How did you get to school? Did you walk, ride a bike, drive a car, or ride a bus?
• Did you eat breakfast? Where (at home or at school)?
• What did you eat for breakfast?
• Do you usually enjoy mornings?

Follow-up: Now change your paragraph about this morning into one about your usual morning.

C. Dictocomp.
Procedure: Use a paragraph like the one in Part A. Read the paragraph aloud several times at normal speed. Then write the key words on the board in sequence (see list below for an example) and ask the students to rewrite the paragraph as they remember it, using the words on the board.

KEY WORDS:

hates	bus	breakfast	understand
get up	later	coffee	
get dressed	car	cereal	

FIG. 7.3. Sample editing activities for beginning-level students.
(Note: Activities developed from suggestions in Brown, 1994b.)

As students progress in their acquisition of English syntax, morphology, and vocabulary, as well as their formal learning of grammatical rules, they can be given more responsibility for correcting errors. An error correction system such as the one advocated in two companion volumes on editing (Bates et al.,1993; Lane & Lange, 1993) may be useful for this intermediate level of editing proficiency. In these texts, teachers and students learn a system of marking papers for 15 different types of errors (Fig. 7.4) and are encouraged to prioritize and keep track of their error patterns. For intermediate-level students, a structured approach to editing such as this one may develop both their knowledge about specific linguistic forms that may be problematic and their ability to diagnose and correct errors. The potential value of such an approach for intermediate students is affirmed by the research of Lalande (1982), who concluded that "instructional feedback" should inform writers "of the location and nature of mistakes, so that they can invoke problem-solving/active correction strategies" (p. 115). However, depending on students' prior educational

SYMBOL	EXPLANATION
vt	incorrect verb tense
vf	verb incorrectly formed
modal	incorrect use or formation of a modal
cond	incorrect use or formation of a conditional sentence
ss	incorrect sentence structure
wo	incorrect or awkward word order
conn	incorrect or missing connector
pass	incorrect formation or use of passive voice
unclear	unclear message
sv	incorrect subject–verb agreement
art	incorrect or missing article
num	problem with the singular or plural of a noun
wc	wrong word choice
wf	wrong word form
nonidiom	nonidiomatic (not expressed this way in English)
cap	capitalization—capital letter needed
coh	coherence—one idea does not lead to the next
cs	comma splice—two independent clauses joined by a comma
dm	dangling modifier
frag	fragment—incomplete sentence
lc	lower case—word(s) incorrectly capitalized
p	punctuation incorrect or missing
pro ref/pro agree	pronoun reference or agreement unclear or incorrect
ro	run-on—two independent clauses joined with no punctuation
sp-	spelling error

FIG. 7.4. Sample grading symbol/editing guide.
(Adapted from Lane & Lange, 1993, pp. xx–xxi.)

Phase 1 (Weeks 1–3): FOCUSING STUDENTS ON FORM
    Goals:
        Students learn to recognize the importance of improving editing skills;
        Students begin to identify their own "sources of error."
    Activities:
        Students write a diagnostic essay; teacher prepares a report of major
        weaknesses and indicates what sort of grade the student is likely to receive
        if such problems persist to the end of the term;
        Students examine sample sentences and essays for the purpose of noting
        what comprehensibility problems are rooted in sentence-level errors.
Phase 2 (Weeks 4–10): TRAINING STUDENTS TO RECOGNIZE MAJOR
ERROR TYPES
    Goals and Activities:
        Students understand and identify major error types in sample essays;
        Students "peer edit";
        Students keep written records of the major types of errors they make,
        turned in with writing projects;
        Instruction on major sources of error is given in class, lab, or through
        independent study, as necessary.
Phase 3 (Weeks 11–15): HELPING STUDENTS TO FIND AND CORRECT
THEIR OWN ERRORS
    Goals and Activities:
        Students edit their own essays and chart their progress;
        Instruction on major sources of error continues.
        (Ferris, 1995a, p. 46)

FIG. 7.5. Teaching editing skills: Overview for a 15-week semester (Ferris, 1995a, p. 46).

experience, especially their English language development, systems such as the one shown in Fig. 7.4 may need to be adapted (or used with adequate explanations) for students' relative knowledge of formal grammar terminology.

Once students have progressed to a point where they can either correct a variety of errors when they are pointed out or find and correct errors themselves, there are several steps that teachers can take to help them move further toward autonomy. In this approach, advanced ESL students can be taught over several phases during the writing course to become self-sufficient as editors (Fig. 7.5).

Phase 1: Focusing Students on Form.   The intent of this stage is to help students realize the importance of improving their editing skills. According to Ferris

(1995c), some teachers assume that ESL writers focus excessively on grammatical form at the expense of developing and organizing their ideas. However, many ESL students have little interest in editing their compositions. Such writers may find editing tedious, may not see it as important, or may have become overly dependent on experts (i.e., teachers, tutors, etc.) to correct their work for them. "Thus, a crucial step in teaching students to become good editors is to convince them of the necessity of doing so" (Ferris, 1995c, p. 18).

There are several ways to raise students' awareness of the importance of editing in general. The first is to utilize in-class activities in which writers look at sentences and/or a short student essay containing a variety of editing problems. Another useful strategy for convincing students of the necessity of developing editing skills is to give them a diagnostic essay assignment early in the term and provide them with comprehensive feedback about their writing, including detailed information about their editing weaknesses so that they have specific grammatical issues to focus on throughout the semester.

Phase 2: Providing Training in Recognizing Major Error Types.   As previously discussed, focusing on patterns of error rather than individual errors is most effective for both teachers and students. At the second stage of the editing process, students are trained to recognize various types of error. These categories may vary depending on the teacher's perception of student needs. However, as already discussed, they should be selected from frequent, serious, and stigmatizing error types. Students are sensitized to these error patterns by reviewing the targeted categories, identifying them in sample student essays, and looking for these errors in peer editing exercises (see Fig. 7.6). Generally speaking, it is easier to find mistakes in others' work than in one's own. This is why publishers and businesses employ proofreaders. The same holds true in composition classes. Exercises in which learners locate and identify error patterns in their peers' work can raise their awareness of parallel problems in their own writing. Such activities can also "lead students away from the frustrating and often counterproductive notion that they can or should attempt to correct every single error in a given essay draft" (Ferris, 1995c, p. 19).

During this stage of the editing process, students may also be given brief, focused instruction on major patterns of error as necessary. This instruction may be given to the whole class if there are particular types of error common to most of the students. When class time is given to grammar/editing instruction, it should be brief and narrowly focused, dealing directly with the specific problems that students are encountering in their writing. Such minilessons can include text analysis, in which students analyze connected pieces of discourse (a paragraph, several paragraphs, or a whole essay) to gain a more thorough understanding of when and how the salient feature is used (see Fig. 7.7 and Frodesen, 1991, for further suggestions). Minilessons can also include a more traditional deductive explanation of the particular grammar point or editing problem being discussed (see Fig. 7.8; for another example, see Ferris, 1995c).

Essay error analysis. Read the attached essay excerpt (in Appendix 7A) and take the following steps to perform an error analysis.

1. With a highlighter, mark errors in the following categories:
   subject–verb agreement
   noun endings (plural or possessive)
   determiner/article error (missing, unnecessary, wrong one)
   verb tense
   verb form
   sentence fragment
   run-on sentence
   comma splice
   (You may find other error types; you may ignore them for this exercise.)
2. Number the highlighted errors consecutively throughout the paper. Use these numbers to complete the attached analysis chart. For each error you will indicate its type and suggest a correction.
3. You will turn in both your highlighted and numbered essay excerpt and your analysis chart.

ERROR ANALYSIS CHART

Error #	Line #	Error type	Possible correction
1			
2			
3			
4			
5			
6			
7			
8			

FIG. 7.6. Sample student exercise: Recognizing major error categories.

$\Rightarrow AA\ 7.6$

An alternative to class-wide instruction is to individualize editing instruction through the use of an editing handbook. In the last few years, several textbooks intended specifically to help students edit their writing have become available (Ascher, 1993; Fox, 1992; Lane & Lange, 1993; Raimes, 1992a). This genre of text is distinct from an ESL grammar text, which attempts to provide comprehensive coverage of grammatical concepts as opposed to focusing on specific editing

Instructions: Using a highlighter, mark every verb phrase in the paragraph shown (verb + any helping words). Then, for each verb you marked, identify the verb tense (simple present, simple past, or past perfect), and be prepared to discuss with your classmates why the verb tense is appropriate in each case. You may assume that they are all correct. The first sentence is done for you.

Clifton Davis tells of a recent event that triggered a significant childhood memory. The recent event was the story of Dondre Green. He was not allowed to play golf at the Caldwell Parish Country Club because it was reserved for whites only. Dondre Green is a black and the management didn't let Negroes enter their private club. About 32 years ago when Clifton Davis was 13 years old the same thing had happened to him. Only that time it was not being able to go to Glen Echo Amusement Park in Maryland because he was a black.

Verb phrase	Tense	Explanation
tells	Present	Present tense is used to report what an author says in a text
triggered	Past	The banquet (where the memory was triggered) happened in the past

FIG. 7.7. Classroom text analysis exercise: Targeted verb tenses in discourse.

problems. In addition, many ESL writing textbooks include an editing section (e.g., Raimes, 1992a; Spack, 1996). When using a handbook, students can be given individualized homework assignments corresponding to their particular area(s) of need as demonstrated in their essay drafts. However, whether a teacher presents a minilesson or assigns individualized editing homework, it is crucial to assess students' prior knowledge of English grammar terms and rules before selecting materials and assigning lessons. Because ESL student populations vary so dramatically from institution to institution and region to region, teachers should not assume that the morphological and syntactic structures covered or the approach taken in a textbook or set of materials will be appropriate for their own students.

Phase 3: Students Finding and Correcting Their Own Errors.   After students have been made aware of their own particular weaknesses in editing through teacher and peer feedback and have practiced identifying error patterns on model student essays and peers' drafts, they should then be instructed to locate and correct errors in their own essay drafts. Also, throughout the semester, the students can keep a log of error frequencies in the different categories to observe their individual improvement and build their confidence as editors. As the semester

Note: Drawing on a variety of sources, this mini-lesson was prepared specifically for a group of high-intermediate to advanced ESL students enrolled in university ESL writing courses. Almost all of these students had been permanent residents of the U.S. for 10 or more years and had been educated in American high schools. Their oral proficiency and comprehension (both listening and reading) were strong, but their knowledge of formal grammar terms and rules was minimal. Thus the definition of terms and the rules/problems outlined are at a relatively basic level and were simpler than many of the sources consulted in preparing the lesson.

I. Important Terms.
    A. *Noun*: a word that describes a person, place, or thing.
    EXAMPLES: *teacher, Mary* (people); *school, Los Angeles* (places); *book, love* (things).
    B. *Pronoun*: a word that can replace a noun in a sentence.
    EXAMPLES:
      1. *The boy* read *the books.*
      2. *He* read *them.*
    C. *Subject*: The noun or pronoun that expresses the topic of the sentence—who or what the sentence is about. The subject is usually at or near the beginning of the sentence.
    EXAMPLES:
      1. *The boy* read the books.
      2. *One* of the students comes in late every day.
    D. *Verb*: A verb is a word that tells you something about the subject of the sentence. The verb comes after the subject of the sentence.
    EXAMPLES:
      1. The *boy ran* quickly.
      2. The *boy is* afraid.
    E. *Subject–Verb Agreement*: Subjects and verbs must *agree*. This means that a singular subject must be followed by a singular verb form, and a plural subject must be followed by a plural verb.
    EXAMPLES:
      1. He goes (singular)   vs. They go (plural)
      2. The boy goes (singular)   vs. The boys go (plural)
      3. I go (singular)   vs. We go (plural)
II. Common subject–verb agreement errors and strategies for avoiding them.
    A. *Problem 1*: The subject and verb do not agree when other words come between them.
    Incorrect: One of the students are coming to the party.
    Correct: One of the students is coming to the party.
    Incorrect: My lack of friends make me feel lonely.
    Correct: My lack of friends makes me feel lonely.

Fig. 7.8 continues

B. *Problem 2*: The verb ending (*-s*) is left off when the subject is third-person singular or uncountable.

Incorrect: The boy go to school every morning.

Correct: The boy goes to school every morning.

Incorrect: Sugar taste very good.

Correct: Sugar tastes very good.

Strategy: Identify all of your verbs. Then ask yourself these questions:

1. What is the subject?
2. Is the subject singular?
3. Is the subject a noncount noun?

After you have identified the subject of each verb, if your answer to questions b or c was yes, use the singular form of the verb (add the *-s* ending).

C. *Problem 3*: An *-s* ending is put on the verb when the subject is plural or

Incorrect: The boys walks home after school.

Correct: The boys walk home after school.

Strategy: Find the subject of the verb. If it is a count noun and it describes more than one person, place, or thing, do not add any ending to the verb.

Note: These explanations were followed by editing practice exercises (at both sentence and paragraph level.)

FIG. 7.8. Deductive minilesson on subject–verb agreement.

Early in the course: The teacher marks all examples of a particular error type in an essay draft (e.g., by underlining), also pointing out in an end comment or on an essay feedback form that the writer has a particular problem to work on (e.g., "Please go through your draft and try to correct all of the noun errors I have underlined").

Mid-course: The teacher underlines a few examples of the error (perhaps only on the first page), again commenting on the error type, and asking the peer editor to underline the rest of the errors of this type in the essay.

Late in the course: The teacher makes a verbal comment (e.g., "You still have too many noun errors—keep working on this!") but doesn't mark any of them, instead asking the writer to find them him or herself.

FIG. 7.9. Teacher's editing feedback. (Adapted from Ferris, 1995c.)

progresses and students accumulate more and more editing practice, the amount of editing feedback provided by the teacher should gradually decrease, with the editing task being turned over first to peer editors and then to the writers themselves.

SUMMARY

Over the past 20 years, ESL writing instruction has swung from one extreme (attempting to eradicate every single student error) to another (primary attention given to writers' ideas and individual writing processes, with linguistic concerns basically left to "take care of themselves") to a middle ground (combining the best of the process approach with increased but selective attention to linguistic accuracy at the final editing stage). ESL writing teachers, ESL students, and subject-matter faculty generally agree on the importance of accuracy in student writing and of teaching students to become self-sufficient as editors. As learners increase their English proficiency, more and more responsibility for editing their own writing can and should be turned over to them. A variety of techniques such as guided writing exercises, identification of error patterns, text analysis, and grammar minilessons can be used to build students' editing skills as they become more proficient in English and as second language writers. The goal of such a discovery approach should not be perfect written products, but rather ESL writers who gradually reduce the occurrence of error in their written production and become increasingly independent as editors. It is also extremely important that teachers take students' first languages, second language development levels, and academic backgrounds (especially prior English language instruction) into account in planning instruction, selecting materials, and providing feedback.

Reflection and Review

1. What are the arguments in favor of providing feedback only on ideas/organization on preliminary drafts of student papers? What are the arguments in favor of also providing grammar feedback on early drafts? Which set of arguments do you find more convincing and why?

2. This chapter argues that teachers or students should not attempt to correct *all* errors in a given piece of writing. What are some arguments against this position?

3. To what extent can or should student preferences affect teachers' decisions regarding error correction and in-class grammar instruction? What are the benefits and drawbacks of varying feedback strategies to accommodate individual students' desires?

4. After arguing that there is no theoretical justification for error correction in L2 writing and that the practical problems with doing so are virtually insurmount-

able, Truscott (1996) further asserted that error correction is worse than useless. He maintained that it is actually harmful because it consumes so much teacher and student energy and attention, taking time away from activities that could help students. Imagine that you are a writing teacher who agrees with Truscott's arguments and have therefore decided not to correct students' written errors any longer. You need to write a memo to your supervisor explaining your new position. What would you say? What counterarguments might your boss offer in response?

5. The discussion of Truscott's (1996) arguments against error correction in this chapter raises a larger issue: If research evidence appears to contradict common sense or intuitions, on which should a teacher rely? What if the research evidence is scarce, conflicting, or incomplete (as in many issues in L2 teaching)? While we are waiting for researchers to come up with conclusive answers (if there ever can be such), what should teachers do in the meantime?

Application Activity 7.1: Assessing Students' and Teachers' Opinions About Grammar Feedback and Instruction

1. Identify several ESL writing students and one or more teachers of ESL writing. Ask them to complete a written questionnaire or an oral interview about their views on error correction.

2. Design a written survey/questionnaire or oral interview questions for use with your participants. Your questions might cover the following topics:
- Views on the importance of error feedback, especially in relation to feedback on other aspects of writing (ideas, organization);
- Views on the importance of grammar instruction in the composition class, especially in relation to other class activities;
- Views on the effectiveness of grammar feedback and instruction.
- Participants' insights into their own editing processes;
- Ideas about grammar feedback and instruction that is helpful and that which is problematic.

Note: You might want to draw on the "Questions for Reflection" at the beginning of this chapter and on the published surveys cited previously (e.g., Ferris, 1995b; Hedgcock & Lefkowitz, 1994, 1996; Leki, 1991a) for ideas for your own questionnaire.

3. Administer your survey or conduct your interviews, being careful to collect the data under consistent conditions (e.g., ensure that all your interviews last 15 minutes, give instructions, and pose interview questions in the same way, etc.).

4. Analyze your data and compare them with your own reflections (from the questions at the beginning of the chapter) and with the results of published studies. At the end of your analysis, reflect on whether you agree, based on your data, with Truscott's (1996) statement that "students believe in correction ... but that does not mean that teachers should give it to them" (p. 359).

Application Activity 7.2: Analyzing a Research Review

Truscott (1996) reviewed numerous studies of L2 error correction, concluding that "grammar correction is not effective" (p. 340). Obtain and carefully read the following studies and then answer the questions below that follow:

1. For each study, note the findings reported and the conclusions drawn by the authors. Compare these to Truscott's summary of that particular study in his review. In your opinion, is Truscott's presentation fair and accurate? Was there any other way to interpret the authors' data?
2. For each study, note the following research elements carefully:
   • How many participants were there?
   • In what pedagogical context were the data collected?
   • What was the duration of the data collection?
   • If the design was experimental, was a control group used?
   • What methods were used to collect and analyze data?
3. Now compare your notes on each study. Do you think this body of research is consistent in either research design or findings? To what extent can the findings of any one of these studies be generalized to all L2 writers? Are all of the studies, taken as a group, generalizable? Why or why not?

Study	Section of Truscott's Review
Cohen and Robbins (1976)	pp. 330–331
Semke (1984)	p. 331
Robb, Ross, and Shortreed (1986)	pp. 331–332
Kepner (1991)	p. 332
Fathman and Whalley (1990)	p. 339
Lalande (1982)	pp. 339–340

Note: Bibliographic information for all of the preceding studies is provided in the References section of this volume.

Application Activity 7.3: Analyzing Errors and Giving Feedback

Appendix 7B contains two student papers written for an advanced university ESL course. Read each one carefully, paying attention to the various error types represented in each paper, then complete the tasks described next.

1. Develop an error analysis form similar to the one used in the student exercise shown in Fig. 7.6. You may wish to add or delete error categories depending on your preliminary reading of the papers.
2. Make two copies of the form and complete an error analysis for each paper.

3. Now imagine that you are going to give each of the two writers feedback about his or her grammar problems.
   a. Use the correction symbols suggested by Lane and Lange (1993) and shown in Fig. 7.4 to mark one of the papers.
   b. For the other paper, use the process suggested in Ferris (1995c, Fig. 7.9) to provide feedback. (Assume that it is early in the semester.)
4. Reflect on your processes for analyzing errors and giving feedback. What was most difficult? What was easiest? Which of the two feedback methods do you prefer and why?

Application Activity 7.4: Assessing the Formal Grammatical Knowledge of a Target Population

Identify an ESL writing course in your community. Imagine that you have been hired to teach this course and that you want to assess the students' grammar problems and their level(s) of formal grammatical knowledge. Complete the following steps to perform a grammar needs analysis.

1. Speak to the teacher to find out the students' general English proficiency level(s) and what he or she perceives to be the most serious and frequent grammar problems among the students. Ask the teacher if you can collect one or more pieces of the following types of data from the students:
   • Copies of their first paper;
   • A brief grammar test, which you design and administer;
   • Results of a written questionnaire in which students assess their own grammar abilities and identify their specific problems;
   • Oral interviews with several of the students.
2. Using the information gathered from the teacher, design one or more needs assessment instruments (e.g., written questionnaire, oral interview questions, error analysis form, grammar test) based on the grammar issues identified by the teacher.
3. Administer the instruments and analyze your results. If this were your class, on what grammar issues would you focus? At what level of explanation would you need to begin? For instance, if you identified verb tenses as a problem, do these students know what a verb is and could they identify different tenses?

Application Activity 7.5: Comparing Reference Sources on a Particular Grammar Point

This activity is intended specifically to follow up the needs analysis exercise in Application Activity 7.4. However, if this activity is undertaken independently, please follow the steps listed next.

Directions. Imagine you are teaching an ESL writing class and you have selected a particular grammar point on which to present a 20 to 30 minute minilesson to the class. Consult several different sources for information on this grammar point (e.g., a reference grammar for teachers, an ESL grammar book, or an editing handbook). After you have examined the sources, decide how you will address the following questions:

- Is one source clearer or more appropriate for this point/group of students than the others? Why?
- What basic information (terms, definitions, examples) will you need to present? Which sources were most helpful in providing these?
- What rules and/or strategies for avoiding errors might you include? Which sources were most helpful in identifying these?
- Did you find any discovery activities or editing exercises that might be helpful for your lesson? How might you need to adapt these for your students?

Application Activity 7.6: Developing Grammar/Editing Lessons

Note: If you have completed Application Activities 7.3 to 7.5, the information you gathered will be helpful in completing this task. If not, you can complete it independently.

Examine the two student papers in Appendix 7B. Imagine that you are teaching a writing class and that these papers are representative of your students' abilities and problems. Design two activities (15–30 minutes each) based on your analyses of the two papers. You may also want to use all or parts of the papers for examples or exercises in your activities.

Activity A should be a discovery/text analysis similar to the exercise in Fig. 7.7.

Activity B should be a deductive mini-lesson similar to that shown in Fig. 7.8.

APPENDIX 7A: ESSAY EXCERPT TO ACCOMPANY FIG. 7.6

The essay I have selected is "College Pressures," By William Zinsser. I chose "College Pressures" because I agree with some of the arguments that the author mentions in his essay. There are two of his points that I need to disagree with, which are parental pressures and professor's attitude toward the students. The rest of Zinsser's pressures pretty much describes the pressures that I face at the university nowadays. For example a big pressure that I noticed all students have is financial. It very hard for most students to go to school and not have to work to support themselves during at school. I realized that working during school time takes some study time away. As I continue reading the essay I realized that he also points out others pressures such as professors pressuring students, parents, peers, and of course the one I am always pressure by is financially.

I need to disagree with Zinsser when he states, "professors who actually like to spend time with students don't have much time to spend.. I noticed that most professors try to spend as much time as possible with their students. So far in all my classes it seems very common for professors to help students after their office hours. I have seen many professor who sometimes are willing to stay half an hour after the class is over to explain to students any misunderstanding they might have on the material the professor is teaching. To me it only proves one thing and that is that the professors only want for the students to succeed in their class.

When I think of peer pressure I see it more as an encouragement for me to succeed in a class. But Zinsser states peer pressure is a disadvantage to a student. I disagree with him completely. When one of my peers receives a higher grade then I do most of the time it does not make me feel jealous or feel pressure, instead it makes me understand that if I try just a little harder that I could do just as well as the other student if not even better. Most of my friend who I have classes with never have rubbed in my face that they did better than me. What they do instead is to encourage me to study hard and sometimes they even give up some of their time to help me in my weaknesses. I have no complains of my peers. I believe that peer pressure does not exist instead I like to think of it as peer encouragement. I think that the pressure that is put on by the student its by herself not by her peers.

APPENDIX 7B: SAMPLE STUDENT PAPERS
FOR APPLICATION ACTIVITIES 7.3 AND 7.6

Essay prompt:

In "A Mason-Dixon Memory," Clifton Davis tells of a recent event that triggered a significant childhood memory. Have you had an experience that brought a former incident to mind? Write an essay in which you describe both experiences, explaining clearly how the more recent one caused you to remember the earlier incident. Also, discuss what was significant about (or what you have learned from) your comparison of the two experiences.

ESSAY 1

Clifton Davis tells of a recent event that triggered a significant childhood memory. The recent event was a story of Dondre Green. He was not allowed to play golf at the Caldwell Parish Country Club because it was reserved for whites only. Dondre Green is a blanck and the management didn't let Negroes to enter their private club. About 32 years ago when Clifton Davis was 13 years old same thing had happened to him. Only that time it was not being able to go to Glen Echo Amusement Park in Maryland because he was a black.

As I was reading <u>A Mason-Dixon Memory</u> by Clifton Davis I was also triggered by a memory. I came to the United States 7 years ago. I guess I've been fortunate and lucky that I didn't have to face those terrible situations like Dondre Green and Clifton Davis. However, my friend from high school had to go through injustices like Dondre Green and Clifton Davis. When she first came to the United States just like many new immigrants she didn't know how to speak English very well. However, do to different school systems back in her country she was well taught compared to her classmates in the United States. She knew so much more and one day she went to her school counselor and asked him to change her classes to little bit more challenging ones. She also told him that she is getting all good grades and turned in every homework assignments as well. However, the counselor took a look at and said "No". My friend was very surprised and wanted to know why. The only reson she got was that she is not good at English like other whites kids in class. The counselor strongly forced the world "whites". She didn't know what the counselor was trying to say but quickly found out that he didn't want her to be in class where only whites were believed to achieve good grades. The counselor didn't even wanted my friend to give the harder class a try. He didn't even give her a chance. Even through she learned everything back in her country she had to waste one high school year because of the counselor at that school. I suddenly remembered my high school friend's story as I was reading about Dondre Green and Clifton Davis.

My high school friend, Dondre Green and Clifton Davis were treated wrong because of their color. They were not even given a chance or rights. I think this is very wrong. Who are we to say some of us are better than others. Who are we to say I'm better than you because I have lighter skin color. Some says that the United States is referred to as "The Melting Pot" because so many different races are intertwined and making this country one. The United States is not just for whites, but for all those who works hard and wanting to be successful. For those who has willingness to make their dreams come true. Everybody should be given a chance no matter what skin color they have because underneth the skin color we are all same.

ESSAY 2: "Passing Away"

There are a lot of events that had happen in my life, but the most memorable is when I loose someone. Recently my grandmother had just pass away because of cancer. When I heard this, I couldn't believe it because I don't want to loose my grandmom. My grandmother death had brought back a very sad memory, which is my uncle death just a few years ag. My uncle die because he was caught in a fire which brought tears to everybody. In just a couple of years I had lost two relative already and it's very hard for me for me to take.

The moment my mom told that my grandmom pass away tears were just running down my eyes and I was very shock. On the day of my grandmom funeral everyone was so sad and the only thing I could heard was my crying. I try not to cry so much, but I just couldn't help it especially, when they brought my grandmom in for us to see. When I saw my grandmom body I started to cry even more and I say to myself that you can not leave me, I really love you. As I was crying another memory just pop up in my mind and that's my uncle death because so far—this is the second funeral I been to in my life and both are my relative.

I remember just a few ago when it was close to father's day and one of my uncle was remodeling his house and a lot of my other relative was also helping. One day while they are eating their lunch outside, two of my uncle was still in the house cleanin. Suddenly the house was caught on fire and because of the gasoline in the house it was burning very fast and my two uncle was trap in there. By the time the fire truck and ambulance got here my two uncle was 60% to 70% burn. A few days later, one of my uncle did and I was very sad because all of his children are young and the oldest was only ten years old. My uncle wife was also pregnant during that time and didn't even know. During that whole summer his family, friends, and relative were very sad. Loosing my uncle was a very sad thing that happen in my life and now, loosing my grandmother is like making the world seem hopeless.

Now every time I think of my grandmother I will always think of my uncle. Loosing them both is a very painful thing for me. From this two experiences, I learn that loosing someone is very painful, but I still have to continue my life because I know they will always be there for me.

In conclusion, my grandmother death had brought back a very sad memories because I'm loosing someon. Every time I think of my grandmom I will also think of my uncle because I'm not able to see them anymore. Now, I learn that loosing someone is very painful, but I know that they will always be in my heart. When I think of my grandmom and uncle tears will always be in my eyes and I can't control it, but I know I really love them.

ESL Writing Assessment: Classroom Perspectives

Questions for Reflection

- In your experience as an academic writer in your primary or second language, what procedures have your instructors used to score and assess your written work? To what extent were these procedures appropriate and why?
- In what ways have the scores or grades you have received on your writing (in L1 or L2) helped you improve your written products? How have scores enhanced your learning and mastery of composing skills?
- If you have had experience as a composition instructor, what do you feel are your greatest challenges in evaluating student writing? If you are a preservice teacher, what are your most significant apprehensions as an evaluator of student writing? Why?
- In your opinion, what should be the role(s) of formal assessment in the teaching of composition? Why?
- Are you familiar with portfolio assessment? If so, under what circumstances? What benefits do you associate with it?

INTRODUCTION

This chapter approaches practices in ESL writing assessment from the perspective that meaningful performance evaluation is an ongoing process involving both teachers and students, not merely a procedure for assigning a quantitative or rank score to a single product (or series of them). As a formative and inherently pedagogical endeavor, therefore, the assessment of students' writing (i.e., their processes as well as their products) is a responsibility that is tightly linked to the other instructional processes already covered in this book, particularly syllabus design, lesson planning, task and assignment development, and feedback procedures. Writing assessment is pedagogical in the sense that, when reliable and valid, its outcomes inform writers in ways that will directly and indirectly promote their progress. In other words, scores, grades, and evaluative feedback should consistently contribute to writers' learning processes and the overall improvement of their measurable writing skills. An extension of this pedagogical function is that assessment should inform teachers of their own effectiveness, as reflected in their students' increasing proficiency and their achievement of programmatic and individual writing goals. This concept is sometimes called *washback*, "the effect a test has on the teaching environment which has preceded it" (Hamp-Lyons, 1991a, p. 337). Assessment is thus an essential teaching task: "We need to know what students do as writers, for both planning and the evaluation of our own teaching. Further, we need to track progress over the course of our teaching" (Hillocks, 1995, p. 132).

PROSPECTS AND PITFALLS IN WRITING ASSESSMENT: SHAPING TOOLS AND TEACHERS' ROLES

Before examining the fundamental premises of L2 writing assessment and their related procedures, we should first acknowledge the ostensible contradictions confronted by many teachers when they face the challenges of evaluating their students' work. For instance, principles and methods of educational assessment are frequently (if not predominantly) framed in terms of testing, in contrast to the day-to-day concerns of performance and progress tracking. Formalized tools for evaluating student writing such as those introduced later are unfortunately (and sometimes notoriously) associated with product-centered scoring that does not assess or value student writing processes (Faigley, Cherry, Jolliffe, & Skinner, 1985; Hamp-Lyons, 1991a). We present these formalized instruments because they offer teachers both systematicity and rigor, although our primary emphasis is on their classroom applications (as opposed to their role in large-scale diagnostic, placement, and exit testing). We likewise acknowledge the need to judge writers' products, particularly in academic settings, but not to the exclusion of feedback on writers' processes and progress (cf. chap. 5). Thus, we view learners' written products as periodic reflections of their ongoing development—a perspective that is particularly appropriate in the context of a portfolio evaluation system.

A further contradiction in the practice of teaching composition concerns the instructor's dual identity as respondent (i.e., audience and coach) and evaluator. That is, teachers often simultaneously provide feedback while assigning scores or grades—objectives that "may operate at cross-purposes" (Hedgcock & Lefkowitz, 1996, p. 288). Thus, classroom evaluation is nearly always problematic because "the audience is usually limited to the person (the teacher) who also **designs, assigns,** and **assesses** that writing" (Kroll & Reid, 1995, p. 18). Teachers can most productively cope with this all-too-common situation by acknowledging the contradiction overtly (rather than by overlooking or ignoring it). As Raimes (1983a) reminded us:

... [students] are aware of the artificiality. They know in their heart of hearts, as we do too, that their readers are only the teacher and perhaps their classmates, too. If a system of credit and grades is involved, then you can be sure they know all that. The teacher is the reader, and the purpose is to improve the students' written English. There's nothing wrong with that. But somehow we don't use it. We circumvent it and pretend it isn't there. (p. 263)

Ways of acknowledging and relieving this inherent tension include devoting explicit attention to assessment issues in the classroom, integrating assessment mechanisms into instructional processes (cf. chaps. 3, 4, and 5), and applying a variety of reliable methods to identify those that are most appropriate and valid for a specific population of writers.

GENERAL PRINCIPLES OF TASK RELIABILITY AND VALIDITY

Whenever student performance is evaluated for the purposes of educational diagnosis, placement, or advancement, the classroom teacher's responsibilities may be no less important than those of a tester or administrator, in the sense that we may be making decisions that could affect students' further training and possibly their careers. For these reasons, it is essential that composition teachers understand the weight of their responsibilities and develop the knowledge and skills to execute them fairly and confidently (cf. Bailey, 1998; Grabe & Kaplan, 1997; Silva, 1997). Although we are less concerned here with testing than with ongoing classroom assessment, there are basic precepts from the field of educational measurement (and language testing, in particular) that provide us with a useful framework for selecting and implementing assessment methods and techniques for everyday use.

In composition, one of the more obvious of these precepts holds that an artifact of student performance that becomes subject to formal measurement must have been produced "through the production of writing" (Hamp-Lyons, 1991b, p. 5). That is, when we measure or score student writing performance or proficiency, the outcome must be based on a student-generated text; this text should consist of 100 words or more and be based on a prompt that gives the writer considerable room in which to generate extended discourse (Hamp-Lyons, 1991b). This is known as *direct assessment,* which contrasts with indirect or objective measurement (Camp, 1993; Grabe & Kaplan, 1996). An indirect measure might attempt to evaluate writing ability by testing verbal reasoning, error recognition, or grammatical accuracy, all of which may be related to writing performance in some way but only indirectly because they do not involve the act of composing. Obviously, our focus here is on direct assessment, which is no less objective than indirect measurement, although indirect tests are often claimed to be less subjective.[1] Admittedly, scoring

---

[1] Hamp-Lyons (1991b) wrote that the term *objective* is a "misnomer, since the test design process is as subjective as it is on a direct test" (p. 6).

student writing generally requires considerably more effort and training than the scoring of indirect instruments simply because raters must be trained to apply standards in a consistent, reliable manner. However, there is no question that direct methods are the most appropriate and potentially valid form of assessment in the writing classroom.

Maintaining reliability is a consistent challenge for classroom teachers as well as professionals concerned with evaluating writing performance at the programmatic or institutional level. In writing assessment, *reliability* refers to the consistency with which a sample of student writing is assigned the same rank or score after multiple ratings by trained evaluators (Carmines & Zeller, 1979; Henning, 1991). In day-to-day practice, achieving this ideal is no easy task because most teachers are the sole evaluators of their students' written work. A number of researchers have discovered that even highly experienced instructors sometimes exhibit wide inconsistencies in their essay rating behaviors and in the standards they apply to student writing (Cumming, 1990a; Freedman, 1979; Nold & Freedman, 1977; Vaughan, 1991; White, 1984). Nonetheless, the systematic application of level-appropriate, clear, and specific scoring criteria can contribute to an instructor's reliability in evaluating student work by focusing his or her attention on specific features of student writing as reflected in course objectives and task goals. Consistent use of such criteria and tools can likewise provide an instructor with practice that, over time, will enable him or her to assign scores and offer feedback with confidence.

Validity is yet another measurement precept crucial to successful writing assessment. Simply stated, the construct refers to the extent to which an instrument "actually measures what it purports to measure" (Cohen, 1994, p. 38). The design and rating of valid measures of ESL writing may require considerable practice and expertise. Validity is nonetheless as essential to meaningful and equitable writing assessment as reliability. In fact, validity depends directly on reliability because no measure "can be valid without first being reliable" (Hamp-Lyons, 1991c, p. 252; cf. Bachman, 1990; Bachman & Palmer, 1996; Bailey, 1998; Moss, 1994a, 1994b). Because a thorough treatment of procedures for verifying both reliability and validity are beyond the scope of this book, we focus here on aspects of these constructs that apply specifically to the day-to-day assessment tasks of classroom teachers.[2]

Perhaps one of the most relevant categories of validity is *face validity,* sometimes called *perceived validity* (Low, 1985) or *surface credibility* (Bachman, 1990). If an instrument has face validity, both teachers and students perceive it to measure what

---

[2]Extensive and thorough sources on reliability measurement and validation procedures include the following: Alderson, Clapham, and Wall (1995); Bachman (1990); Bachman and Palmer (1996); Bailey (1998); Cooper and Odell (1977); Hughes (1989); and McNamara (1996). White (1994) addressed these issues in the context of L1 composition, whereas Hamp-Lyons (1991b) was concerned uniquely with academic ESL writing assessment.

it purports to measure. A writing prompt that aims to elicit writers' argumentative skills, for example, has little or no face validity if the prompt implicitly or explicitly elicits a genre or rhetorical style other than argumentation (although other genres such as description or exposition may be used as part of a writer's argument). Similarly, a composing task that emphasizes the importance of textual organization but that is assessed on the basis of grammatical or mechanical form lacks face validity because it may lack the "appearance of reasonableness or accuracy" (Hamp-Lyons, 1991a, p. 9). Because of the need to demonstrate to students that tasks are neither biased nor unfair, ensuring face validity is perhaps one of the teacher's most salient responsibilities in designing assessment instruments (Silva, 1997). Effective assessment instruments also aim to provide writers with an awareness of their performance on the task and its subtasks (Cohen, 1994).

Criterion validity is a more complex type of validity that classroom teachers should be familiar with, although measuring it is actually only practicable in large-scale testing situations over extended periods of time. In global terms, criterion validity refers to how well an instrument matches other comparable instruments or accepted standards. Criterion validity encompasses both concurrent and predictive validity. If an instrument has concurrent validity, it generates the same rank order of individual writer performances as another previously validated instrument administered under comparable conditions at the same time (Bachman, 1990; Bachman & Palmer, 1996; Hamp-Lyons, 1991a; White, 1994). An instrument that has predictive validity conversely produces the same results (again, in terms of rank order of individual writer performances) at future points in time. It is perhaps unreasonable to expect teachers to achieve criterion validity in their daily practice of assessing writing because composition courses generally require students to produce a variety of text types over the instructional period, rather than a single genre. Thus, the classroom setting is rarely amenable to generating the comparability that is required to measure criterion validity. However, in constructing their own assessment tools, it is useful and informative for teachers to consider how consistently their tasks and instruments match up with prior and future instruments, as well as how closely they parallel those administered by fellow instructors at their institutions.

Related to criterion validity is the concept of *content validity,* which reflects how effectively an assessment instrument activates the kinds of cognitive, rhetorical, and linguistic processes involved in writing (i.e., shaping explicit knowledge, personal experiences, ideas, attitudes, etc. into a text that is logically, rhetorically, and formally acceptable). As Hamp-Lyons (1991a) argued, when we claim that a writing task or instrument has content validity,

> we are not talking about whether the topic upon which the prompt is based is something the [students] can be expected to know about—although that is part of it. We are talking about whether it elicits writing that allows the reader—the judge—to see a sufficient and accurate sample of what the writer can do with the key ideas and skills to be mastered. (p. 11)

Therefore, content validity implies that an instrument should not isolate pieces of knowledge or skill areas, but rather that it should elicit writing that requires students to bring together those components that constitute the composing process (i.e., knowledge, skills, and strategies; Faigley et al., 1985).

In this sense, content validity is almost inseparable from construct validity in the domain of writing assessment. We can claim that a task has construct validity only if we can demonstrate that it measures an underlying capacity or trait (Bachman, 1990; Bachman & Palmer, 1996; Cohen, 1994; Hamp-Lyons, 1991a; White, 1994). Construct validity is essential in direct assessment (which is the normative approach applied in the classroom context) and is tied closely to both face and content validity. Specifically, construct validity is established when an instrument actually tests the skills (or constructs) and component subskills that it is designed to elicit and measure (Allaei & Connor, 1991; Faigley et al., 1985). Admittedly, the contructs that most concern us in the classroom—writing ability, proficiency, and, in many cases, progress—cannot be observed directly; instead, we are forced to make inferences about these constructs based on students' composing performance (Cooper & Odell, 1977; Henning, 1991; White, 1994). Specific textual elements that can be used to make fair and accurate inferences include communicative quality, linguistic accuracy, rhetorical organization, strength of argumentation, referencing, linguistic appropriateness, and reader appeal, among many others. Evaluation of these components can be complemented and enhanced by examining students' processes—a procedure that is discussed in the section on portfolio assessment. Regardless of the components emphasized for assessment in a writing course, teachers should have a working knowledge of the fundamental precepts of validity (particularly face, content, and construct validity) as they design instruments and make decisions about scoring procedures. Without valid instruments, it is difficult if not impossible to ensure that the assessment process will produce the desired washback effects.

ASSESSING ESL WRITING: APPROACHES TO SCORING

Evaluative response to student writing can take a number of forms, each of which offers particular advantages and challenges. This section describes three general approaches to scoring that are both appropriate and practical for use in the classroom context: holistic, analytic, primary trait, and multiple trait scoring. Although these summative methods are also used in large-scale testing, the emphasis here is again on ways in which classroom teachers can apply and adapt them to complement their syllabi and to address their students' particular needs and abilities. We should note that we present these approaches as scoring options from which teachers can select, rather than as preferred or prescribed methods. Just as lesson plans, materials, and assignments should be designed and administered as a function of students' needs and competencies, institutional demands, and the individual teacher's style, scoring procedures should also be adjusted to fit the context in which they are used.

Before exploring scoring procedures in detail, it is worthwhile to recall that the assignments, topics, and prompts used to generate student writing for assessment purposes should be devised with the same care that goes into developing any composing task. That is, teachers should assume that the principles of task construction outlined in chapter 4 also apply to the development of tasks and prompts used in the evaluation process. A distinction is not made between task construction for teaching and task construction for assessment because responsible assessment is also a fundamental part of the teaching process. In this sense, then, summative methods of assessing student writing can also be used formatively. Nonetheless, it is valuable to review several basic task properties that are essential to the application of a systematic and informative scoring procedure. White (1994) observed that most test development committees minimally require the following four features of any prompt or assignment used in large-scale testing: clarity, validity, reliability, and interest.[3] These characteristics are equally useful in developing routine prompts for classroom assessment:

1. *Clarity*—A clearly worded prompt does not require students to waste time understanding what the assignment requires but offers brief and succinct directions that allow them to begin writing quickly and easily;

2. *Validity*—A valid prompt produces written products whose scores reflect the range of writing proficiencies represented in the class. In other words, highly skilled writers receive higher scores than less skilled writers; the range does not show an excessively high proportion of scores in the middle range. Thus, a good prompt allows weaker writers to compose comfortably at their level while challenging the most advanced writers to perform at their best (cf. Reid & Kroll, 1995);

3. *Reliability*—The scoring rubric is transparent and succinct enough to apply consistently across all of the writing samples to be assessed, and multiple readings of the same papers by different raters produce similar (if not identical) scores; and

4. *Interest*—The prompt is interesting and engaging enough to encourage students to write about it with genuine concern, resulting in texts that likewise engage the reader/evaluator. In this way, potential boredom on the part of the reader/evaluator will not unfairly bias his or her scoring. (Adapted from White, 1994.)

---

[3]Readers are encouraged to review chapter 4 for a detailed treatment of features to include in meaningful composing tasks. Kroll and Reid (1994) and Reid and Kroll (1995) also outlined valuable procedures for designing effective writing assignments.

Holistic Scoring

An efficient and increasingly popular approach to writing assessment is holistic (or global) scoring, which aims to rate or rank the overall proficiency level reflected in a given sample of student writing. Holistic scoring rubrics are generally made up of 4 to 10 levels or *bands,* each of which corresponds to a score or rating and a set of descriptors.[4] These descriptors are sometimes general (as in Fig. 8.1) and sometimes fairly detailed (as in Fig. 8.2). A chief advantage of holistic scoring is that it requires readers to respond to a text as a whole, rather than on a dimension of the writing that may stand out to an individual reader as particularly weak or strong (e.g., originality of ideas, grammatical accuracy, etc.). The method is likewise intended to emphasize what the writer has done skillfully, as opposed to the text's perceived deficiencies (Cohen, 1994; Perkins, 1983; White, 1994; Williamson & Huot, 1993). For these reasons, the holistic approach has found favor with process writing proponents because the technique stresses strengths and can easily be built into multidraft instruction.

However, holistic scoring presents several disadvantages about which teachers should be aware. First, a holistic score cannot provide diagnostic information because it does not explicitly reflect components that refer to specific traits of a student text (e.g., content, rhetorical structure, coherence, support, sentence grammar, etc.). A single-value score also reduces reliability, although this problem can be addressed when two or more trained raters score each paper (Camp, 1993; Hamp-Lyons, 1991c; Hughes, 1989; Huot, 1990). In addition, a single score may be difficult to interpret for students and teachers alike unless they share the same understanding of the descriptors in the rubric's bands. Moreover, the same score assigned to two different texts may represent two entirely distinct sets of characteristics even if raters' scores reflect a strict and consistent application of the rubric. This can happen because a holistic score compresses a range of interconnected evaluations about all levels of the texts in question (i.e., content, form, style, etc.). Conversely, raters may not apply the same weighting to certain text features, resulting in uneven (and thus unfair) scores (Lumley & McNamara, 1995; McNamara, 1996). For example, research has shown that longer essays tend to receive higher holistic scores, although longer samples may be comparable in quality and complexity to short essays (Cohen, 1994; Cumming, 1990a).[5] Finally, holistic scoring may produce negative washback by penalizing students' efforts to

---

[4]The following sources contain a wide range of sample scoring rubrics: Bates et al. (1993); Cohen (1994); Educational Testing Service (1996); Hamp-Lyons (1991c); and White (1994).

[5]The training of raters and ensuring interrater reliability are a major concern of testing specialists and administrators, particularly those in charge of administering large-scale standardized instruments such as the Test of Written English (TWE). Although classroom teachers can certainly benefit from developing a familiarity with rater training and reliability monitoring, a detailed treatment of these procedures is beyond the scope of this chapter. For additional resources on this topic, please refer to Cooper and Odell (1977), Educational Testing Service (1996), Hamp-Lyons (1991a), and White (1994).

ESL 051 Paragraph rating scale

5 The main idea of the paragraph directly addresses the topic and is stated clearly and succinctly.

The paragraph is logically organized; its coherence is marked by explicit transitions and/or connectors.

The paragraph contains specific supporting ideas, examples, and/or explanations that are explicitly connected to the main idea.

Choice of vocabulary is excellent.

Grammatical errors, if any, are minor and infrequent.

Spelling and punctuation are generally accurate.

4 The paragraph's main idea is related to the topic and is fairly clear.

The paragraph shows solid organization and use of coherence markers.

The paragraph contains at least two supporting ideas, examples, or explanations that are related to the paragraph's main idea.

Vocabulary use is above average.

There may be minor grammatical errors, but they do not interfere with the main idea.

Errors in spelling and punctuation occur, but do not distract the reader.

3 The paragraph indicates a main idea related to the topic, but in ways that could be clearer and more explicit.

The paragraph's organization may lack logic or coherence because connectors and transition signals are not used consistently or effectively.

Supporting points may be underdeveloped due to a lack of specificity or examples. The paragraph may also lack an adequate number of supporting ideas.

Vocabulary use is average.

The paragraph may contain major grammatical errors that compromise its comprehensibility.

Spelling and punctuation errors may distract the reader.

2 The paragraph's main idea is only marginally related to the topic and/or is difficult to identify.

The paragraph does not have an obvious organizational structure; coherence is weak because connectors and transition signals are inappropriate or absent.

Supporting points are inadequate in number and either unclear or irrelevant.

Vocabulary use is weak.

Grammatical errors may be numerous and major, to the extent that the text cannot be easily read and understood.

Errors in spelling and punctuation consistently distract the reader.

1 The paragraph does not address the topic and/or lacks a main idea.

The text lacks organization and coherence.

Attempts at supporting the main idea are ineffective due to inappropriateness and/or an absence of development; coherence is altogether absent.

Vocabulary use is extremely weak.

Major grammatical errors abound; the text causes the reader major comprehension difficulties.

Spelling and punctuation errors are frequent and highly distracting.

FIG. 8.1. Sample scoring rubric for a low-intermediate ESL composition course.

ENSL 1405—Advanced English writing skills for the social sciences
Evaluation criteria for revised writing assignments

Characteristics of an "A" paper

An "A" paper is admirably thorough and complete. Explicit and clear, the position is strongly and substantially argued with abundant reference to published works. The central issues and their complexity are treated seriously, with alternative viewpoints taken into account. The paper shows rhetorical control at the highest level and displays unity and subtle management. Ideas are balanced with support that is organized according to the content. Textual elements are connected through explicit logical and/or linguistic transitions. Repetition and redundancy are minimal. The paper shows excellent language control, accurate diction, stylistic precision, and meticulous adherence to mechanical conventions.

Characteristics of a "B" paper

A "B" paper is thorough and complete. The text deals effectively with the issues, presenting the position clearly and articulating arguments substantively. References made to published works are ample and appropriate. Alternative perspectives are also addressed competently. The paper shows strong rhetorical control and is well managed. Ideas are generally balanced with support; the whole text shows strong control of organization that is appropriate to the content. Textual elements are generally well connected, although rhetorical fluency may at times need improvement. Occasional repetitions, redundancies and missing transitions may occur, but the paper reflects strong language control and reads smoothly. Grammatical well-formedness and accurate diction are apparent, although minor errors might be present. Stylistic and mechanical errors are minor and do not distract the reader.

Characteristics of a "C" paper

Possibly lacking in thoroughness, a "C" paper is nonetheless complete. The text discusses the issues but requires more focus, development and/or synthesis of published works. The position, while thoughtful, needs to be clarified; arguments may require further substantiation. Repetition, redundancy, and inconsistency sometimes compromise the paper's focus and direction. Alternative viewpoints are minimally addressed and developed. Although the essay shows acceptable rhetorical control, competent management, and appropriate organization, ideas may not be balanced with support. The text shows evidence of planning, although a lack of connectors sometimes interferes with rhetorical fluency. Language is grammatical but may lack fluidity. Whereas the grammatical structures and lexical choices express the writer's intended meanings, more appropriate choices could have been made. Morpho-syntactic, stylistic, and mechanical errors sometimes interfere with the reader's comprehension. Papers assigned a mark of "C" should be revised and resubmitted.

Characteristics of a "D" paper

A "D" paper lacks both completeness and thoroughness. Although the text may consider the issues, it relies heavily on opinions or claims that lack substantial evidence, sometimes leading the reader to wonder if the writer has come to grips with the complexity of the topic. Synthesis of published works is clearly deficient. Superficial and/or inconsistent argumentation, along with inadequate development, seriously compromise the text's ability to convince the reader. Alternative perspectives are given little or no serious attention. Lacking rhetorical control much or most of the time, the paper's overall shape is difficult to discern. The organization suggests a lack of balance of support that leads to noticeable breakdowns in rhetorical fluency. Transitions within and across sentences and paragraphs are attempted, with only partial success. Displaying weak linguistic control, the text contains grammatical, lexical, and mechanical errors that are a serious threat to the reader's comprehension. Papers assigned a mark of "D" must be revised and resubmitted.

<u>Characteristics of an "F" paper</u>
An "F" paper is unsuccessful because it is clearly incomplete and fails to develop and support an argument related to the topic. While the topic may be mentioned, the text digresses and/or does not treat issues of relevance to the assignment. Superficial and inaccurate treatment of published works suggests a failure to read sources carefully and extensively. Demonstrating little rhetorical control, the paper shows virtually no evidence of planning or organization, as exemplified in underdeveloped and/or nonexistent connections and transitions. The text demonstrates inadequate linguistic control, with morpho-syntactic, lexical, and mechanical errors seriously marring the writer's intended meaning. Papers assigned a mark of "F" <u>must</u> be revised and resubmitted.

FIG. 8.2. Sample scoring rubric for an advanced-level social sciences EAP course.

develop their texts and take risks, "since writers may display only novice ability with more complex forms, while those using simpler forms get higher ratings" (Cohen, 1994, p. 315). Classroom teachers can nonetheless avoid a number of these pitfalls by developing clear rubrics, checking their accuracy with the help of peers, reviewing student writing in portfolios, and employing consistent and explicit marking practices.

Although *scoring rubrics* have historically been designed as an aid to raters, they can also be used as an important teaching tool when they are presented to students and referred to by the instructor during the assessment process. Hamp-Lyons (1991c) made the forceful argument that any method of writing assessment that "fails to utilize the educative potential" of the instrument "permits a disjunction between teaching and assessment, a disjunction we have suffered under for all too long, and need suffer no longer" (p. 244). We would similarly maintain that a scoring rubric should reflect the values and expectations of the writer's intended audience (whether real or simulated). A rubric can be used effectively as a teaching tool when fronted in the teaching process (e.g., when it is given to students early in a course and when writers are offered chances to work with it before its criteria are applied to evaluations of their own texts). A well-designed rubric can also serve as a consistent framework for providing meaningful feedback for students to use in revising their papers. To be used productively in this way, however, descriptors must be explicit, comprehensible, and geared specifically toward students' proficiency levels and the rhetorical foci of the writing course. Figures 8.1 and 8.2 provide two illustrations of rubrics whose descriptors are intended to be used as teaching and assessment tools in two distinct contexts. Figure 8.1 shows a five-level holistic scoring rubric for a community college composition course aimed at academic paragraph writing. The rubric in Fig. 8.2, meanwhile, is designed for use in an advanced-level (second semester) EAP course requiring sophisticated and extensive social science writing involving synthesis of theoretical and empirical data. Its five-level scale is intended to parallel the traditional letter-grade marking system used at that institution.

In holistic scoring, the rater reads the writing sample quickly and then assigns a single score or grade to a text based on an overall impression as described in the rubric (see Figs. 8.1 and 8.2). In large-scale writing assessment, two or more raters may assign scores to ensure reliability, particularly if marking is done on a department- or institution-wide basis. In the classroom context, however, the instructor may assign a holistic numerical or letter grade to an assignment after one or more readings; he or she may also provide the student with written and/or oral feedback to supplement the holistic rating or ranking. In day-to-day classroom scoring, teachers sometimes prefer a more finely tuned instrument or a more flexible tool for assigning borderline marks (i.e., those that fall somewhere between bands). This need arises when an essay displays most of the characteristics of one band but simultaneously exhibits one or more features of another. For example, consider how the rubric in Fig. 8.2 might be applied to a thorough and complete essay that deals with the issues and competently addresses alternative perspectives: These are obviously all *B* features. At the same time, however, ideas may not be balanced with support, a lack of connectors may interfere with rhetorical fluency, and the language may lack fluidity. Furthermore, "morpho-syntactic, stylistic and mechanical errors … interfere with … comprehension." These *C* characteristics suggest that neither a mark of *B* nor *C* would be entirely appropriate. A fairer and potentially more informative alternative would be to assign a *B*– or a *C*+, depending on the extent to which the *B* features override the *C* features or vice versa. Although the +/– technique might not be appropriate or efficient for large-scale assessment, it provides a reasonable option for teachers who do not wish to be confined to band-specific scores that may not accurately reflect the quality of all dimensions of a writing sample.

$\boxed{\Rightarrow\!AA\ 8.1}$

Analytic Scoring

Analytic scoring offers advantages similar to those associated with using "+" and "–" marks in conjunction with a holistic rubric. Unlike holistic scoring, however, analytic scoring relies on a rating guide that separates and weights textual components a priori so that the rater's criteria are focused and prioritized before the scoring process begins. Thus, components such as content, organization, cohesion, style, register, vocabulary, grammar, spelling, mechanics, and so on are preassigned a maximum numerical value, with decreasing step scales or bands described within each component. In the widely known ESL Composition Profile (Jacobs, Zingraf, Wormuth, Hartfiel, & Hughey, 1981), for example, each of the five components has a descending four-level scoring scale with its own descriptors. The sample "Essay Rating Profile" in Fig. 8.3, an adaptation of the Jacobs et al. (1981) model, illustrates what such a scoring guide looks like. The scheme in Fig. 8.3 is designed for use in a university NES-NNS freshman composition course; its scale allows for assigning letter grades or numerical values that, when summed, yield a score out of 100.

RHET 105A — Composition I Name: _____

Essay Rating Profile Essay: _____

Score/Grade		Range	Features
Content			
	A	24–27	Superior understanding of topic and writing context; valuable central purpose/thesis defined and supported with sound generalizations and substantial, specific, and relevant details; rich, distinctive content that is original, perceptive, and/or persuasive; strong reader interest
	B	22–23	Accurate grasp of topic and writing context; worthwhile central purpose/thesis clearly defined and supported with sound generalizations and relevant details; substantial reader interest
	C	19–21	Acceptable but cursory understanding of topic and writing context; routine purpose/thesis supported with adequate generalizations and relevant details; suitable but predictable content that is somewhat sketchy or overly general; occasional repetitive or irrelevant material; one or two unsound generalizations; average reader interest
	D/F	5–18	Little or no grasp of the topic or writing context; central purpose/thesis not apparent, weak
Rhetorical structure			
	A	21–23	Exceptionally clear plan connected to thesis/purpose; plan developed with consistent attention to proportion, emphasis, logical order, flow, and synthesis of ideas; paragraphs coherent, unified, and effectively developed; striking title, introduction, and conclusion
	B	18–20	Clear plan related to thesis; plan developed with proportion, emphasis, logical order, and synthesis of ideas; paragraphs coherent, unified, and adequately developed; smooth transitions between paragraphs; effective title, introduction, and conclusion
	C	16–17	Conventional plan apparent but routinely presented; paragraphs adequately unified and coherent, but minimally effective in development; one or two weak topic sentences; transitions between paragraphs apparent but abrupt, mechanical, or monotonous; routine title, introduction, and conclusion
	D/F	5–15	Plan not apparent, inappropriate, undeveloped, or developed with irrelevance, redundancy, inconsistency, or inattention to logical progression; paragraphs incoherent, underdeveloped, or not unified; transitions between paragraphs unclear, ineffective, or nonexistent; weak or ineffective title, introduction, and conclusion
Grammatical form			
	A	18–20	Sentences skillfully constructed, unified, coherent, forceful, effectively varied; deftness in coordinating, subordinating, and emphasizing ideas; harmonious agreement of content and sentence design; impressive use of grammatical structures
	B	16–17	Sentences accurately and coherently constructed with some variety; evident and varied coordination, subordination, and emphasis of ideas; no errors in complex patterns; effective and clear use of grammatical structures
	C	14–15	Sentences constructed accurately but lacking in distinction; minimal skill in coordinating and subordinating ideas; little variety in sentence structure; clarity weakened by occasional awkward, incomplete, fused, and/or improperly predicated clauses and complex sentences; marginal to adequate use of grammatical structures
	D/F	1–13	Sentences marred frequently enough to distract or frustrate the reader; numerous sentences incoherent, fused, incomplete, and/or improperly predicated; monotonous, simple sentence structure; unacceptable use of grammatical structures

Fig. 8.3 continues

Diction & tone			
	A	16–17	Diction distinctive; fresh, precise, concrete, economical, and idiomatic word choice; word form mastery; appropriate, consistent, and engaging tone
	B	14–15	Clear, accurate, and idiomatic diction; minor errors in word form and/or occasional weaknesses in word choice; generally clear, appropriate, and consistent tone
	C	12–13	Satisfactory diction; generally accurate, appropriate, and idiomatic word choice, though occasionally predictable, wordy, or imprecise; limited vocabulary; clarity weakened by errors in S–V and pronoun agreement, point of view, word forms; mechanical and/or inconsistent tone
	D/F	1–11	Diction unacceptable for a college-level essay; inappropriate, nonidiomatic, and/or inaccurate word choice that distracts the reader or obscures content; numerous word form errors; inappropriate and/or inconsistent tone
Mechanics			
	A	12–13	Clarity and effectiveness of expression enhanced by consistent use of conventional punctuation, capitalization, and spelling; appealing manuscript form
	B	10–11	Flow of communication only occasionally diverted by errors in conventional punctuation, capitalization, and spelling; attractive manuscript form
	C	8–9	Adequate clarity and effectiveness of expression, though diminished by punctuation, capitalization, and/or spelling errors; satisfactory manuscript form
	D/F	1–7	Communication hindered or obscured by frequent violations of punctuation, capitalization, and/or spelling conventions; manuscript form unattractive

☐/100 = Overall Score   Grade = ☐

FIG. 8.3. Sample scoring rubric for a university NES/NNS freshman composition course.

Analytic scoring is sometimes recommended as an alternative or complement to holistic scoring for a number of reasons. One of its principal advantages is that analytic guides, by virtue of their explicit descriptors and weighting systems, make the training of raters easier than do holistic rubrics (Cohen, 1994; McNamara, 1996; Omaggio Hadley, 1993; Weir, 1990). Because consistent and reliable holistic scoring often requires regular (and sometimes extensive) norming, novice composition teachers may initially find it easier to work with an analytic scale than a holistic rubric because they can evaluate and respond to specific textual features. Some institutions and departments request that their instructors use analytic scales as a way of standardizing rating procedures across sections and courses (Weir, 1990). A further benefit of analytic scoring is that it prevents the conflation of two or more important text-based categories—one of the common drawbacks of holistic scoring (McNamara, 1996). Analytic guides can also be designed to reflect priorities assigned to specific aspects of student writing (or writing processes) in the syllabus. Not only can descriptors be constructed to represent particular rhetorical and linguistic course objectives (e.g., use of argumentative techniques, figurative language, complex as opposed to simple sentences, etc.), but weightings for particular components can be adjusted to encourage students to direct their efforts toward improving specific skills (cf. Fig. 8.3). For example, in a beginning- or intermediate-level course emphasizing idea development, the scoring guide might assign a 40% to 60% weighting to a content or ideas category, with aspects such as organization and grammar receiving proportionally lower weightings. Finally, the explicitness of analytic scoring guides offers the teacher a potentially valuable tool for providing writers with consistent and direct feedback. Analytic guides generally provide space for each component's score or rating and allow teachers to circle or underline descriptor items that apply to the essay being evaluated. When teachers use these options, complemented by text-specific comments (see chaps. 5 and 7), component scores have meaning beyond mere numerical values or ranks: They are tied directly to identifiable text features and explicit standards.

Nonetheless, critics of analytic scoring point out that the effectiveness of a writing sample is much more than the sum of its parts. Measuring the quality of a text by tallying accumulated subskill scores diminishes the interconnectedness of written discourse and gives the false impression that writing can be understood and fairly assessed by analyzing autonomous text features (Hillocks, 1995; White, 1994). Consequently, component scales may not be used effectively according to their internal criteria, resulting in a halo effect in which one component score may positively (or negatively) influence another. A related disadvantage involves how raters operationalize component scales when their descriptors overlap or when descriptors are overly simplified, misleading, or ambiguous. Hamp-Lyons (1989) reported that even experienced instructors and essay judges sometimes find it difficult to assign numerical scores based on certain descriptors, even when they can refer to benchmark, or model texts. Thus, qualitative judgments about coherence, style, and so on are not always easily accommodated by analytic scoring methods. Finally, analytic scoring may unfairly bias readers in favor of writing samples that contain elements that are easily identified based on the scoring guide's components and descriptors (McNamara, 1996). Because grammatical errors are among the most obvious and salient characteristics of student writing for many readers, grammatical form may receive more attention from raters than other text features, such as idea development and organization, although the latter may have a prominent place in the scoring guide. The unfortunate result of this subtle but powerful bias is that writers might not receive appropriate scores or the type of feedback that will benefit them the most (Cohen, 1994; Hamp-Lyons, 1989).

$\boxed{\Rightarrow AA\ 8.2}$

Primary and Multiple Trait Scoring

Although holistic and analytic scoring rely on preexisting instruments and a priori criteria for assessing and responding to student writing, primary and multiple trait scoring presuppose that the quality of a writing sample can only be judged accurately and fairly with reference to the specific writing context (Hamp-Lyons, 1991c; Lloyd-Jones, 1977; White, 1994). This necessitates devising and deploying a scoring guide that is unique to each prompt and the student writing that it generates. Thus, the overarching goal of this approach is to develop criteria for successful writing on a given topic and/or in a selected genre so that teachers and writers alike can focus on a narrow range of textual aspects or traits (Freedman, 1991). It is important to note that trait- or facet-based instruments "do not claim to assess every element of writing ability that may be manifested in the context" but rather "the most salient criteria or traits" associated with the task (Hamp-Lyons, 1991c, p. 248).

If an essay assignment is designed to elicit persuasive writing, for example, scoring might be based exclusively on the articulation and development of an argument; this would constitute primary trait scoring. In multiple-trait scoring, the principle is the same except that several related traits or facets make up the scoring instrument. In the case of the argumentative essay just mentioned, additional traits might include the directness of the position statement or proposition, the number of supporting points in the argument, the use of counterargument, the credibility of the sources evoked by the writer, and so on. A primary- or multiple-trait approach therefore focuses the reader's attention directly on the purposes of the writing task, as Fig. 8.4 illustrates. When used as part of the instructional cycle, trait-based scoring also offers the advantage of encouraging student writers to limit their attention to a manageable set of rhetorical and/or linguistic characteristics as they compose and revise (Cohen, 1994; Perkins, 1983).

One of the obviously positive attributes of primary- and multiple-trait scoring is that it treats writing samples not as generic but as unique texts grounded in specific, local contexts and motivated by particular purposes. Consequently, the method is highly flexible in that each writing assignment in a given course can theoretically be evaluated according to its own scale. Thus, a carefully designed trait- or facet-based scoring guide is sensitive to the demands of the particular writing task, to a particular group of writers, and to the audience that the writers (and raters) have in mind. The multiple-trait scoring guide reproduced in Fig. 8.4, for example, was originally developed for evaluating a timed writing in which advanced college-level ESL writers compared two short essays expressing opposing points of view (about 500 words each). Students had completed assigned readings on technology's influence on education and the professions and were working toward an upcoming class debate on the topic.

This writing assignment was designed to (a) give students further and more extended practice in analyzing and comparing arguments in writing, and (b) deepen their understanding of the topic. The instructor had selected this topic and the related readings based on students' majors and the next course they would take: an interdisciplinary adjunct writing course entitled, "Reading and Writing for the Applied Sciences." Thus, the prompt and scoring guide are constructed to reflect the rhetorical mode(s) of the assignment (statement of the author's position, comparison), the subtasks involved (summarizing the two reading selections), and the formal features elicited (appropriateness of language, effective lexical use). The descriptors are likewise geared toward measuring the academic and rhetorical skills

Prompt: In their respective essays, Chang and Hunter express conflicting perspectives on how technology has influenced the education and professional training of the modern workforce. You will have 90 minutes in which to explain which author presents the most persuasive argument and why. Based on a brief summary of each author's point of view, compare the two essays and determine which argument is the strongest for you. Be sure to state your position clearly and to give each essay adequate attention.

ENSL 24
Advanced Reading and Composing for Nonnative Speakers
Scoring Guide for Timed Writing 3

Score	Rhetorical soundness	Summary presentation and comparison	Language use
6	The author's position is stated explicitly and substantiated with relevant references to the two essays.	The main idea of each essay is accurately captured and clearly represented; coverage of the two essays is symmetrically balanced.	Language is direct, fluid, and generally accurate; vocabulary use is sophisticated and varied.
5	The author's position is stated clearly and supported with references to the two essays.	The paper effectively paraphrases each essay's main idea; coverage of the two essays is well balanced.	Language control is good; vocabulary use is nicely varied.
4	The author's position is sufficiently explicit but could be stated more clearly; references to the two essays are adequate.	The paper paraphrases each essay's main idea with moderate effectiveness; coverage of the two essays is adequately balanced.	Language shows satisfactory but inconsistent control; vocabulary use shows adequate variety.
3	The author's position is not sufficiently explicit; references to the two essays are sketchy.	The paper merely restates each essay's main idea or captures them inaccurately; coverage of the two essays is not satisfactorily balanced.	Language shows inconsistent control; vocabulary use shows a lack of variety.
2	The author's position is either not explicit or is ineffectively developed; references to the two essays are minimal and inadequate.	The paper only partially restates each essay's main idea; minimal coverage of the two essays.	Language shows inconsistencies that distract the reader; vocabulary use is highly restricted.
1	The author does not state a position; references to the two essays are unacceptable or nonexistent.	The paper fails to capture the main ideas of either essay.	Language control frequently distracts the reader; vocabulary use is highly restricted and/or inaccurate.
0	Not a ratable sample.	Not a ratable sample.	Not a ratable sample.

FIG. 8.4. Sample multiple trait scoring guide (with prompt).

specified in the course objectives. Furthermore, the scoring procedure is specially adapted to the context, purpose, and form of the writing to be elicited. Using this six-level scale, the rater assigns a single score to each of the three traits to determine a cumulative score of 0 to 18 (which can be divided by 3 to arrive at a mean score on a 1–6 scale, if necessary). For example, a student essay may be assigned a 5 for rhetorical soundness, a 4 for summary presentation, and a 6 for language use, yielding a cumulative score of 15/18 (or 5 on a six-level scale).

Because of the flexibility offered by primary- and multiple-trait assessment techniques, scoring criteria can be integrated naturally into the teaching, drafting, feedback, and revision cycle, producing a positive washback on instruction and learning. From the assessment perspective, trait-based scoring simultaneously offers greater face validity than do the more generic holistic and analytic methods because the criteria are directly and explicitly tied to the objectives of specific writing tasks. The practice also offers higher content and construct validity because instruments are based on expectations, textual conventions, and skills associated with a particular setting, such as courses in basic ESL writing, freshman composition, writing for the humanities, writing for business, writing for science and technology, and so on. Primary- and multiple-trait scoring can also yield enhanced concurrent and predictive validity. When raters differ in their evaluations of a writing sample, the precision of trait-based descriptors allows them to resolve discrepancies and reach compromises more easily than with a holistic rubric (which is global and understandably abstract) or analytic guide (which is fixed and may not address particular tasks or genres; Hamp-Lyons, 1991a, 1991c). Thanks to these attributes, trait-based scoring also tends to provide more informative and accurate diagnostic data than do holistic and analytic techniques (Cohen, 1994).

Of course, trait-based scoring is not without its drawbacks, one of the most obvious of which is that the method can be extremely time-consuming (Perkins, 1983). The time and effort required to construct and test scoring guides for each writing assignment may exceed the limits of many classroom teachers. Programs and departments with multiple course sections, however, can reduce individual instructors' workloads to a manageable level by dividing assignment and scoring guide-writing duties evenly among the faculty. In this way, writing tasks and scoring materials are shared across sections so that each instructor may only have to develop one or two scoring guides over a term.

This time-saving option notwithstanding, opponents of trait-based scoring point out that the procedure can sometimes generate subjective, and therefore biased, evaluations of student writing. For example, in primary-trait evaluation, for example, raters may be unable to focus exclusively on the specified trait (e.g., strength of argumentation), implicitly and unknowingly applying criteria related to other facets (e.g., essay length, syntactic complexity, etc.; Hamp-Lyons, 1991c). In addition, a primary-trait model is, by nature, reductionist and therefore cannot integrate writers' strengths and weaknesses. That is, even a sophisticated primary trait scale might award a lower score to an exemplary partial writing sample than to a weak sample that nonetheless fully addresses the prompt (Freedman, 1991). Both primary- and multiple-trait instruments may also simultaneously generate undesirable (and possibly undetected) subjectivity because we may be unable to identify and validate a single facet (or multiple facets) that would be uniquely appropriate for the context, topic, and task. Furthermore, "even if the traits are specific to a local context, the raters may still fall back on traditional generalized concepts in their actual ratings" (Cohen, 1994, p. 323). These are important reservations that should not be overlooked in adopting a trait-based approach to writing assessment.

A number of basic steps can be taken to overcome the pitfalls of primary- and multiple-trait writing assessment. Because a trait- or facet-based scoring guide needs to be developed for each individual writing assignment, construction of the scoring guide should be incorporated directly into the task design process (see chap. 4). As a general guideline, a primary- or multiple-trait assessment tool should contain the following elements:

1. The task or prompt (see chap. 4);
2. A description of the primary rhetorical trait(s) elicited by the task or prompt and featured in the scoring criteria;
3. An interpretation of how the task or prompt will generate the expected writing performance;
4. Identification of the relationship between the task or prompt and the trait(s) to be assessed;
5. A scoring guide (see Fig. 8.4);
6. Benchmark student texts representing each band or score value;
7. A rationale for the scores assigned to the benchmark papers. (Based on Hamp-Lyons, 1991c.)

These elements are mainly intended for the development and implementation of writing tests. Nonetheless, they are useful in routine classroom assessment because they underscore the need to connect scoring as much as possible to the purposes of writing and specific performance expectations. The guidelines also dramatize for teachers and students the principle that writing effectiveness can sometimes depend on specific textual dimensions. Therefore, the use of primary- and multiple-trait instruments "implies a view of writing as a complex and multifaceted activity, and of the response of each reader to text as similarly complex and multifaceted" (Hamp-Lyons, 1991c, p. 248).

$\boxed{\Rightarrow AA\ 8.3}$

PORTFOLIO ASSESSMENT

The scoring methods addressed in the preceding sections offer classroom teachers a range of options from which to choose as they select response and evaluation methods for their courses and writing assignments. These summative procedures, used individually or in combination with one another, can be applied in the framework of portfolio assessment, which is *not* an alternative scoring procedure, but rather an overall model of organizing writing processes and written products for ongoing reflection, dialogue, and evaluation. That is, a portfolio system does not require any particular scoring procedure. In fact, some portfolio assessment models involve no scoring at all, although the process does necessitate ongoing instructor response and evaluation (Bailey, 1998; Elbow, 1993). Portfolio assessment has become increasingly recognized as a valid and valuable tool for teaching and evaluation in a variety of contexts, from elementary and secondary education (Calfee & Perfumo, 1996b; Yancey, 1992) to college-level writing courses (Belanoff & Dickson, 1991).

Recognized widely as an alternative means of assessing learner achievement of all sorts (not just writing), portfolio assessment is intended to feature "production rather than recognition, projects rather than items, and teacher judgment rather than mechanical scoring" (Calfee & Perfumo, 1996a, p. 63). When carefully planned and consistently implemented, portfolio assessment crucially engages both students and teachers in continual discussion, analysis, and evaluation of their *processes* as learners and writers, as well as multiple academic products. Yancey (1992) pointed out that "reflection is perhaps the most critical feature distinguishing portfolios of writing from simple work folders" because a meaningful portfolio consists of much more than "a set of unglossed rough and final drafts assembled willy-nilly" (p. 86). Both teachers and students must bear this in mind if a portfolio process is to be used productively and fairly. To emphasize the fundamentally developmental character of a valid portfolio system, Yancey (1992) set forth the following principles and features:

• A portfolio is a *collection* of work, but it is a collection that is a subset of a larger archive. Theoretically, the archive is the whole of a student's work, but more practically and more frequently, it is a subset of writing completed in a class, a program, a school;

• The process by which the subset is created is one of *selection,* the second principle of portfolios. How entries are selected varies according to the rhetorical situation contextualizing the portfolio. Is the portfolio's purpose to show development only, or both development and achievement? Who will read the portfolio, an insider like a classroom teacher, or a classroom outsider ...? Who has the authority for making the selections?

• A third principle is *reflection,* the process by which a student explains his or her learning: how the portfolio entries were created, for example, how one compares to another, how writing these has changed the writer, what this learning means to him or her;

• A fourth principle is *communication,* in the sense that the writing portfolio, like any portfolio, will communicate something about the writer, about what he or she values, about the context in which the writer has worked, and so on;

• Finally, any portfolio entails *evaluation,* in the sense, again, that it shows processes of valuing taking place, as students make selections, as they arrange them, as they tell the portfolio readers—and themselves—about the entries and the learning connected with them. (p. 86)

Based on these characteristics, it is easy to see how a portfolio system can accommodate and encourage the cyclical, heuristic, and recursive principles of composing pedagogy described and illustrated earlier in this book. Furthermore, the teacher–student transactions and dialogue entailed in portfolio assembly and evaluation underscore the vital role played by assessment in teaching and learning. In particular, the portfolio process offers the following specific benefits:

- A portfolio approach makes a commitment to process-oriented writing instruction real and tangible for both teachers and learners, especially because the process necessitates multidrafting, expert and peer feedback, substantial revision, and reflection (Burnham, 1986);
- A portfolio approach allows students and the instructor to construct a series of assignments that build on and complement one another organically, leading to a culminating array of drafts and revised products that constitute a whole rather than a disjointed set of individual assignments or isolated items (Black, Daiker, Sommers, & Stygall, 1994; Yancey, 1996);
- Because portfolio contents reflect finished products as well as individual processes, a portfolio system enables writers to examine and evaluate their own development and identify specific areas for improvement (Bailey, 1998; Burnham, 1986; Camp, 1992; D'Aoust, 1992; Yancey, 1992);
- "Portfolio evaluation establishes a writing environment rather than a grading environment in the classroom" (Burnham, 1986, p. 139). In this way, instructors can respond to student writing with the central purpose of promoting revision and collaboration (Elbow, 1993);
- A portfolio approach requires writers to view their own processes and products critically, encouraging them to assume responsibility for their own development. As students become more independent as writers, respondents, and critics, they gradually depend less on their instructors to grant approval and direct their revision processes (Burnham, 1986; Klimenkov & LaPick, 1996);
- Because a portfolio approach holds students accountable for their progress and efforts, it reduces the survivalist mentality whereby they attempt merely to get by. That is, in portfolio assessment, writers "find no reward in doing only the minimum required" because they must collaborate with their peers and the instructor to meet their full potential and to succeed in earning a satisfactory mark (Burnham, 1986, p. 139);
- Portfolio assessment reduces the pressure placed on the instructor to give positive and encouraging feedback early in the term, although writing quality at that point may be far from meeting target criteria. Because summative evaluation is postponed until later in the quarter or semester, the instructor can enforce rigorous standards of quality from the beginning by responding to texts frankly, but possibly without assigning scores or grades. In this way, students are given formative, evaluative feedback with which to improve their writing, without being prema-

turely discouraged by low marks (Burnham, 1986; Elbow, 1993; Myers, 1996; Peterson, 1995); and

• In a portfolio model, instructors have the flexibility to focus on particular characteristics of their students' writing and practice with different response and evaluation methods over time (cf. chap. 5). Because writing portfolios contain a variety of genres and assignment types assembled during a school term, instructors can select numerous response (and possibly scoring) procedures that target specific pieces of writing (e.g., holistic feedback and scoring for timed writing, primary-trait scoring for newly introduced rhetorical patterns, etc.). Rather than typecasting or pigeon-holing students, response and evaluation involves ongoing dialogue with students as well as trial and error as the instructor searches for optimal scoring procedures (Burnham, 1986; McCabe, 1996; Yancey, 1992).

Portfolio assessment is, of course, subject to a number of limitations, particularly when used for large-scale performance evaluation. One such limitation concerns how raters can fairly and reliably produce a single score or mark for judging writing quality, particularly when the written products that students include in their portfolios vary widely in terms of genre and complexity. A related problem is comparability: How can grading equivalence be established when individual writers are given the responsibility of selecting from a range of assignments and projects to include in their portfolios? Furthermore, how does one control the variation that might occur when different tasks assigned by different teachers necessitate the rating of portfolios that are not ostensibly comparable (Grabe & Kaplan, 1996)? For example, the tasks created by some teachers might be more compelling and interesting than those assigned by others. A partial solution to this problem is the development of explicit instructions for both students and instructors that ensure consistency and reliability in both the compilation and evaluation of portfolios (Herman, Gearhart, & Aschbacher, 1996). A final aspect that should not be overlooked is authenticity: "How will the portfolio raters know that the students actually wrote all the pieces in the portfolio, and when is editing and revising assistance from others too extensive to represent the student's own writing abilities" (Grabe & Kaplan, 1996, p. 417)? These are all challenges to be confronted directly as portfolio assessment becomes more widely practiced (Camp, 1993; Hamp-Lyons & Condon, 1993; White, 1994, 1995). When implemented thoughtfully and systematically, however, a portfolio approach can furnish both experienced and novice teachers with abundant "room to breathe and grow" (Burnham, 1986, p. 139).

A General Model

Far from being an easy way to grade student writing, designing and implementing a portfolio system requires considerable time, planning, and teacher and learner training, to say nothing of consistent follow-through. The general framework described next, although developed specifically for a particular educational context, illustrates one way in which portfolio assessment can function effectively within and across courses in a given department or institution. Clearly, the extent and complexity of portfolio systems vary widely from one setting to another. A number of secondary and college writing programs, for example, require their instructors to use a program-wide portfolio assessment procedure in their courses and to participate in departmental portfolio rating sessions at the end of each term (and sometimes at midterm). In such situations, the syllabus for each course may set forth program-wide guidelines for students to follow in compiling their portfolios and for instructors to use in teaching, reviewing their students' work, student conferences, and so on. Scoring criteria may likewise be standardized for multiple sections of the same course. In this way, collaborative evaluation of students' portfolios is greatly facilitated because instructors may be expected to grade their own students' work and participate in team grading of the work of students in other sections as well. In other settings, teachers may have the freedom to determine whether they will use portfolios at all. If they do elect to implement a portfolio system, teachers may need to decide the weight of a portfolio in determining course grades depending on the proportion of the course goals that the portfolio will represent.

The model outlined next describes the portfolio process for a course in a multilevel college ESL writing program; its framework is based on the systems pioneered by Burhnam (1986) and Elbow and Belanoff (1991). This model is included here merely to illustrate one of a multitude of approaches to using portfolios in the classroom. Indeed, the literature on portfolio assessment is extensive, increasingly rigorous, and, unfortunately, too vast to synthesize fairly here. Readers are nevertheless encouraged to consult these resources for detailed descriptions of portfolio frameworks, procedures, evaluation methods, and learning outcomes.[6] The following basic questions can serve as a concrete starting point for devising a portfolio process:

1. What are the purposes of the assessment?
2. What tasks and artifacts will be included in the portfolio document?
3. What are the performance standards and how will marking criteria be applied?
4. How will the instructor and/or raters ensure that scoring and feedback will be consistent?
5. To what extent will completed portfolios represent the performances that are reflected in course objectives and students' goals? That is, will the portfolio product have content and construct validity?

---

[6]The following useful and informative sources focus principally on multidisciplinary and/or L1 writing contexts: Belanoff and Dickson (1991); Calfee and Perfumo (1996a, 1996b); Camp and Belanoff (1987); Elbow and Belanoff (1991); Herman, Aschbacher, and Winters (1992); Yancey (1992).

6. How will the outcomes of the evaluation process (i.e., scores or grades, evaluative feedback) affect students' future learning? (based on Herman, Aschbacher, & Winters, 1992; Herman, Gearhart, & Aschbacher, 1996).

Process Overview. The college program for which the following portfolio system was designed comprises four prefreshman composition ESL courses, in addition to two NNS-track freshman composition courses that parallel their NES-track equivalents. The NNS freshman composition courses are taken in a two-semester/one-year sequence (COMP 120 and COMP 121). Although the prefreshman composition courses do not bear credit toward students' degrees, they are graded A–E, as are the freshman composition courses (which do bear academic credit). Portfolio evaluation is used in all courses in the program, with each course establishing required contents and grading criteria appropriate to course-specific objectives and proficiency levels. We focus here on the portfolio model used in the first NNS freshman composition course, COMP 120.

The portfolio process for COMP 120 and all of the courses in the ESL writing program actually begins by acquainting instructors (full- and part-time faculty, as well as graduate teaching associates) with the model's principles and procedures. The orientation for new instructors and periodic faculty-wide in-service workshops offer all instructors a thorough introduction to the program's goals and objectives, which include mastery of the structure and development of paragraphs and multiple forms of extended written discourse (i.e., discipline-specific academic and nonacademic written genres), research techniques, collaborative learning procedures, and the conventions of standard edited English. Although COMP 120 instructors are free to design their own course outlines, the syllabus is constructed and agreed on before the start of each semester. For the sake of consistency across sections, instructors agree on a common textbook or set of materials from which they are free to choose specific readings and design writing assignments; faculty also jointly establish the number and type of revised assignments and timed writings to be included in the COMP 120 portfolio. Deadlines for the midterm and final portfolio documents are also determined collaboratively and announced in the syllabus.

In line with the principles outlined in chapter 3 and earlier in this chapter, the syllabus sets forth assessment criteria that are explicitly linked to course goals and assignment objectives so that students and teachers alike have a clear understanding of how evaluation is to take place over the term. Before students submit their first piece of revised writing, both novice and experienced instructors participate in an essay-norming sessions so that they can familiarize themselves with the COMP 120 holistic scoring rubric (which is similar to the sample in Fig. 8.2) and benchmark papers. The purpose of this early workshop is twofold: (a) It increases the likelihood that grading criteria are applied consistently across sections, and (b) it provides instructors with practice in giving feedback for revision (see chaps. 5 and 7). Participants respond to sample papers for each band in the scoring rubric and discuss techniques for written feedback and conducting individual conferences. Special emphasis is placed on providing students with formative commentary early in their composing processes so that instructors can demonstrate the use of the portfolio as an instrument of change as opposed to a means of static, summative evaluation (Burnham, 1986). Periodic faculty education such as this is crucial to the initiation and maintenance of a portfolio system.

Equally vital to the success of a portfolio model is informing students of their responsibilities as portfolio compilers and of the ways in which they can make the process worthwhile. Before detailing procedures and policies, it is perhaps most valuable to frame the portfolio process in terms of its benefits, not the least of which is that it allows writers to show what and how much they have learned over the term—progress that is difficult to detect or measure when assignments are submitted and evaluated individually. On the first day of class in COMP 120, students are given a handout explaining the portfolio system, its rationale, and its procedures as an attachment to the syllabus. A portion of this handout appears in Fig. 8.5. These guidelines specify what the portfolio will contain, ideas for selecting the most appropriate assignments to include, directions for commentaries and self-assessments, teacher and peer feedback procedures, revision policies, deadlines, and, of course, grading standards (which are supplied with the department's holistic scoring rubric). In keeping with the precept of growth and development, this handout also indicates that assignments later in the semester will become more demanding (and thus that evaluation criteria will be more exacting).

Sequence, Procedures, and Instruments.   Once a portfolio system is in place (or at least sketched out in writing as departmental or classroom policy), it may take two or three drafting–feedback–revision cycles before students adapt to the rhythm of the process and take responsibility for shaping their portfolios. In COMP 120, the portfolio process begins in a fairly structured, formalized way, gradually becoming more flexible to give students increasing independence and autonomy. For example, students are required to revise their first paper twice and include it in their midterm portfolio; they may elect to omit this assignment from their final portfolios, however. Subsequent papers may necessitate only a single revision, although the course requires that students revise all papers that are returned with a mark of "U" (see Fig. 8.5). As the course progresses, students systematically add material to their portfolios, including paper drafts, revisions, peer feedback worksheets, self-assessment commentaries that front papers submitted for instructor feedback, personal and informal writing (e.g., reading responses, journal entries, etc.), and written feedback on their peers' assignments. These materials are assembled systematically over the term to facilitate preparation of midterm and final portfolios for submission. At all times, students are encouraged to include the products that represent their best work and the most significant changes in their composing and thinking skills.

COMP 120: ACADEMIC WRITING I FOR NONNATIVE SPEAKERS

The COMP 120 Portfolio   Fall semester

Background and rationale
The Division of ESL and the English Department have jointly developed a system of Portfolio assessment for all writing courses in the 080, 090 (ESL non-credit), 110 (Academic writing), and 120 (Academic writing for nonnative speakers) series. The COMP 120 Portfolio is designed to help you meet its particular objectives, which include building your mastery of paragraph and essay development, research techniques, collaborative learning procedures, and the conventions of standard edited English. This course is thus designed broadly to develop your academic reading and composing skills. Specifically, you will read texts drawn from literature, the social and physical sciences, and the popular media. You will write about topics using rhetorical techniques that include exposition, explanation, description, comparison, process analysis, and persuasion. When completed, your COMP 120 Portfolio will demonstrate your control of these techniques and your progress as an academic writer.

For specific policies pertaining to the presentation and evaluation of Portfolios, please refer to the *Division of ESL/English Department Portfolio Policy Manual* (Revised edition), which was included as part of the syllabus for this course. The *Policy Manual* includes important information about procedures, confidentiality, grading, etc. Please review this document carefully and refer to it throughout the semester.

This semester's COMP 120 Portfolio requirements
As your syllabus and course outline indicate, COMP 120 will require five revised papers and six timed writings this semester. *You must submit all of these assignments to your instructor on time and in the specified form (or satisfy the make-up policy) in order to earn a grade of "C" or higher this course, as the Policy Manual specifies on page 7.* Assignments receiving a mark of "U" (Unsatisfactory) must be revised and resubmitted; only those that receive a mark of "S" (Satisfactory) are eligible for inclusion in your Portfolio.

Please remember that the Midterm Portfolio and Final Portfolio are not separate documents: Your Midterm Portfolio is an in-progress version of your Final Portfolio. In Comp 120, 85% of your course grade is based on the quality of your Final Portfolio. Please review the *Policy Manual,* pages 9–10, for an explanation of how the individual contents of your Portfolio will be assessed.

Checklist for the Midterm Portfolio
Your Midterm Portfolio will be due at the end of Week 8, October _____. Your instructor will not be authorized to accept your Midterm Portfolio until it contains the following items:
- ❑ Paper 1 (including all intermediate drafts, a peer response worksheet from at least one classmate, cover sheets/self-analyses, and all written instructor feedback)
- ❑ Paper 2 OR Paper 3 (including all intermediate drafts, a peer response worksheet from at least one classmate, cover sheets/self-analyses, and all written instructor feedback)
- ❑ One of your three timed writings (including written instructor feedback). In addition, you may optionally include a revision of this timed writing.
- ❑ One to two pieces of informal, personal, or self-selected writing (e.g., a journal entry, a reading response, a letter to your instructor or a peer, a poem, an editorial for the campus newspaper, etc.).

- ❑ A one-page self-assessment of your performance and progress over the first 7-1/2 weeks of COMP 120. Please use the *Midterm Self-Assessment Guidelines* to compose this document, which should review your work and change as a writer. If you wish to receive a provisional, in-progress grade, please include this request at the end of your self-assessment.

Checklist for the Final Conference
Final Conferences should be scheduled with your instructor during Weeks 12 and 13, November
_____ — _____. You will submit a draft of your two-page final self-assessment to your instructor
in advance of your conference, along with any other materials that s/he requests.

Checklist for the Final Portfolio
Your Final Portfolio will be due at the end of Week 15, December _____. Your instructor will
not be authorized to accept your Final Portfolio until it contains the following items:

❑ Three revised papers (each including intermediate drafts, at least one peer response work-
    sheet, cover sheets/self-analyses, and all written instructor feedback);
❑ Two of your six timed writings (including written instructor feedback). You may also
    optionally include a revision of one of these timed writings, with an appropriate cover sheet
    (Please see your instructor for guidelines);
❑ Two pieces of informal, personal, or self-selected writing related to this course, to another
    course, or to activities outside of your school (e.g., a journal entry, a reading response, a
    letter to your instructor or a peer, a poem, an editorial for the campus newspaper, etc.);
❑ A two-page self-assessment of your performance and progress in COMP 120. Please use the
    Final Self-Assessment Guidelines to compose this document, which should review your work
    and change as a writer and should explain why you have given yourself the grade you have
    indicated. If your instructor has asked you to revise your self-assessment since your Final
    Conference, please include your initial draft as well.

General reminders
• Please submit your Midterm and Final Portfolios in a rigid-cover, 1-inch, three-ring binder,
   as per the *Policy Manual.*
• Please check the *Policy Manual* for specific presentation requirements (i.e., cover sheet,
   typographical conventions, bibliographic style, word-processing formats, headings, etc.).

FIG. 8.5. Sample portfolio process guidelines
for an NNS-track freshman composition course.

An important additional element of the portfolio process is interaction among
students and between individual writers and the instructor. Although group work,
peer feedback sessions, and teacher–student conferences do not lend themselves
easily to the production of artifacts (i.e., written samples to be included in the
portfolio), these interactions are an essential part of the teaching-assessment cycle.
In COMP 120, instructors meet with each student individually for compulsory
midterm and semester-end conferences (usually during scheduled class time). The
semester-end conference occurs in the final weeks of the term so that instructors
can assist students in selecting products to include in their final portfolio submis-
sions. In addition to these more formal meetings, instructors generally hold periodic
(although brief) conferences with students to offer them guidance on individual
drafts and revisions. Rather than providing extensive written feedback on all papers,
some instructors hold brief conferences in which they respond to student writing
orally; students are subsequently required to revise these papers based on the
outcomes of these miniconferences (see chap. 5).

Because of the academic orientation of most of the students, as well as the nature of the course objectives, COMP 120 students are given the option of requesting provisional letter grades on revised assignments and on their midterm portfolios. All of the courses in the ESL program are graded A–E, although for the purposes of ongoing portfolio assessment instructors emphasize formative commentary and oral feedback over summative evaluation. To reinforce the need to revise their work and reflect on its quality, students are initially given only a mark of "S" or "U" on assignments they submit to the instructor for possible inclusion in the portfolio. A mark of "U" represents a paper that is "unsatisfactory" for inclusion in the portfolio in its current form; a mark of "S" suggests that the work satisfactorily meets minimum standards of quality. "S" papers would earn at least a grade of "C" if they were to be assessed on the holistic scoring rubric. In this way, students who complete the minimum number of assignments on time and include in their portfolios only those products that the instructor has deemed satisfactory are assured of passing the course with at least a "C." Nevertheless, instructors only indicate traditional letter grades when students request them, and only then on assignments that have already been assigned a mark of "S." This policy promotes the developmental aspect of the portfolio process and downplays a traditional product orientation in which letter or numerical grades preoccupy students at the expense of genuine growth (Elbow, 1993). These grades are also reported to students as provisional (i.e., no course grade can be assigned until the portfolio is complete and has been evaluated by a team of qualified raters). At the same time, the policy accommodates students who feel insecure without a traditional grade and wish to have a more precise measure of their performance (Burnham, 1986).

When designed efficiently, a portfolio system need not demand more work from the instructor than traditional summative evaluation of disparate individual assignments. However, students may need several weeks to adjust to taking charge of their own progress as writers. This often necessitates allowing extra time at the beginning of the term for acquainting students with policies and procedures, training them to make their own decisions, and preparing them to make revisions independently. In a given semester, the COMP 120 syllabus requires three to six revised papers (of 500–2,000 words) and generally an equal number of timed writings, one or more of which students might revise outside of class. Each of these assignments is read by the instructor and either returned with written feedback or discussed in a conference. The number of revisions per assignment varies from semester to semester and from instructor to instructor, although the first assignment generally requires two revisions, for a total of at least three drafts. As noted earlier, this first assignment is usually a required element for the midterm portfolio, when each student meets with the instructor to discuss his or her progress since the first assignment (see guidelines in Fig. 8.5). At the midterm conference, the instructor compares his or her performance assessment to each individual's self-assessment and offers specific recommendations for improving students' products and strategies to complete the course successfully. Because many students routinely request a provisional course grade at this time, instructors should be prepared to report one, although students are reminded that the final course grade can be determined only when the final portfolio is evaluated.

Because the curriculum and assignments in COMP 120 are revised frequently and because new instructors teach the course nearly every semester, both midterm and final portfolios are evaluated collectively to ensure that the same objectives and standards of quality are met across the multiple sections. At midterm, instructors first collect their students' midterm portfolios by completing an initial evaluation form that features written comments and a provisional grade. Experienced instructors are then paired with less experienced instructors, and portfolios are exchanged and given a second reading by peer instructors, who also complete an evaluation form. Readings are conducted independently following a brief re-norming with benchmark papers; peer raters are strongly encouraged to read holistically, focusing mainly (if not exclusively) on students' revised papers and commentaries (as opposed to initial and intermediate drafts; cf. Belanoff & Dickson, 1991; Burnham, 1986). Teams next meet to compare their results and reconcile feedback that might be ambiguous or inconsistent. The level supervisor or program coordinator then meets with each team to resolve incompatible evaluations before individual instructors return their students' portfolios and conduct midterm conferences. Although somewhat labor-intensive, this process reduces instructor bias, increases reliability, and lends face validity to the feedback that students receive in their midterm conferences because it includes the evaluation of not one but two trained raters.

The process for final portfolio evaluation necessarily requires more elaborate planning but is ultimately intended to relieve some of the frustrations associated with determining course grades. Two to three weeks before the final portfolio deadline, instructors hold individual conferences with students to discuss which papers or projects the portfolios will contain. Prior to this conference, students submit a two-page draft portfolio self-assessment (see Fig. 8.5). In this document, students systematically evaluate the elements of their portfolios, presenting a concise argument for which they feel they deserve a particular grade. In cases where the instructor's preliminary evaluation agrees with the student's, the conference generally focuses on the steps that the student will take to revise any remaining work and present the portfolio for final evaluation by the departmental team. When the instructor's preliminary evaluation differs from the student's self-assessment, the conference generally focuses on informing the student of why his or her self-assessment is inflated or below target. In the former case, the instructor may ask the writer to review the grading criteria carefully and revise his or her work accordingly to enhance his or her chances of earning a higher mark on the final portfolio. Because there is still time left before the final portfolio deadline, students in such circumstances can sometimes make changes in their work that are significant enough to merit a higher overall grade. After the conference and before the submission deadline, students often revise their written self-assessments.

The rating process of the final portfolios is similar to the one used at midterm, except that individual instructors do not read their students' portfolios before they go to the evaluation team, which is made up of two readers who are unfamiliar with the class. Again, less experienced raters are matched with more seasoned readers. Team members perform their readings independently, but they are asked to complete them within a 48- to 72-hour period and compose only the briefest commentaries, which are submitted to the level supervisor or program coordinator. If there are no discrepancies, the supervisor returns the portfolios and results directly to the instructor, who subsequently uses the outcomes to determine students' final course grades. When teams report discrepant written evaluations and/or grades, the supervisor meets with the raters and tries to arrive at a consistent set of results. These arbitrated results are then reported to the instructor at the time that portfolios are returned. Because the instructor has scrutinized the portfolio contents in the process leading up to (and perhaps following) the final conference, he or she is probably already familiar with the portfolio and its quality. Thus, he or she is unlikely to need a final review of the entire document before assigning course grades, which may not be based solely on the portfolio (15% of the course grade in COMP 120 is based on student participation, attendance, on-time performance, etc.).

The COMP 120 portfolio model described herein represents one of many possible designs for a formative writing assessment system that embodies principles emphasized throughout this chapter: Performance evaluation that feeds back into teaching and instruments that hold both writers and teachers accountable for their decisions. In a number of respects, portfolio systems such as this one reflect the general movement in language teaching and general education toward learner-centered assessment. Portfolio assessment involves writers in managing their own processes. An effective portfolio model also answers Elbow's appeal for more formative evaluation and less summative ranking because it engages teachers in a multifaceted response to their students' work. For Elbow (1993),

> Evaluation requires going *beyond* a first response that may be nothing but a kind of ranking ("I like it" or "This is better than that"), and instead looking carefully enough at the performance or person to make distinctions between parts or features or criteria. (p. 187)

Despite its drawbacks (e.g., heavy demands on time, labor-intensiveness, potential unreliability), portfolio evaluation offers many promising possibilities.

$\Rightarrow$ *AA 8.4*

FINAL THOUGHTS: PRACTICAL CONCERNS
IN ASSESSING STUDENT PERFORMANCE

This final section touches on several practical issues in performance assessment that are often overlooked in composition teaching and teacher preparation. Although some of these issues relate directly to responding to written products, others pertain to wider issues of management and record-keeping.

Paper Grading Anxiety

One of our general concerns has to do with overcoming the anxiety that many novice teachers experience when assessing student writing for the first time. Despite being armed with an explicit scoring instrument, many teachers find it difficult to initiate the grading process because they fear making judgments—judgments that may be unfair, unjustified, and/or possibly damaging to the writer. These are wholly natural apprehensions that should not be treated lightly. Frequently, what teachers fear the most are the results of crude and oversimple ranking (i.e., a "B" versus a "C," or a "High Pass" over a "Pass") that does not communicate a meaningful response to students. If we undertake evaluation in Elbow's (1993) sense, however, we do not stop at ranking. At the same time, ranking can be an excellent place for us to start when faced with a typical set of papers to mark, and we will obviously not curtail our efforts at that point. Once we have read through a handful of papers (perhaps not even the whole set), it can be valuable to rank order them from most satisfactory to least satisfactory and then examine our intuitive reactions (Peterson, 1995; Tarvers, 1993; White, 1994).

As Elbow (1993) pointed out, this is part of judgment, and evaluation inherently involves judgment: We cannot avoid it, but we can make it more useful for ourselves and our students. Informative questions to ask ourselves include the following: Why do I think Essay Y is better than Essay X? How do my reactions match up with the descriptors on the scoring rubric? How does my reading of Essay Z affect my re-reading of Essays X and Y? If I read these essays tomorrow, will my rankings be different? By addressing such questions before we move ahead in our grading, we can at least move toward informative evaluation. Ideally, we also calibrate our reading at that moment to some useful external standard (i.e., the task, scoring rubric, quality of individual essays with respect to the others, etc.).

A further recommendation for reducing grading anxiety is actually a simple reminder: Not all writing assignments have to be graded. "Just because conventional institutions oblige us to turn in a single quantitative course grade at the end of every marking period, it doesn't follow that we need to grade individual papers" (Elbow, 1993, p. 191). This is as true in settings where teachers evaluate individual assignments summatively as in portfolio systems. As long as the syllabus allows for some flexibility in terms of how many assignments get quantitative scores or letter grades, teachers should take full advantage of their prerogative to focus essentially (and perhaps only) on providing evaluative feedback from time to time and not on traditional ranking (although it is our view that both methods are necessary and useful).

Assigning Course Grades

Determining individual course grades can be as anxiety-provoking for teachers as grading student writing for the first time. Needless to say, the two processes should be undertaken with the same care and systematicity. However, arriving at fair and informative course grades need not cause undue worry for teachers or students. As noted in chapter 3, the process can be facilitated by establishing assessment standards, weighting policies, and grade calculation procedures in the course syllabus. In many postsecondary settings, weightings are fixed for certain courses; in others, individual instructors might have the freedom to assign variable weights to a certain percentage of the course grade. At the same time, many instructors may have complete freedom to weight grades as they wish. When there is some flexibility, teachers should first examine course goals and the objectives of graded work: Weighting of assignments in the grade should first reflect their importance in the syllabus and, second, the effort and time required for students to complete them satisfactorily (Peterson, 1995). For example, a revised research paper should legitimately receive proportionally more weight in the grade if research writing is featured as a major course goal; it should likewise be weighted more heavily than a short explanatory essay requiring no research at all. If a writing course emphasizes reading and thus requires extensive reading assignments, the grading scale might assign a corresponding weight to reading tasks such as journals or quizzes (cf. Appendix 3A) .

A related concern of many teachers is rewarding students for their measurable progress, particularly when their syllabus professes a process orientation emphasizing revision. Without compromising evaluation criteria or standards of quality, teachers can make room in their grading policies for fair assessment of both products and progress. This can be done by weighing assignments given later in the term more heavily than those given at the beginning. In a course that leads to the drafting and revision of an original research paper, for example, the initial assignments might target skills necessary for composing and polishing that final product. Early assignments might require students to analyze, paraphrase, and synthesize sources as practice for more extensive work with new material and a more demanding research process later in the term. Therefore, the initial essays might be weighted 15% or 20%, whereas the final research paper might be weighted 30% or even more to reflect increasing demands and accumulation of skills. In this way, students whose performance is initially weak still have opportunities to improve their marks over time. At the same time, students who begin with more solid skills still have ample incentive to complete the assigned work and improve their skills. Variable weighting can be a useful tool in traditional courses as well as in courses that rely on portfolio assessment (Herman, Gearhart, & Aschbacher, 1996).

An additional recommendation for easing the distress of determining course grades is a purely pragmatic one: Keep accurate and detailed records of student performance. Whether you use a gradebook, loose grade sheets, individual progress charts, or a computer database, keep records current and accurate. Not only should all assignments be noted and a score or grade recorded (in the case of graded assignments), so should attendance, participation, peer critiques, intermediate drafts, and so on if these components are assessed in your course or program. As soon as you have finished marking students' papers, record the grades in the form in which you will use them at the end of the term. For example, if your grading system is based on percentages or numerical scores, record these values instead of converting them to letter grades or symbols. This will prevent having to reconstruct these notations later. If course grades are weighted, organize the columns of your gradebook, charts, or database to reflect these categories. In this way, you can easily convert cumulative scores or means into weighted scores that can subsequently be summed to calculate a composite score or grade.

Managing the Workload

Responding efficiently to the volume of student writing is sometimes the primary concern of novice and experienced teachers, for whom the workload can be simply overwhelming. Tarvers (1993) offered two obvious but frequently ignored pieces of advice: "Be realistic" and "don't keep promises you can't keep" (p. 117). In other words, allow enough time to read and respond to the assignments you have given and plan adequate buffer time in your syllabus and revision sequences to allow for possible delays. Novice teachers may spend 30 minutes or more on a typical 500-word paper; experienced instructors may spend 15 to 20 minutes. Even at that rate, a stack of 30 papers can easily consume up to a full 8-hour work day (or more). With practice, experience, and a trusted and reliable scoring instrument, grading time can be reduced to a manageable level. Still, it may often be necessary to restrict the time you spend on each paper to a fixed period (e.g., 15–20 minutes per essay). Alternatively, you might divide your workload into smaller chunks so that you read 5 to 10 essays a day over a 3- or 4-day period, rather than reading a stack of papers all in one day. Similarly, announce return dates to your students based on a reasonable timetable; if essays require revision, try to return them early enough to allow students several days before the revision due date.

SUMMARY

This chapter has outlined fundamental principles of classroom-based writing assessment and described theoretical and procedural aspects of three major scoring methods. In addition to examining finer points of techniques for rating student writing, we have presented an overview of portfolio assessment in the context of composition instruction. Finally, we have offered some specific, practical suggestions for managing paper marking and facilitating the evaluation of student performance. Throughout this chapter, we have emphasized the essentially *pedagogical* role of assessment in the teaching of writing. In our view, responding to and evaluating student writing is as essential to successful composition instruction as careful materials design, course planning, and lesson execution. Further, the establishment of clear and systematic scoring criteria is as useful for students as for teachers. Major points related to this generalization can be summarized in the following statements:

- Whatever scoring method(s) they select for marking their students' work, teachers should aim for the highest standards of validity and reliability;
- Each of the three scoring methods discussed in this chapter (holistic, analytic, and trait based) presents particular advantages and disadvantages that should be weighed in light of (a) each method's reliability and validity, as well as (b) how satisfactorily the method will inform students about the quality of their work;
- Portfolio assessment offers distinct advantages over traditional summative evaluation of individual writing assignments and can maximize the interactive, heuristic, recursive elements of process-based composing pedagogy introduced and explained throughout this book; and
- Fair, effective, and informative writing assessment and evaluation of students' progress can be facilitated by adopting efficient planning, paper-marking, and record-keeping practices.

Reflection and Review

1. How do face, criterion (concurrent and predictive), content, and construct validity differ? Which of these are of the greatest relevance in ESL writing assessment? Why?
2. Describe the relationship between validity and reliability. Why are both of these constructs important for classroom teachers to understand as they assess student writing and overall writing performance?
3. Identify and compare the general principles underlying holistic, analytic, and trait-based scoring. Of these three scoring methods, which offers the greatest advantages for you in your current or future teaching context? Why?
4. In what ways can assessment criteria and scoring procedures be integrated into the syllabus and curriculum of a composition course to promote positive washback? What advantages does such integration offer teachers and student writers?

5. To what extent can formative portfolio assessment be claimed as a more valid means of evaluating writing products and skills than traditional summative evaluation? Explain.

Application Activity 8.1: Holistic Essay Scoring Practice

Directions.

1. Select a pair or set of sample student essays from those provided in Appendixes 5B–5D. Alternatively, select two or three sample essays written by students in an ESL course at your institution. These samples should represent as diverse a range of quality as possible.

2. Depending on the proficiency level of the students who composed the sample essays, rate the samples using the holistic rubric in either Fig. 8.1 or Fig. 8.2. Make comments on a copy of the rubric or on the sample essays as you would if you were evaluating the essays in a classroom setting.

3. Make copies of your comments and holistic scores for each of the essays and distribute this material to one or more classmates for comparison.

4. In a pair or group discussion, compare your scores and comments with those of your peers. Use the following prompts to guide you:

   a. On what points did you agree or disagree? Why?

   b. If you disagreed, try to arrive at a consensus evaluation of each of the essays.

   c. After identifying the sources of your agreement and disagreement, formulate a list of future suggestions for using holistic scoring rubrics.

Application Activity 8.2: Analytic Essay Scoring Practice—Option 1

Directions.

1. As you did in Application Activity 8.1, select a pair or set of sample student essays from those provided in Appendixes 5B–5D. Alternatively, select two or three sample essays written by students in an ESL course at your institution. These samples should represent as diverse a range of quality as possible.

2. Depending on the proficiency level of the writers, rate the samples using the analytic scoring rubric in Fig. 8.3. Make comments on a copy of the scoring sheet or on the sample essays as you would if you were evaluating the essays in a classroom setting.

3. Make copies of your comments and scoring sheet for each of the essays and distribute this material to one or more classmates for comparison.

4. In a pair or group discussion, compare your component and composite scores as well as your comments with those of your peers. Use the following prompts to guide you:

   a. On what points did you agree or disagree? Why?

   b. Where you disagreed, try to arrive at a consensus evaluation of each of the essays.

   c. After identifying the sources of your agreement and disagreement, formulate a list of future suggestions for using analytic scoring scales.

Analytic Essay Scoring Practice—Option 2

Directions.

1. Using the same sample essays that you evaluated and discussed in Application Activity 8.1, rate and comment on these using the analytic scale in Fig. 8.3.

2. Follow the discussion and comparison guidelines outlined in Option 1, Items 2–4.

3. In your final discussion (Option 1, Item 4), consider these questions:

   a. How well do your composite analytic ratings match with your holistic ratings?

   b. Where do the two sets of scores and comments differ? Why?

   c. Given the nature of the writing tasks you evaluated, which of the two scales do you feel is most appropriate? Why?

   d. How might you modify one or both of the scales to suit your educational setting?

Application Activity 8.3: Designing and Testing a Rubric or Scale

Directions.

1. Identify a specific ESL (or NES/NNS) composition course in your program or at a nearby institution. Individually or with a classmate, use this context to design one of the following:

   a. A holistic scoring rubric intended for systematic use in the course;

   b. An analytic scoring scale intended for systematic use in the course;

   c. A primary or multiple trait scoring scale intended for evaluating a specific writing assignment given in the course.

2. Use one of the models in Figs. 8.1 to 8.4 as a starting point. Also, consult one or more of the sources cited in this chapter for additional ideas and sample

instruments. If you are not teaching the course, consult with the instructor to familiarize yourself with the students, curriculum, and course goals.

3. In addition to the scoring guide, prepare a scoring package that includes essential elements such as benchmark papers for the bands in your scale, a rationale for the scores assigned to those papers, and an explanation of how the instrument reflects and promotes specific course goals (i.e., an analysis of the instrument's validity). If you construct a primary or multiple trait scale, also include the task/prompt, a description of the traits elicited by the task/prompt, and an interpretation of how the task/prompt generates the expected writing performance (cf. Hamp-Lyons, 1991c).

4. If possible, pilot your instrument by using it to evaluate one or more sets of student papers. Use this experience to revise and refine your instrument for future use in this course or another one like it.

Application Activity 8.4: Designing a Writing Portfolio Plan

Directions.

1. Select an ESL (or NES/NNS) composition course (in your program or at a nearby institution) in which the current method of assessment relies on traditional summative evaluation of individual writing assignments.

2. Conduct a small-scale study of the course design, syllabus, curriculum, and learner population (see Application Activities 3.1 and 3.2 for possible frameworks and guidelines). Your fundamental goal in this step of the process is to assess the feasibility of integrating a portfolio system into the course.

3. Based on the portfolio model for COMP 120 described in this section (and on other sources on portfolio assessment—see references and footnotes), sketch a simple portfolio plan tailored to the writing course you have selected. In your proposal, include descriptions of the following elements: sequences, procedures, and instruments. Also include a set of written guidelines for students, similar to the sample materials presented in Fig. 8.5.

4. Share and discuss your proposal with your classmates, instructor, and instructor(s) of the course under study. If you teach the course, consider ways in which you might integrate your portfolio plan into the course and pilot it successfully.

<table>
<tr><td>

CHAPTER

9

</td><td>

Technology
in the Writing Class:
Uses and Abuses

</td></tr>
</table>

Questions for Reflection

- Do you use a computer regularly for your own writing? If so, do you do all of your planning, composing, revising, and editing at the computer? Or do you undertake some of these tasks with pen and paper?
- If you use computers for writing, in what ways has your writing benefited from word processing or other computer-based writing tools? What frustrations or disadvantages have you experienced?
- What do you think are the greatest advantages computers offer to second language writers? What are potential drawbacks?

THE BRIEF, TUMULTUOUS HISTORY
OF COMPUTER-ASSISTED WRITING RESEARCH
AND INSTRUCTION

About the applications of the personal computer for education, it has been said that "not since the invention of the printing press has a technological device borne such implications for the learning process" (Bork, 1985, p. 1). As computers became widely available in the 1980s in U.S. schools, colleges, and universities, writing teachers and researchers expressed virtually limitless optimism and enthusiasm about the potential of word processing and other computer-based writing tools to facilitate students' writing processes and improve their end products. Within a few short years, however, this enthusiasm was tempered by reality. Some researchers (e.g., Barker, 1987; Haas, 1989; Hawisher, 1987) claimed that student writers planned less, revised less (or at least not more), and paid more attention to sentence-level concerns when composing with computers. Others pointed out that contextual variables such as access to computers, screen size, user-friendliness of software, and distractions present in the computer lab may make word processing less desirable under some circumstances than traditional pen-and-paper methods. Faced with such a variety of negative evidence and conclusions, researchers in the early 1990s began offering a more moderate view of computer-assisted writing instruction, and a judicious middle ground for technology in the writing class was established. It is now understood that computers cannot teach novice writers how to think, plan, or revise, nor can they magically transform inexperienced writers into proficient ones or replace teachers in giving instruction and feedback. Nonetheless, computers can make many facets of the writing process easier, making writing more enjoyable, improving student attitudes, and lowering anxieties about writing, especially those of basic and ESL writers.

In summary, over the past 20 years, composition researchers have been "either wildly enthusiastic or vehement in their rejection of the new medium" (Pennington, 1993a, p. 227). Today's writing instructors and researchers generally hold a cautiously positive view of computer-assisted writing that takes the conclusions of previous research and the inherent limitations of the medium into careful consideration. From this brief history, only one implication seems certain: Computers in education and in writing programs are here to stay, and "either we take the opportunity this new machine affords to rethink the ways we write and teach writing, or we soon risk seeming as anachronistic as a piece of parchment to our students" (Curtis, 1988, p. 344).

ADVANTAGES AND DISADVANTAGES
OF COMPUTER-ASSISTED WRITING INSTRUCTION

A number of reviewers and researchers have outlined potential benefits and drawbacks to the use of computers for writing instruction (Fig. 9.1). In her review of L1 studies of computers and writing, Pennington (1993a) noted a number of potential benefits for students:

Advantages	Disadvantages
• Increased motivation to revise (because of the ease of doing so)	• Increased anxiety due to lack of familiarity with hardware or software
• Greater consciousness of writing as process	• Unequal or limited student access to computers
• Quicker, more fluent, less self-conscious writing	• Limited student typing and/or word-processing abilities
• Increased writing quantity	• Subversion of individual student writing processes (some prefer pen-and-paper; some are distracted by writing in a lab setting)
• Increased collaboration (teacher–student and student–student) in the computer writing lab	• Increased student focus on surface features of texts because corrections are so easy
• Greater motivation because writing is easier, more interesting, and more enjoyable	
(Teichman & Poris, 1989, p. 93)	(Balestri, 1988; Barker, 1987; Bernhardt, Edwards, & Wojahn, 1989; Bernhardt, Wojahn, & Edwards 1990; Brady, 1990; Bridwell-Bowles, Johnson, & Brehe, 1987; Haas, 1989; Hawisher, 1987)

FIG. 9.1. Potential advantages and disadvantages of computer-assisted writing.

1. Quality of written work:

   • More thorough development of content;
   • Higher analytic ratings on content, organization, and language;
   • Higher holistic ratings of compositions.

2. Writing activity:

   • More time spent writing and longer compositions;
   • More experimentation with language/more flexible writing processes.

3. Revision behavior:

   • Greater number and variety of revisions;
   • More discourse- and meaning-level revision;
   • Fewer surface errors.

4. Affective/social outcomes:

   • Less writing apprehension and better attitudes;
   • Greater objectivity toward own writing;
   • More collaboration among student writers. (p. 230)

However, detractors (and proponents who are less enthusiastic about computers) point out that some studies have reported less positive results. For instance, some researchers have found no differences between groups of computer users and groups of pencil-and-paper users in number or quality of revisions or overall writing quality (Etchison, 1989; Hawisher, 1987; Kurth, 1987; Peterson, 1993; Teichman & Poris, 1989). Others have reported decreased collaboration among students in the computer writing lab (Bernhardt et al., 1989; Bernhardt et al., 1990). It is important to note here that studies of computer-assisted writing are highly inconsistent in terms of the number of participants studied, duration of data collection, participants' level of education, and so on. Only when there is a more complete and systematic body of research can we argue with any certainty that word processing helps novice writers improve their written products and develop their composing skills.

RESEARCH ON COMPUTER-ASSISTED WRITING

To examine the research in L1 and L2 composition on the use of word processing and other computer-based tools and to understand its classroom implications, three major questions must be addressed: (a) What are the effects of word processing on instruction, the writing process, the quality of students' writing, and student attitudes? (b) What are the effects of other computer-based tools on writing instruction and outcomes? and (c) What special advantages and drawbacks are associated with using computer-based composing tools with L2 writers? Related pedagogical concerns include the specifics of implementing word processing in the ESL writing class, the use of other types of writing software, computer-based response to student writing, and issues of security, cheating, and plagiarism.

It is important at the beginning of this discussion to offer two caveats. First, because research on computers and writing is a relatively new phenomenon and because the technology has changed dramatically over a short period of time, studies on any single aspect of computer-assisted writing are scarce. Moreover, current investigations become dated rapidly. Second, the computer scene is changing. As time goes by, more and more students are becoming computer literate, and warnings offered in the mid-1980s about students' inability to do word processing and about their discomfort with the technology are becoming less salient. Instead, we increasingly focus our attention on maximizing the advantages of computers for novice writers who have used microcomputers since childhood or adolescence. Thus, there is much that we do not yet know about the effects of computer use on student writers. Our lack of knowledge can only be remedied by time—time in which computer technology will continue to advance and become more widely available, and time in which, it is to be hoped, researchers will ask the right questions and use the right methodological tools to assess how writers can (and cannot) benefit from using computers.

What Are the Effects of Word Processing?

Effects on Writing Instruction. Bernhardt et al. (1989) and Bernhardt et al. (1990) examined the differences between freshman composition classes taught in the traditional classroom setting and those taught partially in a computer lab. The first, labeled a program evaluation study, analyzed 24 writing classes taught by 12 teachers. Each teacher taught one traditional writing course and one computer-assisted course (in which half of the instructional time took place in the computer lab). Results show that students in the computer sections revised more effectively and generally outperformed the control group (the 12 classes taught in the traditional setting). Also, student attitudes toward the writing course were more favorable in the computer setting. However, lack of access to computers (i.e., long waits to use the lab outside of class) and a lack of familiarity with word-processing commands led to frustration among students. Further, some students did not like writing in the lab during class and felt that lab days were a waste of time.

In their ethnographic case study, Bernhardt et al. (1990) examined two writing instructors (four classes) who participated in their larger 1989 study. From these studies in particular, together with evidence from other reports, clear differences can be seen between writing instruction in traditional classes and computer lab classes:

1. The time spent writing in the computer lab can greatly decrease the proportion of teacher-fronted instructional time;
2. More one-on-one time between teacher and students is possible in the computer lab;
3. Students in the lab setting may be less willing to attend to administrative announcements, do exercises, or participate in discussion; and
4. Some teachers may be less comfortable than others in adapting to the computer lab setting.

Effects on the Writing Process. Studies of how computer-based writing affects the writing process have examined issues of planning, revision, and student–student collaboration. Haas (1989) studied 10 experienced writers and 10 novice writers using think-aloud methodology to contrast the amounts and types of planning evidenced when the writers used word processors versus pen and paper for composing. She concluded that less planning was done with word processing and speculated that word processing may inhibit planning in three ways: (a) Writers have so much fun playing with fonts and formatting that they begin using the computer more quickly (thus spending less time planning), (b) computers inhibit rereading because of limited screen size, and (c) planning notes can be more difficult to manipulate on a computer than with pen and paper. However, Haas also pointed out that "writers may begin writing sooner and spend less time planning because making changes is easier with word processing" (1989, p. 202). She also made the important qualification that "the relationship of planning to text quality has not been established. It is not clear ... if the differences in planning ... would result in texts of lower judged quality" (p. 202). Bridwell-Bowles et al. (1987) similarly studied eight experienced writers as they wrote four different papers: one with pen and paper and three with computers. In their study, writers who planned and drafted on paper and then entered the draft into the computer for further revision and editing had the most successful and satisfying writing experiences.

A number of studies have examined the issue of whether word processing leads to more extensive and effective revisions. Such studies presuppose, of course, that computers greatly facilitate revision because word processors make the mechanics of revision so much easier. Nevertheless, as Curtis (1988) noted, assuming that "given word processors and sent out on their own, inexperienced student writers will compose better essays ... is similar to assuming that, given a two horsepower table saw, writing teachers will build credenzas" (p. 338). In fact, a number of studies have found that students exhibit improved or superior revising behaviors when using computers (e.g., Daiute, 1985; McAllister & Louth, 1988; also see Pennington, 1993a). In contrast, others have found either no significant differences (between pen and paper and computer revision) or negative effects of word processing on revision (Benesch, 1987; Harris, 1985; Hawisher, 1987; Kurth, 1987).

Several writers (Chadwick & Bruce, 1989; Cochran-Smith, 1991; Curtis, 1988; Pennington, 1993a) have pointed out the difficulty inherent in documenting revision carried out on a computer. Of necessity, most studies focus only on changes made on consecutive hard copy drafts. Because a great deal of revision takes place online during the shaping of the initial hard copy draft, counting only changes made between the first printout and the second may greatly underestimate the amount and nature of revisions made on screen but never printed out. As Cochran-Smith (1991) reminded us, "excluding the revisions made as a text is initially shaped is probably tantamount to excluding the very aspect of writing with word processing that makes it unusual" (p. 126).

Empirical findings also conflict with regard to whether conducting composition classes in computer writing labs leads to more or less peer interaction. Computer enthusiasts initially believed that interaction and collaboration would increase and be greatly facilitated by the lab setting because of the open, informal atmosphere of the computer lab and because collaboration is so easy. That is, partners and groups can gather around a screen and send one another files over electronic mail or over a local area network (LAN). In addition, word-processed texts are more attractive and easier to read than handwritten drafts. However, Bernhardt et al. (1989, 1990) actually report decreased peer collaboration in the lab because of time pressures and students' lack of interest in doing anything but their own writing. Nonetheless, it is important to note that other studies have found evidence of increased collaboration among students in computer lab settings (Barker, 1987; Brady, 1990; Selfe & Wahlstrom, 1986; Teichman & Poris, 1989). Other researchers have also pointed out the rich potential of the medium for effective peer interaction (Sirc, 1989). Of course, whether in or out of the computer lab, peer response activities must be carefully planned and executed (see chap. 6 for a more extensive discussion of peer response).

$\boxed{\Rightarrow AA\ 9.1}$

Effects on Writing Quality. Again, it was initially taken as a given that student writing would automatically improve with computers because the process of writing is presumably easier and because students tend to be more highly motivated to write using a keyboard, screen, and CPU. Not surprisingly, the research evidence on this point is also contradictory. In a meta-analysis of 14 studies comparing word processing with pen-and-paper composing, Schramm (1989) acknowledged a small but statistically significant advantage for writing quality with word processing. The large-scale Bernhardt et al. (1989) program review study also concluded that students in computer writing sections outperformed students in traditional writing classes. Reporting parallel results, McAllister and Louth (1988) studied 102 college basic writers, among whom the computer users produced higher quality revisions than did those in the traditional method control group. In contrast,

Etchison (1989), Hawisher (1987), Kurth (1987), and Teichman and Poris (1989) presented outcomes showing no significant differences between control and experimental groups in overall text quality or quality of revisions. In considering these contradictory results, we must again consider the recommendations of Barker (1987) and Pennington (1993a) that we carefully examine the contextual variables affecting such studies to assess the reliability, validity, and applicability of the results.

Effects on Student Attitudes.   One area of inquiry on which there is little disagreement is the issue of student reactions to word processing. Notwithstanding student complaints about long waits to use the computer lab (Bernhardt et al., 1989; Dalton & Hannafin, 1986), unfamiliarity with hardware and software (Barker, 1987; Bernhardt et al., 1989), difficulty with rereading due to small screen size (Barker, 1987; Haas, 1989), and lack of typing skills (Brady, 1990; Dalton & Hannafin, 1986), "almost all researchers in word processing note that using a word processor improves student attitudes" (Barker, 1987, p. 112).

Even studies reporting no significant differences between composing with word processors and with pen and paper (as seen in revision behavior and text quality) often admit (if grudgingly) that student attitudes toward writing improve when they use computers. For instance, Teichman and Poris (1989), who indicated no major differences between control and experimental groups in either overall essay quality or in writing anxiety, concluded that "if the computer makes writing a less onerous, more satisfying experience for many students, there is at least the possibility that improvement in writing will follow. Positive attitudes generally lead to positive results" (p. 100). In other words, even in the absence of clear and convincing distinctions between students using different media for writing (as manifest in text quality and composing behaviors), the improved attitudes and increased motivation resulting from students who use computers may, in and of themselves, be compelling arguments for using them in composition courses.

$\Rightarrow AA\ 9.2$

$\Rightarrow AA\ 9.3$

What Are the Effects of Other Computer-Based Writing Tools?

Alhough word processing is the most frequently studied and used computer application in composition research and instruction, there are many other computer-based writing tools currently in use. Such tools include interactive, adaptive software that walks students through various aspects of the composing process (e.g., invention heuristics, organization tools, revision questions, etc.), text analyzers (e.g., spelling, grammar, and style checkers), and response programs that enable teachers and peers to insert comments and corrections into student files. Finally, the ever-increasing availability of electronic mail and LANs (in writing labs) has created new options for teachers and students, potentially affecting all aspects of the composing process.

Computer-Assisted Writing Instruction. In a review of various types of writing tools, Kozma (1991) suggested that software that models or prompts learners for scaffolding purposes (i.e., idea organizers and process prompters) may be helpful to novice writers. Such software can provide guidance (especially if software is interactive), display intermediate processes, and provide model texts. However, Kozma also warned that "it is not clear that novices have enough skill to use the capabilities of process prompters or that prompting is a sufficient intervention for novices" (1991, p. 38). Sirc (1989) characterized CAI programs as being oversimplified, forcing individual writers into the molds of invention heuristics. In Sirc's view, teachers need to exercise extreme caution in utilizing software that requires students "to engage in various predrafting, drafting, and postdrafting strategies" (p. 194), as if all students had similar strategies and compose in exactly the same way. Clearly, bad instruction can result from CAI programs just as easily as it can from poor classroom pedagogy, but one could make that argument about any medium. A compromise position between CAI enthusiasts and detractors might be that writers should be introduced to a variety of composing tools (whether or not on the computer) but not required to continue using them if they do not find them helpful and complementary to their own writing strategies.

Text Analyzers. When student texts have been word processed, text analysis applications can search and examine documents for various features, count them, and give the writer or teacher quantitative information about textual features. Smith (1989) presented an overview of various types of text analysis programs. One of these includes *Chunkers*, which "offer an alternative perspective on the text by isolating, by highlighting, by breaking up, or by rearranging its parts" (p. 68). A second form of text analyzer is the *Simple Checker*, such as spelling checkers and diction/usage checkers, which can flag texts for "wordy phrases, overused words, incorrect words or phrases, sexist words, clichés, slang, and the like" (p. 69). Text analysis software may also include counters, which tabulate the number of words in a text, average word or sentence length, quotation marks, exclamation points, and so on. Text counters may also include standards or thresholds against which the writer can measure his or her text, such as readability grades. Finally, Smith discussed parsers, which are "programs for determining parts of speech and grammatical structures in input text" (p. 73).

Although Smith clearly favored the use of text analyzers for composition (particularly the *Writer's Workbench* program), other authorities have expressed considerably less enthusiasm about such tools. For instance, in their review of three popular grammar/style checkers, Lewis and Lewis (1987) concluded that these applications "use fixed grammatical rules and canned phrases when analyzing a document and are limited by their inability to 'understand' context or logic" (p. 246). As a result, these tools are fallible and most effectively employed by "users with enough knowledge of grammar to sort accurate advice from misplaced assertions" (p. 246). Nelson (1987) similarly characterized style checkers as "far too rule-bound to serve higher forms of communication" (p. 49). Thus, there are two potentially irreconcilable problems with grammar/style checkers: They are at once too simple (applying formulaic, limited, prescriptive rules uncritically to all texts regardless of the genre, content, or context) and too difficult (requiring a great deal of sophistication on the part of the user to separate good advice from bad).

The greatest problem, of course, is that novice writers generally need to focus their attention on their ideas and logic rather than on grammatical and stylistic surface errors. Along these lines, Kozma (1991) warned that "Text analyzers should be used carefully with novice writers.... While such packages may facilitate editing and proofreading tasks, these are not the problems that plague novice readers most" (p. 37). It could also be argued that text analyzers are actually more harmful to student writers than to experienced writers: Because they may lack confidence as well as linguistic and rhetorical sophistication, novice writers are more likely to accept uncritically the suggestions, prescriptions, and corrections offered by an apparently all-knowing computer application.

Response Programs.   Sirc (1989) discussed the use by teachers of computer programs to respond to student writing, identifying three general types of computer response: (a) programs that allow a teacher's grading and commentary to be done on the computer, (b) programs that analyze and count surface errors in student texts, and (c) programs that respond in preprogrammed dialogue to student writing. Sirc offered pointed criticism of the second and third types, arguing that error counting response programs send the wrong message to students (i.e., that surface textual features are of primary importance) and that preprogrammed interaction between the computer and student writer is excessively oversimplified and generic: "Why would one want a student's paper, the potentially fragile first steps of a developing writer, to be 'read' and 'responded to' by a medium that can't read?" (p. 189). However, both Sirc (1989) and Kozma (1991) see great potential in response programs that allow teachers to insert commentary into a student text, either online (over e-mail or a network) or offline (on a student's floppy disk), allowing peers to collaborate electronically and offer authentic, real-time responses to one another's texts. Examples include Daedalus, which allows writers to conduct text-based discussions over a computer network, and SEEN, which "creates a virtual network among stand-alone machines by using a message or mailbox system that students pass around on disk" (Kozma, 1991, pp. 39–40). Kozma argued that such programs "may provide novice writers with information, motivation, and feedback they may not otherwise have" (p. 40). Sirc similarly concluded his review of computer response applications by saying that, "computers per se have nothing to tell my students. But I have much to tell them, and they have much to tell each other; if computers can aid in this endeavor, so much the better" (p. 203).

Other Applications of Electronic Mail for Writing Instruction. E-mail offers more than an alternative forum for teacher and peer response. It can also provide opportunities for writers to build their fluency and confidence by composing in a convenient and relatively low-risk setting (Sullivan, 1993). For instance, e-mail allows students to send journal entries to their teacher and to one another, setting up an authentic real-time dialogue between writers and readers. Students also can e-mail prewriting ideas and completed essay drafts over a class network, facilitating subsequent in-class peer response sessions (see chap. 6). In addition, the use of one-to-one e-mail and/or class discussion lists can encourage students to practice their writing and discuss interesting topics. Students can also be encouraged to explore student chat rooms and bulletin boards on the Internet for authentic opportunities to communicate through writing. Finally, by using e-mail, students can receive *cyber-tutoring* from graduate students or instructors either at their institutions or elsewhere (Goodwin, Hamrick, & Stewart, 1993).

$\boxed{\Rightarrow AA\ 9.4}$

Effects and Implications of Computer-Assisted Instruction for L2 Writers

Effects of Word Processing. Research on the use of word processing with L2 writers has reported findings similar to those of L1 studies. For example, students cannot be expected to improve their planning, revision, or overall writing simply by be‰o½g exposed to computers; they need careful instruction both in writing strategies and in how to exploit the capabilities of word-processing tools. However, ESL students appear to reap tremendous affective benefits from word processing (Jones & Fortescue, 1987; Neu & Scarcella, 1991; Pennington, 1990, 1991, 1993a, 1993b; Phinney, 1989, 1991; Piper, 1987). Specifically, students' attitudes and motivations toward writing in English appear to benefit from computer use (Neu & Scarcella, 1991; Phinney, 1989; Piper 1987), and their anxieties appear to decrease because computers reduce the fear of errors and worries about legibility (Phinney, 1989). Pennington (1993b) pointed out that word processors may also "free up some of the novice writer's time and attention, making it easier to concentrate on the non-mechanical aspects of composing" (p. 151). For L2 writers in particular, because writing at a computer is faster and easier (in most cases) than writing by hand, word processing may encourage writers to produce more text and for longer periods of time (Pennington, 1993b; Phinney, 1989). Additionally, the mechanical ease of the computer benefits L2 students who may be struggling to master the Roman alphabet or who face a cognitive/memory overload while trying to compose in their L2 because the computer memory supplements the human brain's storage capacity (Jones & Tetroe, 1987; Pennington, 1993b). Finally, because a lack of grammatical or lexical accuracy can be a major issue for L2 writers (see chap. 7), the ease of revision facilitated by computers may encourage students to revise more frequently, leading to improved, more well-formed papers (Pennington, 1993b).

Some researchers have expressed concern that both basic and ESL writers experience difficulty in learning how to use word-processing applications, adding frustration with technology to their overall lack of confidence and competence in writing. At the same time, other investigations show that L1 basic writers and ESL writers can master the technology with relative ease and that doing so gives them a feeling of success and competence that may improve their attitudes toward and success in writing (Etchison, 1989; McAllister & Louth, 1988; Neu & Scarcella, 1991). However, ESL specialists caution that students must be given adequate instruction and assistance in using word-processing tools for them to be more help than hindrance (Pennington, 1993b; Phinney, 1991).

Text Analysis in L2 Writing.   A number of researchers and theorists have examined the value of text analyzers in training ESL writers. Several classroom studies have reported some positive effects of the systematic use of text analysis. Reid (1986) reported that ESL students who used Writer's Workbench significantly improved their editing and writing skills over those who did not use the application, but also admitted that other variables may have contributed to this outcome. In an experimental study of the effects of two commercial text analyzers on 39 EFL writers, Liou (1992) found that participants in the experimental group responded positively to the use of the programs and that weaker writers tended to benefit the most from using them. However, she also reported that there was no difference in writing quality between control and experimental groups. Several studies (Bland, Noblitt, Armington, & Gay, 1990; Noblitt & Bland, 1991; Scott & New, 1993) examined the effects of a French L2 software program called *Système-D*, finding that this application, which also tracks students' requests for information about their texts, provided valuable insights about students' editing strategies.

Other researchers have examined the accuracy of text analysis programs in assessing L2 writing. Brock (1990a) examined the commercial grammar checker *Grammatik III*, finding that it was inappropriate for L2 text analysis. Ferris (1993) argued that algorithms written for L1 text analysis may be inaccurate and may underestimate both ESL student errors and students' developing competence (as expressed through interlanguage structures). In a follow-up study, Brock (1990b) discovered that *Grammatik IV* could be customized to address certain problems encountered by ESL writers, but questioned whether the effort was worthwhile given other problems with text analyzers (i.e., that they are too rigid, prescriptive, and focused on surface features of texts).

Even more troubling than the limitations of the software applications may be their effects on developing L2 writers. Pennington and Brock (1990) reported that when ESL students used a text analyzer alone (without feedback from a teacher), the results were shorter sentences, shorter drafts, and fewer revisions. They also noted that writers tended to accept the analyzer's suggestions, even when inappropriate, and did not correct errors that the analyzer did not flag. Further, students became increasingly dependent on feedback—a finding that casts doubts on claims that such programs promote self-monitoring and self-correction. Similarly, Poulsen (1991) noted that, although a spell checker caught about 80% of student spelling errors, the ESL students did not always use the correct form suggested by the spell checker. In addition, if a correct alternative was not offered, students rarely tried to solve the problems in other ways. Despite these concerns and problems, Sampson and Gregory (1991) warned that ESL writing teachers cannot simply proscribe or ignore the use of spelling and grammar checkers by ESL students, noting that many students are computer literate and aware of the existence of these aids (which tend to be widely available in campus computer labs in the United States). Rather than "leading these students down the technological primrose path" (p. 36), teachers need to engage in frank discussions with their students concerning the advantages, drawbacks, and pitfalls of using text analyzers.

$\Rightarrow AA\ 9.4$

Pennington (1992) critiqued research on text analyzers and ESL writing by arguing that such analysis programs are (a) not generalizable, (b) ineffective in training students to develop editing strategies, (c) unable to enhance writing quality, (d) lacking in a clear educational rationale, and (e) highly inaccurate. She went on to suggest that effective text analysis software should:

1. Be clearly grounded in a theoretical, empirical, and practical base;
2. Have as its primary goal the development of editing skills through training in the analysis and decision processes involved;
3. Offer on-line helps and models of the editing process;
4. Allow for individualized learning and inductive discovery;
5. Encourage active involvement and independence, so that the locus of control is internal rather than external;
6. Incorporate collaborative work to develop a sense of audience;
7. Focus on both discourse-level and sentence-level revision;
8. Treat the editing process as an interplay of form and meaning. (Pennington, 1992, p. 429)

Other Computer-Assisted Writing Tools.   Other researchers and teachers have reported that computer-assisted writing software has helped their students' writing and attitudes. For instance, Hanson-Smith (1990) reported that the use of a program called *Constructing the Paragraph*, which contains 125 sample paragraphs and exercises for analyzing their discourse structures, improved student interaction and attitudes in the context of a process-oriented collaborative college composition course. Liou, Wang, and Hung-Yeh (1992) reported that, "the combined effect of classroom instruction and grammatical CALL is helpful for writing instruction" (p. 23). The interactive, adaptive software that was used contained drill, practice, and instruction based on Chinese EFL students' common written errors. Butler (1990) suggested that concordancing errors from computerized corpora of student texts "may provide a new way of analyzing errors and of helping language teachers to help students" (p. 343). Finally, Sullivan (1993) reported that the use of a computer network to provide peer feedback can improve student motivation, participation, interaction, and collaboration, pointing out that electronic discussion groups are "freer of risk than a traditional teacher-centered classroom" (p. 34), relieving ESL students of their anxieties about being understood and using culturally inappropriate language.

PEDAGOGICAL ISSUES IN COMPUTER-ASSISTED WRITING INSTRUCTION

From this review of the research on various aspects of computer use in L2 writing classes, several generalizations should emerge: (a) There are many potential benefits for student writers, especially for ESL writers, in the use of word processing; (b) these benefits are unlikely to materialize without careful preparation and instruction by the writing instructor; and (c) due to the many pitfalls in the uses of other types of writing software with L2 students, especially text analyzers, teachers must be alert to the possible dangers and communicate these drawbacks to their learners. Considering these issues, ESL writing teachers who wish to use computers as an integral part of their writing courses have several practical decisions to make (see Fig. 9.2).

How Frequently and in What Ways Will WP and CAI Be Used?

There are three general models of computer-assisted writing instruction:

1. Class is taught exclusively in a computer laboratory;
2. Class sessions are divided between traditional classrooms and computer labs, with the computer lab being utilized regularly (e.g., once a week); and
3. Class sessions are held exclusively in a regular classroom, but students are expected to use computers (on their own time) for their writing assignments.

1. Provide computer lab sections (which students can select) in programs for ESL students who are at an intermediate (or higher) level of English proficiency and who can produce paragraph- to essay-length assignments.
2. Provide training in the use of the computer, word-processing software, and e-mail applications (as applicable).
3. In initial stages of computer lab instruction, provide tutors to help with technical questions, and/or arrange students so that more experienced computer users can sit near and assist novices.
4. Ideally, provide access to a computer lab with the following characteristics:
   - ample time to use the computers (whether during class time or at other times);
   - large and clear display screens;
   - separate carrels or work stations with moveable dividers to allow for privacy when needed or to allow for student-student interaction when desired;
   - user-friendly word-processing software;
   - access to e-mail and the Internet;
   - networking capabilities;
   - an overhead projector connected to a computer so that exercises and writing samples can be displayed for whole-class activities.
5. Integrate peer work into the curriculum through networking or through trading disks for computerized feedback.
6. Provide structure for the computer lab sessions by giving guidelines for writing activities (e.g., "Work on your first draft of the next essay assignment") or by providing files with in-class activities (process prompters, idea generators, organizing heuristics, etc.).
7. Talk to students about the benefits and drawbacks of using spelling and grammar checkers (see Figs. 9.4 and 9.5, and Application Activity 9.5).

FIG. 9.2. General guidelines for computer-assisted ESL writing instruction (adapted from Pennington, 1990, and Phinney, 1989).

The quantitative and microethnographic studies conducted by Bernhardt et al. (1989, 1990) demonstrated that there are strengths and weaknesses in the first two models. Classes conducted entirely in the computer lab tend to function as writers' workshops. That is, students see class sessions as a time to write, rather than to be instructed in writing, and there may be a great deal of informal teacher–student interaction as the teacher moves about the computer lab helping individual students. However, peer interaction may be minimal because students tend to be more interested in completing their own writing projects than in responding to others' work. Some students may object to so much in-class writing, feeling that it is a waste of class time (when the teacher could be telling them something) and that they prefer to write in a quiet, solitary environment when they have a larger block of time. The second model, in which the class alternates between a regular classroom and a computer lab (as in the Bernhardt et al. studies), has the potential of providing the best or the worst of both worlds. Students benefit from getting both in-class instruction (in the regular class) and in-class writing time (in the lab), but students and teacher may feel that they do not have enough time for either priority and thus do nothing well.

Structuring Instruction Within the Computer Setting. Once a teacher decides to utilize the computer lab for classroom instruction, whether for all or part of the class time, experts agree that lab time should be carefully planned. Although unstructured lab time has its benefits (students get extended periods of time to write and the teacher can conduct individual conferences), there are several important drawbacks to relinquishing the class time spent in the lab to free writing. First, students may feel resentful that their time is being wasted because they aren't doing anything in class or they may prefer to do their thinking and writing at a different time of day, in a quieter setting, and for longer or shorter blocks of time (Bernhardt et al., 1989, 1990). Thus, students may object to being forced to write in conditions that are not optimal for them. Second, researchers in computer-assisted writing agree that computers cannot and should not replace instruction by the teacher. Novice writers need instruction, modeling, and practice in various aspects of the composing process and of technical aspects of writing (e.g., citing sources, grammar use, etc.). This is especially true for ESL students, who need more extensive introduction to the linguistic and rhetorical forms of written academic English than do NESs (Ferris, 1994; Leki, 1990a; Reid, 1994; Silva, 1993). Phinney (1989) warned that, "without specific instruction in using the computer to facilitate the writing process, from prewriting to revision, the computer alone appears to have little effect in changing writing behavior ... whether they are writing in their first or second language" (p. 87). Finally, there is some evidence that, in both L1 and L2 settings, students' willingness to collaborate and respond to peers' writing decreases in a computer lab (Bernhardt et al., 1990; Piper, 1987).

Although an instructor can and probably should allow students some unstructured free writing time in the computer lab, there are steps that a teacher can take to utilize computer lab time for maximal benefit. For ESL writers, experts such as Phinney (1989) and Pennington (1990) advised that students be given instruction and practice early in the term in the use of computers and software. Pennington further advised that teachers, tutors, and peers who are expert in using the computer for writing be assigned to help student writers individually as they become familiar with word processing. Moreover, the curriculum should be designed so that students can progressively develop their computer writing skills over the course of a semester (or longer). Phinney (1989) suggested that the teacher develop or adapt exercise files that provide "writing heuristics, suggestions for strategies in content generation and organization, revision and editing exercises, and exercises which teach various aspects of the software" (p. 87). Figure 9.3 provides an example of such an exercise, which can also be done on paper. Nevertheless, completing prewriting and revision exercises on a computer allows the student to save and adapt files for later use. The teacher can adapt any activity (e.g., for peer response, organization, self-evaluation, etc.)

Answer the following questions about your topic. When you have answered the questions, save this file under a different name on your disk and print out a copy of it. If you think one of the questions does not apply to your topic, write **NA** (not applicable) after the question.

What is the topic of your paper? State it briefly.
WHO is involved in your topic?
WHAT things are involved?
WHEN do the events take place?
WHERE do the events take place?
WHY do the events happen?
HOW do things happen?
What can you **DESCRIBE** about your topic?
What **CHANGES** have occurred in it?
Can you relate an **INCIDENT** about it?
What do you **REMEMBER** about it?
What are its **PARTS, SECTIONS, or ELEMENTS?**
Can you give **INSTRUCTIONS** for making or doing it?
How do you **FEEL** about it?
Why is it **IMPORTANT or VALUABLE?**What **CAUSES** it?
What **RESULTS** from it?
Can you **COMPARE** it to something?
Do you **AGREE or DISAGREE** with it? Why?

FIG. 9.3. Example of a student prewriting exercise for the word processor
(adapted from Phinney, 1989).

and leave instructions in word-processing files for student use. Generally, "almost anything that can done with pencil and paper can be transferred to a computer" (Phinney, 1989, p. 88). The advantage of this practice is that doing writing activities on the computer saves time (the student can write more quickly and give copies to the teacher or classmates more easily) and builds familiarity and comfort with the computer along with composing skills.

Whatever the teacher decides to include during computer lab sessions, whether it be word-processing instruction, composing activities, free writing, online peer response, or teacher–student conferences, it is important that he or she plan lab time carefully and not simply assume that a traditional lesson plan can be transferred to a computer lab with little or no modification (see chap. 3). As Bernhardt et al. (1990) pointed out, "Teaching in a computer lab is a more pressured situation than teaching a regular classroom, and … teachers need to approach the new environment deliberately and with ample planning" (p. 372). Specifically, teachers need to limit classroom administration talk (collecting homework, discussing assignments, etc.) by making efficient announcements at the beginning of the class before students become distracted by the computers (and possibly missing important information). Teachers also should sell the instructional strategy of using the computer lab by making certain learners "understand why class time is being given to writing and what the expectations are for both preparation and participation" (Bernhardt et al.,

1990, p. 365). Similarly, it may be even harder to obtain students' cooperation and attention to peer review activities in a computer lab setting, so teachers need to ensure that students understand why such activities are valuable and structure the review activities carefully, regardless of their form (see chap. 6).

Grammar/Style Checkers and Other Dangers. As previously discussed, L2 computer writing experts warn against the use of grammar checkers for ESL writers because they tend to be inaccurate in assessing L2 writing and because students become excessively dependent on them, to the detriment of the development of their own editing strategies. However, it is probably naïve, especially in a college or university setting where such programs are widely available on campus networks, to ignore grammar checkers or forbid students to use them. Teachers should probably meet this problem head-on by candidly discussing with students the problems and pitfalls of grammar checkers. This can be done by showing students the results of a grammar checker's analysis of a sample ESL student paper and pointing out what errors were overlooked by the program and ways in which suggested corrections might actually lead students astray (Brock, 1990a; Sampson & Gregory, 1991). Figure 9.4 provides an example of such an exercise. Although L2 writing experts are less wary of spell checkers and thesaurus use by ESL writers, students may use them more accurately and effectively if the teacher points out their strengths and limitations during a regular session (Fig. 9.5).

Another possible abuse of computer-assisted writing involves cheating and plagiarism. Writing teachers often complain about student paper networks for essays and term papers. Assuming that such networks exist (and both authors have seen evidence of them during their teaching careers), they become even more problematic when papers can be quickly copied from a floppy disk or hard drive or can be e-mailed from one student to another. The student can easily make a few changes and print the paper for submission. However, there are a few precautions that a teacher can take against computer-assisted cheating, such as requiring parts of each assignment to be composed in class (where the teacher can monitor it and perhaps initial a draft printout) and preliminary drafts to be submitted in a folder with the final paper so that the teacher can note, by looking at the fossil record of the paper, any sudden, dramatic changes in content, style, or accuracy. The teacher should also have some baseline and periodic samples of each student's in-class writing so that if computer-facilitated peer-tutoring sessions result in excessive correction by a classmate or friend, the teacher can compare the in- and out-of-class writing samples. Although L1 and L2 students do occasionally cheat (and do so regardless of whether a computer is being used), this knowledge should inform, but not control, a teacher's pedagogical choices. That some forms of dishonesty may be facilitated by the use of computers should not, in and of itself, discourage teachers from using them.

The following student paper was written in 35 minutes on the topic of "culture shock."

1. Read the paper and highlight, underline, or circle any grammar errors you find.

Culture Shock

Nothing is easy after arriving in another country. There are many things that are different from my own country. It takes time to cope with. I think that studying in the United States could be tremendously interesting, from overcoming the language gap, getting used to the weather, and leading an independent life.

English is the first thing I need to pay much attention to. Even though I am comfortable with my English reading and writing skills, but conversing with Americans still make me a little nervous. In order to improve my conversation, I have been spending watching television 3 hours everyday since I arrived in the United States. Besides, I catch every opportunity to speak with Americans. Now, I enjoy talking in English.

The weather here is the only thing that I appreciate most. The weather here is not so humid as that of Taiwan. Because of the aridity, I seldom perspire and feels comfortable. It is hot during the day, but cool during the night. Cool night always brings me a good sleep.

I have to do everything new. The life I lead now is opposite to the life I had in Taiwan. Washing clothes, buying food, cooking, and cleaning living room are all my chores.

There is an old saying in China: "The more places you travel, the more things you learn". I understand the meaning now. I have to learn here not only from textbook, but also from ordinary life.

---

2. Now you will examine the same paper after it has been analyzed by a computer grammar checker (Grammatik). (Note: The paper with analysis may be found in Appendix 9A.) Compare your analysis with the computer's suggestions:

   What was the same?

   What was different? Did you mark errors that were not marked by the computer? Did the computer mark errors that you did not?

   In places where you and the computer disagreed, who do you think was right—you or the computer? (If you are not sure, discuss the problem with your classmates and teacher.)

3. After going through this exercise, discuss with your classmates and teacher whether you think grammar checkers are helpful for student writers. If not, why not? If so, what can a student to do to avoid the problems you discovered in this exercise?

FIG. 9.4. Example of an in-cl;ass exercise demonstrating the limits of grammar checkers.

SUMMARY AND IMPLICATIONS

It is tempting for many writing teachers simply to dismiss computers from their instructional plans, even if they are devoted computer users. The logistical problems—providing adequate computer facilities and training, increased constraints on lesson planning, a (perceived) increase in student dishonesty that may follow from computer-assisted writing—may discourage teachers from attempting to incorporate computer technology into the writing curriculum. Further, for teachers who are not especially computer literate, the challenge of developing computer-based activities may seem overwhelming.

Yet the evidence is strong that computer use improves student attitudes, confidence, and motivation and that these benefits may be even more significant for L2 writers. Clearly, as Bernhardt et al. (1989) pointed out, not all teachers are comfortable or effective in a computer lab setting, but we would encourage readers whose students have adequate computer facilities available to consider holding some computer lab sessions as part of their writing course. The intervention may be as minimal as a session or two to show students how to save and print files; block, move, add, and delete text; and use a spelling or grammar checker. This assistance can surely help a number of students write for longer durations, write more frequently, write longer drafts, and ultimately write better. Regardless of how

---

1. Read the paper below and circle any spelling errors that you find. You may ignore other types of errors. For the errors you circled, suggest correct spellings.

CULTURE SHOCK

When I first came to America, it was five years ago. I was only thirteen years old, and I experience a lot of "culture shock."

There are a lot of things that were totally strange to me. For example, the chees, rock music, and even people kissing on the street.

The thing that effect me the most is the language different. I only have taken one year of basic English class before I came to America. When I want to talk to the teacher in class, I have to use hand sign to help, so that teacher can understand what I'm trying to say.

Also, the food is another problem. I have never taste chees before I came to America, and it seem to me that my stomach does not fited too will to American food. So about once a week, I have to go to chinese resturan for some "home taste."

Also, the people kissing, hugging in public place was also a unbelieveable thing in my country. But, as times gose by now I can solve all this problems.

2. Now you will examine the same paper after it has been analyzed by a computer spell checker (WordPerfect 6.0/DOS). (Note: The paper with analysis may be found in Appendix 9B.)

   Compare your analysis with the computer's suggestions:

   What was the same?

   What was different? Did you mark errors that were not marked by the computer? Did the computer mark errors that you did not?

   When the computer marked a spelling error, were correct choices offered? If so, was the correction you made in Step 1 on the list?

   In places where you and the computer disagreed, who do you think was right—you or the computer? (If you are not sure, discuss the problem with your classmates and teacher.)

3. After going through this exercise, discuss with your classmates and teacher whether you think spell checkers are helpful for student writers. If not, why not? If so, what can a student to do to avoid the problems you discovered in this exercise? What, for instance, would you do if a computer marked a spelling error but provided no suggested corrections? And how would you deal with the limitations of the spell checker? (For instance, this writer used effect instead of affect, which would be correct in other contexts, so the speller wouldn't mark it.)

FIG. 9.5. Example of an in-class exercise demonstrating the uses of spell checkers.

much or how little the computer lab is used (if it is utilized at all), it is important to recognize that novice writers still need the teacher to plan the instructional time so that they can improve their composing and word-processing skills. Finally, teachers who are just beginning to introduce computer-assisted writing to their students should remember that "the effects of computers on writing ability may not be a matter of quick transfer, but of subtle and incremental evolution over the life of a writer" (Bernhardt et al., 1989, p. 129).

Reflection and Review

1. What are some hypothetical arguments in favor of holding class sessions in a computer lab instead of a regular classroom? What arguments favor implementing both?

2. After reflecting on your own experience and reviewing the findings presented in this chapter, what do you think is the single greatest potential benefit for students in a computer-assisted composition class? Can you think of any conditions or circumstances that could prevent this advantage from being realized?

3. After reflecting on your own experience and reading in this chapter, what do you think is the single greatest potential drawback for students in a computer-assisted composition course? Can you think of any steps that a teacher could take to solve this problem or prevent it from occurring?

4. Imagine you are about to teach an ESL writing class and have decided to conduct all or some of your class sessions in a computer lab. What effects do you think this decision might have on:
- your syllabus;
- your day-to-day lesson plans;
- the textbook(s) and other materials you will use;
- your own interaction with students, including your responses to their writing;
- peer interaction; and
- the ratio of in-class to out-of class writing?

5. Consider some of the in-class activities illustrated in chapters 3, 4, 6, 7, and 8 (and/or the application activities you completed in conjunction with those chapters). Could these activities be adapted for use on a computer? If so, what changes (if any) might need to be made? If not, why not?

6. Consider the principles and examples of written and oral teacher response discussed in chapter 5 (and/or application activities you completed in conjunction with that chapter). How would you adapt written feedback (or teacher–student conferencing) to a computer lab setting? If you do not think you could adapt your feedback strategies, why not?

Application Activity 9.1: Comparing Research Studies on Computers and Revision

1. Locate and read Hawisher (1987) and McAllister and Louth (1988), both published in *Research in the Teaching of English*.

2. After reading both studies carefully, write an essay in which you compare and contrast them, considering the following issues:
   - What are the research questions in each study? To what extent are they similar (or different)?
   - How many participants were involved, and who were they?
   - What was the duration of each study? Over what period of time were the effects of word processing assessed?
   - What analysis methods did the authors use to assess revision strategies and/or the quality of student revisions?
   - What findings do the researchers report and what conclusions do they draw?
   - After considering your responses to the previous questions, why do you think the two studies, conducted during the same time period and published in the same journal, arrived at such divergent conclusions?

Note: As you read the studies and develop your essay, consider the recommendations of Pennington (1993), who argued that, in evaluating and constructing studies on computers and writing, the following contextual factors need to be considered:
   - the characteristics of the students;
   - the orientation and experience of the teacher;
   - the characteristics of the setting in which the computer is used;
   - the amount of time spent in computer-assisted writing;
   - the nature and quantity of instruction offered in computer use and writing process;
   - the types of hardware and software used by the students; and
   - the ways in which outcomes and effectiveness of computer use are measured.

Application Activity 9.2: Reflecting on Your Own Computer-Assisted Writing Process

1. Choose a writing task that you do regularly and that you can do at two different times (letters, journal entries, class papers, designing lesson plans/handouts, etc.). Complete two separate examples of the task (e.g., two different letters) at different times. Do one using pen and paper and one using a computer.

2. As you complete the two tasks, audio- or videotape yourself as you think aloud about how you are carrying out the task (or have a partner observe you as

you write and think aloud). You may wish to consult Bridwell-Bowles et al. (1987) and Haas (1989) for examples and analyses of think-aloud data.

3. Based on your own observations, your taped think aloud (or partner's notes), and the two texts you produced, reflect on your experience of writing using the two media:

- How much and what types of planning did you do before beginning your writing?
- What changes/revisions did you make, and when in the process did you make them?
- Did you produce a longer text using either medium? Do you feel that one text is of higher quality than the other?
- How did you feel as you completed the two tasks? Did you find one more enjoyable, difficult, frustrating, and so on than the other?
- How would you feel if you were a writing student and were forced to use one medium exclusively?

4. Write a paper in which you discuss your analysis, relating it to the research and ideas presented in this chapter and explaining how the experience will (or will not) affect your present or future teaching of writing.

Application Activity 9.3: Surveying Student Writers About Their Experiences With Computers

In considering whether to use word processing and other computer-based tools in a writing class, one issue that arises is equity: that students with prior experience with and easier access to computers will have an inherent advantage over other students. As computer usage and ownership becomes increasingly widespread throughout the United States and the world, this may become less and less of an issue. In this activity, you will survey a group of ESL writers about their prior and current experiences with computers. To do so, follow these steps:

1. Identify a group of ESL writers in a particular setting (e.g., permanent resident students at a high school or community college, international students at a university, an EFL class in another country).

2. Make arrangements with the writing teacher to administer a survey to the students.

3. Design a survey that assesses:
    a. the extent and nature of students' prior experience with computers (include questions about word processing and other educational/writing software applications, electronic mail, LAN use, and Internet experience);
    b. students' current access to computers, including hardware and software, computer instruction and support, electronic mail, and the Internet; and
    c. students' current comfort level with and attitudes toward computer use (for writing or in general).

4. Imagine that you are writing a position paper to a dean, principal, or other program administrator, in which you present your findings and discuss why it would or would not be a good idea to conduct this particular writing course totally or partially in a computer writing lab.

Application Activity 9.4: "Cybertutoring" an ESL Student Writer

Identify an ESL student writer currently enrolled in a composition course who has access to a computer and e-mail. Obtain the permission of the classroom teacher and the cooperation of the student and complete the following steps to become a cybertutor:

1. If the student is not computer literate or experienced with using e-mail, meet with him or her to go over the basics of sending and receiving e-mail messages and attaching, uploading, and downloading word-processed documents. (If the student is already an experienced e-mail user, you can skip this step.)

2. Have the student e-mail you a partial or completed draft of a paper he or she is working on for the writing class.

3. Respond online to the paper's ideas and/or organization by inserting comments either in the margins or between paragraphs (whatever your e-mail editor will accommodate) and by writing a summary comment (like a brief letter) at the end of the paper. Respond to the paper according to the principles for written response discussed in chapter 5. E-mail the annotated paper back to the student.

4. Ask the student to send you a follow-up message indicating:
   • What comments were most helpful;
   • Any feedback that was confusing; and
   • Any comments with which he or she disagreed.

Also ask the student to e-mail you any revisions of the paper so that you can assess the student's progress and the effects of your comments.

5. Reflect on the experience: Did you find responding online different from handwriting comments on paper or in a face-to-face writing conference? What did you like about communicating with the student in this way? What did you find difficult?

If you want to extend or adapt this project, you might do so in the following ways:
   • Exchange additional iterations of drafts–comments–revisions with the same student;
   • Repeat the process with other student writers, noting variation across students;

- Request that the student send you (and you provide feedback on) texts from other class activities (e.g, journal entries, responses to readings, etc.) that you provide feedback on; and
- Exchange messages with the student in which he or she poses questions about grammar, vocabulary, organization, the writing process, and so on, and in which you provide tutoring through your answers.

Application Activity 9.5: Using a Spelling/Grammar Checker to Analyze Student Writing

Obtain one or more ESL student papers containing both spelling and grammar errors and type or scan it into a computer. Analyze it by following these steps:

1. Print out a copy of the paper and highlight all spelling and grammar errors you find.
2. Run a spell check. Did the spell checker find all of the spelling errors that you marked? Did it identify other words as being misspelled? Were there any identified spelling errors for which no correct alternatives were offered by the program? When alternatives were offered, do you think they were appropriate (Was the word you think the student intended on the list of choices)? After considering all of this information, what would be the benefits and drawbacks for this student writer of using a computer spell checker with this paper?
3. Run a grammar check. Did the computer find all of the grammar errors you marked? Did it identify other constructions (that you did not mark) as erroneous? Were the suggested corrections accurate? Appropriate?
4. Imagine you are going to use this paper and the text analyses (spelling and grammar checks) in a lesson in which you point out the strengths and weaknesses of text analyzers to your students (as in Fig. 9.3). What specific information and points might you include?

APPENDIX 9A: SAMPLE STUDENT PAPER
WITH GRAMMATIK ANALYSIS

Culture Shock

Nothing is easy after arriving in another country. There are many things that are different from my own country. It takes time to cope with. I think that studying in the United States could be tremendously interesting, from overcoming the language gap, getting used to the weather, and leading an independent life.

English is the first thing I need to pay much attention ⊢—('TO' MUST BE A _PREPOSITION_ ("TO THE PARK"), PART OF A _PHRASAL VERB_ ("HE CAME TO AFTER A FEW MINUTES"), OR PART OF AN _INFINITIVE_ ("TO GO"). YOU MAY MEAN 'TOO' OR 'TWO' HERE.)—⊢ to. ⊢—(SIMPLIFY.)—⊢ Even though I am comfortable with my English reading and writing skills, but ⊢—(THERE APPEARS TO BE AN EXTRA _NOUN PHRASE_ IN THIS SEQUENCE. CHECK FOR MISSING WORDS OR PUNCTUATION.)—⊢ conversing with ⊢—('MAKE' SEEMS TO BE AN _APPOSITIVE_. CONSIDER SETTING THE _PHRASE_ OFF WITH COMMAS.)—⊢ Americans ⊢—(THE _ADVERB_ 'STILL' DOES NOT USUALLY MODIFY THE _NOUN_ 'MAKE'.)—⊢ still make me a little nervous. ⊢—(CONSIDER SIMPLIFYING.)—⊢ In order to improve my conversation, I have been spending watching television ⊢—(WHOLE NUMBERS IN THIS RANGE SHOULD BE SPELLED OUT, EVEN AS PART OF LARGER NUMBERS ('EIGHT MILLION').)—⊢ 3 hours ⊢—(THE _ADJECTIVE_ 'EVERY-DAY' OCCURS ONLY BEFORE A _NOUN_. IF YOU MEAN "EACH DAY," WRITE 'EVERY DAY'.)—⊢ everyday since I arrived in the United States. Besides, I catch every opportunity to speak with Americans. Now, I enjoy talking in English.

The weather here is the only thing that I appreciate most. The weather here is not so humid as that of Taiwan. Because of the aridity, ⊢—(THE _SUBJECT_ 'I' RE-QUIRES A PLURAL VERB, NOT THE SINGULAR VERB 'FEELS'.)—⊢ I seldom perspire and feels comfortable. ⊢—(THE SINGULAR _SUBJECT_ 'IT' TAKES A SINGULAR _VERB_, NOT THE PLURAL VERB 'COOL'.)—⊢ It is hot during the day, but cool during the night. Cool night always brings me a good sleep.

I have to do everything new. ⊢—(THIS DOESN'T SEEM TO BE A COMPLETE SENTENCE.)—⊢ The life ⊢—('I' IS NOT USUALLY FOLLOWED BY 'LEAD'.)—⊢ ⊢—(THE _PRONOUN_ 'I' IS USED WITH 'AM' AND 'WAS'.)—⊢ I lead now is opposite to the life I had in Taiwan. Washing clothes, buying food, cooking, and cleaning living room are all my chores.

There is an old saying in China: "The more places you travel, the more things you learn⊢—(ALWAYS PLACE THE '.' INSIDE THE CLOSING QUOTATION MARK ('""').)—⊢ ". I understand the meaning now. I have to learn here not only from ⊢—(AN _ARTICLE_ OR OTHER _MODIFIER_ USUALLY PRECEDES THE WORD 'TEXTBOOK'. CHECK ALSO FOR ERRORS IN HYPHENATION, POSSESSIVE FORM, AND MODIFIER AGREEMENT.)—⊢ textbook, but also from ordinary life.

APPENDIX 9B: STUDENT PAPER
WITH SPELL-CHECKER SUGGESTIONS

Note: Misspelled words are in bold in the text. Analysis follows the text.

When I first came to America, it was five years ago. I was only thirteen years old, and I experience a lot of "culture shock."

There are a lot of things that were totally strange to me. For example, the **(1) chees**, rock music, and even people kissing on the street.

The thing that **(2) effect** me the most is the language different. I only have taken one year of basic English class before I came to America. When I want to talk to the teacher in class, I have to use hand sign to help, so that teacher can understand what I'm trying to say.

Also, the food is another problem. I have never taste **(3) chees** before I came to America, and it seem to me that my stomach does not **(4) fited** too **(5) will** to American food. So about once a week, I have to go to chinese **(6) resturan** for some "home taste."

Also, the people kissing, hugging in public place was also a **(7) unbelieveable** thing in my country.

But, as times **(8) gose** by now I can solve all this problems.

Analysis

Error #	Marked?	Suggestions
1	yes	Correct choice ("cheese") is #8 of 35 suggestions
2	no	
3	See #1	
4	yes	Correct choice ("fitted") is #6 of 17 suggestions
5	no	
6	yes	none
7	yes	Correct choice is #1 of two suggestions
8	yes	Correct choice is #1 of 15

REFERENCES

Aaron, J. E. (1997). *The Little, Brown essential handbook for writers* (2nd ed.). New York: Longman.

Alderson, J. C. (1984). Reading in a foreign language: A reading problem or a language problem? In J. Alderson & A. Urquhart (Eds.), *Reading in a foreign language* (pp. 1–27). New York: Longman.

Alderson, J. C., Clapham, C., & Wall, D. (1995). *Language test construction and evaluation.* Cambridge, England: Cambridge University Press.

Aljaafreh, A., & Lantolf, J. P. (1994). Negative feedback as regulation and second language learning in the zone of proximal development. *The Modern Language Journal, 78,* 465–483.

Allaei, S. K., & Connor, U. (1990). Exploring the dynamics of cross-cultural collaboration. *The Writing Instructor, 10,* 19–28.

Allaei, S. K., & Connor, U. (1991). Using performative assessment instruments with ESL student writers. In L. Hamp-Lyons (Ed.), *Assessing second language writing in academic contexts* (pp. 227–240). Norwood, NJ: Ablex.

Anderson, D., Benjamin, B., Busiel, C., & Paredes-Holt, B. (1996). *Teaching on-line: Internet research, conversation and composition.* New York: HarperCollins College Publishers.

Anson, C. M. (Ed.). (1989). *Writing and response.* Urbana, IL: National Council of Teachers of English.

Anson, C. M., & Schwegler, R. A. (1997). *The Longman handbook for writers and readers.* New York: Longman.

Applebee, A. N. (1978). Teaching high-achievement students: A survey of the winners of the 1977 NCTE Achievement Awards in writing. *Research in the Teaching of English, 1,* 41–53.

Applebee, A. N. (1981). *Writing in the secondary school* (NCTE Research Rep. No. 21). Urbana, IL: National Council of Teachers of English.

Applebee, A. N. (1984). *Contexts for learning to write.* Norwood, NJ: Ablex.

Applebee, A. N. (1986). Problems in process approaches: Toward a reconceptualization of process instruction. In A. Petrosky & D. Bartholomae (Eds.), *The teaching of writing: Eighty-fifth yearbook of the National Society for the Study of Education, Part II* (pp. 49–70). Chicago: University of Chicago Press.

Ascher, A. (1993). *Think about editing.* Boston: Heinle & Heinle.

Atkinson, D., & Ramanathan, V. (1995). Cultures of writing: An ethnographic comparison of L1 and L2 university writing/language programs. *TESOL Quarterly, 29,* 539–568.

Atwell, N. (1984). Writing and reading literature from the inside out. *Language Arts, 61,* 240–252.

Atwell, N. (1987). *In the middle: Writing, reading, and learning with adolescents.* Portsmouth, NH: Heinemann.

Axelrod, R. B., & Cooper, C. R. (1993). *The concise guide to writing.* New York: St. Martin's.

Axelrod, R. B., & Cooper, C. R. (1997). *The St. Martin's guide to writing* (5th ed.). New York: St. Martin's.

Bachman, L. (1990). *Fundamental considerations in language testing.* Oxford: Oxford University Press.

Bachman, L., & Palmer, A. (1996). *Language testing in practice: Designing and developing useful language tests.* Oxford: Oxford University Press.

Bailey, K. M. (1996). The best laid plans: Teachers' in-class decisions to depart from their lesson plans. In K. M. Bailey & D. Nunan (Eds.), *Voices from the language classroom* (pp. 15–40). Cambridge, England: Cambridge University Press.

Bailey, K. M. (1998). *Learning about language assessment: Dilemmas, decisions, and directions.* Boston: Heinle & Heinle.

Bailey, K. M., & Nunan, D. (Eds.). (1996). *Voices from the language classroom.* Cambridge, England: Cambridge University Press.

Balestri, D. P. (1988). Softcopy and hard: Wordprocessing and writing process. *Academic Computing, 2*(1), 14–17, 41–45.

Barker, T. T. (1987). Studies in word processing and writing. *Computers in the schools, 4,*(1) 109–121.

Bartholomae, D. (1986). Words from afar. In A. R. Petrosky & D. Bartholomae (Eds.), *The teaching of writing: Eighty-fifth yearbook of the National Society for the Study of Education, Part II* (pp. 1–7). Chicago: National Society for the Study of Education.

Bartholomae, D., & Petrosky, A. (Eds.). (1986). *The language of teaching and learning.* Portsmouth, NH: Heinemann.

Bates, L., Lane, J., & Lange, E. (1993). *Writing clearly: Responding to ESL compositions.* Boston: Heinle & Heinle.

Bazerman, C. (1985). Physicists reading physics: Schema-laden purposes and purpose-laden schema. *Written Communication, 2,* 3–24.

Bazerman, C. (1988). *Shaping written knowledge: The genre and activity of the experimental article in science.* Madison, WI: The University of Wisconsin Press.

Beach, R. (1979). The effects of between-draft teacher evaluation versus student self-evaluation on high school students' revising of rough drafts. *Research in the Teaching of English, 13,* 111–119.

Beach, R., & Liebman-Kleine, J. (1986). The writing/reading relationship: Becoming one's own best reader. In B. T. Petersen (Ed.), *Convergences: Transactions in reading and writing* (pp. 64–81). Urbana, IL: National Council of Teachers of English.

Beason, L. (1993). Feedback and revision in writing across the curriculum classes. *Research in the Teaching of English, 27,* 395–421.

Beason, L., & Lester, M. (1997). *Now I get it: A commonsense guide to grammar and usage.* New York: St. Martin's.

Beck, M.-L. (1997). Why syntactic theory? In K. Bardovi-Harlig & B. Hartford (Eds.), *Beyond methods: Components of second language teacher education* (pp. 42–66). New York: McGraw-Hill.

Behrens, L., & Rosen, L. J. (1997). *Writing and reading across the curriculum* (6th ed.). New York: Longman.

Belanger, J. (1987). Theory and research into reading and writing connections: A critical review. *Reading-Canada-Lecture, 5,* 10–18.

Belanoff, P., & Dickson, M. (Eds.). (1991). *Portfolios: Process and product.* Portsmouth, NH: Boynton/Cook-Heinemann.

Bell, J. S. (1995). The relationship between L1 and L2 literacy: Some complicating factors. *TESOL Quarterly, 29,* 687–704.

Benesch, S. (1987, March). *Word processing in English as a second language: A case study of three non-native college students.* Paper presented at the Conference on College Composition and Communication, Atlanta, GA (EDRS No. ED 281 381).

Benesch, S. (Ed.). (1988). *Ending remediation: Linking ESL and content in higher education.* Washington, DC: TESOL.

Benesch, S., Rakijas, M., & Rorschach, B. (1987). *Academic writing workshop.* Belmont, CA: Wadsworth.

Bereiter, C., & Scardamalia, M. (1987). *The psychology of written composition.* Hillsdale, NJ: Lawrence Erlbaum Associates.

Berger, V. (1990). The effects of peer and self-feedback. *CATESOL Journal, 3,* 21–35.

Berkenkotter, C., & Huckin, T. N. (1993). Rethinking genre from a sociocognitive perspective. *Written Communication, 10,* 475–509.

Berlin, J. A. (1987). *Rhetoric and reality: Writing instruction in American colleges, 1900–1985.* Carbondale, IL: Southern Illinois University Press.

Berlin, J. A. (1988). Rhetoric and ideology in the writing class. *College English, 50,* 477–494.

Berlin, J. A., & Inkster, R. (1980). Current-traditional rhetoric: Paradigm and practice. *Freshman English News, 8,* 1–5, 14.

Bernhardt, E. (1991). *Reading development in a second language: Theoretical, empirical, & classroom perspectives.* Norwood, NJ: Ablex.

Bernhardt, S. A., Edwards, P. R., & Wojahn, P. G. (1989). Teaching college composition with computers: A program evaluation study. *Written Communication, 6,* 108–133.

Bernhardt, S. A., Wojahn, P. G., & Edwards, P. R. (1990). Teaching college composition with computers: A timed observation study. *Written Communication, 7,* 342–374.

Biber, D. (1988). *Variation across speech and writing.* Cambridge, England: Cambridge University Press.

Birnbaum, J. (1982). The reading and composing behavior of selected fourth- and seventh-grade students. *Research in the Teaching of English, 16,* 241–260.

Bizzell, P. (1982). College composition: Initiation into the academic discourse community. *Curriculum Inquiry, 12,* 191–207.

Bizzell, P. (1987). Language and literacy. In T. Enos (Ed.), *A sourcebook for basic writing teachers* (pp. 125–137). New York: Random House.

Bizzell, P. (1992). *Academic discourse and critical consciousness.* Pittsburgh, PA: University of Pittsburgh Press.

Black, L., Daiker, D. A., Sommers, J., & Stygall, G. (Eds.). (1994). *New directions in portfolio assessment.* Portsmouth, NH: Heinemann.

Bland, S. K., Noblitt, J. S., Armington, S., & Gay, G. (1990). The naive lexical hypothesis: Evidence from computer-assisted language learning. *The Modern Language Journal, 74,* 440–450.

Blanton, L. (1993). Reading as performance: Reframing the function of reading. In J. Carson & I. Leki (Eds.), *Reading in the composition classroom: Second language perspectives* (pp. 234–246). Boston: Heinle & Heinle.

Bogel, F. V., Carden, P., Cox, G. H., Davis, S., Freedman, D. P., Gottschalk, K. K., Hjortshoj, J., & Shaw, E. E. (Eds.). (1988). *Teaching prose: A guide for writing instructors.* New York: Norton.

Bork, A. (1985). *Personal computers for education.* New York: Harper & Row.

Bossers, B. (1991). On thresholds, ceilings and short-circuits: The relation between L1 reading, L2 reading, and L2 knowledge. *AILA Review, 8,* 45–60.

Boutwell, M. (1983). Reading and writing process: A reciprocal agreement. *Language Arts, 60,* 723–730.

Bowen, R., Madsen, H., & Hilferty, A. (1985). *TESOL techniques and procedures.* Cambridge, MA: Newbury House.

Brady, L. (1990). Overcoming resistance: Computers in the writing classroom. *Computers and Composition, 7*(2), 21–33.

Braine, G. (1988). A reader reacts. *TESOL Quarterly, 22,* 700–702.

Brannon, L., & Knoblauch, C. H. (1982). On students' rights to their own texts: A model of teacher response. *College Composition and Communication, 33,* 157–166.

Bridges, C. (Ed.). (1986). *Training the new teacher of college composition.* Urbana, IL: National Council of Teachers of English.

Bridwell, L. (1980). Revising strategies in twelfth grade students' transactional writing. *Research in the Teaching of English, 14,* 197–222.

Bridwell-Bowles, L., Johnson, P., & Brehe, S. (1987). Composing and computers: Case studies of experienced writers. In A. Matsuhashi (Ed.), *Writing in real time: Modelling production processes.* Norwood, NJ: Ablex.

Briggs, C. L., & Elkind, D. (1977). Characteristics of early readers. *Perceptual and Motor Skills, 44,* 1231–1237.

Briggs, C. L., & Bauman, R. (1992). Genre, intertextuality, and social power. *Journal of Linguistic Anthropology, 2,* 131–172.

Brinton, D., Snow, M. A., & Wesche, M. B. (1989). *Content-based second language instruction.* Boston: Heinle & Heinle.

Brock, M. N. (1990a). Can the computer tutor? An analysis of a disk-based text analyzer. *System, 18,* 351–359.

Brock, M. N. (1990b). Customizing a computerized text analyzer for ESL writers: Cost versus gain. *CALICO Journal, 8*(2), 51–60.

Brookes, A., & Grundy, P. (1990). *Writing for study purposes: A teacher's guide to developing individual writing skills.* Cambridge, England: Cambridge University Press.

Brooks, E., & Fox, L. (1995). *Making peace: A reading/writing/thinking text on global community.* New York: St. Martin's.

Brown, H. D. (1994a). *Principles of language learning and teaching* (3rd ed.). Englewood Cliffs, NJ: Prentice-Hall.

Brown, H. D. (1994b). *Teaching by principles.* Englewood Cliffs, NJ: Prentice-Hall.

Brown, J. D. (1995). *The elements of language curriculum: A systematic approach to program development.* Boston: Heinle & Heinle.

Browning, G. (1996). Challenges facing California ESL students and teachers across the segments. *CATESOL Journal, 9,* 15–46.

Bruffee, K. A. (1986). Social construction, language, and the authority of knowledge—A bibliographical essay. *College English, 48,* 773–790.

Burnham, C. (1986). Portfolio evaluation: Room to breathe and grow. In C. Bridges (Ed.), *Training the new teacher of college composition* (pp. 125–139). Urbana, IL: National Council of Teachers of English.

Burt, M. K. (1975). Error analysis in the adult EFL classroom. *TESOL Quarterly, 9,* 53–62.

Burt, M. K., & Kiparsky, C. (1972). *The gooficon: A repair manual for English.* Rowley, MA: Newbury House.

Butler, J. (1990). Concordancing, teaching, and error analysis: Some applications and a case study. *System, 18,* 343–349.

Calfee, R., & Perfumo, P. (1996a). A national survey of writing portfolio practice: What we learned and what it means. In R. Calfee & P. Perfumo (Eds.), *Writing portfolios in the classroom: Policy and practice, promise and peril* (pp. 63–81). Hillsdale, NJ: Lawrence Erlbaum Associates.

Calfee, R., & Perfumo, P. (Eds.). (1996b). *Writing portfolios in the classroom: Policy and practice, promise and peril.* Hillsdale, NJ: Lawrence Erlbaum Associates.

Calkins, L. M. (1983). *Lessons from a child.* Portsmouth, NH: Heinemann.

Camp, R. (1992). Portfolio reflections in middle and secondary school classrooms. In K. B. Yancey (Ed.), *Portfolios in the writing classroom* (pp. 61–79). Urbana, IL: National Council of Teachers of English.

Camp, R. (1993). Changing the model for direct assessment of writing. In M. Williamson & B. Huot (Eds.), *Holistic scoring: Theoretical foundations and validation research* (pp. 56–69). Cresskill, NJ: Hampton.

Camp, R., & Belanoff, P. (1987). Portfolios as proficiency tests. *Notes from the National Testing Network in Writing, 7,* 8.

Canale, M., Frenette, N., & Belanger, M. (1988). Evaluation of minority student writing in first and second language. In J. Fine (Ed.), *Second language discourse: A textbook of current research.* Norwood, NJ: Ablex.

Cardelle, M., & Corno, L. (1981). Effects on second language learning of variations in written feedback on homework assignments. *TESOL Quarterly, 15,* 251–261.

Carmines, E. G., & Zeller, R. A. (1979). *Reliability and validity assessment.* Beverly Hills, CA: Sage.

Carnicelli, T. A. (1980). The writing conference: A one-to-one conversation. In T. R. Donovan & B. W. McClelland (Eds.), *Eight approaches to teaching composition* (pp. 101–131). Urbana, IL: National Council of Teachers of English.

Carrell, P. L. (1981). Culture-specific schemata in L2 comprehension. In R. Orem & J. Haskell (Eds.), *Selected papers from the Ninth Illinois TESOL/BE Convention, the First Midwest TESOL Conference* (pp. 123–132). Chicago, IL: TESOL/BE.

Carrell, P. L. (1983a). Three components of background knowledge in reading comprehension. *Language Learning, 33,* 183–207.

Carrell, P. L. (1983b). Background knowledge in second language comprehension. *Language Learning and Communication, 2,* 25–34.

Carrell, P. L. (1984). Evidence of a formal schema in second language comprehension. *Language Learning, 34,* 87–112.

Carrell, P. L. (1987). Text as interaction: Some implications of text analysis and reading research for ESL composition. In U. Connor & R. Kaplan (Eds.), *Writing across languages: Analysis of L2 text* (pp. 47–56). Reading, MA: Addison-Wesley.

Carrell, P. L. (1990). Reading in a foreign language: Research and pedagogy. *JALT Journal, 12,* 53–74.

Carrell, P. L. (1991). Second language reading: Reading ability or language proficiency? *Applied Linguistics, 12,* 159–179.

Carrell, P. L., Devine, J., & Eskey, D. (Eds.). (1988). *Interactive approaches to second language reading.* Cambridge, England: Cambridge University Press.

Carrell, P. L., & Eisterhold, J. C. (1983). Schema theory and ESL reading pedagogy. *TESOL Quarterly, 17,* 553–574.

Carrell, P. L., & Monroe, L. (1995). ESL composition and learning styles. In J. Reid (Ed.), *Learning styles in the ESL/EFL classroom* (pp. 148–157). New York: Heinle & Heinle.

Carroll, S., Swain, M., & Roberge, Y. (1992). The role of feedback in adult second language acquisition: Error correction and morphological generalizations. *Applied Psycholinguistics, 13,* 173–198.

Carson, J. (1993). Reading for writing: Cognitive perspectives. In J. Carson & I. Leki (Eds.), *Reading in the composition classroom: Second language perspectives* (pp. 85–104). Boston: Heinle & Heinle.

Carson, J. E., Carrell, P. L., Silberstein, S., Kroll, B., & Kuehn, P. A. (1990). Reading–writing relationships in first and second language. *TESOL Quarterly, 24,* 245–266.

Carson, J. G., & Leki, I. (Eds.). (1993). *Reading in the composition classroom: Second language perspectives.* Boston: Heinle & Heinle.

Carson, J. G., & Nelson, G. L. (1996). Chinese students' perceptions of ESL peer response group interaction. *Journal of Second Language Writing, 5,* 1–19.

Carson, J. G., & Nelson, G. L. (1994). Writing groups: Cross-cultural issues. *Journal of Second Language Writing, 3,* 17–30.

Celce-Murcia, M. (Ed.). (1991). *Teaching English as a second or foreign language* (2nd ed.). New York: Newbury House.

Celce-Murcia, M., & Larsen-Freeman, D. (1983). *The grammar book: An ESL/EFL teacher's course.* Rowley, MA: Newbury House.

Chadwick, S., & Bruce, N. (1989, April). The revision process in academic writing: From pen and paper to word processor. *Hong Kong Papers in Linguistics and Language Teaching, 12,* 1–27.

Chastain, K. (1988). *Developing second language skills: Theory and practice.* San Diego, CA: Harcourt Brace Jovanovich.

Chaudron, C. (1983, March). *Evaluating writing: Effects of feedback on revision.* Paper presented at the 17th annual TESOL Convention, Toronto, Canada (EDRS No. ED 227 706).

Ching, R., McKee, S., & Ford, R. (1996). Passages between the community college and the California State University. *CATESOL Journal, 9,* 79–98.

Christiansen, M. (1965). Tripling writing and omitting readings in freshman English: An experiment. *College Composition and Communication, 16,* 122–124.

Clarke, M. (1978). Reading in Spanish and English: Evidence from adult ESL students. *Language Learning, 29,* 121–150.

Clayton, T. (1993). Using background knowledge to stimulate composition in Malay students. In M. N. Brock & L. Walters (Eds.), *Teaching composition around the Pacific Rim: Politics and pedagogy* (pp. 48–60). Bristol, England: Multilingual Matters.

Cochran-Smith, M. (1991). Word processing and writing in elementary classrooms: A critical review of related literature. *Review of Educational Research, 61,* 107–155.

Coe, R. M. (1987). An apology for form: Or, who took the form out of process? *College English, 49,* 13–28.

Cohen, A. (1987). Student processing of feedback on their compositions. In A. L. Wenden & J. Rubin (Eds.), *Learner strategies in language learning* (pp. 57–69). Englewood Cliffs, NJ: Prentice-Hall.

Cohen, A. (1990). *Second language learning: Insights for teachers, learners, and researchers.* New York: Newbury House/Harper & Row.

Cohen, A. (1994). *Assessing language ability in the classroom* (2nd ed.). Boston: Heinle & Heinle.

Cohen, A., & Cavalcanti, M. (1990). Feedback on compositions: Teacher and student verbal reports. In B. Kroll (Ed.), *Second language writing: Research insights for the classroom* (pp. 155–177). New York: Cambridge University Press.

Cohen, A. D., & Robbins, M. (1976). Toward assessing interlanguage performance: The relationship between selected errors, learners' characteristics, and learners' expectations. *Language Learning, 26,* 45–66.

Coles, W. E. (1974a). *Composing: Writing as a self-creating process.* Upper Montclair, NJ: Boynton/Cook.

Coles, W. E. (1974b). *Teaching composing: A guide to teaching writing as a self-creating process.* Rochelle Park, NJ: Hayden.

Coles, W. E. (1978). *The plural I: The teaching of writing.* New York: Holt, Rinehart & Winston.

Coles, W. E. (1980). *Composing II: Writing as a self-creating process.* Upper Montclair, NJ: Boynton/Cook.

Collette, C. P., & Johnson, R. (1997). *Finding common ground: A guide to personal, professional, and public writing* (2nd ed.). New York: Longman.

Connor, U. (1996). *Contrastive rhetoric: Cross-cultural aspects of second-language writing.* Cambridge, England: Cambridge University Press.

Connor, U., & Asenavage, K. (1994). Peer response groups in ESL writing classes: How much impact on revision? *Journal of Second Language Writing, 3,* 257–276.

Connor, U., & Farmer, M. (1990). The teaching of topical structure analysis as a revision strategy for ESL writers. In B. Kroll (Ed.), *Second language writing: Research insights for the classroom* (pp. 126–139). Cambridge, England: Cambridge University Press.

Connor, U., & Kaplan, R. B. (Eds.). (1987). *Writing across languages: Analysis of L2 text.* Reading, MA: Addison-Wesley.

Connors, R., & Lunsford, A. (1993). Teachers' rhetorical comments on student papers. *College Composition and Communication, 44,* 200–223.

Cook, V. J., & Newson, M. (1996). *Chomsky's Universal Grammar: An introduction.* Oxford: Blackwell.

Cooper, C., & Odell, L. (Eds.). (1977). *Evaluating writing: Describing, measuring, judging.* Urbana, IL: National Council of Teachers of English.

Cooper, C. R. (1975). Measuring growth in writing. *English Journal, 64,* 111–120.

Cross, D. (1991). *A practical handbook of language teaching.* Englewood Cliffs, NJ: Prentice-Hall/Regents.

Cumming, A. (1985). Responding to the writing of ESL students. *Highway One, 8,* 58–78.

Cumming, A. (1989). Writing expertise and second language proficiency. *Language Learning, 39,* 81–141.

Cumming, A. (1990a). Expertise in evaluating second language compositions. *Language Testing, 7,* 31–51.

Cumming, A. (1990b). The thinking, interactions, and participation to foster in adult ESL literacy instruction. *TESL Talk, 20,* 34–51.

Cummins, J. (1981). The role of primary language development in promoting educational success for language minority students. In *Schooling and language minority students: A theoretical framework* (pp. 3–49). Los Angeles: California State University Evaluation, Dissemination, and Assessment Center.

Cummins, J. (1984). *Bilingualism and special education.* San Diego, CA: College Hill.

Curtis, M. S. (1988). Windows on composing: Teaching revision on word processors. *College Composition and Communication, 39,* 337–344.

Cziko, G. (1978). Differences in first and second language reading: The use of syntactic, semantic and discourse constraints. *Canadian Modern Language Review, 34,* 473–489.

D'Aoust, C. (1992). Portfolios: Process for students and teachers. In K. B. Yancey (Ed.), *Portfolios in the writing classroom* (pp. 39–48). Urbana, IL: National Council of Teachers of English.

Daiker, D., Kerek, A., Morenberg, M., & Sommers, J. (1994). *The writer's options: Combining to composing* (5th ed.). New York: HarperCollins College Publishers.

Daiute, C. (1985). *Writing and computers.* Reading, MA: Addison-Wesley.

Dalton, D. W., & Hannafin, M. J. (1986). The effects of word processing on written composition. *Journal of Educational Research, 80,* 338–342.

Dawe, C. W., & Dornan, E. A. (1997). *One to one: Resources for conference-centered writing* (5th ed.). New York: Longman.

Davis, C. (1993, March). A Mason–Dixon memory. *Reader's Digest, 142* (851), 49–53.

Day, S. X., McMahan, E., & Funk, R. (1997). *The practical writer's guide with additional readings.* Boston: Allyn & Bacon.

DeFord, D. (1981). Literacy: Reading, writing, and other essentials. *Language Arts, 58,* 652–658.

Delpit, L. (1988). The silenced dialogue: Power and pedagogy in educating other people's children. *Harvard Educational Review, 58,* 280–298.

Devine, J. (1993). The role of metacognition in second language reading and writing. In J. Carson & I. Leki (Eds.), *Reading in the composition classroom: Second language perspectives* (pp. 105–127). Boston: Heinle & Heinle.

Devine, J., Carrell, P., & Eskey, D. (Eds.). (1987). *Research in reading English as a second language.* Washington, DC: TESOL.

DeVries, T. (1970). Reading, writing, frequency, and expository writing. *Reading Improvement, 7,* 14–19.

Dodds, J. (1997). *The ready reference handbook: Writing, revising, editing.* Boston: Allyn & Bacon.

Donalson, K. (1967). Variables distinguishing between effective and ineffective writers in the tenth grade. *Journal of Experimental Education, 4,* 37–41.

Doxiadis, D. (1990). Facing a different culture. In R. Spack (Ed.), *Guidelines: A cross-cultural reading/writing text* (pp. 98–100). New York: St. Martin's.

Doyle, W. (1983). Academic work. *Review of Educational Research, 52,* 159–199.

Dubin, F., Eskey, D., & Grabe, W. (Eds.). (1986). *Teaching second language reading for academic purposes.* Reading, MA: Addison-Wesley.

Dubin, F., & Olshtain, E. (1986). *Course design: Developing programs and materials for language learning.* Cambridge, England: Cambridge University Press.

Dumicich, J., & Root, C. (1996). *Drawing on experience: The fundamentals of good writing.* New York: McGraw-Hill.

Dupuy, B., Tse, L., & Cook, T. (1996). Bringing books into the classroom: First steps in turning college-level ESL students into readers. *TESOL Journal, 5*(4), 10–15.

Dyson, A. H. (Ed.). (1989). *Collaboration through writing and reading: Exploring possibilities.* Urbana, IL: National Council of Teachers of English.

Ede, L., & Lunsford, A. (1984). Audience addressed/audience invoked: The role of audience in composition theory and pedagogy. *College Composition and Communication, 35,* 155–171.

Edelsky, C. (1982). Writing in a bilingual program: The relation of L1 and L2 texts. *TESOL Quarterly, 16,* 211–228.

Ediger, A., Ching, R., & Poole, D. (Eds.). (1996). Why ESL articulation is a burning issue [Special issue]. *CATESOL Journal, 9,* 1.

Educational Testing Service. (1996). *Test of Written English Guide* (4th ed.). Princeton, NJ: Educational Testing Service.

Eisterhold, J. C. (1990). Reading-writing connections: Toward a description for second language learners. In B. Kroll (Ed.), *Second language writing: Research insights for the classroom* (pp. 88–101). Cambridge, England: Cambridge University Press.

Elbow, P. (1973). *Writing without teachers.* New York: Oxford University Press.

Elbow, P. (1981a). *Embracing contraries: Explorations in learning and teaching.* New York: Oxford University Press.

Elbow, P. (1981b). *Writing with power: Techniques for mastering the writing process.* New York: Oxford University Press.

Elbow, P. (1993). Ranking, evaluating, and liking: Sorting out three forms of judgment. *College English, 55,* 187–206.

Elbow, P., & Belanoff, P. (1991). SUNY Stony Brook portfolio-based evaluation program. In P. Belanoff & M. Dickson (Eds.), *Portfolios: Process and product* (pp. 3–16). Portsmouth, NH: Boynton/Cook.

Elley, W. (1984). Exploring the reading difficulties of second language learners and second languages in Fiji. In J. Alderson & A. Urquhart (Eds.), *Reading in a foreign language* (pp. 281–297). London: Longman.

Elley, W. (1991). Acquiring literacy in a second language: The effect of book-based programs. *Language Learning, 41,* 375–411.

Elley, W., & Mangubhai, F. (1983). The impact of reading on second language learning. *Reading Research Quarterly, 19,* 53–67.

Ellis, R. (1994). *The study of second language acquisition.* Oxford: Oxford University Press.

Emig, J. (1971). *The composing processes of twelfth graders.* Urbana, IL: National Council of Teachers of English.

Eschholz, P. A. (1980). The prose models approach: Using products in the process. In T. R. Donovan & B. W. McClelland (Eds.), *Eight approaches to teaching composition.* Urbana, IL: National Council of Teachers of English.

Eskey, D. E. (1983). Meanwhile, back in the real world ... Accuracy and fluency in second language teaching. *TESOL Quarterly, 17,* 315–323.

Eskey, D. E. (1986). Theoretical foundations. In F. Dubin, D. Eskey, & W. Grabe (Eds.), *Teaching second language reading for academic purposes* (pp. 3–21). Reading, MA: Addison-Wesley.

Eskey, D. E. (1993). Reading and writing as both cognitive process and social behavior. In J. Carson & I. Leki (Eds.), *Reading in the composition classroom: Second language perspectives* (pp. 221–233). Boston: Heinle & Heinle.

Eskey, D. E., & Grabe, W. (1988). Interactive models for second language reading: Perspectives on instruction. In P. Carrell, J. Devine, & D. Eskey (Eds.), *Interactive approaches to second language reading* (pp. 223–238). Cambridge, England: Cambridge University Press.

Etchison, C. (1989). Word processing: A helpful tool for basic writers. *Computers and Composition, 6*(2), 33–43.

Evanechko, P., Ollila, L., & Armstrong, R. (1974). An investigation of the relationships between children's performance in written language and their reading ability. *Research in the Teaching of English, 8,* 315–326.

Fader, D. (1976). *Hooked on books.* New York: Berkeley Books.

Faigley, L. (1986). Competing theories of process: A critique and a proposal. *College English, 48,* 527–542.

Faigley, L., & Witte, S. (1981). Analyzing revision. *College Composition and Communication, 32,* 401–414.

Faigley, L., Cherry, R. D., Jolliffe, D. A., & Skinner, A. M. (1985). *Assessing writers' knowledge and processes of composing.* Norwood, NJ: Ablex.

Fathman, A., & Whalley, E. (1990). Teacher response to student writing: Focus on form versus content. In B. Kroll (Ed.), *Second language writing: Research insights for the classroom* (pp. 178–190). New York: Cambridge University Press.

Ferris, D. R. (1992, April). *Turning ESL writers into editors: A process approach.* Paper presented at the CATESOL State Conference, Sacramento, CA.

Ferris, D. R. (1993). The design of an automatic analysis program for L2 text research: Necessity and feasibility. *Journal of Second Language Writing, 2,* 119–129.

Ferris, D. R. (1994). Rhetorical strategies in student persuasive writing: Differences between native and non-native English speakers. *Research in the Teaching of English, 28,* 45–65.

Ferris, D. R. (1995a). Can advanced ESL students become effective self-editors? *CATESOL Journal, 8,* 41–62.

Ferris, D. R. (1995b). Student reactions to teacher response in multiple-draft composition classrooms. *TESOL Quarterly, 29,* 33–53.

Ferris, D. R. (1995c). Teaching ESL composition students to become independent self-editors. *TESOL Journal, 4*(4), 18–22.

Ferris, D. R. (1997). The influence of teacher commentary on student revision. *TESOL Quarterly, 31,* 315–339.

Ferris, D. R., Pezone, S., Tade, C. R., & Tinti, S. (1997). Teacher commentary on student writing: Descriptions and implications. *Journal of Second Language Writing, 6,* 155–182.

Ferris, D. R., & Tagg, T. (1996). Academic oral communication needs of EAP learners: What subject-matter instructors actually require. *TESOL Quarterly, 30,* 31–58.

Findlay, C. A., & Nathan, L. A. (1980). Functional language objectives. *TESOL Quarterly, 14,* 221–231.

Finegan, E. (1994). *Language: Its structure and use* (2nd ed.). Fort Worth, TX: Harcourt, Brace.

Finocchiaro, M., & Brumfit, C. (1983). *The functional-notional approach: From theory to practice.* Oxford: Oxford University Press.

Flachman, K., & Pluta, K. (1996). Building bridges: Articulating writing programs between two- and four-year colleges. *CATESOL Journal, 9,* 227–236.

Flahive, D., & Bailey, N. (1993). Exploring reading/writing relationships in adult second language learners. In J. Carson & I. Leki (Eds.), *Reading in the composition classroom: Second language perspectives* (pp. 128–140). Boston: Heinle & Heinle.

Flower, L. (1979). Writer-based prose: A cognitive basis for problems in writing. *College English, 41,* 19–38.

Flower, L. (1985). *Problem-solving strategies for writing* (2nd ed.). San Diego: Harcourt Brace Jovanovich.

Flower, L. (1989). *Problem-solving strategies for writing* (3rd ed.). San Diego: Harcourt Brace Jovanovich.

Flower, L. S., & Hayes, J. R. (1980). The cognition of discovery: Defining a rhetorical problem. *College Composition and Communication, 31,* 21–32.

Flower, L. S., & Hayes, J. R. (1981). A cognitive process theory of writing. *College Composition and Communication, 32,* 365–387.

Flower, L., Stein, V., Ackerman, J., Kantz, M., McCormick, K., & Peck, W. (1990). *Reading-to-write: Exploring a cognitive and social process.* New York: Oxford University Press.

Fox, L. (1992). *Focus on editing.* London: Longman.

Frank, M. (1990). *Writing as thinking: A guided process approach.* Englewood Cliffs, NJ: Prentice-Hall.

Freedman, S. W. (1979). How characteristics of student essays influence teachers' evaluations. *Journal of Educational Psychology, 71,* 328–338.

Freedman, S. W. (1987). *Response to student writing.* Urbana, IL: National Council of Teachers of English.

Freedman, S. W. (1991). Evaluating writing: Linking large-scale testing and classroom assessment. *Center for the Study of Writing, Occasional Paper, 27.* Berkeley, CA: University of California.

Freedman, S. W., & Katz, A. (1987). Pedagogical interaction during the composing process: The writing conference. In A. Matsuhasi (Ed.), *Writing in real time: Modeling production processes* (pp. 58–80). New York: Academic Press.

Freedman, S. W., & Sperling, M. (1985). Written language acquisition: The role of response and the writing conference. In S. W. Freedman (Ed.), *The acquisition of written language* (pp. 106–130). Norwood, NJ: Ablex.

Friedlander, A. (1990). Composing in English: Effects of a first language on writing in English as a second language. In B. Kroll (Ed.), *Second language writing: Research insights for the classroom* (pp. 109–125). Cambridge, England: Cambridge University Press.

Fries, C. (1945). *Teaching and learning English as a second language.* Ann Arbor, MI: University of Michigan Press.

Frodesen, J. (1991). Grammar in writing. In M. Celce-Murcia (Ed.), *Teaching English as a second or foreign language* (2nd ed., pp. 264–276). Boston: Heinle & Heinle.

Frodesen, J. (1995). Negotiating the syllabus: A learning-centered, interactive approach to ESL graduate writing course design. In D. Belcher & G. Braine (Eds.), *Academic writing in a second language: Essays on research & pedagogy* (pp. 331–350). Norwood, NJ: Ablex.

Gajdusek, L., & van Dommelen, D. (1993). Literature and critical thinking in the composition classroom. In J. Carson & I. Leki (Eds.), *Reading in the composition classroom: Second language perspectives* (pp. 197–217). Boston: Heinle & Heinle.

Garlow, K. (1996). The challenge of articulating ESL courses in postsecondary education: Policy and legislative issues. *CATESOL Journal, 9,* 153–174.

Garrison, R. (1974). One-to-one: Tutorial instruction in freshman composition. *New Directions for Community Colleges, 2,* 55–83.

Gaskill, B. (1996). Articulation agreements between intensive ESL programs and postsecondary institutions. *CATESOL Journal, 9,* 117–127.

Gee, J. P. (1992). *The social mind: Language, ideology, and social practice.* New York: Bergin & Garvey.

Gee, J. P. (1996). *Social linguistics and literacies: Ideologies in discourses* (2nd ed.). Bristol, PA: Taylor & Francis.

Goldman, S., Reyes, M., & Varnhagen, C. (1984). Understanding fables in first and second languages. *NABE Journal, 8*(1), 35–66.

Goldman, S., & Trueba, H. (Eds.). (1987). *Becoming literate in English as a second language.* Norwood, NJ: Ablex.

Goldstein, L. M. (1993). Becoming a member of the "teaching foreign languages" community: Integrating reading and writing through an adjunct/content course. In J. Carson & I. Leki (Eds.), *Reading in the composition classroom: Second language perspectives* (pp. 290–298). Boston: Heinle & Heinle.

Goldstein, L. M., & Conrad, S. (1990). Student input and the negotiation of meaning in ESL writing conferences. *TESOL Quarterly, 24,* 443–460.

Goodman, K. S., Goodman, Y. M., & Hood, W. J. (Eds.). (1989). *The Whole Language evaluation book.* Portsmouth, NH: Heinemann.

Goodwin, A. A., Hamrick, J., & Stewart, T. C. (1993). Instructional delivery via e-mail. *TESOL Journal, 3*(1), 24–27.

Goshgarian, G., & Krueger, K. (1997). *Crossfire: An argument rhetoric and reader* (2nd ed.). London: Longman.

Gower, R., & Walters, S. (1983). *Teaching practice handbook: A reference book for EFL teachers in training.* Portsmouth, NH: Heinemann.

Grabe, W. (1988). Reassessing the term "interactive." In P. Carrell, J. Devine, & D. Eskey (Eds.), *Interactive approaches to second language reading* (pp. 56–70). Cambridge, England: Cambridge University Press.

Grabe, W. (1991). Current developments in second language reading research. *TESOL Quarterly, 25,* 375–406.

Grabe, W., & Kaplan, R. B. (1996). *Theory and practice of writing.* London: Longman.

Grabe, W., & Kaplan, R. B. (1997). The writing course. In K. Bardovi-Harlig & B. Hartford (Eds.), *Beyond methods: Components of second language teacher education* (pp. 172–197). New York: McGraw-Hill.

Graves, R. L. (Ed.). (1990). *Rhetoric and composition: A sourcebook for teachers and writers* (3rd ed.). Portsmouth, NH: Boynton Cook/Heinemann.

Greenhalgh, A. M. (1992). Voices in response: A postmodern reading of teacher response. *College Composition and Communication, 43,* 401–410.

Grobe, S., & Grobe, C. (1977, October). Reading skill as a correlate of writing ability in college freshmen. *Reading World,* 50–54.

Gunderson, L. (1991). *ESL literacy instruction: A guidebook to theory and practice.* Englewood Cliffs, NJ: Regents/Prentice-Hall.

Haas, C. (1989). How the writing medium shapes the writing process: Effects of word processing on planning. *Research in the Teaching of English, 23,* 181–207.

Hacker, D. (1995). *A writer's reference* (3rd ed.). New York: St. Martin's/Bedford Books.

Hafiz, F., & Tudor, I. (1989). Extensive reading and the development of language skills. *ELT Journal, 43,* 1–13.

Hairston, M. (1982). The winds of change: Thomas Kuhn and the revolution in the teaching of writing. *College Composition and Communication, 33,* 76–88.

Hairston, M. (1986). Using nonfiction literature in the composition classroom. In B. Petersen (Ed.), *Convergences: Transactions in reading and writing* (pp. 179–188). Urbana, IL: National Council of Teachers of English.

Hakuta, K. (1976). Becoming bilingual: A case study of a Japanese child learning English. *Language Learning, 26,* 321–351.

Hakuta, K. (1986). *Mirror of language: The debate on bilingualism.* New York: Basic Books.

Hakuta, K., & D'Andrea, D. (1992). Some properties of bilingual maintenance and loss in Mexican background high-school students. *Applied Linguistics, 13,* 72–99.

Hamp-Lyons, L. (1985). Two approaches to teaching reading: A classroom-based study. *Reading in a Foreign Language, 3,* 363–373.

Hamp-Lyons, L. (1989). Raters respond to rhetoric in writing. In H. W. Dechert & M. Raupauch (Eds.), *Interlingual processes* (pp. 229–244). Tübingen: Gunter Narr.

Hamp-Lyons, L. (Ed.). (1991a). *Assessing second language writing in academic contexts.* Norwood, NJ: Ablex.

Hamp-Lyons, L. (1991b). Basic concepts. In L. Hamp-Lyons (Ed.), *Assessing second language writing in academic contexts* (pp. 5–15). Norwood, NJ: Ablex.

Hamp-Lyons, L. (1991c). Scoring procedures for ESL contexts. In L. Hamp-Lyons (Ed.), *Assessing second language writing in academic contexts* (pp. 241–276). Norwood, NJ: Ablex.

Hamp-Lyons, L., & Condon, W. (1993). Questioning assumptions about portfolio-based assessment. *College Composition and Communication, 44,* 176–190.

Hanson-Smith, E. (1990). Word-processed composition. *TESOL Newsletter, 24*(3), 23.

Harris, J. (1985). Student writers and word processing: A preliminary evaluation. *College Composition and Communication, 36,* 323–330.

Harris, M. (1986). *Teaching one-to-one: The writing conference.* Urbana, IL: National Council of Teachers of English.

Harste, J. (1988). *Creating classrooms for authors: The reading–writing connection.* Portsmouth, NH: Heinemann.

Hashimoto, I. Y. (1991). *Thirteen weeks: A guide to teaching college writing.* Portsmouth, NH: Boynton/Cook Heinemann.

Hawisher, G. E. (1987). The effects of word processing on the revision strategies of college freshmen. *Research in the Teaching of English, 21,* 145–159.

Hayes, J. R., & Flower, L. (1983). Uncovering cognitive processes in writing: An introduction to protocol analysis. In P. Mosenthal, L. Tamar, & S. A. Walmsley (Eds.), *Research in writing* (pp. 206–220). New York: Longman.

Heath, S. B. (1986). Sociocultural contexts of language development. In *Beyond language: Social and cultural factors in schooling language minority students* (pp. 145–186). Los Angeles: California State University Evaluation, Dissemination, and Assessment Center.

Hedgcock, J., & Atkinson, D. (1993). Differing reading–writing relationships in L1 and L2 literacy development. *TESOL Quarterly, 27,* 329–333.

Hedgcock, J., & Lefkowitz, N. (1992). Collaborative oral/aural revision in foreign language writing instruction. *Journal of Second Language Writing, 1,* 255–276.

Hedgcock, J., & Lefkowitz, N. (1994). Feedback on feedback: Assessing learner receptivity to teacher response in L2 composing. *Journal of Second Language Writing, 3,* 141–163.

Hedgcock, J., & Lefkowitz, N. (1996). Some input on input: Two analyses of student response to expert feedback in L2 writing. *The Modern Language Journal, 80,* 287–308.

Hedgcock, J., & Pucci, S. (1993). Whole language applications to ESL in secondary and higher education. *TESOL Journal, 3*(2), 22–26.

Hendrickson, J. (1976). *Error analysis and selective correction in the adult ESL classroom: An experiment.* Washington, DC: Educational Resources Information Center. (ERIC Document Reproduction Service No. ED 135 260).

Hendrickson, J. (1978). Error correction in foreign language teaching: Recent theory, research, and practice. *The Modern Language Journal, 62,* 387–392.

Henning, G. (1991). Issues in evaluating and maintaining an ESL writing assessment program. In L. Hamp-Lyons (Ed.), *Assessing second language writing in academic contexts* (pp. 279–291). Norwood, NJ: Ablex.

Herman, J. L., Aschbacher, P. R., & Winters, L. (1992). *A practical guide to alternative assessment.* Alexandria, VA: Association for Supervision and Curriculum Development.

Herman, J. L., Gearhart, M., & Aschbacher, P. R. (1996). Portfolios for classroom assessment: Design and implementation issues. In R. Calfee & P. Perfumo (Eds.), *Writing portfolios in the classroom: Policy and practice, promise and peril* (pp. 27–59). Hillsdale, NJ: Lawrence Erlbaum Associates.

Heys, F. (1962). The theme-a-week assumption: A report of an experiment. *English Journal, 51,* 320–322.

Hill, C. E. (1990). *Writing from the margins: Power and pedagogy for teachers of composition.* New York: Oxford University Press.

Hillocks, G., Jr. (1982). The interaction of instruction, teacher comment, and revision in teaching the composing process. *Research in the Teaching of English, 16,* 261–278.

Hillocks, G., Jr. (1986). *Research on written composition: New directions for teaching.* Urbana, IL: ERIC Clearinghouse on Reading and Communication Skills and the National Conference on Research in English.

Hillocks, G., Jr. (1995). *Teaching writing as reflective practice.* New York: Teachers College Press.

Hinds, J. (1983a). Contrastive rhetoric: Japanese and English. *Text, 3,* 183–195.

Hinds, J. (1983b). Linguistics in written discourse in particular languages: Contrastive studies in Japanese and English. In R. B. Kaplan (Ed.), *Annual review of applied linguistics, III* (pp. 78–84). Rowley, MA: Newbury House.

Hinds, J. (1987). Reader vs. writer responsibility: A new typology. In U. Connor & R. B. Kaplan (Eds.), *Writing across languages: Analysis of L2 text* (pp. 141–152). Reading, MA: Addison-Wesley.

Hirsch, E. D. (1977). *The philosophy of composition.* Chicago: University of Chicago Press.

Hodges, E. (1992). The unheard voices of our responses to students' writing. *Journal of Teaching Writing, 11,* 203–218.

Horowitz, D. (1986a). The author responds to Liebman-Kleine. *TESOL Quarterly, 20,* 788–790.

Horowitz, D. (1986b). Process, not product: Less than meets the eye. *TESOL Quarterly, 20,* 141–144.

Horowitz, D. (1986c). What professors actually require: Academic tasks for the ESL classroom. *TESOL Quarterly, 20,* 445–462.

Horowitz, D. (1990). Fiction and nonfiction in the ESL/EFL classroom: Does the difference make a difference? *English for Specific Purposes, 9,* 161–168.

Huang, S. (1994). Learning to critique and revise in an English-as-a-foreign-language university writing class. *Dissertation Abstracts International, 55*(10), 3120–A.

Hughes, A. (1989). *Testing for language teachers.* Cambridge, England: Cambridge University Press.

Hughey, J., Wormuth, D., Hartfiel, F., & Jacobs, H. (1983). *Teaching ESL composition: Principles and techniques.* Rowley, MA: Newbury House.

Hulstijn, J. (1991). How is reading in a second language related to reading in a first language? *AILA Review, 8,* 5–14.

Hunter, M. (1984). Knowing, teaching, and supervising. In P. Hosford (Ed.), *Using what we know about teaching* (pp. 169–192). Alexandria, VA: Association for Supervision and Curriculum Development.

Hunter, M., & Russell, D. (1977). How can I plan more effective lessons? *Instructor, 87,* 74–75.

Huot, B. (1990). Reliability, validity, and holistic scoring: What we know and what we need to know. *College Composition and Communication, 41,* 201–213.

Hyland, K. (1990). Providing productive feedback. *ELT Journal, 44,* 279–285.

Ihde, T. W. (1994, March). *Feedback in L2 writing.* Revised version of a paper presented at the American Association for Applied Linguistics, Baltimore, MD. (ERIC Document Reproduction Service No. ED 369 287).

Illo, J. (1976). From senior to freshman: A study of performance in English composition in high school and college. *Research in the Teaching of English, 10,* 127–136.

Jacobs, H. L., Zingraf, S., Wormuth, D., Hartfiel, V., & Hughey, J. (1981). *Testing ESL composition: A practical approach.* Rowley, MA: Newbury House.

Jacobs, S., & Karliner, A. (1977). Helping writers to think: The effect of speech roles in individual conferences on the quality of thought in student writing. *College English, 38,* 489–505.

James, M. (1987). ESL reading pedagogy: Implications of a schema-theoretical approach. In J. Devine, P. Carrell, & D. Eskey (Eds.), *Research in reading in English as a second language* (pp. 177–188). Washington, DC: TESOL.

Janopoulos, M. (1986). The relationship of pleasure reading and second language writing proficiency. *TESOL Quarterly, 20,* 763–768.

Janopoulos, M. (1992). University faculty tolerance of NS and NNS writing errors. *Journal of Second Language Writing, 1,* 109–122.

Jensen, G. H., & DiTiberio, J. K (1989). *Personality and the teaching of composition.* Norwood, NJ: Ablex.

Johns, A. M. (1986). Coherence and academic writing: Some definitions and suggestions for teaching. *TESOL Quarterly, 20,* 247–266.

Johns, A. M. (1988a). Another reader reacts. *TESOL Quarterly, 22,* 705–707.

Johns, A. M. (1988b). The discourse communities dilemma: Identifying transferable skills for the academic milieu. *English for Specific Purposes, 7,* 55–60.

Johns, A. M. (1990). L1 composition theories: Implications for developing theories of L2 composition. In B. Kroll (Ed.), *Second language writing: Research insights for the classroom* (pp. 24–36). Cambridge, England: Cambridge University Press.

Johns, A. M. (1991). Faculty assessment of student literacy skills: Implications for writing assessment. In L. Hamp-Lyons (Ed.), *Assessing second language writing in academic contexts* (pp. 167–179). Norwood, NJ: Ablex.

Johns, A. M. (1993). Reading and writing tasks in English for academic purposes classes: Products, processes, and resources. In J. Carson & I. Leki (Eds.), *Reading in the composition classroom: Second language perspectives* (pp. 274–289). Boston: Heinle & Heinle.

Johns, A. M. (1995a). Genre and pedagogical purposes. *Journal of Second Language Writing, 4,* 181–190.

Johns, A. M. (1995b). Teaching classroom and authentic genres: Initiating students into academic cultures and discourses. In D. Belcher & G. Braine (Eds.), *Academic writing in a second language: Essays on research and pedagogy* (pp. 277–291). Norwood, NJ: Ablex.

Johns, A. M., & Davies, F. (1981). Text as a vehicle for information. *Reading in a Foreign Language, 1,* 1–19.

Johnson, D. M., & Roen, D. H. (Eds.). (1989). *Richness in writing: Empowering ESL students.* New York: Longman.

Johnson, P. (1986). Acquisition of schema for comprehension and communication: A study of the reading–writing relationships in ESL. *RELC Journal, 17,* 1–13.

Jones, C., & Fortescue, S. (1987). *Using computers in the classroom.* London: Longman.

Jones, S. (1985). Problems with monitor use in second language composing. In M. Rose (Ed.), *Studies in writer's block and other composing process problems* (pp. 96–118). New York: Guilford.

Jones, S., & Tetroe, J. (1987). Composing in a second language. In A. Matsuhashi (Ed.), *Writing in real time: Modeling production processes* (pp. 34–57). Norwood, NJ: Ablex.

Just, M., & Carpenter, P. (1987). *The psychology of reading and language comprehension.* Boston: Allyn & Bacon.

Kadesch, M. C., Kolba, E. D., & Crowell, S. C. (1991). *Insights into academic writing: Strategies for advanced students.* New York: Longman.

Kantz, M. (1990). Helping students use textual sources persuasively. *College English, 52,* 74–91.

Kaplan, R. B. (1966). Cultural thought patterns in intercultural communication. *Language Learning, 16,* 1–20.

Kaplan, R. B. (1967). Contrastive rhetoric and the teaching of composition. *TESOL Quarterly, 1,* 10–16.

Kaplan, R. B. (1983). *Annual Review of Applied Linguistics III.* Rowley, MA: Newbury House.

Kaplan, R. B. (1987). Cultural thought patterns revisited. In U. Connor & R. B. Kaplan (Eds.), *Writing across languages: Analysis of L2 text* (pp. 9–27). Reading, MA: Addison-Wesley.

Kaplan, R. B. (1988). Contrastive rhetoric and second language learning: Notes toward a theory of contrastive rhetoric. In A. C. Purves (Ed.), *Writing across languages and cultures: Issues in contrastive rhetoric* (pp. 275–304). Newbury Park, CA: Sage.

Kassen, M. A. (1988). Native and non-native speaker teacher response to foreign language learner writing: A study of intermediate-level French. *Texas Papers in Foreign Language Education, 1*(1), 1–15.

Keh, C. (1990). Feedback in the writing process: A model and methods for implementation. *ELT Journal, 44,* 294–304.

Kennedy, X. J., Kennedy, D. M., & Holladay, S. A. (1997). *The compact Bedford guide for college writers* (4th ed.). Boston: Bedford Books/St. Martin's.

Kepner, C. G. (1991). An experiment in the relationship of types of written feedback to the development of second-language writing skills. *The Modern Language Journal, 75,* 305–313.

Kinsella, K., & Sherak, K. (1995). Classroom work style survey. In J. M. Reid (Ed.), *Learning styles in the ESL/EFL classroom* (pp. 235–237). Boston, MA: Heinle & Heinle.

Kirszner, L. G., & Mandell, S. R. (1996). *Windows on writing: Practice in context (with additional readings).* New York: St. Martin's.

Klimenkov, M., & LaPick, N. (1996). Promoting student self-assessment through portfolios, student-facilitated conferences, and cross-age interaction. In R. Calfee & P. Perfumo (Eds.), *Writing portfolios in the classroom: Policy and practice, promise and peril* (pp. 239–259). Hillsdale, NJ: Lawrence Erlbaum Associates.

Knoblauch, C. H., & Brannon, L. (1981). Teacher commentary on student writing: The state of the art. *Freshman English News, 10,* 1–4.

Knoblauch, C. H., & Brannon, L. (1984). *Rhetorical traditions and the teaching of writing.* Upper Montclair, NJ: Boynton/Cook Publishers.

Koch, R. (1982). Syllogisms and superstitions: The current state of responding to writing. *Language Arts, 59,* 464–471.

Kozma, R. B. (1991). Computer-based writing tools and the cognitive needs of novice writers. *Computers and Composition, 8*(2), 31–45.

Krapels, A. R. (1990). An overview of second language writing process research. In B. Kroll (Ed.), *Second language writing: Research insights for the classroom* (pp. 37–56). Cambridge, England: Cambridge University Press.

Krashen, S. D. (1984). *Writing: Research, theory, and application.* Oxford: Pergamon.

Krashen, S. D. (1985a). *The input hypothesis: Issues and implications.* New York: Longman.

Krashen, S. D. (1985b). *Inquiries & insights: Second language teaching, immersion & bilingual education, literacy.* Englewood Cliffs, NJ: Alemany/Prentice-Hall.

Krashen, S. D. (1988). Do we learn to read by reading? The relationship between free reading and reading ability. In D. Tannen (Ed.), *Linguistics in context: Connecting observation and under-standing* (pp. 269–298). Norwood, NJ: Ablex.

Krashen, S. D. (1993). *The power of reading.* Englewood, CO: Libraries Unlimited.

Krashen, S. D. (1994). *The pleasure hypothesis.* Paper presented at the Georgetown Round Table on Language and Linguistics, Washington, DC.

Kroll, B. (1978). Cognitive egocentrism and the problem of audience awareness in written discourse. *Research in the Teaching of English, 12,* 269–281.

Kroll, B. (1991). Teaching writing in the ESL context. In M. Celce-Murcia (Ed.), *Teaching English as a second or foreign language* (2nd ed., pp. 245–263). New York: Newbury House.

Kroll, B. (1993). Teaching writing IS teaching reading: Training the new teacher of ESL composition. In J. Carson & I. Leki (Eds.), *Reading in the composition classroom: Second language perspectives* (pp. 61–81). Boston: Heinle & Heinle.

Kroll, B., & Reid, J. (1994). Guidelines for designing writing prompts: Clarifications, caveats, and cautions. *Journal of Second Language Writing, 3,* 231–255.

Kroll, B., & Reid, J. (1995). Designing and assessing effective classroom writing assignments for NES and ESL students. *Journal of Second Language Writing, 4,* 17–41.

Kucer, S. (1985). The making of meaning: Reading and writing as parallel processes. *Written Communication, 2,* 317–336.

Kucer, S. (1989). Reading a text: Does the author make a difference? In B. Lawson, S. Sterr Ryan, & W. R. Winterowd (Eds.), *Encountering student texts: Interpretive issues in reading student writing* (pp. 159–168). Urbana, IL: National Council of Teachers of English.

Kucer, S. (1991). Authenticity as the basis for instruction. *Language Arts, 68,* 532–540.

Kurth, R. J. (1987). Using word processing to enhance educational strategies during student writing activities. *Educational Technology, January,* 13–19.

Lalande, J. F. (1982). Reducing composition errors: An experiment. *The Modern Language Journal, 66,* 140–149.

Land, R., & Evans, S. (1987). What our students taught us about paper marking. *English Journal, 76,* 113–116.

Lane, J., & Lange, E. (1993). *Writing clearly: An editing guide.* Boston: Heinle & Heinle.

Larsen-Freeman, D., & Long, M. (1991). *An introduction to second language acquisition research.* London: Longman.

Latulippe, L. D. (1992). *Writing as a personal product.* Englewood Cliffs, NJ: Prentice-Hall.

Lauer, J. (1970). Heuristics and composition. *College Composition and Communication, 21,* 396–404.

Leeds, B. (Ed.). (1996). *Writing in a second language: Insights from first and second language teaching and research.* New York: Longman.

Lees, E. O. (1979). Evaluating student writing. *College Composition and Communication, 30,* 370–374.

Leki, I. (1990a). Coaching from the margins: Issues in written response. In B. Kroll (Ed.), *Second language writing: Research insights for the classroom* (pp. 57–68). New York: Cambridge University Press.

Leki, I. (1990b). Potential problems with peer responding in ESL writing classes. *CATESOL Journal, 3,* 5–19.

Leki, I. (1991a). Building expertise through sequenced writing assignments. *TESOL Journal, 1,* 19–23.

Leki, I. (1991b). The preferences of ESL students for error correction in college-level writing classes. *Foreign Language Annals, 24,* 203–218.

Leki, I. (1991c). Twenty-five years of contrastive rhetoric: Text analysis and writing pedagogies. *TESOL Quarterly, 25,* 123–143.

Leki, I. (1992). *Understanding ESL writers: A guide for teachers.* Portsmouth, NH: Boynton/Cook Publishers.

Leki, I. (1995a). *Academic writing: Exploring processes and strategies* (2nd ed.). New York: St. Martin's.

Leki, I. (1995b). Good writing: I know it when I see it. In D. Belcher & G. Braine (Eds.), *Academic writing in a second language: Essays on research and pedagogy* (pp. 23–46). Norwood, NJ: Ablex.

Leki, I., & Carson, J. (1994). Students' perceptions of EAP writing instruction and writing needs across the disciplines. *TESOL Quarterly, 28,* 81–101.

Lewin, K. (1951). *Field theory in social science.* New York: Harper Torchbooks.

Lewis, B., & Lewis, R. (1987). Do style checkers work work? *PC World, 5,* 247–252.

Lightbown, P. M., & Spada, N. (1994). Focus-on-form and corrective feedback in communicative language teaching. In H. D. Brown & S. Gonzo (Eds.), *Readings on second language acquisition* (pp. 306–329). Englewood Cliffs, NJ: Prentice-Hall.

Lindemann, E. (1987). *A rhetoric for writing teachers* (2nd ed.). New York: Oxford University Press.

Liou, H.-C. (1992). Investigation of using text-critiquing programs in a process-oriented writing class. *CALICO Journal, 10*(4), 17–38.

Liou, H.-C., Wang, S. H., & Hung-Yeh, Y. (1992). Can grammatical CALL help EFL writing instruction? *CALICO Journal, 10*(1), 23–44.

Lloyd-Jones, K. (1977). Primary trait scoring. In C. Cooper & L. Odell (Eds.), *Evaluating writing: Describing, measuring, judging* (pp. 96–124). Urbana, IL: National Council of Teachers of English.

Loban, W. (1976). *Language development: Kindergarten through grade twelve.* Urbana, IL: National Council of Teachers of English.

Lockhart, C., & Ng, P. (1995). Analyzing talk in peer response groups: Stances, functions, and content. *Language Learning, 45,* 605–655.

Long, M. H. (1994). The least a second language acquisition theory needs to explain. In H. D. Brown & S. Gonzo (Eds.), *Readings on second language acquisition* (pp. 470–487). Englewood Cliffs, NJ: Prentice-Hall.

Long, M. H., & Porter, P. (1985). Group work, interlanguage talk, and second language acquisition. *TESOL Quarterly, 19,* 207–228.

Low, G. (1985). Validity and the problem of direct language proficiency tests. In J. C. Alderson (Ed.), *Lancaster practical papers in English language education, 6* (pp. 151–168). Oxford: Pergamon.

Lumley, T., & McNamara, T. (1995). Rater characteristics and rater bias: Implications for training. *Language Testing, 12,* 54–71.

Lunsford, A., & Connors, R. (1992). *The St. Martin's handbook* (2nd ed.). New York: St. Martin's.

Lynch, B. K., & Hudson, T. (1991). EST reading. In M. Celce-Murcia (Ed.), *Teaching English as a second or foreign language* (2nd ed., pp. 216–232). New York: Newbury House.

MacDonald, R. E. (1991). *A handbook of basic skills and strategies for beginning teachers.* White Plains, NY: Longman.

Mace-Matluck, B., Dominguez, D., Holtzman, W., & Hoover, W. (1983). *Language and literacy in bilingual instruction.* Austin, TX: Southwest Educational Laboratory.

MacGowan-Gilhooly, A. (1991). Fluency first: Reversing the traditional ESL sequence. *Journal of Basic Writing, 10.*

Macrorie, K. (1980). *Searching writing.* Portsmouth, NH: Boynton/Cook Heinemann.

Macrorie, K. (1984). *Writing to be read* (rev. 3rd ed.). Portsmouth, NH: Boynton/Cook Heinemann.

Mager, R. F. (1975). *Preparing instructional objectives.* Belmont, CA: Fearon-Pitman.

Mallonee, B. C., & Breihan, J. R. (1985). Responding to students' drafts: Interdisciplinary consensus. *College Composition and Communication, 36,* 213–231.

Mangelsdorf, K. (1989). Parellels between speaking and writing in second language acquisition. In D. M. Johnson & D. H. Roen (Eds.), *Richness in writing: Empowering ESL students* (pp. 134–145). New York: Longman.

Mangelsdorf, K. (1992). Peer reviews in the ESL composition classroom: What do the students think? *ELT Journal, 46,* 274–284.

Mangelsdorf, K., & Posey, E. (1997). *Your choice: A basic writing guide with readings.* New York: St. Martin's.

Mangelsdorf, K., & Schlumberger, A. L. (1992). ESL student response stances in a peer-review task. *Journal of Second Language Writing, 1,* 235–254.

Master, P. (1996). *Systems of English grammar: An introduction for language teachers.* Englewood Cliffs, NJ: Prentice-Hall.

Mathews, E., Larsen, R., & Butler, G. (1945). Experimental investigation of the relation between reading training and achievement in college composition classes. *Journal of Educational Research, 38,* 499–505.

Matthews, A., Spratt, M., & Dangerfield, L. (Eds.). (1985). *At the chalkface: Practical techniques in language teaching.* London: Edward Arnold.

McAllister, C., & Louth, R. (1988). The effect of word processing on the quality of basic writers' revisions. *Research in the Teaching of English, 22,* 417–427.

McCabe, C. (1996). Restructuring student assessment and living to tell about it. In R. Calfee & P. Perfumo (Eds.), *Writing portfolios in the classroom: Policy and practice, promise and peril* (pp. 327–346). Hillsdale, NJ: Lawrence Erlbaum Associates.

McCarthy, M., & Carter, R. (1995). *Language as discourse: Perspectives for language teaching.* London: Longman.

McCormick, K., Waller, G., & Flower, L. (1987). *Reading texts: Reading, responding, writing.* Lexington, MA: D.C. Heath.

McKay, S. (Ed.). (1984). *Composing in a second language.* Rowley, MA: Newbury House.

McKay, S. (1993). *Agendas for second language literacy.* Cambridge, England: Cambridge University Press.

McKay, S. (1994). Developing ESL writing materials. *System, 22,* 195–203.

McLaughlin, B. (1987). Reading in a second language: Studies with adult and child learners. In S. Goldman & H. Trueba (Eds.), *Becoming literate in English as a second language* (pp. 57–70). Norwood, NJ: Ablex.

McNamara, T. (1996). *Measuring second language performance*. London: Longman.

McQuillan, J. (1994). Reading versus grammar: What students think is pleasurable for language acquisition. *Applied Language Learning, 5,* 95–100.

Mendonça, C. O., & Johnson, K. E. (1994). Peer review negotiations: Revision activities in ESL writing instruction. *TESOL Quarterly, 28,* 745–769.

Meyers, A. (1997). *Composing with confidence* (4th ed.). New York: Longman.

Milner, E. (1951). A study of the relationship between reading readiness in grade one school children and patterns of parent–child interaction. *Child Development, 22,* 95–112.

Mittan, R. (1989). The peer review process: Harnessing students' communicative power. In D. M. Johnson & D. H. Roen (Eds.), *Richness in writing: Empowering ESL students* (pp. 207–219). New York: Longman.

Mohan, B. (1986). *Language and content*. Reading, MA: Addison-Wesley.

Moore, L. (1986). Teaching students how to evaluate writing. *TESOL Newsletter, 20*(5), 23–24.

Moran, M. G., & Lunsford, R. F. (Eds.). (1984). *Research in composition and rhetoric: A bibliographical sourcebook*. Westport, CT: Greenwood.

Moss, P. (1994a). Can there be validity without reliability? *Educational Researcher, 23*(2), 5–12.

Moss, P. (1994b). Validity in high stakes writing assessment. *Assessing Writing, 1,* 109–129.

Moxley, J. M. (1989). Responding to student writing: Goals, methods, alternatives. *Freshman English News, 17,* 3–11.

Mulderig, G. P. (1995). *The Heath guide to grammar and usage*. Lexington, MA: D. C. Heath.

Murray, D. E. (1992). Collaborative writing as a literacy event: Implications for ESL instruction. In D. Nunan (Ed.), *Collaborative language learning and teaching* (pp. 100–117). Cambridge, England: Cambridge University Press.

Murray, D. E. (1996). Is remediation an articulation issue? *CATESOL Journal, 9,* 175–182.

Murray, D. M. (1978). Write before writing. *College Composition and Communication, 29,* 375–382.

Murray, D. M. (1985). *A writer teaches writing* (2nd ed.). Boston: Houghton Mifflin.

Murray, D. M. (1986). *Colleague in the classroom*. New York: Houghton Mifflin.

Murray, D. M. (1987). *Write to learn*. New York: Holt, Rinehart & Winston.

Myers, G. (1990). *Writing biology: Texts in the social construction of scientific knowledge*. Madison, WI: The University of Wisconsin Press.

Myers, M. (1996). Sailing ships: A framework for portfolios in formative and summative systems. In R. Calfee, & P. Perfumo, (Eds.), *Writing portfolios in the classroom: Policy and practice, promise and peril* (pp. 149–178). Hillsdale, NJ: Lawrence Erlbaum Associates.

Neeld, E. C. (1986). *Writing* (2nd ed.). Glenview, IL: Scott, Foresman.

Nelson, G. L., & Murphy, J. M. (1992). An L2 writing group: Task and social dimensions. *Journal of Second Language Writing, 1,* 171–193.

Nelson, G. L., & Murphy, J. M. (1992/1993). Writing groups and the less proficient ESL student. *TESOL Journal, 2*(2), 23–26.

Nelson, G. L., & Murphy, J. M. (1993). Peer response groups: Do L2 writers use peer comments in revising their drafts? *TESOL Quarterly, 27,* 135–142.

Nelson, R. (1987, August). Let's hear it for CAW. *Personal Computing, August,* 49–52.

Neu, J., & Scarcella, R. (1991). Word processing in the ESL classroom: A survey of student attitudes. In P. Dunkel (Ed.), *Computer-assisted language learning and testing: Research issues and practice* (pp. 169–187). Rowley, MA: Newbury House.

Newkirk, T. (1984). Direction and misdirection in peer response. *College Composition and Communication, 35,* 301–311.

Newkirk, T. (Ed.). (1986). *Only connect: Uniting reading and writing*. Upper Montclair, NJ: Boynton/Cook.

Newkirk, T. (1995). The writing conference as performance. *Research in the Teaching of English, 29,* 193–215.

Noblitt, J. S., & Bland, S. K. (1991). Tracking the learner in computer-aided language learning. In B. F. Freed (Ed.), *Foreign language acquisition and the classroom* (pp. 120–132). Lexington, MA: D.C. Heath.

Nold, E., & Freedman, S. (1977). An analysis of readers' responses to essays. *Research in the Teaching of English, 11,* 164–174.

North, S. M. (1987). *The making of knowledge in composition: Portrait of an emerging field.* Upper Montclair, NJ: Boynton/Cook.

Nunan, D. (1989). *Communicative task design.* Cambridge, England: Cambridge University Press.

Nunan, D. (1991). *Syllabus design.* Oxford: Oxford University Press.

Omaggio Hadley, A. (1993). *Teaching languages in context* (2nd ed.). Boston: Heinle & Heinle.

Oxford, R. L. (1990). *Language learning strategies: What every teacher should know.* New York: Newbury House.

Oxford, R. L., & Ehrman, M. (1993). Second language research on individual differences. *Annual Review of Applied Linguistics, 13,* 188–205.

Oxford, R. L., Holloway, M. E., & Horton-Murillo, D. (1992). Language learning styles and strategies in the multicultural, tertiary L2 classroom. *System, 20,* 439–456.

Parker, R. (1985). The "language across the curriculum" movement: A brief overview and bibliography. *College Composition and Communication, 36,* 173–178.

Patthey-Chavez, G. G., & Ferris, D. R. (1997). Writing conferences and the weaving of multi-voiced texts in college composition. *Research in the Teaching of English, 31,* 51–90.

Paulson, D. (1992). *Assessment of FL learners' writing ability: Formulation of tasks and evaluation.* Washington, DC: Educational Resources Information Center. (ERIC Reproduction Service No. ED 342 249).

Pennington, M. C. (1990). An evaluation of word processing for ESL writers. *University of Hawaii Working Papers in ESL, 9*(1), 77–113.

Pennington, M. C. (1991). Positive and negative potentials of word processing for ESL writers. *System, 19,* 267–275.

Pennington, M. C. (1992). Beyond off-the-shelf computer remedies for student writers: Alternatives to canned feedback. *System, 20,* 423–477.

Pennington, M. C. (1993a). A critical examination of word processing effects in relation to L2 writers. *Journal of Second Language Writing, 2,* 227–255.

Pennington, M. C. (1993b). Exploring the potential of word processing for non-native writers. *Computers and the Humanities, 27,* 149–163.

Pennington, M. C., & Brock, M. N. (1990). Process and product approaches to computer-assisted composition. In M. C. Pennington & V. Stevens (Eds.), *Computers in applied linguistics* (pp. 79–109). Clevedon: Multilingual Matters.

Peregoy, S. F., & Boyle, O. F. (1997). *Reading, writing, & learning in ESL: A resource book for K–12 teachers* (2nd ed.). New York: Longman.

Perkins, K. (1983). On the use of composition scoring techniques, objective measures, and objective tests to evaluate ESL writing ability. *TESOL Quarterly, 17,* 651–671.

Perl, S. (1979). The composing process of unskilled college writers. *Research in the Teaching of English, 13,* 317–339.

Petersen, B. T. (Ed.). (1986). *Convergences: Transactions in reading and writing.* Urbana, IL: National Council of Teachers of English.

Peterson, A. (1989). The writing–reading connection: Taking off the hand-cuffs. In A. H. Dyson (Ed.), *Collaboration through writing and reading: Exploring possibilities* (pp. 249–253). Urbana, IL: National Council of Teachers of English.

Peterson, R. (1995). *The writing teacher's companion: Planning, teaching, and evaluating in the composition classroom.* Boston: Houghton Mifflin.

Peterson, S. (1993). A comparison of student revisions when composing with pen and paper versus word processing. *Computers in the Schools, 9*(4), 55–69.

Phinney, M. (1989). Computers, composition, and second language teaching. In M. C. Pennington (Ed.), *Teaching languages with computers: The state of the art* (pp. 81–96). La Jolla, CA: Athelstan.

Phinney, M. (1991). Computer-assisted writing and apprehension in ESL students. In P. Dunkel (Ed.), *Computer-assisted language learning and testing: Research issues and practice* (pp. 189–204). Rowley, MA: Newbury House.

Pianko, S. (1977). *The composing acts of college freshman writers: A description.* Unpublished doctoral dissertation, Rutgers, The State University.

Pica, T. (1984). Second language acquisition theory in the teaching of writing. *TESOL Newsletter, 18*(2), 5–6.

Piper, A. (1987). Helping learners to write: A role for the word processor. *ELT Journal, 41,* 119–125.

Poulsen, E. (1991). Writing processes with word processing in teaching English as a foreign language. *Computers in Education, 16,* 77–81.

Prabhu, N. S. (1992). The dynamics of the language lesson. *TESOL Quarterly, 26,* 225–241.

Pratt, D. (1980). *Curriculum design and development.* New York: Harcourt Brace Jovanovich.

Prior, P. (1995). Redefining the task: An ethnographic examination of writing and response in graduate seminars. In D. Belcher & G. Braine (Eds.), *Academic writing in a second language: Essays on research and pedagogy* (pp. 47–82). Norwood, NJ: Ablex.

Purgason, K. B. (1991). Planning lessons and units. In M. Celce-Murcia (Ed.), *Teaching English as a second or foreign language* (2nd ed., pp. 419–431). New York: Newbury House.

Purves, A. C. (Ed.). (1988). *Writing across languages and cultures: Issues in contrastive rhetoric.* Newbury Park, CA: Sage.

Quindlen, A. (1988, April 28). Life in the 30s. *The New York Times,* pp. C3, C5.

Radecki, P., & Swales, J. (1988). ESL student reaction to written comments on their written work. *System, 16,* 355–365.

Raimes, A. (1983a). Anguish in a second language? Remedies for composition teachers. In A. Freedman, I. Pringle, & J. Yalden (Eds.), *Learning to write: First language/second language* (pp. 258–272). New York: Longman.

Raimes. A. (1983b). *Techniques in teaching writing.* New York: Oxford University Press.

Raimes, A. (1985). What unskilled ESL students do as they write: A classroom study of composing. *TESOL Quarterly, 19,* 229–258.

Raimes, A. (1987). Language proficiency, writing ability, and composing strategies: A study of ESL college student writers. *TESOL Quarterly, 19,* 229–258.

Raimes, A. (1990). *How English works: A grammar handbook with readings.* New York: St. Martin's.

Raimes, A. (1991). Out of the woods: Emerging traditions in the teaching of writing. *TESOL Quarterly, 25,* 407–430.

Raimes, A. (1992a). *Grammar troublespots.* New York: St. Martin's.

Raimes, A. (1992b). *Exploring through writing: A process approach to ESL composition* (2nd ed.). New York: St. Martin's.

Ramage, J. D., & Bean, J. C. (1997). *The Allyn & Bacon guide to writing.* Boston: Allyn & Bacon.

Reid, J. M. (1984a). Comments on Vivian Zamel's "The composing processes of advanced ESL students: Six case studies." *TESOL Quarterly, 18,* 149–153.

Reid, J. M. (1984b). The radical outliner and the radical brainstormer: A perspective in composing processes. *TESOL Quarterly, 18,* 529–533.

Reid, J. M. (1986). Using the Writer's Workbench in composition teaching and testing. In C. W. Stansfield (Ed.), *Technology and language testing* (pp. 167–188). Washington, DC: TESOL.

Reid, J. M. (1987). The learning style preferences of ESL students. *TESOL Quarterly, 21,* 87–111.

Reid, J. M. (1989). English as a second language composition in higher education: The expectations of the academic audience. In D. Johnson & D. Roen (Eds.), *Richness in writing: Empowering ESL students* (pp. 220–234). New York: Longman.

Reid, J. M. (1993a). Historical perspectives on writing and reading in the ESL classroom. In J. Carson & I. Leki (Eds.), *Reading in the composition classroom: Second language perspectives* (pp. 33–60). Boston: Heinle & Heinle.

Reid, J. M. (1993b). *Teaching ESL writing.* Englewood Cliffs, NJ: Regents/Prentice-Hall.

Reid, J. M. (1994). Responding to ESL students' texts: The myths of appropriation. *TESOL Quarterly, 28,* 273–292.

Reid, J. M. (1995a). Environmental writing inventory. In J. M. Reid (Ed.), *Learning styles in the ESL/EFL classroom* (pp. 218–219). Boston, MA: Heinle & Heinle.

Reid, J. M. (Ed.). (1995b). *Learning styles in the ESL/EFL classroom.* Boston, MA: Heinle & Heinle.

Reid, J. M., & Kroll, B. (1995). Developing and assessing effective classroom writing assignments for NES and ESL students. *Journal of Second Language Writing, 4,* 17–41.

Reid, J. M., & Lindstrom, M. (1985). *The process of paragraph writing.* Englewood Cliffs, NJ: Prentice-Hall.

Resh, C. A. (1994). A study of the effect of peer responding on the responder as writer-reviser. *Dissertation Abstracts International, 55*(12), 3771A–3772A.

Reynolds, A. L. (1993). *Explorations in basic writing.* New York: St. Martin's.

Richard-Amato, P. A. (1988). *Making it happen: Interaction in the second language classroom.* New York: Longman.

Richards, J. (1990). *The language teaching matrix.* New York: Cambridge University Press.

Richards, J., & Lockhart, C. (1994). *Reflective teaching in second language classrooms.* Cambridge, England: Cambridge University Press.

Richards, J., & Rodgers, T. (1982). Method: Approach, design, and procedure. *TESOL Quarterly, 16,* 153–168.

Rivers, W. (1968). *Teaching foreign language skills.* Chicago: University of Chicago Press.

Robb, T., Ross, S., & Shortreed, I. (1986). Salience of feedback and its effect on EFL writing quality. *TESOL Quarterly, 20,* 83–93.

Roberts, D., Bachen, C., Hornby, M., & Hernandez-Ramos, P. (1984). Reading and television: Predictors of reading achievement at different age levels. *Communication Research, 11,* 9–49.

Roller, C. (1988). Transfer of cognitive academic competence and L2 reading in a rural Zimbabwean primary school. *TESOL Quarterly, 22,* 303–328.

Rooks, G. (1988). *Share your paragraph.* Englewood Cliffs, NJ: Prentice-Hall.

Rosa, A., & Eschholz, P. (1995). *Models for writers: Short essays for composition* (5th ed.). New York: St. Martin's.

Rose, M. (1980). Rigid rules, inflexible plans, and the stifling of language: A cognitivist analysis of writer's block. *College Composition and Communication, 31,* 389–401.

Rose, M. (1983). Remedial writing courses: A critique and a proposal. *College English, 45,* 109–128.

Rose, M. (Ed.). (1985). *Studies in writer's block and other composing process problems.* New York: Guilford.

Rosenblatt, L. (1988). Writing and reading: The transactional theory. *Reader, 20,* 7–31.

Rumelhart, D. E. (1980). Schemata: The building blocks of cognition. In R. J. Spiro, B. C. Bruce, & W. F. Brewer (Eds.), *Theoretical issues in reading comprehension* (pp. 33–58). Hillsdale, NJ: Lawrence Erlbaum Associates.

Russell, D. R. (1990). Writing across the curriculum in historical perspective: Toward a historical interpretation. *College English, 52,* 52–73.

Ruth, L., & Murphy, S. (1984). Designing topics for writing assessment: Problems of meaning. *College Composition and Communication, 35,* 410–422.

Ruth, L., & Murphy, S. (1988). *Designing writing tasks for the assessment of writing.* Norwood, NJ: Ablex.

Ryan, J. (1977). Family patterns of reading problems: The family that reads together. In M. Douglas (Ed.), *Claremont Reading Conference, 41st Yearbook* (pp. 159–163). Claremont, CA: Claremont Graduate School.

Salyer, M. (1987). A comparison of the learning characteristics of good and poor ESL writers. *Applied Linguistics Interest Section Newsletter, TESOL, 8,* 2–3.

Sampson, D. E., & Gregory, J. F. (1991). A technological primrose path? ESL students and computer-assisted writing programs. *College ESL, 1*(2), 29–36.

Santos, T. (1988). Professors' reactions to the academic writing of nonnative-speaking students. *TESOL Quarterly, 22,* 69–90.

Sarig, G. (1987). High-level reading in the first and in the foreign language: Some comparative process data. In J. Devine, P. Carrell, & D. Eskey (Eds.), *Research in reading in English as a second language* (pp. 105–120). Washington, DC: TESOL.

Sarig, G. (1993). Composing a study-summary: A reading–writing encounter. In J. G. Carson & I. Leki (Eds.), *Reading in the composition classroom: Second language perspectives* (pp. 161–182). Boston: Heinle & Heinle.

Sasser, L. (1996). Articulation between segments: Secondary to postsecondary programs. *CATESOL Journal, 9,* 61–74.

Scarcella, R., & Oxford, R. (1993). *The tapestry of language learning: The individual in the communicative classroom.* Boston, MA: Heinle & Heinle.

Schramm, R. M. (1989). The effects of using word-processing equipment in writing instruction: A meta-analysis. *Dissertation Abstracts International, 50,* 2643A.

Scollon, R., & Scollon, S. B. (1981). *Narrative, literacy, and face in interethnic communication.* Norwood, NJ: Ablex.

Scott, V. M., & New, E. (1993). Computer-aided analysis of foreign language writing process. *CALICO Journal, 11*(3), 5–18.

Selfe, C. L., & Wahlstrom, B. J. (1986). An emerging rhetoric of collaboration: Computers, collaboration, and the composing process. *Collegiate Microcomputer, 4*(4), 289–295.

Semke, H. D. (1984). The effects of the red pen. *Foreign Language Annals, 17,* 195–202.

Shanahan, T. (1984). Nature of the reading–writing relation: An exploratory multivariate analysis. *Journal of Educational Psychology, 76,* 466–477.

Shanahan, T., & Lomax, R. (1986). An analysis and comparison of theoretical models of the reading–writing relationship. *Journal of Educational Psychology, 78,* 116–123.

Sheldon, L. E. (1988). Evaluating ELT textbooks and materials. *English Language Teaching Journal, 42,* 237–246.

Sheldon, W., & Carillo, L. (1952). Relation of parents, home, and certain developmental characteristics to children's reading ability. *The Elementary School Journal, 52,* 262–269.

Shen, F. (1989). The classroom and the wider culture: Identity as a key to learning English composition. *College Composition and Communication, 40,* 459–466.

Sheppard, K. (1992). Two feedback types: Do they make a difference? *RELC Journal, 23,* 103–110.

Shih, M. (1986). Content-based approaches to teaching academic writing. *TESOL Quarterly, 20,* 617–648.

Shrum, J. L., & Glisan, E. W. (1994). *Teacher's handbook: Contextualized language instruction.* Boston: Heinle & Heinle.

Silva, T. (1990). Second language composition instruction: Developments, issues, and directions in ESL. In B. Kroll (Ed.), *Second language writing: Research insights for the classroom* (pp. 11–23). Cambridge, England: Cambridge University Press.

Silva, T. (1993). Toward an understanding of the distinct nature of L2 writing: The ESL research and its implications. *TESOL Quarterly, 27,* 657–671.

Silva, T. (1997). On the ethical treatment of ESL writers. *TESOL Quarterly, 31,* 359–363.

Sirc, G. (1989). Response in the electronic medium. In C. Anson (Ed.), *Writing and response: Theory, practice, and research* (pp. 187–205). Urbana, IL: National Council of Teachers of English.

Skehan, P. (1989). *Individual differences in second-language learning.* London: Edward Arnold.

Skehan, P. (1991). Individual differences in second language learning. *Studies in Second Language Acquisition, 13,* 275–298.

Skierso, A. (1991). Textbook selection an evaluation. In M. Celce-Murcia (Ed.), *Teaching English as a second or foreign language* (2nd ed., pp. 432–453). New York: Newbury House.

Skutnabb-Kangas, T., & Cummins, J. (1988). *Minority education: From shame to struggle.* Clevedon: Multilingual Matters.

Smalley, R. L., & Ruetten, M. K. (1995). *Refining composition skills: Rhetoric and grammar* (4th ed.). Boston: Heinle & Heinle.

Smalzer, W. R. (1996). *Write to be read: Reading, reflection, and writing.* New York: Cambridge University Press.

Smith, B. (1997). *Bridging the gap: College reading* (5th ed.). New York: Longman.

Smith, C. R. (1989). Text analysis: The state of the art. *Computer-Assisted Composition, 3,* 68–77.

Smith, F. (1982). *Writing and the writer.* New York: Holt, Rinehart & Winston.

Smith, F. (1983). Reading like a writer. *Language Arts, 60,* 558–567.

Smith, F. (1984). *Reading like a writer.* Victoria, BC: Abel.

Smith, F. (1985). *Reading without nonsense* (2nd ed.). New York: Teachers College Press.

Smith, F. (1986). *Understanding reading: A psycholinguistic analysis of reading and learning to read* (3rd ed.). Hillsdale, NJ: Lawrence Erlbaum Associates.

Smith, F. (1988). *Joining the literacy club: Further essays into education.* Portsmouth, NH: Heinemann.

Snow, M. A., & Brinton, D. (1988). The adjunct model of language instruction: An ideal EAP framework. In S. Benesch (Ed.), *Ending remediation: ESL and content in higher education* (pp. 33–52). Washington, DC: TESOL.

Sokmen, A. A. (1988). Taking advantage of conference-centered writing. *TESOL Newsletter, 22*(1), 1, 5.

Sommers, N. (1982). Responding to student writing. *College Composition and Communication, 33,* 148–156.

Spack, R. (1984). Invention strategies and the ESL college composition student. *TESOL Quarterly, 18,* 649–670.

Spack, R. (1988). Initiating ESL students into the academic discourse community: How far should we go? *TESOL Quarterly, 22,* 29–52.

Spack, R. (1990). *Guidelines: A reading–writing text.* New York: St. Martin's.

Spack, R. (1993). Student meets text, text meets student: Finding a way into academic discourse. In J. Carson & I. Leki (Eds.), *Reading in the composition classroom: Second language perspectives* (pp. 183–196). Boston: Heinle & Heinle.

Spack, R. (1994). *The international story: An anthology with guidelines for reading and writing about fiction.* New York: St. Martin's.

Spack, R. (1996). *Guidelines: A reading–writing text* (2nd ed.). New York: St. Martin's.

Sperling, M. (1991). Dialogues of deliberation: Conversation in the teacher–student writing conference. *Written Communication, 8,* 131–162.

Sperling, M. (1994). Constructing the perspective of teacher-as-reader: A framework for studying response to student writing. *Research in the Teaching of English, 28,* 175–207.

Sperling, M., & Freedman, S. W. (1987). A good girl writes like a good girl: Written response to student writing. *Written Communication, 4,* 343–369.

Squire, J. R., & Applebee, R. K. (1968). *High school English instruction today.* New York: Appleton.

Stahl, S. A., & Hayes, D. (Eds.). (1997). *Instructional models in reading.* Hillsdale, NJ: Lawrence Erlbaum Associates.

Stanley, J. (1992). Coaching student writers to be effective peer evaluators. *Journal of Second Language Writing, 1,* 217–233.

Steiner, F. (1975). *Performing with objectives.* Cambridge, MA: Newbury House.

Stevenson, C. (1985). *Challenging illiteracy: Reading and writing disabilities in the British army.* New York: Teachers College Press.

Stewart, D. (1993). *Immigration and education: The crisis and the opportunities.* New York: Lexington.

Stotsky, S. (1983). Research on reading/writing relationships: A synthesis and suggested directions. *Language Arts, 60,* 627–642.

Stufflebeam, D. L., McCormick, C. H., Brinkerhoff, R. O., & Nelson, C. O. (1985). *Conducting educational needs assessments.* Boston: Kluwer-Nijhoff.

Sullivan, N. (1993). Teaching writing on a computer network. *TESOL Journal, 3*(1), 34–35.

Swaffar, J. (1988). Readers, texts, and second languages: The interactive process. *The Modern Language Journal, 72,* 123–149.

Swales, J. M. (1990). *Genre analysis: English in academic and research settings.* Cambridge, England: Cambridge University Press.

Swales, J. M., & Feak, C. (1994). *Academic writing for graduate students: A course for nonnative speakers of English.* Ann Arbor, MI: University of Michigan Press.

Tannacito, D. (1995). *A guide to writing in English as a second or foreign language: An annotated bibliography of research and pedagogy.* Alexandria, VA: TESOL.

Tarvers, J. K. (1993). *Teaching writing: Theories and practice* (4th ed.). New York: HarperCollins College Publishers.

Tate, G., & Corbett, E. P. (Eds.). (1988). *The writing teacher's sourcebook* (2nd ed.). New York: Oxford University Press.

Taylor, B. P. (1981). Content and written form: A two-way street. *TESOL Quarterly, 15,* 5–13.

Teichman, M., & Poris, M. (1989). Initial effects of word processing on writing quality and writing anxiety of freshman writers. *Computers and the Humanities, 23,* 93–101.

Thorne, S. (1993). Prewriting: A basic skill for basic writers. *Teaching English in the Two-Year College, 20,* 31–36.

Tibbetts, C., & Tibbetts, Z. (1997). *Strategies: A rhetoric and reader with handbook* (5th ed.). New York: Longman.

Tierney, R. J., & Pearson, P. D. (1983). Toward a composing model of reading. *Language Arts, 60,* 568–580.

Truscott, J. (1996). The case against grammar correction in L2 writing classes. *Language Learning, 46,* 327–369.

Tsui, A. B. M. (1996). Learning how to teach ESL writing. In D. Freeman & J. Richards (Eds.), *Teacher learning in language teaching* (pp. 97–119). Cambridge, England: Cambridge University Press.

Tumposky, N. R. (1984). Behavioral objectives, the cult of efficiency and foreign language learning: Are they compatible? *TESOL Quarterly, 18,* 295–310.

Turkenik, C. (1995). *Choices: Writing projects for students of ESL.* New York: St. Martin's.

Valdes, G. (1992). Bilingual minorities and language issues in writing. *Written Communication, 9,* 85–136.

VanPatten, B. (1988). How juries get hung: Problems with the evidence for focus-on-form in teaching. *Language Learning, 38,* 243–260.

van Lier, L. (1994). Some features of a theory of practice. *TESOL Journal, 4*(1), 6–10.

van Lier, L. (1995). *Introducing language awareness.* London: Penguin Books.

van Lier, L. (1996). *Interaction in the language curriculum: Awareness, autonomy, & authenticity.* London: Longman.

van Naerssen, M. (1985). Relaxed reading in ESL. *TESOL Newsletter, 19,* 2.

Vann, R., Lorenz, F., & Meyer, D. (1991). Error gravity: Faculty response to errors in written discourse of nonnative speakers of English. In L. Hamp-Lyons (Ed.), *Assessing second language writing in academic contexts* (pp. 181–195). Norwood, NJ: Ablex.

Vann, R., Meyer, D., & Lorenz, F. (1984). Error gravity: A study of faculty opinion of ESL errors. *TESOL Quarterly, 18,* 427–440.

Vaughan, C. (1991). Holistic assessment: What goes on in the rater's mind? In L. Hamp-Lyons (Ed.), *Assessing second language writing in academic contexts* (pp. 111–125). Norwood, NJ: Ablex.

Villamil, O. S., & de Guerrero, M. C. M. (1996). Peer revision in the L2 classroom: Social-cognitive activities, mediating strategies, and aspects of social behavior. *Journal of Second Language Writing, 5,* 51–75.

Vygotsky, L. (1986). *Thought and language* (A. Kozulin, Trans. & Ed.). Cambridge, MA: MIT Press. (Original work published 1962)

Wagner, D., Spratt, J., & Ezzaki, A. (1989). Does learning to read in a second language always put the child at a disadvantage? Some counter evidence from Morocco. *Applied Psycholinguistics, 10,* 31–48.

Wajnryb, R. (1992). *Classroom observation tasks.* Cambridge, England: Cambridge University Press.

Walker, C. P., & Elias, D. (1987). Writing conference talk: Factors associated with high- and low-rated writing conferences. *Research in the Teaching of English, 21,* 266–285.

Watson-Reekie, C. (1982). The use and abuse of models in the ESL writing class. *TESOL Quarterly, 16,* 5–14.

Weaver, C. (1994). *Reading process and practice* (2nd ed.). Portsmouth, NH: Heinemann.

Weir, C. J. (1990). *Communicative language testing.* New York: Prentice-Hall.

Wertsch, J. (1987). *Vygotsky and the social formation of mind.* Cambridge, MA: Harvard University Press.

Whichard, N. W., Gamber, C., Lester, V., Leighton, G., Carlberg, J., & Whitaker, W. (1992). Life in the margin: The hidden agenda of commenting on student writing. *Journal of Teaching Writing, 11,* 51–64.

White, E. M. (1984). Holisticism. *College Composition and Communication, 35,* 400–409.

White, E. M. (1994). *Teaching and assessing writing: Recent advances in understanding, evaluating, and improving student performance* (2nd rev. ed.). San Francisco: Jossey-Bass.

White, E. M. (1995). An apologia for the timed impromptu essay test. *College Composition and Communication, 46,* 30–45.

White, L. (1994). Universal grammar: Is it just a new name for old problems? In H. D. Brown & S. Gonzo (Eds.), *Readings on second language acquisition* (pp. 451–468). Englewood Cliffs, NJ: Prentice-Hall.

Widdowson, H. (1983). *Learning purpose and language use.* New York: Oxford University Press.

Williams, D. (1981). Factors relating to performance in reading English as a second language. *Language Learning, 31,* 31–50.

Williams, D. (1983). Developing criteria for textbook evaluation. *English Language Teaching Journal, 37,* 251–261.

Williams, J. D. (1996). *Preparing to teach writing.* Mahwah, NJ: Lawrence Erlbaum Associates.

Williamson, M., & Huot, B. (Eds.). (1993). *Holistic scoring: Theoretical foundations and validation research.* Cresskill, NJ: Hampton.

Witbeck, M. C. (1976). Peer correction procedures for intermediate and advanced ESL composition lessons. *TESOL Quarterly, 10,* 321–326.

Wong-Fillmore, L., Ammon, P., McLaughlin, B., & Ammon, M. (1985). *Learning English through bilingual instruction.* Final report to the National Institute of Education, Contract #400-80-0030.

Woodward, J., & Phillips, A. (1967). A profile of the poor writer. *Research in the Teaching of English, 1,* 41–53.

Yagelski, R. (1995). The role of classroom context in the revision strategies of student writers. *Research in the Teaching of English, 29,* 216–238.

Yancey, K. B. (Ed.). (1992). *Portfolios in the writing classroom.* Urbana, IL: National Council of Teachers of English.

Young, R. (1978). Paradigms and problems: Needed research in rhetorical invention. In C. Cooper & L. Odell (Eds.), *Research on composing: Points of view* (pp. 29–47). Urbana, IL: National Council of Teachers of English.

Zamel, V. (1976). Teaching composition in the ESL classroom: What we can learn from research in the teaching of English. *TESOL Quarterly, 10,* 67–76.

Zamel, V. (1982). Writing: The process of discovering meaning. *TESOL Quarterly, 16,* 195–209.

Zamel, V. (1983). The composing processes of advanced ESL students: Six case studies. *TESOL Quarterly, 17,* 165–187.

Zamel, V. (1985). Responding to student writing. *TESOL Quarterly, 19,* 79–102.

Zamel, V. (1987). Recent research on writing pedagogy. *TESOL Quarterly, 21,* 697–715.

Zamel, V. (1992). Writing one's way into reading. *TESOL Quarterly, 26,* 463–485.

Zamel, V. (1997). Toward a model of transculturation. *TESOL Quarterly, 31,* 341–352.

Zebroski, J. (1986). The uses of theory: A Vygotskian approach to composition. *The Writing Instructor, 5,* 57–67.

Zeman, S. (1969). Reading comprehension and writing of second and third graders. *Reading Teacher, 23,* 144–150.

Zhang, S. (1995). Reexamining the affective advantage of peer feedback in the ESL writing class. *Journal of Second Language Writing, 4,* 209–222.

Zinsser, W. (1990). College pressures. In R. Spack (Ed.), *Guidelines: A cross-cultural reader/writing text* (pp. 132–139). New York: St. Martin's Press.

AUTHOR INDEX

SUBJECT INDEX